EXPLANATORY NOTE

The sources of translations given at the beginning of each selection are rendered as concisely as possible. Full bibliographical data can be obtained from the list of sources in the clothbound edition. In the reference at the head of each selection, unless otherwise indicated, the author of the book is the writer whose name precedes the selection. Where excerpts have been taken from existing translations, they have sometimes been adapted or edited in the interests of uniformity with the book as a whole.

Chinese words and names are rendered according to the modified Wade-Giles system of romanization which has become standard in American sinological publications. An exception to this appears in the names of certain Neo-Confucian philosophers where the syllable *i* has been converted to *yi* in order to avoid possible confusion for the non-sinologist. Indic words appearing in the chapters on Buddhism as technical terms or titles in italics follow the standard system of transliteration found in Louis Renou's *Grammaire Sanskrite* (Paris, 1930), pp. xi–xiii, with the exception that here ś is regularly used for ç. To facilitate pronunciation, other Sanskrit terms and proper names appearing in roman letters are rendered according to the usage of Webster's New International Dictionary, 2d edition, Unabridged, except that here the macron is used to indicate long vowels and the Sanskrit symbols for ś (ç) and ṣ are uniformly transcribed as sh. Similarly, the standard Sanskrit transcription of c is given as ch.

Chinese names are rendered in their Chinese order, with the family name first and the personal name last. Dates given after personal names are those of birth and death except in the case of rulers whose reign dates are preceded by "r." Generally the name by which a person was most commonly known in Chinese tradition is the one used in the text. Since this book is intended for the general reader, rather than the specialist, we have not burdened the text with a list of the alternate names or titles which usually accompany biographical reference to a scholar in Chinese or Japanese historical works.

W. T. DE B.

INTRODUCTION TO
ORIENTAL CIVILIZATIONS

WM. THEODORE DE BARY, EDITOR

Sources of

Chinese Tradition

VOLUME II

COMPILED BY

Wm. Theodore de Bary
Wing-tsit Chan
Chester Tan

COLUMBIA UNIVERSITY PRESS *New York*

The addition to the "Records of Civilization: Sources and Studies" of a group of translations of Oriental historical materials in a cloth-bound edition, from which this volume is taken, was made possible by funds granted by Carnegie Corporation of New York. That Corporation is not, however, the author, owner, publisher, or proprietor of this publication, and is not to be understood as approving by virtue of its grant any of the statements made or views expressed therein.

UNESCO COLLECTION OF REPRESENTATIVE WORKS, CHINESE SERIES
This volume has been accepted in the Chinese Translation Series of the United Nations Educational, Scientific, and Cultural Organization (UNESCO).

Text edition in two volumes published 1964

ISBN 0-231-08603-2
Printed in the United States of America

p 20 19 18 17

SOURCES OF CHINESE TRADITION

VOLUME II

CONTENTS

[vii]

[ix]

CHRONOLOGICAL TABLE

China and the New World

1839–1842   Anglo-Chinese (Opium) War.
1839   Lin Tse-hsü (1785–1850), Imperial Commissioner at Canton.
1844   First publication of *Illustrated Gazetteer of the Maritime Countries* by Wei Yüan (1794–1856).
1850–1864   Taiping Rebellion.
1861   Essay on reform by Feng Kuei-fen (1809–1874).
1862–1874   T'ung-chih reign. Rise of influence of Empress Dowager Tz'u-hsi. Suppression of Taiping, Nien, and Muslim rebellions. Calls for reform by Wang T'ao (1828–1897), Tseng Kuo-fan (1811–1872), and Li Hung-chang (1823–1901).
1894–1895   Sino-Japanese War.
1897   Publication of *Confucius as a Reformer* by K'ang Yu-wei (1858–1927).
1898   Peak of European scramble for concessions. The Hundred Days of Reform, ending in exile of K'ang Yu-wei and Liang Ch'i-ch'ao (1873–1929) and death of T'an Ssu-t'ung (1865–1898). *Exhortation to Learn,* by Chang Chih-tung (1837–1909).
1900   Boxer Rebellion.
1902   Liang Ch'i-ch'ao's journal, *A New People,* begun.
1905   *T'ung-meng hui* founded, Sun Yat-sen (1866–1925), president; its manifesto on Three People's Principles issued.
1906   Traditional civil service examination abolished.
1911   Republic proclaimed.
1916   Failure of Yüan Shih-k'ai's attempt to restore monarchy. Ch'en Tu-hsiu (1879–1942), editor of *The New Youth.*
1917   Literary revolution proposed by Hu Shih (1891—).
1919   May 4 Movement.
1921   Chinese Communist Party founded.
1923   Debate on science and the philosophy of life. Reorganization of Kuomintang with Soviet help and advice.
1924   Sun Yat-sen's lectures on Three People's Principles.
1926   Beginning of northern expedition of Kuomintang.
1927   Mao Tse-tung's "Report" on the Hunan Peasant Movement.
1931   Japanese expansion in Manchuria.
1934   Suppression of Kiangsi Soviet and beginning of Long March of Communists. Launching of Chiang Kai-shek's New Life Movement.

1935	Establishment of Communist headquarters at Yenan.
1936	Sian incident: kidnapping of Chiang Kai-shek followed by United Front of Nationalist government and Communist Party.
1937	Marco Polo Bridge incident, expanding into Japanese occupation of coastal China and Yangtze valley.
1938	Chungking made wartime capital.
1943	Chiang Kai-shek's *China's Destiny*. Beginning of Communist Party reform movement at Yenan.
1945	End of Pacific War.
1949	Withdrawal of Nationalist government to Taiwan; founding of Communists' "People's Republic." Mao's "Dictatorship of the People's Democracy."
1957	The "Hundred Flowers" campaign launched by Mao Tse-tung's speech on "The Correct Handling of Contradictions Among the People."

CHAPTER XX

THE OPENING
OF CHINA
TO THE WEST

The year 1839, which saw the opening of the Opium War between Britain and China, is the great turning point in China between old and new. It marks the end of China's long existence as an independent civilization, free to disregard what took place beyond the borders of the Central Kingdom, and its emergence into a world of rapid, irresistible change. The new China might be slow in coming and still constantly stalked by its past, but the outcome of this historic encounter was to insure that, eventually and inevitably, dynamic forces from the West would have a large part in shaping its future.

Up to this time, for almost three centuries since the first arrival of the Portuguese off South China, the Chinese cou.t had succeeded in dealing with Westerners on its own terms. Trade was confined to a few ports where agents of the court could regulate it strictly and tax it heavily. This indeed was the traditional pattern of state control over commerce, whether foreign or domestic—a system designed to hold it under close supervision, to keep the merchant in an inferior status, to subordinate commerce to the interests of the state, and to obtain a maximum in revenue while assuming a minimum of responsibility on the part of the imperial bureaucracy for the actual conduct of trade (which was handled by licensed merchants in accordance with the age-old practice for state monopolies). Many of the disadvantages of such a system from the trader's point of view were not, therefore, disabilities specially imposed on foreigners and calculated to harrass them, but simply limitations inherent in the "regular" conditions of doing business in China. Chinese merchants, for their part, had long since learned to live with them. Westerners, especially British traders in the early nineteenth century, remained restive under these restrictions and resentful of them. Imbued with the spirit of a rising English middle class, believing in free trade and the near-sacredness of property, they ran up against a regime which recognized neither of these as basic principles and a way of life in which the pursuit of profit was actually scorned as ignoble.

If the established pattern for foreign trade had such disadvantages for the merchant, it involved difficulties for the government as well. Burdensome taxes and restrictions were an invitation for enterprising and resourceful persons to engage in smuggling. Smuggling, moreover, could prove lucrative not only for the direct participants but for local officials as well, who could be bribed to keep hands off the illegal traffic. These factors help to explain why it should have proven so difficult for the government to put an end to the opium trade in spite of repeated bans on its importation and sale. The state was not merely in conflict with foreigners, who found opium from India and the Near East a wonder-drug in curing the chronic imbalance of trade with China, but with its own members whose self-interest led them to "squeeze" the traffic for their personal benefit rather than stamp it out for the good of all.

On the other hand, the "self-interest" of foreigners participating in the China trade was not wholly bound up with the marketing of opium, and it is possible that intelligent negotiation would have brought about gradual reduction in imports of the drug, while other articles, especially manufactured goods, took the place of opium in the trade. Unfortunately, the traditional conduct of foreign relations by the Chinese court was confined largely to tribute-relations with states looked upon as "vassals" of the emperor. There was no inclination to establish equal relations with the Western powers or to enter into negotiations which might lead to an abridgement of the emperor's absolute power to deal with foreigners as he would with his own subjects. For want of such a middle ground on which to meet, the means were lacking whereby to resolve the constant conflicts which arose in contacts between Chinese and foreigners over differing conceptions of justice and equity.

Under these circumstances a stalemate was no solution. The evils of the opium traffic were so far-reaching that the Chinese could ignore them only at great peril. Meanwhile the impossibility of China's maintaining its traditional isolationist policy made imperative the finding of a new *modus vivendi* with the West. Some sort of showdown was inevitable.

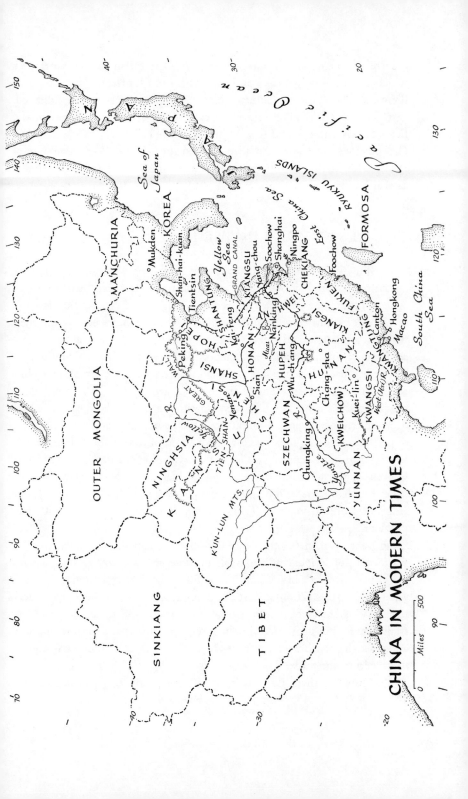

CHINA IN MODERN TIMES

Here we shall concern ourselves less with the merits of the issues over which war eventually broke out than with the Chinese understanding of them and the effect on Chinese thinking of the events which followed. Instructive for this purpose are the cases of two Chinese leaders in the fields of government and scholarship: Lin Tse-hsü (1785–1850), Imperial Commissioner at Canton in 1839–40, and the scholar, Wei Yüan (1794–1856), who helped to interpret for Chinese minds the meaning of this fateful conflict.

THE LESSON OF LIN TSE-HSÜ

Lin Tse-hsü, a native of the southeast coastal province of Fukien, was an exemplary product of the Chinese educational and civil service system. After winning the *chin-shih* degree in 1811, he rose rapidly through the official ranks and served with particular distinction in posts concerned with fiscal matters and public works, gaining a wide reputation for his competence, integrity and humaneness. By the late thirties, when opium smuggling became a pressing question, Lin had already established himself as an able governor and then governor-general of rich and populous provinces in Central China. In such a position a man less deeply concerned over the fate of his people might have been content to enjoy the measure of personal success which was already assured him. But Lin, having taken strong measures to end the traffic in his own sphere of jurisdiction, placed himself in the forefront of those who called upon the court for a full-scale assault on the opium menace. The result was his appointment as Imperial Commissioner at Canton with full powers to deal with the problem.

On his arrival in Canton in March of 1839, Lin demonstrated that he was a man of serious and inflexible purpose, not the type of official who could be wheedled, bribed, or stalled off. Within a few months he had taken such strong action against the Hong merchants and Western traders that existing stocks of opium had been destroyed and the cessation of the traffic was all but guaranteed by the foreigners. It was at this time that Lin addressed his celebrated letter to Queen Victoria demanding assurances of an end to the trade.

Were opium, then, the sole or chief issue between the Chinese and

British, there would presumably have been no cause for the outbreak of the first Anglo-Chinese War later that same year. To the British on the scene, however, Lin's uncompromising policies seemed not just firm or tough but arrogant and unreasonable. Though ready to make substantial concessions with regard to the drug traffic in order not to lose all opportunities for trade, for them the lure of profits did not suffice to overcome strong feelings in what they regarded as matters of principle. The lack of treaty relations meant that there was no established procedure for the administration of justice in incidents involving Chinese and foreigners. Commissioner Lin was determined that Chinese authorities should mete out punishment for crimes on Chinese soil of which foreigners had been accused. The British were equally adamant in refusing to turn over suspects, whose guilt was by no means established, to the mercies of Chinese officials whom they considered vindictive and inhumane. When Lin countered with the breaking off of all trade and expulsion of the British from China, full-scale hostilities broke out.

The Chinese, as is well known, were pitifully unprepared on land and sea to resist the force of British arms, and it was only a matter of weeks before the underlying weakness of Lin's "get-tough" policy became fully exposed. Officially disgraced, the erstwhile viceroy and commissioner was eventually banished to Chinese Turkestan. In the meantime, he had become fully persuaded of the need for strengthening China through the adoption of Western arms and methods of warfare, though he could make no progress in gaining acceptance of this view at court. Even when later restored to the official ranks, partly on account of his accomplishments in flood control and land reclamation work, Lin lacked any real opportunity to influence state policy in the direction of greater realism and reform. The lesson he had learned in Canton remained largely his own. It would be decades more before the court could be moved by further misfortunes to take such warnings to heart.

LIN TSE-HSÜ
Letter to the English Ruler

In this celebrated letter to Queen Victoria (1839), Lin argues against the opium trade with all the moral earnestness of the Confucian scholar and lofty condescension of one speaking for the imperial court. On its own terms, of course, Lin's argument is unanswerable. Yet his tone indicates how unready the Chinese were to deal with the British as diplomatic equals or to negotiate outstanding differences on other scores.

Intransigent as he appeared, Lin nonetheless compelled admiration. His likeness appeared later in Mme. Tussaud's Wax Museum in London, and the distinguished British consular official and sinologist, H. A. Giles, said of Lin: "He was a fine scholar, a just and merciful official, and a true patriot."

[From Teng and Fairbank, *China's Response to the West*, pp. 24–27]

A communication: magnificently our great emperor soothes and pacifies China and the foreign countries, regarding all with the same kindness. If there is profit, then he shares it with the peoples of the world; if there is harm, then he removes it on behalf of the world. This is because he takes the mind of Heaven and earth as his mind.

The kings of your honorable country by a tradition handed down from generation to generation have always been noted for their politeness and submissiveness. We have read your successive tributary memorials saying: "In general our countrymen who go to trade in China have always received His Majesty the Emperor's gracious treatment and equal justice," and so on. Privately we are delighted with the way in which the honorable rulers of your country deeply understand the grand principles and are grateful for the Celestial grace. For this reason the Celestial Court in soothing those from afar has redoubled its polite and kind treatment. The profit from trade has been enjoyed by them continuously for two hundred years. This is the source from which your country has become known for its wealth.

But after a long period of commercial intercourse, there appear among the crowd of barbarians both good persons and bad, unevenly. Consequently there are those who smuggle opium to seduce the Chinese people and so cause the spread of the poison to all provinces. Such persons who only care to profit themselves, and disregard their harm to others, are not tolerated by the laws of Heaven and are unanimously hated by human beings. His Majesty the Emperor, upon hearing of this, is in a towering rage. He has especially sent me, his commissioner, to come to Kwangtung, and together with the governor-general and governor jointly to investigate and settle this matter. . . .

We find that your country is sixty or seventy thousand *li* from China. Yet there are barbarian ships that strive to come here for trade for the

[6]

purpose of making a great profit. The wealth of China is used to profit the barbarians. That is to say, the great profit made by barbarians is all taken from the rightful share of China. By what right do they then in return use the poisonous drug to injure the Chinese people? Even though the barbarians may not necessarily intend to do us harm, yet in coveting profit to an extreme, they have no regard for injuring others. Let us ask, where is your conscience? I have heard that the smoking of opium is very strictly forbidden by your country; that is because the harm caused by opium is clearly understood. Since it is not permitted to do harm to your own country, then even less should you let it be passed on to the harm of other countries—how much less to China! Of all that China exports to foreign countries, there is not a single thing which is not beneficial to people: they are of benefit when eaten, or of benefit when used, or of benefit when resold: all are beneficial. Is there a single article from China which has done any harm to foreign countries? Take tea and rhubarb, for example; the foreign countries cannot get along for a single day without them. If China cuts off these benefits with no sympathy for those who are to suffer, then what can the barbarians rely upon to keep themselves alive? Moreover the woolens, camlets, and longells [i.e., textiles] of foreign countries cannot be woven unless they obtain Chinese silk. If China, again, cuts off this beneficial export, what profit can the barbarians expect to make? As for other foodstuffs, beginning with candy, ginger, cinnamon, and so forth, and articles for use, beginning with silk, satin, chinaware, and so on, all the things that must be had by foreign countries are innumerable. On the other hand, articles coming from the outside to China can only be used as toys. We can take them or get along without them. Since they are not needed by China, what difficulty would there be if we closed the frontier and stopped the trade? Nevertheless our Celestial Court lets tea, silk, and other goods be shipped without limit and circulated everywhere without begrudging it in the slightest. This is for no other reason but to share the benefit with the people of the whole world.

The goods from China carried away by your country not only supply your own consumption and use, but also can be divided up and sold to other countries, producing a triple profit. Even if you do not sell opium, you still have this threefold profit. How can you bear to go further, selling products injurious to others in order to fulfill your insatiable desire? . . .

We have further learned that in London, the capital of your honorable rule, and in Scotland (Ssu-ko-lan), Ireland (Ai-lun), and other places, originally no opium has been produced. Only in several places of India under your control such as Bengal, Madras, Bombay, Patna, Benares, and Malwa has opium been planted from hill to hill, and ponds have been opened for its manufacture. For months and years work is continued in order to accumulate the poison. The obnoxious odor ascends, irritating Heaven and frightening the spirits. Indeed you, O King, can eradicate the opium plant in these places, hoe over the fields entirely, and sow in its stead the five grains [i.e., millet, barley, wheat, etc.]. Anyone who dares again attempt to plant and manufacture opium should be severely punished. This will really be a great, benevolent government policy that will increase the common weal and get rid of evil. For this, Heaven must support you and the spirits must bring you good fortune, prolonging your old age and extending your descendants. All will depend on this act. . . .

Now we have set up regulations governing the Chinese people. He who sells opium shall receive the death penalty and he who smokes it also the death penalty. Now consider this: if the barbarians do not bring opium, then how can the Chinese people resell it, and how can they smoke it? The fact is that the wicked barbarians beguile the Chinese people into a death trap. How then can we grant life only to these barbarians? He who takes the life of even one person still has to atone for it with his own life; yet is the harm done by opium limited to the taking of one life only? Therefore in the new regulations, in regard to those barbarians who bring opium to China, the penalty is fixed at decapitation or strangulation. This is what is called getting rid of a harmful thing on behalf of mankind.

Moreover we have found that in the middle of the second month of this year [April 9] Consul [Superintendent] Elliot of your nation, because the opium prohibition law was very stern and severe, petitioned for an extension of the time limit. He requested a limit of five months for India and its adjacent harbors and related territories, and ten months for England proper, after which they would act in conformity with the new regulations. Now we, the commissioner and others, have memorialized and have received the extraordinary Celestial grace of His Majesty the Emperor, who has redoubled his consideration and compassion. All those who within the period of the coming one year (from England) or six months (from India) bring opium to China by mistake, but who voluntarily confess and completely surrender their opium, shall be exempt from their punishment. After this limit of time, if there are still those who bring opium to China then they will plainly have committed a willful violation and shall at once be executed according to law, with absolutely no clemency or pardon. This may be called the height of kindness and the perfection of justice.

Our Celestial Dynasty rules over and supervises the myriad states, and surely possesses unfathomable spiritual dignity. Yet the Emperor cannot bear to execute people without having first tried to reform them by instruction. Therefore he especially promulgates these fixed regulations. The barbarian merchants of your country, if they wish to do business for a prolonged period, are required to obey our statutes respectfully and to cut off permanently the source of opium. They must by no means try to test the effectiveness of the law with their lives. May you, O King, check your wicked and sift out your vicious people before they come to China, in order to guarantee the peace of your nation, to show further the sincerity of your politeness and submissiveness, and to let the two countries enjoy together the blessings of peace. How fortunate, how fortunate indeed! After receiving this dispatch will you immediately give us a prompt reply regarding the details and circumstances of your cutting off the opium traffic. Be sure not to put this off. The above is what has to be communicated. [Vermilion endorsement:] This is appropriately worded and quite comprehensive (*Te-t'i chou-tao*).

The Need for Western Guns and Ships

This letter to his friend Wu Tzu-hsü, written two years after the debacle at Canton, expresses Lin's realization of the need for adopting modern weapons and methods of warfare. As one in official disgrace, however, Lin dared not speak out nor even communicate his thoughts privately except in guarded fashion. Under such circumstances it is understandable that the advocacy of reform should have been hampered and the taking of concrete steps so long delayed.

[From Teng and Fairbank, *China's Response to the West*, p. 28]

The rebels' ships on the open sea came and went as they pleased, now in the south and now suddenly in the north, changing successively between morning and evening. If we tried to put up a defense everywhere, not only would we toil and expend ourselves without limit, but also how could we recruit and transport so many troops, militia, artillery, and ammunition, and come to their support quickly? . . .

When I was in office in Kwangtung and Kwangsi, I had made plans regarding the problems of ships and cannon and a water force. Afraid that there was not enough time to build ships, I at first rented them. Afraid that there was not enough time to cast cannon and that it would not be done according to the regulations, I at first bought foreign ones. The most painful thing was that when the Hu-men [the Bogue or "Tiger's mouth," the entrance to the Canton River] was broken into, a large number of good cannon fell into the hands of the rebellious barbarians. I recall that after I had been punished two years ago, I still took the risk of calling the Emperor's attention to two things: ships and guns. At that time, if these things could have been made and prepared, they still could have been used with effect to fight against the enemy in Chekiang last fall [1841]. Now it is even more difficult to check the wildfire. After all, ships, guns, and a water force are absolutely indispensable. Even if the rebellious barbarians had fled and returned beyond the seas, these things would still have to be urgently planned for, in order to work out the permanent defense of our sea frontiers. . . .

But at this time I must strictly observe the advice to seal my lips as one corks the mouth of a bottle. However, toward those with identical aims and interests, I suddenly spit out the truth and am unable to control myself. I extremely regret my foolishness and carelessness. Nevertheless, when I turn my thoughts to the depth of your attention to me, then I cannot conceal these things from myself. I only beg you to keep them confidential. By all means, please do not tell other persons.

WEI ᵛÜAN AND THE WEST

The *Illustrated Gazetteer of the Maritime Countries,* by Wei Yüan (1794–1856), is a landmark in China's relations with the West, since it represents the first systematic attempt to provide educated men with a realistic picture of the outside world. A sizeable compilation running to sixty chapters, this gazetteer owed its inception to the pioneering work of Lin Tse-hsü who, while in Canton, made strenuous efforts to gather information about the West, taking notes himself, collecting materials, arranging translations, and compiling a *Gazetteer of the Four Continents,* which Wei used as the basis for his own work after Lin's dismissal.

Wei was exceptional in his alertness to the situation confronting China and his realization of the need for serious study of the West. He was not, however, a man whose intellectual importance derived from inadvertent involvement in what proved to be a momentous issue. A classicist and historian of the first rank, Wei combined the finest traditions of Ch'ing scholarship with the serious concern of the dedicated Confucian official in matters of state. By 1842 he had already published his military history of the Ch'ing dynasty, *Sheng-wu chi,* a work regarded as authoritative and often reprinted. Consequently, he spoke as one commanding scholarly respect, not as a mere opportunist or crackpot, and the tone of his work reflects his serious purpose—to provide information upon which to base practical state policies rather than simply to peddle curious notions about the strange world outside.

Wei's general thesis in the *Gazetteer* is this: the Western barbarians, bent on power and profit, have devised techniques and machines by which to subvert or conquer the civilized world. China, dedicated as she is to virtue, learning, and the ways of peace, possesses a spiritual and moral strength which can yet triumph over the enemy if only the Chinese awaken to the danger and apply themselves to the practical problems involved. Traditional military science suggests that the first requisite is intelligence of the enemy—of his strengths and weaknesses. The second requisite is to match these strengths and exploit the weaknesses. If the natural abilities of the Chinese are devoted to the study and adoption of Western military methods, and there is not too great an impatience with the achievement of immediate results, the time will come when China can reassert herself. In the meantime, she should seek to exploit the prime weakness of the West—its inherent disunity, which derives from the lack of a common moral basis and consequent anarchy of selfish ambitions among the nations. To play the Western powers off against one another is then the obvious strategy.

Despite the violent and contemptuous tone of his language, Wei is careful to state that his is a policy valid either for war or for peace. He admits of the possibility that China's military preparations may not enable her soon to resist or attack the West. Peace negotiations could prove necessary again as they had in the Opium War. Yet a policy of playing the Western powers off against each other, while gaining time for reform and strengthening within, would be appropriate even in these circumstances.

[11]

Wei's official career, though one of genuine distinction, was limited to relatively minor posts and matters of more traditional concern to the bureaucratic class: internal (and particularly local) administration, flood control and irrigation, water transport, and salt administration. His *Illustrated Gazetteer of the Maritime Countries* was reprinted many times, expanded and supplemented. Japanese editions of this work and Wei's *Sheng-wu chi* came to the attention of the samurai reformer Sakuma Shōzan, who spoke of Wei as "a comrade in another land." Sakuma also commented, however, that in practical matters like gunnery Wei lacked firsthand experience and his information was often inaccurate.[1]

Thus Wei's approach to the problem of national defense may be said to reflect his Confucian concern for the state, a more realistic estimate of Western power, and the Ch'ing scholar's penchant for works of compilation based on critical, though not necessarily empirical, research. He had neither the opportunity, nor perhaps the inclination, to take up the practical art of war which in the past had proven so uncongenial to Chinese Confucian tastes. Wei's own urgings to the contrary, this same lack of practical efforts remained a weakness of China for years to come.

WEI YÜAN
Preface to the Illustrated Gazetteer of the Maritime Countries

In the preface to his work, Wei, characteristically for the Ch'ing scholar, starts with a discussion of the sources he has drawn upon. Then he explains the nature and purposes of the work, and provides a conspectus of the contents, chapter by chapter. The whole is in a highly rhetorical style, replete with classical allusions and the usual pretensions in regard to Chinese cultural superiority and world sovereignty.

[From *Hai-kuo t'u-chih,* Original Preface, 1a–6b]

The present work, *Illustrated Gazetteer of the Maritime Countries (Hai-kuo t'u-chih)* contains sixty chapters. Upon what is it based? It is based, on the one hand, upon the *Gazetteer of the Four Continents (Ssu chou chih)* which was translated by Secretary [of War], Lin [Tse-hsü], former Governor-General of Kwangtung and Kwangsi, and, on the other hand, upon the histories and gazetteers of different previous dynasties, and the different series of *Island Gazetteers* published since the Ming

[1] Cf. Tsunoda, de Bary, and Keene, *Sources of Japanese Tradition,* Chapter XXIV.

period, and also upon many barbarian atlases and books published in recent years. They were brought together, and thoroughly searched. Many difficulties had to be worked out in order that this pioneer work might be published.

At a rough estimate, about eighty percent of the source materials used in this book covering the Southeastern Ocean [Southeast Asia] and the Southwestern Ocean [South and West Asia] and about sixty percent covering the Great Western Ocean [Western Europe], the Little Western Ocean [North Africa], the Northern Ocean [Russia and Eastern Europe], and the Outer Great Western Ocean [North and South America] are new materials supplementing the original [Lin's] book covering the same areas. They are also illustrated with maps, tables, and diagrams. A variety of opinion from different schools is presented in the interests of broad coverage.

In what respect does this work differ from the gazetteers of earlier writers? The answer is that those earlier works all described the West as it appeared to Chinese writers, while this book describes the West as it appears to Westerners.

What is the purpose of the present work? Its purpose is to show how to use barbarians to fight barbarians, how to make the barbarians pacify one another [to our advantage], and how to employ the techniques of the barbarians in order to bring the barbarians under control. The *Book of Changes* says: "Depending upon the mutual influence of love and hate, there may be fortune or misfortune; depending upon the mutual influence of approach and withdrawal, there may be repentance or regret; depending upon the mutual influence of honesty and dishonesty, there may be gain or loss." [2] So it is in defending against an enemy: depending upon whether one knows the enemy's position or not, there may be absolute gain or total loss. In ancient times those who succeeded in driving off the barbarians knew the enemy's position as clearly as if it were spread out upon their own desk or carpet; they were informed of the enemy's condition as intimately as if the enemy were dining or sleeping with them.

With this book in hand, then, will it be possible to drive off the barbarians?

Perhaps so, perhaps not. This book provides only military tactics, not the basic strategy. It provides the tangible means for making war, but not

[2] Hsi hsia 9 (Legge, 405).

the intangible ones. There were ministers of state in the Ming period who said that in order to deal with the menace of Japanese pirates on the high seas, it was first necessary to pacify the hearts of the people, embittered by an accumulation of grievances. But what are the accumulated grievances now? They come neither from flood nor from fire; they are stirred up neither by swords nor by other metal weapons. They are due not to traitorous elements along the coast; nor to the opium smokers or opium smugglers [but to misgovernment]. Therefore the gentleman [as he reads the *Book of Odes*] turns to the chapters of *Yün-han* and *Ch'e-kung* [which were written to praise King Hsüan of the Chou dynasty for his efforts to restore the great virtue of his ancestors] before he reads the chapters of *Ch'ang-wu* and *Chiang-han* [which praise the same king for his successful expedition against the Huai tribes]. By so doing he is able to understand the zealous concern of the poets who wrote the two sections, Ta ya and Hsiao ya, of the *Book of Odes*. In the same way, when he studies the interpretations of King Wen and the Duke of Chou [in the *Book of Changes*] with regard to "adjusting man's inward thoughts and external acts" and "the seasonal rotations of growth and diminution," he is able to understand the anxious concern of the authors and annotators of the *Book of Changes*. Man's zealousness and sense of concern are the means by which Heaven in the natural course of things brings peace out of chaos, by which human hearts are converted from ignorance to enlightenment, and by which man's abilities are turned from what is vain to what is practical.

Previously, the Chun-k'o-erh tribes were very unruly during the periods K'ang-hsi and Yung-cheng (1662–1735), but were suppressed with lightning speed in the middle of the Ch'ien-lung period (1736–1796). Yet the steady poisoning of our people by the barbarians with their opium represents a crime ten thousand times worse than that of the Chun-k'o-erh tribes. However, our present emperor, His Majesty, is so benevolent and diligent. His virtue matches that of His ancestors. The operations of Heaven in time and of man through his own efforts are conjoined for our advantage. Why should we fear that the time is not ripe for extermination of the barbarians; why should we fear that there may be no chance to show our might? Thus all of our courageous people must show their eagerness for the achievement of such a task, and anyone who has not lost his senses must devise some means for its accomplishment. Away with hypocrisy! Away with all window dressing! Away with the dread of difficulty! Away with the nurturing of internal evils and the tolerating of private gain at the expense of the public interest! Then the minds of men will be aroused from their ignorant lethargy.

First of all, through practical projects we must advance practical effort; and through practical effort advance practical projects. The mugwort must be kept in dry storage for three years [before it can be applied as an effective medicine]. Our nets must be made ready before we can go fishing in the lake. We must not try to drown ourselves in the river merely to show our heroism, nor must we try to appease our hunger by drawing picture-cakes. Then we shall no longer be plagued by a dearth of men with practical abilities.

Secondly, once rid of our ignorant lethargy, the sun will shine more brightly in the sky; once the dearth of men with practical abilities is remedied, government orders will be carried out with the speed of wind and lightning. There is a statement in the commentary:[3] "Bring all the waste land in the country under cultivation; let all farms be under good care; so that the people within the four seas will be contented, and even the Yüeh-shang tribes [the most remote barbarians] will be our loyal subjects." With this concern in mind, I wrote this preface for the *Hai-kuo t'u-chih*.

. . . .

Defensive measures may serve offensive purposes as well as purposes of peaceful negotiation. Use the barbarians to control the barbarians, so that all our borders may be strongly held. Thus the first section of this book deals with maritime defense.

Down through three thousand years [of world history]; over the ninety thousand *li* of the world's circumference, both vertically in time and horizontally in space, with geographical charts and historical data, the second section presents a general survey of historical and territorial changes for all nations in the world.

Neither the barbarian religion nor the barbarian opium can penetrate the borders of our vassal states [to the South]. Alas, that they can show their will to resist [while we cannot]. So the third section deals with the nations along the coast of the Southeastern Seas [i.e., Indo-China, Siam, etc.].

[3] Which "commentary" (*chuan*) is unspecified; we have been unable to locate the source.

The Isles of Luzon and Java [i.e., the Philippines and the East Indies] are equal in extent to Japan, but they are either encroached upon or absorbed [by Western barbarians]. Taking heed of the overturned cart ahead [to avert a similar disaster for ourselves], the fourth section deals with the Isles of the Southeastern Ocean [Southeastern Asia].

The religion has been changed three times, and the land cut into Five Regions. The magpie's nest is now occupied by the turtle doves,[4] which are also a threat to China. The fifth section deals with India.

Both the whites and the blacks are from remote and isolated areas. They are forced to serve as advance guards, collaborating with the seafarers of the West. The sixth section deals with Africa of the Little Western Ocean.

The western part of the Mediterranean Sea is inhabited by many barbarian tribes, who cherish only profits and power, and indeed are as treacherous as the owls. The seventh section deals with the European countries in the Great Western Ocean.

Her [Russia's] tail lies in the East and her head in the West; her northern borders extend to the sea of ice. If we make alliances with the nearby countries in order to attack those afar, she may be our friend in a land war. The eighth section deals with Russia in the Northern Ocean. [In this section Wei sets forth his hope that Russia may distract England by invading India. In the next he suggests that the United States would be a natural ally in naval warfare.]

She has effectively resisted the violent invasion of the English barbarians and faithfully guarded the central plain. If we make alliances with those afar, in order to attack those nearby, she may be of assistance in a sea war. The ninth section deals with the United States in the Outer Great [Western] Ocean.

Every man has Heaven as his source; religious teachings derive from the sages. Though the different teachings meet and part, agree and disagree, they are all orderly and logical. The tenth section deals with religions of the Western nations.

It is China alone which embraces ten thousand *li* under one sovereignty. In contact with one another but unconnected—are Europe and Arabia. The eleventh section presents a chronological table of events in China and the West.

[4] So stupid they cannot make a nest for themselves.

[16]

The Chinese calendar has been supplemented by the Western; the Western calendar differs from the Chinese. As a guide for the people in their seasonal labors, ours takes the place of honor. The twelfth section presents a table of similarities and differences between the Chinese and the Western calendars.

In war topography is of first importance, however remote and wild the region. By the gathering of supplies and sketching of plans, a war can be won in the office. The thirteenth section presents a general survey of geographical conditions in each country.

Topography, important though it be, is nothing compared to cooperation among men. Surprise tactics and orthodox strategy are to be used according to circumstances, so that there will be the least expenditure of force and a maximum of concerted planning. The fourteenth section presents a program for controlling the barbarians.

Knowing one's own plans and being familiar with those of the enemy, one may judge whether to wage war or negotiate peace. Without knowing the right medicine, how can one cure the disease of shortsightedness and stupidity? The fifteenth section offers a compilation of data on the barbarian situation.

Maritime warfare depends upon warships, as land warfare depends upon battlements. Without mastering the best techniques, how can the stormy seas be tamed? The sixteenth section presents a detailed discussion of warships.

The Five Elements are able to subdue one another. Among them metal and fire are the most fierce. A thunder blast from the earth can serve both offensive and defensive purposes. The seventeenth section presents a detailed discussion of firearms and their use in warfare.

The languages and conveyances of different peoples are not the same, but their currencies are similar. To make a skillful use of them, one must make the utmost use of one's intelligence. The eighteenth section deals with [Western] currency, goods, and contrivances.

This preface is written by Wei Yüan of Shao-yang, Secretary to the Cabinet, on the 12th moon of the 22d year of Tao-kuang (February, 1843) at Yangchow.

重 玉 全 爵 洪 王 天

CHAPTER XXI

THE HEAVENLY KINGDOM OF THE TAIPINGS

In the writings of Lin Tse-hsü and Wei Yüan we have seen the impact of the West on two men who exemplified the finest traditions of Chinese statecraft and Confucian scholarship—representatives of that elite group which had served for centuries as the custodians of the Chinese government and of Confucian values in thought and scholarship. On another level of society, in these years just after China's defeat in the Opium War, there were signs of an even more powerful and striking reaction to the West in the great Taiping Rebellion, a mass movement so remarkable that it has continued to excite and perplex historians in recent years almost as much as it did Chinese and Western observers in the mid-nineteenth century. If on closer acquaintance this great popular uprising has seemed to reflect less of Western influence than of native traditions and internal unrest, it remains a fascinating example of the interplay between Chinese and Western ideas in an historical event of the first magnitude.

Hung Hsiu-ch'üan (1813–1864), the leader of this rebellion which swept up like a whirlwind from the southernmost regions of China, was the son of a poor peasant family belonging to the Hakka minority group and living not far from Canton. Hung had enough promise as a student so that his family joined together in providing him with an education and sending him on to take the provincial civil service examinations. Though repeatedly unsuccessful, on one of these visits to Canton (1836) Hung heard a Christian missionary preach and picked up some religious tracts. When the following year he failed again at the examinations, he seems to have suffered a nervous collapse and during his illness to have had certain visions. In one of them a fatherly old man appeared to him and complained that men, instead of worshiping him, were serving demons. In another Confucius was scolded for his faithlessness, and repented his ways. In still another a middle-aged man appeared and instructed Hung in the slaying of demons. These apparitions he later understood as signifying that God the Heavenly Father (whom he identified with the supreme god, Shang-ti, of ancient Chinese tradition) and Jesus Christ, his Elder Brother, had commissioned him as the Younger Brother to stamp out demon worship. To some Hung might have appeared to be the victim of his own fevered imaginings, but others were impressed by his quiet earnestness and deep sense of conviction. Perhaps most significant from the Chinese point of view was his ability to persuade members of his own family of the rightness of his cause.

These ideas continued to ferment in Hung's mind, yet it was only seven years later that he took the trouble to read more carefully the tracts given him in Canton, containing translations and summaries from the Bible and sermons on scriptural texts. Later still he spent two months studying in Canton with the Reverend Issachar J. Roberts, an American Southern Baptist missionary, whose fundamentalist teachings provided Hung with what limited knowledge he gained of Christianity. In the meantime, Hung, who earned a livelihood teaching in village schools, had been joined by some of his relatives in idol-breaking missions which aroused local feelings and the displeasure of the authorities. Forced to shift their activities westward, these prophets without honor in their own country met with a far better reception among the Hakkas of Kwangsi. By the late 1840s Hung found himself the leader of a growing band known as the God Worshipers. Here, too, however, the iconoclasm and strange teachings of the God Worshipers provoked official intervention and attempts at suppression.

In the mind of Hung the Manchu regime seems to have become identified quite early with the demonic forces which had to be destroyed in order to establish the Kingdom of Heaven on earth. But it was more than Hung's iconoclasm which led this new religious movement increasingly to take on a political and military aspect. Famine and economic depression in the late 1840s, burdensome taxation, the decline in dynastic prestige as a result of defeat at the hands of the British and the consequent impairment of governmental functions, especially in the more remote regions like Kwangsi, contributed to a situation in which the survival of any group depended upon its ability to defend and provide for itself in the midst of growing confusion and lawlessness. The God Worshipers were only one such group, but they proved better organized and possessed of a greater sense of purpose than most.

Under pressure of constant official harassment, Hung and his closest collaborators finally worked out a plan for full-fledged revolt. In effect it put the God Worshipers on a total-war footing. A military organization was created which would mobilize all of the resources of the community for prosecution of the war effort. Personal property had to be turned over to a communal treasury (the "Sacred Treasury"), religious observances were strictly enforced, and a detailed code of military discipline and ethical conduct was established with heavy penalties for any violations.

Systematically the leaders of the uprising set about consolidating their forces, making weapons, indoctrinating their followers, and training the militia. By December of 1850 the new army was able successfully to withstand a full assault by government troops, and in the flush of this first victory Hung formally proclaimed, at the start of the new year, his rebel regime, the Heavenly Kingdom of Great Peace. He himself assumed the title of Heavenly King, and others of the leaders, including several with military and organizational talents probably superior to those of Hung, were ranked as subordinate kings or princes.

The name of the new regime suggests that it was meant to fulfill the highest ideals of the Chinese political tradition (Taiping, or "Great Peace" designated a period of perfect peace and order according to one cyclical view of ancient history), along with the realization of a Kingdom of Heaven in which all worshiped the one True God. It was thus to be a theocratic state with military, political, and religious authority concentrated in a single hierarchy. Such an all-embracing, monolithic structure was congenial enough to the Chinese political scene and particularly suited to the requirements of a revolutionary situation. As a political venture the Taiping movement had a broad appeal to anti-Manchu, nationalist sentiment. As a program of economic reform, it attracted the overburdened and destitute, particularly among the peasants. As a new community—indeed a great family in which all the members were "brothers" and "sisters"—it had an appeal to rich and poor alike who suffered from the social dislocation and insecurity of the times. The Taiping cause, in other words, became a rallying point for all those elements which traditionally have attached themselves to a new dynastic movement.

Even in the powerful appeal of its religious *mystique* the Taiping Rebellion had something in common with peasant uprisings and dynastic revolutions in the past. Where it differed, however, was in the intensity and sectarian fanaticism with which Taiping religious teachings were insisted upon. Great importance was attached to the indoctrination of new recruits, and volunteers who refused to accept the Taiping faith—however genuine might be their antipathy to the Manchus—were turned away. In fact, the extraordinary discipline of the Taiping armies, the heroism of many in battle, and their readiness to meet death—for which there could be no earthly reward—all suggest that a sense of religious purpose, rather than simply economic gain or political ambition, was what held together this motley assemblage of malcontents and misfits, missionaries and messiahs.

From the military standpoint the Rebellion enjoyed startling success in its early years. It had the advantage of tight organization, firm discipline, talented commanders, and a high degree of mobility which derived from the cutting of all personal ties to home and property. Nevertheless, if Taiping progress northward was devastatingly swift, through Hunan to the central Yangtze valley and thence eastward to Nanking, this rapid advance came about only by the adoption of a strategy which had its own limitations—notably the bypassing of large centers of resistance. The Taipings concerned themselves little with organizing the countryside as they passed through. No permanent envelopment of these bypassed strongholds and eventual reduction of them was seriously attempted. Local opposition and temporary setbacks, instead of suggesting the need for caution and consolidation, were interpreted as signs from God that they should push on in other directions toward new and greater triumphs. The chief military commander, Yang Hsiu-ch'ing, who had the title of Eastern King, frequently claimed direct revelation from God the Father in support of his strategic moves, and Taiping accounts of the campaign make it appear that the triumphal course of the rebellion reflects the direct intervention of God in history through the instrumentality of chosen deputies like Hung and Yang.

Once established in their capital at Nanking, occupied March, 1853, and renamed "Heavenly Capital" (T'ien-ching), the Taipings sent out an

[21]

expedition to take Peking which again made striking gains initially, but was eventually slowed, isolated, and defeated. A similar expedition to the West was more successful in enlarging the area under Taiping control, but for the most part the new regime found itself engaged in a protracted struggle to maintain its position in the lower Yangtze valley, a rich and populous region which posed formidable problems of defense and administration. For ten years the fortunes of war waxed and waned, with the exploits of some Taiping commanders resulting in heavy defeats for imperial armies, while, on the other hand, increasing pressure was exerted against them by the reorganized and revitalized forces of regional leaders loyal to the Manchu cause—leaders such as Tseng Kuo-fan, Tso Tsung-t'ang, and Li Hung-chang, who were to play a dominant role in the subsequent history of the dynasty.

A significant loss for the Taipings was their failure to enlist the support of the West. There was early sympathy for the rebel cause on the part of some Westerners in the treaty ports, based on a favorable impression of Taiping morale and discipline, as well as the hope that the Taiping religion might prove genuinely Christian. However, contacts with the leaders of the revolt soon disillusioned and alienated them. The fanaticism, ignorance, and arrogant pretensions of the latter to a special divine commission, to which even foreign Christians must submit, quickly dispelled any illusions that the Taipings would be easier for the Western powers to deal with than the Manchus. Subsequently Taiping moves threatening Shanghai brought the active intervention of the West against them.

A far more serious weakness of the Taipings was internal—a failure in political leadership. The Taiping "kings" paid little attention to systematic organization of the countryside, preferring to establish themselves in the larger towns and cities. Moreover, educated men with experience in civil administration, whose services might have been highly useful, were repelled by the Taipings' uncouthness, their superstitious adherence to a "foreign" faith, and apparent repudiation of Confucian orthodoxy. A civil service examination based on official Taiping literature did little to remedy the lack of trained personnel. Increasingly, too, the cohesion and capacities of the Taiping leadership were severely strained. After the capture of Nanking, Hung steadily withdrew from active direction of affairs, and assumed a role reminiscent of the Taoist sage-emperor who ruled by his magic potency—in this case his divine virtue. Yet in fact

Hung's whole personality disintegrated rapidly, as he devoted himself more and more to the pleasures of the palace. There, in violation of the strict sexual morality and monogamy enjoined upon the Taipings, the Heavenly King kept a virtual harem.

In the meantime, the Eastern King, Yang Hsiu-ch'ing, steadily arrogated greater powers to himself and even aspired to the imperial dignity, before he lost his life in the first of a series of blood-baths which deprived the regime of several top leaders and many of their adherents. Thereafter Hung tended to place his own relatives in key positions, being more concerned for their trustworthiness than their ability. One such relative was Hung Jen-kan, prime minister in the last years of the regime, who had far more acquaintance with Christianity and the West than the other "kings," but who proved unable to effectuate any of his plans for the reorganization of the regime along more Western lines.

One of the great ironies of the Taiping Rebellion was revealed at the time of its final collapse in the summer of 1864. Nanking had been in danger for months when Li Hsiu-ch'eng, an able general whose military successes had not turned his head from a devoted loyalty to Hung, advised abandonment of the capital and escape to the south. The Heavenly King chose to remain, insisting that God would protect and provide for the Taipings. Yet by June of 1864 Hung had himself despaired of his cause, taken poison and died, his body being found later, draped in imperial yellow, in a sewer under the palace. Hung's faithful followers held out another month in the midst of the worst privation and suffering, and when finally overwhelmed by the Manchu forces, gave up their lives in a great slaughter rather than submit. Tseng Kuo-fan, leader of the victorious armies, is authority for the statement that not one surrendered.

There can be no doubt then that an intense, if misguided, religious faith was a crucial element in the Taiping movement, the most distinguishing feature of which was its monotheism. In the past China had not lacked for gods or popular religious movements, nor had the imperial court been without its own cult linking dynastic rule to the will of Heaven. But it was Hung who first proclaimed a belief in one God who was the Father of all, a God who was at once accessible to the prayers of the individual and actively concerned with the governing of the world. In Taiping documents, as will be seen from the selections which follow, this point is particularly stressed: that whereas the old cult of Heaven was a one-family affair, jealously guarded by the ruling house, the True God was the ruler, father and friend of all. His direct accessibility to men, however, proved both a boon and a bane to the Taipings. For if this conception stimulated a genuine piety in many, it also provided a dangerous weapon to a few of their leaders who claimed divine inspiration for their actions and God's sanction for their own ambitions.

Western influence can be clearly seen in some of the practices adopted by the Taipings, such as a calendar with a seven-day week and observance of the sabbath. It may have been responsible in part also for the greater equality accorded to women, the condemnation of polygamy and adultery, and the bans on slavery, foot-binding, gambling, wine, and tobacco. The coincidence, however, of a strait-laced Protestant fundamentalism with a degree of native puritanism among the Chinese peasantry (the latter reflected also in the professedly anti-Christian Communist movement of the mid-twentieth century) makes it difficult to assess precisely the degree of foreign influence.

In its combination of militant monotheism, prophetic inspiration, and drive for power in the name of God, the Taiping movement is perhaps most reminiscent of the rise of Islam in the seventh-century Near East. Where in the latter case, however, cultural traditions were less deeply rooted among the nomadic Arabs who enlisted in Muhammad's cause, even the peasant Chinese who so largely made up the forces of Hung Hsiu-ch'üan were already deeply imbued with ethical and religious traditions rooted in the past. To a considerable extent the Taipings were compelled, in spite of their early hostility to Confucianism, to compromise with many of its customs and values, or, more accurately, unconsciously to accept them without sensing any incompatibility between traditional ethics and the new faith. Such accommodations, nonetheless, proved insufficient to bridge the gap between Taiping ideology and the Chinese tradition, or to equip the revolutionary leadership for the stupendous task of ruling a mature and complex society. In the end it was the defenders of tradition and those schooled in Chinese statecraft who emerged victorious to guide China's destinies for another half-century.

The Book of Heavenly Commandments (T'ien-t'iao shu)

This text, officially promulgated by the Taiping regime in 1852, was probably written several years earlier to serve as a basic statement of the God Worshipers' creed and religious practice when they were first organized. It bespeaks a simple and unpretentious faith, constantly reiterating the hope of Heaven and fear of hell in a manner reminiscent more of the Qur'ān than of the Bible. Much of it is devoted to forms which are to be used in the saying of prayers, grace at meals, etc., and to an explanation of the Ten Commandments. Under the latter we find provisions for segregation of the sexes, and prohibitions against opium smoking and gambling, which reflect a strong puritanical strain in the early Taiping movement.

When a translation of this work by W. H. Medhurst appeared in the English-language *North China Herald* on May 14, 1853, the editor commented: "We cannot help thinking that this is a most extraordinary document, and can see in it little to object against. Two things strike us on reading it carefully through: the one is that with the exception of occasional references to redemption by Christ and apparent extracts from the Lord's Prayer, the ideas seem to be generally taken from the Old Testament, with little or nothing from the New; the other is that it appears to be mainly a compilation drawn up by the rebels themselves, for if a Christian missionary had had anything to do with it, he certainly would not have directed the offering up of animals, wine, tea, and rice even though these offerings were presented to the Great God. As it is, we repeat, it is a most extraordinary production, and were the rebels to act up to everything therein contained, they would be the most gentle and moral set of rebels we ever met with."

The translation given here is adapted and revised from that of Medhurst as emended on the basis of other early editions of the text by members of the Modern Chinese History Project, Far Eastern and Russian Institute, University of Washington, as a part of a documentary history of the Taiping Rebellion, which is soon to be published.

[From Hsiao I-shan, *T'ai-p'ing t'ien-kuo ts'ung-shu,* Series I, ts'e 1, pp. 1a–2b]

Who in this mortal world has not offended against the Heavenly Commandments? If one was not aware of his offense in former times, he can still be excused; now, however, as the Lord God has already issued a gracious proclamation, henceforth whoever knows how to repent of his sins in the presence of the Lord God, not to worship false spirits, not to practice perverse things, and not to transgress the Heavenly Commandments, shall be permitted to ascend to Heaven and to enjoy happiness, and for thousands and myriads of years to enjoy dignity and honor without end. Whoever does not know how to repent of his sins . . . will most certainly be punished by being sent down to hell to suffer bitterness, and for thousands and myriads of years to suffer sorrow and pain without end. Which is gain and which is loss, we ask you to think over. Our brothers and sisters throughout the mortal world, ought not all of you to awaken from your lethargy? If, however, you continue unroused, then are you truly base-born, truly deluded by the devil, and truly is there bliss which you do not know how to enjoy. [1a]

Now, those whose minds have been deluded by the demons always say that only the monarch can worship the Lord God. However, the Lord God is the universal Father of all in the mortal world. Monarchs are his able children, the good his filial children, the commoners his ignorant children, and the violent and oppressive his disobedient children. If you say that monarchs alone can worship the Lord God, we beg to ask you, as for the parents of a family, is it only the eldest son who can be filial and obedient to his parents?

Again it has been falsely said that to worship the Great God is to follow barbarians' ways. They do not know that in the ancient world monarchs and subjects alike all worshiped the Lord God. As for the great Way of worshiping the Lord God, from the very beginning, when the Lord God created in six days Heaven and earth, mountains and seas, man and things, both China and the barbarian nations walked together in the great Way; however, the various barbarian countries of the West have continued to the end in the great Way. China also walked in the great Way, but within the most recent one or two thousand years, China has erroneously followed the devil's path, thus being captured by the demon of hell. Now, therefore, the Lord God, out of compassion for mankind, has extended his capable hand to save the people of the world, deliver them from the devil's grasp, and lead them out to walk again in the original great Way. [1a–b]

A FORM TO BE OBSERVED IN REPENTING SINS

Let the suppliant kneel down in the sight of Heaven and pray to the Lord God to forgive his sins. He may use a written form of prayer, and when the prayer is over, he may either take a basin of water and wash his whole body clean, or he may perform his ablutions in the river, which will be still better. After repenting his sins, let him morning and evening worship the Lord God, beseeching that the Lord God look after him, and grant him His Holy Spirit to transform his heart. When taking his meals, he should give thanks to God, and every seventh day worship and praise God for His grace and virtue. Let him also constantly obey the ten Heavenly Commandments. Do not on any account let him worship all the false spirits that are in the world, still less let him do any of the corrupt things of the world. In this manner, the people may become the sons and daughters of the Lord God. While in the world the Lord God will look after them, and after ascending to Heaven the Lord God will graciously love them, and in high Heaven they will eternally enjoy bliss. [2a–b]

THE TEN HEAVENLY COMMANDMENTS

1. Honor and worship the Lord God. . . .[1]
2. Do not worship false gods. . . .
3. Do not take the name of the Lord God in vain. . . .
4. On the seventh day, worship and praise the Lord God for his grace. . . .
5. Be filial and obedient to thy Father and Mother. . . .
6. Do not kill or injure men. . . .
7. Do not indulge in wickedness and lewdness.

In the world there are many men, all brothers; in the world there are many women, all sisters. For the sons and daughters of Heaven, the men have men's quarters and the women have women's quarters; they are not allowed to intermix. Men or women who commit adultery or who are licentious are considered monsters; this is the greatest possible transgression of the Heavenly Commandments. The casting of amorous glances, the harboring of lustful imaginings about others, the smoking of opium, and the singing of libidinous songs are all offenses against the Heavenly Commandment.

8. Do not steal or rob.

Poverty and riches are granted by the Lord God, and whosoever steals or plunders the property of others, transgresses the Heavenly Commandment.

9. Do not tell [or spread] falsehoods.

All those who speak wildly, falsely, or treacherously, and those who use coarse and vile language trangress against the Heavenly Commandment.

10. Do not think covetous thoughts.

When a man looks upon the beauty of another's wife or daughter

[1] The commentary of the Taiping expositor has been omitted except for the last four commandments.

and then covets that man's wife or daughter; when a man looks upon the richness of another man's possessions and then covets that man's possessions; or when a man engages in gambling and buys lottery tickets and bets on names,[2] all these are transgressions of the Heavenly Commandment. [6b–8a]

A Primer in Verse (Yu-hsüeh shih)

This official text, first published in 1851, offers simple and concise formulations—easily put to memory—of basic religious and moral principles which the Taiping leaders wished to inculcate in their followers. Although opposed to Confucianism in so far as it was identified with the established regime or took on the appearance of a religious cult, the Taipings unconsciously accepted much that is readily recognizable as Confucian in social and political ethics.
[From Hsiao I-shan, T'ai-p'ing t'ien-kuo ts'ung-shu, Series I, t'se 4, pp. 1a–5b, 14a-b]

PRAISING GOD

> The Lord God-on-High, the divine Being,
> Is respectfully worshiped in all countries.
> Men and women throughout the world,
> Pay homage to Him morning and evening.
>
> All that we see, above and below,
> Basks in the Lord's favor.
> In the beginning it took only six days
> For the creation of all things to be completed.
>
> Is there anyone, circumcised or uncircumcised,
> Not created by God?
> Give thanks [to Him] for the heavenly favor
> That you may obtain everlasting glory.

PRAISING JESUS CHRIST

> Jesus was a Crown Prince,
> Whom God sent to earth in ancient times.

---

[2] It was a common practice of the time, especially in Kwangtung, to bet on who would succeed in the state examinations. Gambling clubs were established for this purpose. The Kwangtung government first fined such gambling and later collected a gambling tax from the clubs.

He sacrificed His life for the sins of men,
Being the first to offer meritorious service.

It was hard to bear the Cross;
Grieving clouds darkened the sun.
The noble Prince from Heaven,
Died for you—men and women.

Having returned to Heaven after His resurrection,
In His glory, He holds all power.
Upon Him we are to rely—
Be saved and enter Paradise!

PRAISING PARENTS

[Just as] the storing up of grain provides against starvation,
[So] the raising up of children provides against old age.
He who is filial to his parents will have filial sons.
Thus, mysteriously, is recompense made.

You should ask yourself,
How you were able to grow up.[3]
Respect the teaching of the Fifth Heavenly Commandment;
Honor and wealth will shower down on you from the Heavenly Court.

THE IMPERIAL COURT

The imperial court is an awesome place.
With fear and trembling heed the imperial authority as if it reached
  into your very presence.
The power of life and death belongs to the Son-of-Heaven.
Among the officials none should oppose Him.

THE WAY OF A KING

If one man, aloft, upholds the Right,
The myriad states all enjoy repose.[4]
Let the king alone hold power;
And all slander and depravity will disappear forever.

[3] Through the loving care of your parents.
[4] These two lines are adapted from the opening passage of the *Book of Changes*.

The more virtuous the Master, the more honest will be His subjects.
Wise kings produce good officials.
I [Yin] and [Duke] Chou have set the example [for ministers].
Upholding justice, they maintained discipline at court.

THE WAY OF THE FAMILY

> Kinsfolk within the household—
> Be cheerful and happy!
> Be harmonious and united as one body,
> Blessings will shower down upon you from Heaven.

There follow similar maxims for eleven other family relationships from mother, son, etc., to older and younger sister-in-law, as well as injunctions with regard to sexual chastity and fidelity, and disciplining of the senses. For the most part these are of a traditional Chinese character, and largely Confucian, like the verses above. Finally the primer concludes with the following:

PARADISE

> Whether to be noble or mean is for you to choose.
> To be a real man you must make an effort to improve yourself.
> Follow the teaching of the Ten Commandments;
> You will enjoy the blessings of Paradise.

The Taiping Economic Program

The following selection is taken from *The Land System of the Heavenly Kingdom* (*T'ien-ch'ao t'ien-mu chih-tu*), which was included in the list of official Taiping publications promulgated in 1853. Its precise authorship is uncertain, and there is no evidence of a serious attempt having been made to put this system into effect in Taiping-controlled areas. Nevertheless, as a statement of Taiping aims the document carried with it all the weight of Hung Hsiu-ch'üan's authority and that of the Eastern King, Yang Hsiu-ch'ing, then at the height of his power. It reflects one of the chief appeals which the movement made to the Chinese peasantry.

The plan set forth here amounts to a blueprint for the total organization of society, and especially of its human resources. If its initial concern is with the land problem, as the title indicates, it quickly moves on to other spheres of human activity and brings them under a single pattern of control. The basic organization is military in nature, reminiscent of the farmer-soldier militia of earlier dynasties. In its economic egalitarianism, totalitarian communism, authoritarian hierarchy and messianic zeal, this Taiping manifesto seems to foreshadow the Chinese Communist movement of the twentieth century, while at the same time it echoes reformers and rebels in the past. Most typically it recalls the fondness of earlier Chinese thinkers for what might be described as the "completely-designed" society—their vision of a neat symmetrical system embodying the supreme values of Chinese thought: order, balance, and harmony.

Nevertheless, we can appreciate how conservative Confucianists would have recoiled at the thought of so much economic regimentation. Tseng Kuo-fan, their great leader in the struggle against the Taipings, commented: "The farmer cannot till his own land and [simply] pay taxes on it; the land is all considered to be the land of the Heavenly King [and all produce goes directly to the communal treasury]. The merchant cannot engage in trade for himself and profit thereby; all goods are considered to be the goods of the Heavenly King."

The organizational note is struck at the outset with an explanation of the system of army districts and military administration (omitted here). We reproduce below only the basic economic program.

[From Hsiao I-shan, *T'ai-p'ing t'ien-kuo ts'ung-shu*, Series I, t'se 4, pp. 1a–3a]

All officials who have rendered meritorious service are to receive hereditary stipends from the court. For the later adherents to the Taiping cause, every family in each military district (*chün*) is to provide one man to serve as a militia man. During an emergency they are to fight under the command of their officers to destroy the enemy and to suppress bandits. In peacetime they are to engage in agriculture under the direction of their officers, tilling the land and providing support for their superiors.

All land [in the country] is to be classified into nine grades. Land that produces 1,200 catties of grain per *mu* during the two harvest seasons of the year is to be classified as A-A Land. That which produces 1,100 per *mu* during the same periods is to be classified as A-B Land; that which produces 1,000 catties is to be classified as A-C Land, 900 catties as B-A Land, 800 as B-B Land, 700 as B-C Land, 600 as C-A Land, 500 as C-B Land, and 400 as C-C Land.[5]

---

[5] This classification of the land into nine grades follows the form found in the "Tribute of Yü" section of the *Book of History;* the general method of land allocation follows the principle set forth in the *Rites of Chou,* Ti kuan hsia (SPTK ed., 4:24).

[For the purposes of land distribution], one *mu* of A-A Land is equal to 1.1 *mu* of A-B Land, 1.2 *mu* of A-C Land, 1.35 *mu* of B-A Land, 1.5 *mu* of B-B Land, 1.75 *mu* of B-C Land, 2 *mu* of C-A Land, 2.4 *mu* of C-B Land, or 3 *mu* of the C-C Land.

The distribution of all land is to be based on the number of persons in each family, regardless of sex. A large family is entitled to more land, a small one to less. The land distributed should not be all of one grade, but mixed. Thus for a family of six, for instance, three are to have fertile land and three barren land—half and half of each.

All the land in the country is to be cultivated by the whole population together. If there is an insufficiency [of land] in this place, move some of the people to another place. If there is an insufficiency in another place, move them to this one. All lands in the country are also to be mutually supporting with respect to abundance and scarcity. If this place has a drought, then draw upon the abundant harvest elsewhere in order to relieve the distress here. If there is a drought there, draw upon the abundant harvest here in order to relieve the distress there. Thus all the people of the country may enjoy the great blessings of the Heavenly Father, Supreme Ruler, and Lord God-on-High. The land is for all to till, the food for all to eat, the clothes for all to wear, and money for all to spend. Inequality shall exist nowhere; none shall suffer from hunger or cold.

Every person sixteen or over, whether male or female, is entitled to a share of land; those fifteen or under should receive half the share of an adult. For instance, if a person of sixteen is given a *mu* of land in the A-A class, a person under that age can only receive half of that amount, namely, 0.50 *mu* of land of the same class. Or if a person sixteen or over is given 3 *mu* of C-C land, then a person fifteen or under would receive half of that, or 1.5 *mu* of C-C land.

Mulberry trees are to be planted along the walls [of villages] throughout the country. All women are required to grow silkworms, to do weaving, and to make clothes. Every family of the country is required to raise five hens and two hogs, in keeping with the proper breeding seasons.[6]

During the harvest season, the Group Officer[7] should direct [the grain collection by] the sergeants. Deducting the amount needed to feed the twenty-five families until next harvest season, he should collect the rest of the produce for storage in state granaries. The same method of collec-

[6] A paraphrase of *Mencius*, I A, 7.
[7] The *liang ssu-ma*, official in charge of each 25-family group.

tion is applicable to other kinds of products, such as barley, beans, ramie fiber, cotton clothes, silk, domestic animals, silver and copper cash, etc., for all people under Heaven are of one family belonging to the Heavenly Father, the Supreme Ruler, the Lord God-on-High. Nobody should keep private property. All things should be presented to the Supreme Ruler, so that He will be enabled to make use of them and distribute them equally to all members of his great world-family. Thus all will be sufficiently fed and clothed. That is the will of the Heavenly Father, the Supreme Ruler, the Lord God-on-High, who has dispatched the True Ruler of Great Peace to save the men of the world.

The Group Officer must keep a record of the amount of grain and cash he has collected and report them to the Treasurers and Receiving and Disbursing Tellers. A state treasury and a church are to be established among every twenty-five families, under the direct administration of the Group Officer. All expenditures of the twenty-five families for weddings, births, or other festival occasions are to be paid for out of the state treasury. But there is to be a fixed limit; not a penny is to be spent beyond that. For each festival occasion, such as a wedding or the birth of a child, a family is to be allowed 1,000 copper cash and 100 catties of grain, so that there will be a uniform rule throughout the country. In sum, nothing should be wasted, in order that there will be provision against any exigency of war or drought. Thus, throughout the land in the contracting of marriages, wealth need be no consideration.

In the twenty-five family units pottery-making, metal-working, carpentry, masonry and other such skilled work should be performed by the sergeants and militiamen in the off-seasons from farming and military service.

In conducting the different kinds of festival ceremonies for the twenty-five families under his administration, the Group Officer should hold religious services to pray to the Heavenly Father, the Supreme Ruler, and Lord God-on-High. All the bad customs of the past must be completely abolished.

The Principles of the Heavenly Nature (T'ien-ch'ing tao-li shu)

This official work, dated 1854, was written after the Taipings had established their capital at Nanking and the first flush of victory gave way to a seeming let-down in morale, discipline, and zeal for the cause. It served to restate the religious creed of the Taipings and emphasize those qualities—self-sacrifice, loyalty, and solidarity—which had contributed to their amazing successes. The appeal throughout is to a dedicated and crusading military elite.

Another important purpose of the book was to enhance and consolidate the position of the Taiping leadership, especially that of the Eastern King, Yang Hsiu-ch'ing, who was virtual prime minister of the regime and the one who inspired the writing of this document. We see here in a strange new garb the old conception of the ruler as commissioned with divine powers to unite the world and establish peace. Both Hung and Yang are thus represented as in some degree sharing the role of Jesus Christ as saviors of the world. Since it would not have done for any of the "kings" to engage openly in such self-glorification, nominal authorship is attributed to the "marquises" and "chancellors" who constituted the next highest ranks in the Taiping hierarchy.

Extant editions of the text appear to date from about 1858, by which time rivalries and mistrust had split the leadership, Yang had been assassinated, and his assassin, the Northern King, murdered by Hung. Though there are many direct and indirect evidences of dissension, the text has not been amended or adjusted to these later developments except to strip the Northern King of his rank.

The translation here has been adapted from that of C. T. Hu for the documentary history of the Taiping Rebellion being prepared by the Modern Chinese History Project of the Far Eastern and Russian Institute, University of Washington.

[From Hsiao, *T'ai-p'ing t'ien-kuo ts'ung-shu,* ts'e 5, pp. 1–37]

With regard to human life, reverence for Heaven and support of the Sovereign begin with loyalty and uprightness; to cast off the devil's garb and become true men—this must come about through an awakening. Now, the Heavenly Father and the Heavenly Elder Brother have displayed the heavenly favor and specially commanded our Heavenly King to descend into the world and be the true Taiping sovereign of the ten thousand states of the world; they have also sent the Eastern King to assist in court policy, to save the starving, to redeem the sick, and, together with the Western and Northern Kings, [Wei] Ch'ang-hui,[8] and the Assistant King, to take part in the prosperous rule and assist in the grand design. As a result, the mortal world witnesses the blessings of resurrection, and our bright future is the symbol of renewal. [1a-b]

We marquises and chancellors hold that our brothers and sisters have been blessed by the Heavenly Father and the Heavenly Elder Brother,

[8] Former King of the North who, having assassinated the Eastern King and in turn been murdered by Hung, was no longer referred to by his title when this edition was published.

[34]

who saved the ensnared and drowning and awakened the deluded; they have cast off worldly sentiments and now follow the true Way. They cross mountains and wade rivers, not even ten thousand *li* being too far for them to come, to uphold together the true Sovereign. Armed and bearing shield and spear, they carry righteous banners that rise colorfully. Husband and wife, men and women, express common indignation and lead the advance. It can be said that they are determined to uphold Heaven and to requite the nation with loyalty. [2a–b]

You younger brothers and sisters have now experienced the heavenly days of Great Peace (Taiping), and have basked in the glory of the Heavenly Father, the Supreme Ruler and Lord God-on-High. You must be aware of the grace and virtue of the Heavenly Father, the Supreme Ruler and Lord God-on-High, and fully recognize that the Heavenly Father, the Supreme Ruler and Lord God-on-High, is alone the one true God. Aside from the Heavenly Father, the Supreme Ruler and Lord God-on-High, there is no other god. Moreover, there is nothing which can usurp the merits of the Heavenly Father, the Supreme Ruler and Lord God-on-High. In the ten thousand nations of the world everyone is given life, nourished, protected, and blessed by the Heavenly Father, the Supreme Ruler and Lord God-on-High. Thus the Heavenly Father, the Supreme Ruler and Lord God-on-High, is the universal father of man in all the ten thousand nations of the world. There is no man who should not be grateful, there is no man who should not reverently worship Him. Have you not seen the Heavenly King's "Ode on the Origin of Virtue and the Saving of the World," which reads: "The true God who created Heaven and earth is none but God; all, whether noble or mean, must worship Him piously"? This is precisely our meaning! [4a–5a]

There follow citations from the Confucian Classics referring to the Lord-on-High (*Shang-ti*) which are taken here as showing that God was known to and worshiped by the ancient Chinese. Subsequently, however, various forms of idolatry arose.

However, worldly customs daily degenerated. There were even those who likened themselves to rulers, and, being deluded in heart and nature, arrogant yet at fault, and falsely self-exalted, forbade the prime minister and those below to sacrifice to Heaven. Then [these men] competed in establishing false gods and worshiping them, thus opening up the ways of the devilish demons. The people of the world all followed in like fashion, and this became firmly fixed in their minds. Thereupon, after a considerable time, they did not know their own errors. Hence the Heavenly Father, the Lord God, in view of mortal man's serious crime of disobedience, at his first anger, sent down forty days and forty nights of heavy rain, the vast waters spreading in all directions and drowning mortal man. Only Noah and his family had unceasingly worshiped the Heavenly Father, the Supreme Ruler and Lord God-on-High; therefore, relying on the heavenly grace, they were fortunate and they alone were preserved. In this, the first instance of the Heavenly Father's great anger, was the great proof of his great powers displayed.

After the Flood, the devilish king of Egypt, whose ambition was mediocrity and who was possessed by the demons, envied the Israelites in their worship of God and bitterly persecuted them. Therefore, the Heavenly Father in his great anger led the Israelites out of Egypt. In this, the second instance of the Heavenly Father's great anger, was the great proof of his great powers displayed.

However, the rulers and people of that time still had not completely forgotten the heavenly grace. But since the emergence of Taoism in the Ch'in [dynasty] and the welcoming of Buddhism in the Han [dynasty], the delusion of man by the demons has day by day increased, and all men have forgotten the grace and virtue of the Heavenly Father. The Heavenly Father's merits were falsely recognized as the merits of demons. Therefore, the Heavenly Father, observing this from above, saw that the people of the mortal world followed the demons and were being transformed into demons; strange and peculiar, they were no longer men. The Heavenly Father once again became greatly angered; yet if he were to annihilate them completely, he could not bear it in his heart; if he were to tolerate them, it would not be consonant with righteousness. At that time, the elder son of the Heavenly Father, the Heavenly Elder Brother Jesus, shouldered the great burden and willingly offered to sacrifice his life to redeem the sins of the men of the world. The Heavenly Father, the Supreme Ruler and Lord God-on-High, sincere in his pity for the world and profound in his love for man, spared not his eldest son, but sent him down to be born in Judea, and to redeem our sins in order to propagate the true Way. At the time of his redemption of our sins, he was falsely accused and nailed upon the cross, so that mortal man could rely upon his precious blood and be cleansed of all sin. Thereby did he make complete the grace of the Heavenly Father, who had sent him down to be sacrificed for the world. [6a–7a]

Let us ask your elder and younger brothers: formerly the people sacrificed only to the demons; they worshiped the demons and appealed to the demons only because they desired the demons to protect them. Yet how could they think that the demons could really protect them? Let us consider one example. During a drought, no man failed to worship the demons and to pray for rain. Certainly they did not realize that this is all within the power of the Heavenly Father; when He decrees a drought, a drought follows; when He decrees rain, rain follows. If the Heavenly Father did not decree sweet rain, then even though they worshiped the demons of the mortal world, one and all, still the drought would continue as before. A popular saying has it: "If beating a drum can bring rain, then mountain peaks can be opened to cultivation;[9] if the burning of incense can bring protection, then a smoking kiln can satisfy opium smokers; if a vegetarian diet can bring immortality, then bulls can ascend to heaven; if taking opium can satiate hunger, then a fart can fertilize a field." Another popular saying goes: "The bean curd is only water, the king of hell is only a demon." In view of this, it can be seen that the demons are not responsive and are unable to protect men. The people pray for rain, yet they cannot send down rain. To worship them is of no avail. However, the men of the world sank even deeper, not knowing how to awaken themselves. Therefore, the Heavenly Father again became angry.

In the *ting-yu* year [1837], our Heavenly Father displayed the heavenly grace and dispatched angels to summon the Heavenly King up to Heaven. There He clearly pointed out the demons' perversities and their deluding of the world. He also invested the Heavenly King with a seal and a sword; He ordered the Savior, the Heavenly Elder Brother, Jesus, to take command of the heavenly soldiers and heavenly generals and to aid the Heavenly King, and to attack and conquer from Heaven earthward, layer by layer, the innumerable demons. After their victory they returned to Heaven and the Heavenly Father, greatly pleased, sent

---

[9] That is, it is as unlikely that beating a drum could bring rain as that mountain peaks could be cultivated.

the Heavenly King down upon the earth to become the true Taiping Sovereign of the ten thousand nations of the world, and to save the people of the world. He also bade him not to be fearful and to effect these matters courageously, for whenever difficulties appeared, the Heavenly Father would assume direction and the Heavenly Elder Brother would shoulder the burden. [8a–9a]

Several instances are then given of the way in which God's power was manifested in the triumphant campaigns of the Taiping forces, and of how His will was made known to them. The account concludes with these episodes:

In the *jen-tzu* year [1852], at Yung-an-chou, our food supplies were almost exhausted, nor was there even any red powder [gunpowder]. The demons, several hundred thousand in number, rank upon rank, encircled the city from all directions. There was no avenue of escape. By this time the devilish demons knew of our situation and became unusually fierce, all believing their plan would succeed. In the third month, the Heavenly Father greatly displayed his powers and ordered us younger brothers and sisters, one and all, to uphold the true Sovereign and attack Kuei-lin. We then moved the camps and broke through the encirclement; and, because the Heavenly Father had changed our hearts, we one and all with utmost energy and disregard for our persons struck through the iron passes and copper barriers, killing innumerable devilish demons, and directly arrived at the Kwangsi provinical capital. Thereupon Kuei-lin was encircled. Later, because the people of the city came out and spoke to the Eastern King, reporting that the city granaries were empty and that provisions were deficient, the Eastern King, seeing that their strength was exhausted, showed great mercy and immediately ordered a temporary lifting of the siege until another good plan of attack could be contrived.

You all should know of the Heavenly Father's power, his omniscience, omnipotence, and omnipresence. Why was it that the one city of Kuei-lin alone could not be attacked and secured? This was because our Heavenly Father secretly made it so—something not easily understood by man.

Thereafter, from Kuei-lin we moved on to capture Hsing-an, Ch'üan-chou, Tao-chou, Ch'en-chou, and other moated cities. Wherever the Heavenly Army went, battles were won and objectives taken; wherever it went, the enemy scattered, our strength being as [irresistible as] a knife splitting bamboo. We moved from Ch'en-chou to Ch'ang-sha; the latter city was attacked several times, and again we rushed by the city; this also was the result of the Heavenly Father's having secretly willed it so. If the army had entered Ch'ang-sha and had been stationed there long, then the boatmen at I-yang and other places along the river, being unable to avoid the trickery and intimidation of the demons, would have had to flee to distant localities. How then could we have obtained boats for a million brave soldiers, that we might float downstream to capture Wu-ch'ang? From this we can see that our Heavenly Father's power secretly made it so.

From Wu-ch'ang to Chin-ling [Nanking] the land extends as far as a thousand *li;* how strategic and important are the passes and river crossings, and how strong and firm are the cities and moats! To attack and capture the cities seemed difficult; even if victory could have been secured, it appeared that it would take a very long time. Yet in not more than one month's time, we had followed the stream eastward from Wu-ch'ang, passing Kiangsi, crossing Anhwei, and pushing directly up to Chin-ling, without the least resistance. After reaching this provincial capital, we found the height and thickness of the city walls and the vastness of the land to be indeed twice that of other provincial cities; to attack it seemed far more difficult. Who would have known that within ten days one single effort would bring success? Chin-ling was captured with our hands hanging at our sides. Had it not been for our Heavenly Father's power, how could things have been so quick and easy? From this we can again see the Heavenly Father's power to predetermine things. [12b–14a]

There follow accounts of the individual Taiping leaders showing how each triumphed over adversities and suffered great hardships in order to advance the cause.

Even the Eastern King in his holiness and the several Kings in their eminence had to undergo cleansing and polishing and repeatedly demonstrate great fortitude before they could enjoy true happiness. How much more must we elder and younger brothers preserve our fortitude in order that we may seek abundant blessings. Do we not see the Heavenly King's edict which says: "All things are predetermined by the Heavenly Father and the Heavenly Elder Brother; the ten thousand hardships are all the Heavenly Father's and Heavenly Elder Brother's means of testing our hearts; thus each of us must be true-hearted, firm and patient; we must cleave to the Heavenly Father and the Heavenly Elder Brother"? The Heavenly King has also said: "How can it be easy to ascend to Heaven? The first prerequisite is patience of mind and will. You will certainly ascend to Heaven if you are resolute at heart." [17a–b]

Recollecting the past, from the righteous uprising in Chin-t'ien to the capture of Chin-ling, we have received great mercy from our Heavenly Father and Heavenly Elder Brother; we have established our Heavenly Capital and in a few years we have been able to enjoy the great happiness of our Heavenly Father. All this has been due to the work of our Heavenly Father and our Heavenly Elder Brother, who alone can bring such speedy results. Hence, if, with additional efforts toward improvement and perfection, we, with united hearts, combine our strength for the immediate extermination of the demons, our Heavenly Father will display his great powers and instantaneously the seas and lands will be cleared and the hills and rivers united under one command. Then our younger brothers and sisters will be reunited with their families, and blood relations will again be together. How fortunate that will be! [19a–b]

There follows a long section dealing with disobedient and traitorous officers who serve as object lessons of the futility of deserting or betraying the Taiping cause. It is shown how God, who knows and sees all, revealed their wicked designs to the Taiping leaders. Thus their cowardice and self-seeking brought them only the most severe punishment.

We brothers and sisters, enjoying today the greatest mercy of our Heavenly Father, have become as one family and are able to enjoy true blessings; each of us must always be thankful. Speaking in terms of our ordinary human feelings, it is true that each has his own parents and there must be a distinction in family names; it is also true that as each has his own household, there must be a distinction between this boundary and that boundary. Yet we must know that the ten thousand names derive from the one name, and the one name from one ancestor. Thus our origins are not different. Since our Heavenly Father gave us birth and nourishment, we are of one form though of separate bodies, and we breathe the same air though in different places. This is why we say: "All are brothers within the four seas." [10] Now, basking in the profound mercy of Heaven, we are of one family. Brothers and sisters are all of the same parentage; as all are born of one Spiritual Father, why should there be the distinctions of "you and I," or "others and ourselves"? When there is clothing, let all wear it; when there is food, let all eat of it. When someone is ill, others should ask a doctor to treat him and take care of his medicine. We must treat parentless boys and girls and persons of advanced age with more care, bathing them and washing and changing their clothes. Thus we will not lose the idea of sharing joys and sorrows, as well as mutual concern over pain and illness. Safety for the old, sympathy for the young, and compassion for the orphaned, all emerge from the Eastern King's understanding of our Heavenly Father's love for the living and from the Heavenly King's treating all as brothers and fellow beings. [27b–28b]

As for [maintaining] our brothers' peace in the camps, everyone must be kind, industrious, and careful. When the skies are clear the soldiers should be drilled, and when it rains the heavenly books should be read, clearly expounded, and mutually discussed, so that everybody will know the nature of Heaven and forever abide by the true Way. If the demons advance, at the first beat of the signal drums, everyone must hurriedly arm himself with gun, sword, or spear, and hasten to the palace to receive orders. In charging forward, each must strive to be in the front, fearing to be left behind, and none must shirk responsibilities. Thus will we be of one virtue and of one heart. Even if there are a million demons, they will not be hard to exterminate instantly. [28b–29a]

We brothers, our minds having been awakened by our Heavenly Father, joined the camp in the earlier days to support our Sovereign, many bringing parents, wives, uncles, brothers, and whole families. It is a matter of course that we should attend to our parents and look after our wives and children, but when one first creates a new rule, the state must come first and the family last, public interests first and private interests last. Moreover, as it is advisable to avoid suspicion [of improper conduct] between the inner [female] and the outer [male] and to distinguish between male and female, so men must have male quarters and women must have female quarters; only thus can we be dignified and avoid

[10] *Analects*, XII, 5.

confusion. There must be no common mixing of the male and female groups, which would cause debauchery and violation of Heaven's commandments. Although to pay respects to parents and to visit wives and children occasionally are in keeping with human nature and not prohibited, yet it is only proper to converse before the door, stand a few steps apart and speak in a loud voice; one must not enter the sisters' camp or permit the mixing of men and women. Only thus, by complying with rules and commands, can we become sons and daughters of Heaven. [29a–30a]

At the present time, the remaining demons have not yet been completely exterminated and the time for the reunion of families has not yet arrived. We younger brothers and sisters must be firm and patient to the end, and with united strength and a single heart we must uphold God's principles and wipe out the demons immediately. With peace and unity achieved, then our Heavenly Father, displaying his mercy, will reward us according to our merits. Wealth, nobility, and renown will then enable us brothers to celebrate the reunion of our families and enjoy the harmonious relations of husband and wife. Oh, how wonderful that will be! The task of a thousand times ten thousand years also lies in this; the happiness and emoluments of a thousand times ten thousand years also lie in this; we certainly must not abandon it in one day. [37b–38a]

CHAPTER XXII

REFORM AND REACTION UNDER THE MANCHUS

趙啓霖　為有廳　同嗣瓛

The defeat of the Taipings was only one of the more hopeful signs for the Manchus in the early 1860s, after two decades of defeat and near-disaster for the dynasty. The foreign occupation of Peking in 1860 had been followed by a reorganization of leadership at court, with stronger and more flexible men rallying forces loyal to the dynasty and working toward better relations with the foreign powers. The new diplomatic missions established in the capital and foreign concessions in treaty ports up and down the coast, though forced upon the court originally, had now made it both necessary and possible for the Chinese to come into closer contact with Westerners—contacts which slowly and imperceptibly widened their horizons on the world. In the provinces able commanders like Tseng Kuo-fan, Tso Tsung-t'ang, and Li Hung-chang, who had shown great personal resourcefulness and determination in suppressing the rebels and had even demonstrated a readiness to adopt Western guns and naval vessels for use against the Taipings, continued individually to promote modernization projects which would strengthen their military positions and enhance the basis of their own regional power.

If, to Western observers, these developments suggested some hope for China's future, to the Chinese there were other grounds for encouragement—enough to justify calling this period a "revival" or "restoration" in the life of the nation and the ruling dynasty. In foreign relations, the Chinese could at most be gratified by a respite from the constant pressure of the Western powers; a widening of foreign influence, certainly, was nothing to congratulate themselves upon. In internal affairs, however, they could observe with satisfaction the restoring of peace and stability after several major revolts (besides the Taipings, the Nien rebellion in Anhwei and Shantung, 1853–1868, and the Muslim rebellions in the southwest, 1855–1873, and northwestern provinces, 1862–1877); so too a gradual improvement in local administration, and steps taken to rehabilitate the economy along more or less traditional lines—the encouragement of agriculture, land reclamation and development, irrigation, flood control, tax reform, etc. The genuine effectiveness of such time-honored measures can be appreciated in terms of their contribution to the traditional agrarian economy (upon which, obviously, so many millions of Chinese depended for their daily life), even if such methods fell far short of meeting the economic challenge of the West.

To conservative Confucianists there was reassurance in all this, not only that age-old methods and institutions seemed to stand the test of these times, but that men of ability and character had appeared who could make them effective. It was leadership, rather than the techniques or institutions themselves, in which the Confucianist placed hope. It was the "gentleman," pursuing virtue and learning rather than power and profit, who would save China. From such a point of view no more basic or radical a change could take place than that which transformed the people inwardly and united them in support of worthy rulers. To talk of drastic changes in social or political institutions was almost unthinkable, and certainly uncalled for.

On this fundamental point there was virtually unanimous agreement, even among those who felt that the danger from the West prompted fundamental re-examination and reform. They might believe it necessary to adopt Western guns and ships—even to master the languages, the knowledge, the techniques required for the production and use of these weapons—but such measures would be indispensably linked to a regeneration of the national life, a reassertion of traditional values in government, a renewed concern for the livelihood of the people, and a kind of moral rearmament based on self-cultivation and tightened social discipline. A re-examination in these terms tended, therefore, to focus on two types of weakness: military inferiority to the West, which called for the employment of new methods, and moral inadequacy with respect to traditional ideals, which called for self-criticism and an intensified effort to uphold old standards.

SELF-STRENGTHENING AND THE THEME OF UTILITY

Reform along these lines was most strikingly exemplified in the so-called "Self-strengthening" movement. Its immediate objective was a build-up in military power; its ultimate aim was to preserve and strengthen the traditional way of life. In the following selections are presented the views of men prominently identified as exponents of reform on this basis: namely, that the adoption of Western arms could be justified on grounds of utility and practicality, as a means of defending China and preserving Chinese civilization.

FENG KUEI-FEN
On the Manufacture of Foreign Weapons

Feng Kuei-fen (1809–1874), a classicist, teacher and official, came to recognize the need for modernization and the importance of scientific studies when forced to take refuge in Shanghai from the Taipings and brought into contact with Westerners defending the city. Later as an adviser to some of the leading statesmen of his time, Feng demonstrated an acute grasp of both state and foreign affairs. His essays advocating a wide variety of reforms were highly regarded by some leaders and became increasingly influential toward the end of the century. It was at his suggestion that a school of Western languages and sciences was established in Shanghai in 1863.

Feng had few illusions regarding the ease with which China might undertake reform. He appreciated the difficulty of adopting weapons which presupposed a considerable scientific knowledge and technological development. Even more he recognized the disturbing fact that Western superiority lay not in arms alone but also in leadership. In his eyes, however, the qualities of character and mind displayed by Westerners were simply those long recognized as essential to leadership within the Chinese tradition. The foreigners' example might be edifying, and indeed a reproach to the deplorable state of Chinese public life, but it was not a lesson in the sense that China had anything new to learn from the West. The lesson was simply that she had more to make of her own learning.

Such is the two-pronged attack by Feng on Chinese complacency, as expressed in these excerpts from his book of essays, *Protests from the Study of Chiao-pin* (1861). Note again that when a Confucian reformer seeks to make changes, he must come to grips with the civil service system, which has so pervasive an influence on the Chinese mentality.

[From *Chiao-pin lu k'ang-i, Chih yang-ch'i i,* pp. 58b–63a]

According to a general geography compiled by an Englishman, the territory of China is eight times that of Russia, ten times that of the United States, one hundred times that of France, and two hundred times that of Great Britain. . . . Yet we are shamefully humiliated by the four nations, not because our climate, soil, or resources are inferior to theirs, but because our people are inferior. . . . Now, our inferiority is not something allotted us by Heaven, but is rather due to ourselves. If it were allotted us by Heaven, it would be a shame but not something we could do anything about. Since the inferiority is due to ourselves, it is a still greater shame, but something we can do something about. And if we feel ashamed, there is nothing better than self-strengthening. . . .

Why are the Western nations small and yet strong? Why are we large and yet weak? We must search for the means to become their equal, and that depends solely upon human effort. With 'regard to the present situation, several observations may be made: in not wasting human talents, we are inferior to the barbarians; in not wasting natural resources, we are inferior to the barbarians; in allowing no barrier to come between the ruler and the people, we are inferior to the barbarians; and in the matching of words with deeds, we are also inferior to the barbarians. The remedy for these four points is to seek the causes in ourselves. They can be changed at once if only the emperor would set us in the right direction. There is no need to learn from the barbarians in these matters. [58b–59a]

We have only one thing to learn from the barbarians, and that is strong ships and effective guns. . . . Funds should be allotted to establish a shipyard and arsenal in each trading port. A few barbarians should be employed, and Chinese who are good in using their minds should be selected to receive instruction so that in turn they may teach many craftsmen. When a piece of work is finished and is as good as that made by the barbarians, the makers should be rewarded with an official *chü-jen* degree, and be permitted to participate in the metropolitan examinations on the same basis as other scholars. Those whose products are of superior quality should be rewarded with the *chin-shih* degree [ordinarily conferred in the metropolitan examinations], and be permitted to participate in the palace examinations like others. The workers should be paid double so that they will not quit their jobs.

Our nation's emphasis on civil service examinations has sunk deep into people's minds for a long time. Intelligent and brilliant scholars have exhausted their time and energy in such useless things as the stereotyped examination essays, examination papers, and formal calligraphy. . . . We should now order one-half of them to apply themselves to the manufacturing of instruments and weapons and to the promotion of physical studies. . . . The intelligence and ingenuity of the Chinese are certainly superior to those of the various barbarians; it is only that hitherto we have not made use of them. When the government above takes delight in something, the people below will pursue it further: their response will be like an echo carried by the wind. There ought to be some people of extraordinary intelligence who can have new ideas and improve on Western methods. At first they may take the foreigners as their teachers and models; then they may come to the same level and be their equals; finally they may move ahead and surpass them. Herein lies the way to self-strengthening. [60a–61a]

It may be argued: "Kuan Chung repeled the barbarians and Confucius acclaimed his virtue; the state of Chu adopted barbarian ways and [Confucius in] the *Spring and Autumn Annals* condemned them. Is not what you are proposing contrary to the Way of the sages?" No, it is not. When we speak of repeling the barbarians, we must have the actual means to repel them, and not just empty bravado. If we live in the present day and speak of repeling the barbarians, we should ask with what instruments we are to repel them. . . . [The answer is that] we should use the instruments of the barbarians, but not adopt the ways of the barbarians. We should use them so that we can repel them.

Some have asked why we should not just purchase the ships and man them with [foreign] hirelings, but the answer is that this will not do. If we can manufacture, repair, and use them, then they are our weapons. If we cannot manufacture, repair, or use them, then they are still the weapons of others. . . . In the end the way to avoid trouble is to manufacture, repair, and use weapons by ourselves. Only thus can we pacify the empire; only thus can we become the leading power in the world;

only thus can we restore our original strength, redeem ourselves from former humiliations, and maintain the integrity of our vast territory so as to remain the greatest country on earth. [61a–62b]

On the Adoption of Western Learning
[From *Chiao-pin lu k'ang-i, Ts'ai hsi-hsüeh i,* pp. 67b–70]

Western books on mathematics, mechanics, optics, light, and chemistry contain the best principles of the natural sciences. In the books on geography, the mountains, rivers, strategic points, customs, and native products of the hundred countries are fully listed. Most of this information is beyond the reach of the Chinese people. . . .

If we wish to use Western knowledge, we should establish official translation bureaus in Canton and Shanghai. Brilliant students not over fifteen years of age should be selected from those areas to live and study in these schools on double allowances. Westerners should be appointed to teach them the spoken and written languages of the various nations, and famous Chinese teachers should be engaged to teach them classics, history, and other subjects. At the same time they should learn mathematics. (Note: All Western knowledge is derived from mathematics. . . . If we wish to adopt Western knowledge, it is but natural that we should learn mathematics). . . . China has many brilliant people. There must be some who can learn from the barbarians and surpass them. [67b–68a]

It is from learning that the principles of government are derived. In discussing good government, the great historian Ssu-ma Ch'ien said (following Hsün Tzu): "Take the latter-day kings as your models." This was because they were nearer in time; their customs had changed from the past and were more similar to the present; and their ideas were not so lofty as to be impracticable. It is my opinion that today we should also take the foreign nations as our examples. They live at the same time and in the same world with us; they have attained prosperity and power by their own efforts. Is it not fully clear that they are similar to us and that their methods can easily be put into practice? If we let Chinese ethics and Confucian teachings serve as the foundation, and let them be supplemented by the methods used by the various nations for the attainment of prosperity and power, would it not be the best of all solutions?

Moreover, during the past twenty years since the opening of trade, a great number of foreign chiefs have learned our written and spoken language, and the best of them can even read our classics and histories. They are generally able to speak on our dynastic regulations and civil administration, on our geography and the condition of our people. On the other hand, our officers from the governors down are completely ignorant of foreign countries. In comparison, should we not feel ashamed? The Chinese officers have to rely upon stupid and preposterous interpreters as their eyes and ears. The mildness or severity of the original statement, its sense of urgency or lack of insistence, may be lost through their tortuous interpretations. Thus frequently a small grudge may develop into a grave hostility. At present the most important political problem of the empire is to control the barbarians, yet the pivotal function is entrusted to such people. No wonder that we understand neither the foreigners nor ourselves, and cannot distinguish fact from untruth. Whether in peace negotiations or in deliberating for war, we are unable to grasp the essentials. This is indeed the underlying trouble of our nation. [69a–70a]

TSENG KUO-FAN AND LI HUNG-CHANG
On Sending Young Men Abroad to Study

Tseng Kuo-fan (1811–1872) and his protege Li Hung-chang (1823–1901) were, in the practical sphere, the outstanding exponents of "self-strengthening" during the latter half of the nineteenth century. Acclaimed as the conqueror of the Taipings, and long viceroy in Central China, Tseng was also admired as a scholar in the classical tradition and as a Confucian "gentleman" who exemplified the traditional virtues in government: industry, frugality, honesty and integrity in office, and loyalty to the dynasty. He was the type of "superior man" whose learning and personal character inspired the devotion of his subordinates and gave Confucianists a confidence that such personal qualities could meet the challenge of the times. Intellectually an eclectic, Tseng minimized doctrinal differences and sought agreement on the ethical bases of action. His support of certain types of modernization for purposes of national defense also reflected a readiness to make compromises for the achievement of practical ends.

In this letter, submitted to the Tsungli Yamen, which handled foreign affairs, in March, 1871, Tseng and Li emphasize not only China's practical need to learn from the West but also the pre-eminent practicality of the Westerners. They are convinced that Western methods can only be mastered through prolonged and intensive study abroad, and propose sending a select group of young men for this purpose. In Japan at this time, the top leaders were themselves visiting the West and preparing to re-educate a whole nation. The aims of Tseng and Li are much more circumscribed—to train an elite corps with a combination of classical Chinese and Western studies, carefully directed and controlled in the interests of the state. Yet even so modest a proposal met with strong opposition at court before it was put into effect in 1872.

[From *Li Wen-chung kung ch'üan-chi, I shu han-kao*, 1:19b–21b]

Last autumn when I [Tseng] was at Tientsin, Governor Ting Jih-ch'ang frequently came to discuss with me proposals for the selection of intelligent youths to be sent to the schools of various Western countries to study military administration, shipping administration, infantry tactics, mathematics, manufacturing, and other subjects. We estimated that after more than ten years their training would have been completed, and they could return to China so that other Chinese might learn thoroughly the superior techniques of the Westerners. Thus we could gradually plan for self-strengthening. . . . After Mr. Pin Ch'un and two other gentlemen, Chih-kang and Sun Chia-ku, had traveled in various countries at imperial command, they saw the essential aspects of conditions overseas, and they found that cartography, mathematics, astronomy, navigation, shipbuilding, and manufacturing are all closely related to military defense. It is the practice of foreign nations that those who have studied abroad and have learned some superior techniques are immediately invited upon their return by academic institutions to teach the various subjects and ·to develop their fields. Military administration and shipping are considered as important as the learning that deals with the mind and body, and nature and destiny of man. Now that the eyes of the people have been opened, if China wishes to adopt Western ideas and excel in Western methods, we should immediately select intelligent boys and send them to study in foreign countries. . . .

Some may say: "Arsenals have been established in Tientsin, Shanghai and Foochow for shipbuilding and the manufacturing of guns and ammunition. The T'ung-wen College [for foreign languages] has been established in Peking for Manchu and Chinese youths to study under

Western instructors. A language school has also been opened in Shanghai for the training of young students. It seems, therefore, that a beginning has been made in China and that there is no need for studying overseas." These critics, however, do not know that to establish arsenals for manufacturing and to open schools for instruction is just the beginning of our effort to rise again. To go to distant lands for study, to gather ideas for more advantageous use, can produce far-reaching and great results. Westerners seek knowledge for practical use. Whether they be scholars, artisans, or soldiers, they all go to school to study and understand the principles, to practice on the machines, and to participate personally in the work. They all exert themselves to the utmost of their ingenuity, and learn from one another, in the hope that there will be monthly progress and yearly improvement. If we Chinese wish to adopt their superior techniques and suddenly try to buy all their machines, not only will our resources be insufficient to do so, but we will be unable to master the fundamental principles or to understand the complicated details of the techniques, unless we have actually seen and practiced with them for a long time. . . .

We have heard that youths of Fukien, Kwangtung, and Ningpo also occasionally have gone abroad to study, but they merely attempted to gain a superficial knowledge of foreign written and spoken languages in order to do business with the foreigners for the purpose of making a living. In our plan, we must be doubly careful at the beginning of selection. The students who are to be taken to foreign countries will all be under the control of the commissioners. Specializing in different fields, they will earnestly seek for mastery of their subjects. There will be interpreters, and instructors to teach them Chinese literature from time to time, so that they will learn the great principles for the establishment of character, in the hope of becoming men with abilities of use to us.

HSÜEH FU-CH'ENG
On Reform

A one-time secretary and adviser to both Tseng Kuo-Fan and Li Hung-chang, Hsüeh Fu-ch'eng (1838–1894) achieved no high rank or position in the bureaucracy (not having competed in the examinations for the higher civil service degrees). He did, however, become an influential advocate of reform through the circulation of his essays and memorials in official circles, and, besides assisting in the negotiation of the Chefoo Convention (1876), helped to draft plans for a new Chinese navy.

This excerpt is taken from Hsüeh's *Suggestions on Foreign Affairs* (*Ch'ou-yang ch'u-i*), which was submitted to Li in 1879 and forwarded by him to the Tsungli Yamen. Hsüeh argues for reform on the ground that change is inevitable and nothing new to Chinese history. But if he is tempted to accept the idea of progress as a law of history, there is no indication of it here. Rather his premise is the thoroughly traditional one of cyclical or pulsatory change at calculable intervals, which may be for good or ill but in any case must be coped with, as indeed even the sage-kings had to cope with it. A great change in circumstances, therefore, calls for a great change in methods (*fa,* which can also be understood as "laws" or "institutions").

Hsüeh nevertheless contends that changes in method do not mean abandonment of the "immutable" Way of the sages. Indeed it is the use of new methods which will preserve that Way inviolate. Thus a dichotomy is established between ends and means. Here the means Hsüeh has in mind adopting is "the study of machines and mathematics." Consequently the dichotomy is between the Way and "instruments" (*fa* in the sense of methods). How far he would go toward changing *fa* in the sense of basic institutions is left unclear. Where general concepts are used so equivocally—where inevitable change can be understood to imply desired reforms, and methods can mean anything from "instruments" to "institutions"—there is much room for ambiguity and often more scope for rhetoric than logic.

[From *Ch'ou-yang ch'u-i*, in *Yung-an ch'üan chi*, ts'e 12, 46b–49a]

It is the way of Heaven that within several hundred years there are small changes and within several thousand years great changes. . . . In several thousand years [under the early sage-kings] there was change from a primitive world to a civilized world. From the age of the sage-kings through the Three Dynasties there was most truly peace and order. Then the First Emperor of the Ch'in swallowed up the feudal states, abolished the feudal lords, broke up the well-fields, and destroyed the laws of the early kings. Thus it was two thousand years from the time of [the sage-kings] Yao and Shun that the feudal world was changed into a world of [centrally administered] prefectures and districts. . . . As we come down to the present, the European states suddenly rise up and assert themselves overseas because of their knowledge of machinery and mathematics. . . . In ninety thousand *li* around the globe there is no place where they do not send their envoys and establish trade relations. Confronted with this situation, even Yao and Shun would not have been able to close the doors and rule the empire in isolation. And this likewise is now two thousand years from the time of Ch'in and Han. Thus there has been a change from a world in which the Chinese and barbarians were isolated from each other into a world in which China and foreign countries are in close contact. . . . When change in the world is small, the laws governing the world will accordingly undergo small change; when change in the world is great, the laws will accordingly undergo great change. [46b]

Sometimes in the succession of one sage to another there cannot but be changes in the outward forms of government. Sometimes when a sage has to deal with the world, sooner or later there must be changes made. Thus only a sage can pattern himself after another sage, and only a sage can change the laws of another sage. The reason for his making changes is not that he likes change, but that he is obliged to do so by the circumstances of the time. Now there is rapid change in the world. It is my opinion that with regard to the immutable Way we should change the present so as to restore the past [the Way of the sages]; but with regard to changeable laws, we should change the past system to meet present needs. Alas! If we do not examine the differences between the two situations, past and present, and think in terms of practicability, how can we remedy the defects? [47a]

Western nations rely on intelligence and energy to compete with one another. To come abreast of them, China should plan to promote commerce and open mines; unless we change, the Westerners will be rich and we poor. We should excel in technology and the manufacture of machinery; unless we change, they will be skillful and we clumsy. Steamships, trains, and the telegraph should be adopted; unless we change, the Westerners will be quick and we slow. The advantages and disadvantages of treaties, the competence and incompetence of envoys, and the improvement of military organization and strategy should be discussed. Unless we change, the Westerners will cooperate with each other and we shall stand isolated; they will be strong and we shall be weak. [47b]

Some may ask: "If such a great nation as China imitates the Westerners, would it not be using barbarian ways to change China?" Not so. For while in clothing, language, and customs China is different from foreign countries, the utilization of the forces of nature for the benefit of the people is the same in China as in foreign countries. The Western people happen to be the first in adopting this new way of life, but how can we say that they alone should monopolize the secrets of nature? And how do we know that a few decades or a hundred years later China may not surpass them? . . . Now if we really take over the Westerners' knowledge of machinery and mathematics in order to protect the Way of our sage-kings Yao and Shun, Yü and T'ang, Wen and Wu, and the Duke of Chou and Confucius, and so make the Westerners not dare to despise China, I know that if they were alive today, the sages would engage themselves in the same tasks, and their Way would also be gradually spread to the eight bounds of the earth. That is what we call using the ways of China to change the barbarians.

Some may also say: "In making changes one should aim to surpass others and not pursue them. Now the Western methods are superior, and we imitate them; if we follow others helplessly, by what means then are we to surpass them?" This, too, is not so. If we wish to surpass others, it is necessary to know all their methods before we can change; but after we have changed, we may be able to surpass them. We cannot expect to surpass others merely by sitting upright in a dignified attitude. Now if seeing that others are ahead of us we contemptuously say that we do not care to follow them, the result is that we will not be able to move even a small step. Moreover, they have concentrated the ability and energy of several million people, have spent millions of dollars, and have gone through prolonged years and generations before they acquired their knowledge. If we want to excel them in one morning, is it really possible or is it not impossible? A large river may begin with the overflow from small bogs, and a great mound may be built up from overturned baskets of soil. Buddhism came from India and yet it flourished in the East. Mathematics began in China,[1] and yet it has reached its highest development in Western countries. If we compare the ability and wisdom of the Chinese with those of the Westerners, there is no reason to think that we should be unable to surpass them. It all depends on how we exert ourselves.

Alas! There are endless changes in the world, and so there are endless variations in the sages' way of meeting these changes. To be born in the present age but to hold fast to ancient methods, is to be like one who in the age of Shen Nung [when people had learned how to cook] still

[1] A widely held view of which Juan Yüan was a leading exponent.

ate raw meat and drank blood, or like one who lived in the age of the Yellow Emperor [when weapons were available] and yet, in resisting the violence of Ch'ih-yu, struggled against him with bare hands. Such a one would say: "I am following the methods of the ancient sages." But it is hardly possible that he should not become exhausted and fall. Moreover, the laws [or methods] which ought to be changed today can still [in their new form] embody the essence of the laws of the ancient sages. [48a–49a]

WANG T'AO
On Reform

Wang T'ao (1828–1897) represents a new type of reformer on the Chinese scene. In contrast to the great reformers of the past (e.g., Wang Mang, Wang An-shih) who were scholar-officials, and in contrast also to his contemporaries, Feng Kuei-fen and Hsüeh Fu-ch'eng, who wrote as officials and worked closely with statesmen like Tseng Kuo-fan and Li Hung-chang, Wang T'ao was an independent scholar and journalist. Sometimes, indeed, he is called "the father of Chinese journalism." His work was done mainly in the ports of Hongkong and Shanghai, under foreign protection and in close touch with foreigners. For years he assisted the eminent British sinologue, James Legge, in his translations from the Chinese classics, and with Legge's help visited England and Western Europe, observing and writing on developments there. Later, too, Wang visited Japan, where he was well-received as a scholar and reformer. When finally he settled down to a career as journalist, he did so as a man with foreign contacts, a wide knowledge of the outside world, and a freedom to express himself unknown in the past—when not only the right to criticize but even the means (a public press) and the audience (an influential public opinion) were lacking.

The following is taken from an essay of Wang's written about 1870, which anticipates some of Hsüeh Fu-ch'eng's basic points but carries them even further. There is the argument from cyclical change to the need for adapting to the current situation. There is the assertion that Confucius himself would have advocated change under such circumstances. There is the distinction between the Way of the sages, which must be preserved, and the instruments (weapons, methods) of the West which should be adopted for its defense. At the same time, Wang insists that change must go deeper and further than mere imitation of the West in externals, and suggests, however vaguely, that a thorough renovation of society is necessary. Though his specific recommendations here relate primarily to education, eventually he advocated basic governmental change as well. Consequently the ambiguity in Wang's use of the term *pien-fa* for "reform" is even more pronounced than in Hsüeh Fu-ch'eng's essay. Though he speaks of adopting from the West only "instruments," he intends that change should extend not only to technology ("methods") but to *fa* in the sense of "basic institutions." Wang therefore presages, intellectually, the transition from reformism conceived in terms of immediate utility to a more radical view of institutional change.

The following excerpt is preceded by a discussion of previous changes in Chinese history which we have already seen echoed by Hsüeh. Here, however, Wang is consciously re-examining Chinese history to refute the assertion of "Western scholars that China has gone unchanged for 5,000 years." Contending in effect, that China's stagnation was a comparatively recent development, he then goes on to deal with the present situation.

[From *Pien-fa* in *T'ao-yüan wen-lu wai-pien,* 1:11a–15b]

I know that within a hundred years China will adopt all Western methods and excel in them. For though both are vessels, a sailboat differs in speed from a steamship; though both are vehicles, a horse-drawn carriage cannot cover the same distance as a locomotive train. Among weapons, the power of the bow and arrow, sword and spear, cannot be compared with that of firearms; and of firearms, the old types do not have the same effect as the new. Although it be the same piece of work, there is a difference in the ease with which it can be done by machine and by human labor. When new methods do not exist, people will not think of changes; but when there are new instruments, to copy them is certainly possible. Even if the Westerners should give no guidance, the Chinese must surely exert themselves to the utmost of their ingenuity and resources on these things.

However, they are all instruments; they are not the Way, and they cannot be called the basis for governing the state and pacifying the world. The Way of Confucius is the Way of Man. As long as humankind exists, the Way will remain unchanged. The three moral obligations and the five human relations began with the birth of the human race. When a man fulfills his duty as man, he need have no regrets in life. On this is based the teaching of the sages. [1:11a]

I have said before that after a few hundred years the Way will achieve a grand unity. As Heaven has unified the south, north, east, and west under one sky, it will harmonize the various teachings of the world and bring them back to the same source. . . .

Alas! People all understand the past, but they are ignorant of the future.

[56]

Only scholars whose thoughts run deep and far can grasp the trends. As the mind of Heaven changes above, so do human affairs below. Heaven opens the minds of the Westerners and bestows upon them intelligence and wisdom. Their techniques and skills develop without bound. They sail eastward and gather in China. This constitutes an unprecedented situation in history, and a tremendous change in the world. The foreign nations come from afar with their superior techniques, contemptuous of us in our deficiencies. They show off their prowess and indulge in insults and oppression; they also fight among themselves. Under these circumstances, how can we not think of making changes? Thus what makes it most difficult for us not to change is the mind of Heaven, and what compels us unavoidably to change is the doings of men. [1:11b-12a]

If China does not make any change at this time, how can she be on a par with the great nations of Europe, and compare with them in power and strength? Nevertheless, the path of reform is beset with difficulties. What the Western countries have today are regarded as of no worth by those who arrogantly refuse to pay attention. Their argument is that we should use our own laws to govern the empire, for that is the Way of our sages. They do not know that the Way of the sages is valued only because it can make proper accommodations according to the times. If Confucius lived today, we may be certain that he would not cling to antiquity and oppose making changes. . . .

But how is this to be done? First, the method of recruiting civil servants should be changed. The examination essays, coming down to the present, have gone from bad to worse and should be discarded. And yet we are still using them to select civil servants. . . .

Second, the method of training soldiers should be changed. Now our army units and naval forces have only names registered on books, but no actual persons enrolled. The authorities consider our troops unreliable, and so they recruit militia who, however, can be assembled but cannot be disbanded. . . . The arms of the Manchu banners and the ships of the naval forces should all be changed. . . . If they continue to hold on to their old ways and make no plans for change, it may be called "using untrained people to fight,"[2] which is no different from driving them to their deaths. . . .

[2] Mencius, IV B, 8.

Thirdly, the empty show of our schools should be changed. Now district directors of schools are installed, one person for a small town and two for a large city. It is a sheer waste of government funds, for they have nothing to do. The type of man in such posts is usually degenerate, incompetent, senile, and with little sense of shame. [1:13a–14a]

Fourthly, the complex and multifarious laws and regulations should be changed. . . . The government should reduce the mass of regulations and cut down on the number of directives; it should be sincere and fair and treat the people with frankness and justice. . . .

After the above four changes have been made, Western methods could be used together with others. But the most important point is that the government above should exercise its power to change customs and mores, while the people below should be gradually absorbed into the new environment and adjusted to it without their knowing it. This reform should extend to all things—from trunk to branch, from inside to outside, from great to small—and not merely to Western methods. [1:14b]

Formerly we thought that the foundation of our wealth and strength would be established if only Western methods were stressed, and that the result would be achieved immediately. . . . Now in various coastal provinces there have been established special arsenals to make guns and ships. Young boys have been selected and sent to study abroad. Seen from outside, the effort is really great and impressive. Unfortunately, we are merely copying the superficialities of the Western methods, getting only the name but very little substance. The ships which were formerly built at Foochow were entirely based on the older methods of Western countries, not worth the faint praise of those who know about such things. . . .

The advantage of guns lies in the techniques of discharging them; that of ships in the ability to navigate them. The weapons we use in battle must be effective, but the handling of effective weapons depends upon people. . . . Yet those regarded as able men have not necessarily been able, and those regarded as competent have not necessarily been competent. They are merely mediocrities who accomplish something through the aid of others. Therefore, the urgent task of our nation today lies primarily in the governance of the people, and next in the training of soldiers. And in these two the essential point is to gather men of abilities. Indeed, superficial imitation in concrete things is not so good as arousing intellectual curiosity. The forges and hammers of the factories cannot be compared with the apparatus of people's minds. [1:15a–b]

INSTITUTIONAL REFORM

When we attempt to assess the aims and accomplishments of Chinese reformers in the 1870s and '80s, the comparison to Meiji Japan is almost inevitable. In aims there is a strong general resemblance between the two; in the scope and effectiveness of their reforms a striking difference. Where the Chinese self-strengtheners sought to preserve the Confucian Way through the adoption of Western techniques, Japanese modernizers talked of combining "Eastern ethics and Western science" or spoke of preserving their distinctive "national polity" (*kokutai*) in the midst of an intense program of modernization. Yet, given this general similarity of aims, the process of change in Japan went further and faster than in China, and to a very different result. In the one case there was rapid industrialization, political centralization, educational reform, and social change—all of these involving a much fuller participation of the Japanese people in the national effort and contributing to a degree of unity and strength unprecedented in Japanese history. In China, by the 1890s, it was evident that the self-strengtheners had not only failed to achieve such an effective national unity and concerted action, but had perhaps only contributed further to the processes of disintegration which typically marked the last years of a great dynasty.

The reasons for this obvious difference are complex and profound, and it is not our purpose to examine them here. One relevant observation may be made, however, in distinguishing the Chinese problem from the Japanese. It is the far greater challenge to reform presented by a vast, sprawling China, whose ostensible political unity was perhaps more of a liability than an asset—whose imperial structure, with its centralized administration, bureaucratic organization and procedures, unwieldiness and inflexibility, proved more intractable to reformers in China than did the comparatively decentralized and less stable feudal structure of Japan to the leaders of the Meiji Restoration.

If to Wang T'ao a great nemesis of reform lay in the "multiplicity of governmental regulations and endless number of directives," his complaint represented not only the traditional protest of the Confucian reformer, but a direct recognition that bureaucratic red tape and centralized control left little room for even piecemeal reform. If, in his mind too, the most important thing was for the court to exercise its power and authority in the direction of reform, this came from a realization that, lacking such leadership from above, little initiative could be taken below.

Under these circumstances, reformers might prescribe change for the empire as a whole, but the individual self-strengtheners in positions of limited authority could hardly plan for a truly national program of reform. Within their own spheres of jurisdiction or influence they might inaugurate projects for the modernizing of their personal armies, the manufacturing of arms, the building of ships, the promoting of business, the opening of schools for technical and language training, as well as for the improvement of the more traditional functions of government in China; yet the tendency was for even these worthwhile ventures to take on a strongly bureaucratic character—to become part of an official sub-empire—without, however, enjoying any of the benefits of centralized planning or coordination. The net result is typified by the utter failure of Li Hung-chang's new army and navy, owing to "squeeze," corruption and inefficiency in the supply system, when put to the test by the Japanese in the war of 1894–95. It was this failure that led directly to demands for more drastic change.

K'ANG YU-WEI AND THE REFORM MOVEMENT

China's humiliating defeat in the Sino-Japanese War and the seeming danger of her imminent partition by the foreign powers would have been cause enough for an outcry of alarm and protest. To these were added a growing sense of dissatisfaction and frustration among the younger generation of students, who by now had been exposed to reformist writings and had their eyes opened to the outside world. This group was by no means large. The educated class had always constituted a small minority of Chinese, and those affected by new ideas represented a still smaller fraction. Thus, rather than their numbers, it was their role as recruits or members of the bureaucratic elite, which gave them influence. Significantly, among the leaders of the reform group were several from the Kwangtung region, where, like Hung Hsiu-ch'üan before them and Sun Yat-sen after, they were stimulated by close contact with the West in Hongkong and Canton. Increasingly, toward the end of the century, these young men were being challenged and inspired by the brilliant journalism of a writer like Wang T'ao. Youthful impressions, once wholly formed by the Confucian Classics and native tradition, were now being formed also by the translations of men like Yen Fu (1853-1921), who made available in Chinese the works of Thomas Huxley, John Stuart Mill, Herbert Spencer, and Adam Smith.

More even than by such ideas as evolution, progress, and liberty—radically new though these were and certain to stir intellectual ferment—this generation was disturbed, and profoundly so, just by the shock of events. Not only the handful of active reformers, but officialdom generally, found its pride and self-confidence shaken. This loss of poise and self-assurance may have helped to provide the rare, if momentary, opportunity which innovators seized upon in the famous Hundred Days of Reform in 1898. Yet it also created a deeply felt need among educated Chinese somehow to be reassured that China's cultural identity would not be wholly lost amid these changes—a need which the reformers themselves felt more acutely even than those who opposed them.

K'ang Yu-wei (1858-1927), the dominant figure of the Reform Movement, was born near Canton into a world of crisis. The Taiping Rebellion raised up by K'ang's fellow provincial was still agonizing the empire from within, while from without the British and French, who had moved again into Canton only the year before, were pressing a campaign that would lead to the occupation of Peking itself in 1860.

As the scion of a distinguished gentry-official family, K'ang was provided with an education along traditional lines, but at the age of fifteen he made known his distaste for the business of mastering the "eight-legged essay" so indispensable to success in the civil service examinations. Two years later he was reading about Western geography and in time became a voracious reader of Chinese books on the history and geography of the West. Probably the chief influence on K'ang in these early years was exerted by a teacher of the old school, who aroused in him a passion for classical scholarship and a sense of complete dedication to the Confucian ideals of personal virtue and service to society. An episode recounted in K'ang's *Autobiographical Chronology* shows, nevertheless, that his independence and iconoclasm were already quite marked:

My Master praised highly the writings of Han Yü and so I read and studied the collected works of Han [Yü] and Liu [Tsung-yüan], emulating him in this as well. By this time I had read the books of the philosophers and had learned the [various] methods of [seeking] the Way. Thus I presented myself in person before the Master and said to him that Han Yü's methods of [seeking] the Way were shallow, and that in searching for concrete substance in the writings of all the great names in scholarship down through the Sung, Ming, and the present dynasty, [I had found that] they were all empty and lacking in substance. I ventured to say that when one spoke of the Way, it should be like Chuang Tzu or Hsün Tzu; when one spoke of governing, it should be like Kuan Tzu or Han Fei Tzu; while as regards medicine, the *Su-wen* would constitute a separate subject. But as to Han Yü, he was no more than a literary craftsman skilled in the undulation of broad and sweeping cadences which, while they appealed to the ear, had nothing to do with the Way. Thus his *Yüan-tao* was extremely superficial. . . . The Master, who was usually correct and stern, in this case laughingly chided me for being wrongheaded. From the time he had first seen me he had often cautioned me about my undue feelings of superiority, and after this I was [more] humble, but nevertheless my fellow-students came to be shocked at my intractability.

With the arrival of autumn and winter, I had learned in their broad outlines the general meaning of the important books in the four divisions [of literature]. My intelligence and comprehension became confused, for every day I was buried amid piles of old papers, and I developed a revulsion for them. Then one day I had a new idea. I thought: scholars engaged in textual research, such as Tai Chen, filled their homes with the books that they had written, but in the end what was the use of all this? Thus I gave it up and in my own heart I fancied seeking a place where I might pacify my mind and determine my destiny. Suddenly I abandoned my studies, discarded my books, shut my door, withdrew from my friends, and sat in contemplation, nurturing my mind. My schoolmates thought me very queer, for there had been no one who had done this, inasmuch as the Master upheld the individual's actual practice [of the Confucian virtues] and detested the study of Ch'an [Buddhism]. While I was sitting in contemplation, all of a sudden I perceived that Heaven, earth, and the myriad things were all of one substance with myself, and in a great release of enlightenment I beheld myself a sage and laughed for joy; then suddenly I thought of the sufferings and hardships of all living beings, and I wept in melancholy; abruptly I thought: why should I be studying here and neglecting my parent? and that I should pack up immediately and go back to the thatched hut over my grandfather's grave. The students, observing that I sang and wept for no apparent reason, believed that I had gone mad and was diseased in mind.[3]

This experience of K'ang's was not unusual in the Chinese intellectual tradition. Neo-Confucianists like Wang Yang-ming before him had suddenly found themselves suffocated and overburdened by the kind of exhaustive scholarship Chu Hsi had seemed to encourage—scholarship which often exhausted one's mind and spirit before one began to exhaust the sources. What is significant here for our understanding of K'ang is, first, the evidence of an early tendency toward syncretism, stronger certainly than his sense of orthodoxy; and second, the conception of himself as somehow set apart from the rest of men and, indeed, above them. The impulse toward quietism and mysticism, on the other hand, proved a passing one. After a few months in lonely isolation and meditation, K'ang's sense of a special destiny to save mankind through active involvement in the affairs of the world took command of him. Subsequent visits to Hongkong and Shanghai impressed him with the orderliness and prosperity of Western civilization. Intensifying his pursuit of Western learning, he also became involved in efforts toward practical reform, like his movement to abolish foot-binding. Meanwhile the young reformer had by no means abandoned classical Confucian studies, but had begun to identify himself with the so-called "New Text School" of textual criticism. The purpose of this, for K'ang, was not so much to determine by critical methods what must have been the original teaching of Confucius, but, whether consciously or not, to justify his new view of the sage as essentially a reformer and to discredit all else that passed for Confucianism.

By the mid-1880s K'ang, still only twenty-seven, had already formulated in his mind the ideas which became the basis of his two most famous works, the *Grand Unity* (*Ta t'ung shu*) and *Confucius As a Reformer* (*K'ung Tzu kai-chih k'ao*). By 1887 he had succeeded, after an earlier failure, in winning the second degree in the civil service examinations, and by 1895, the highest regular (*chin-shih*) degree. He had also begun to attract talented students, who helped in the revising and publishing of his works and later in the organizing of reformist societies which spread his ideas and made him the center of violent controversy. Japan, whose defeat of China created an atmosphere of crisis and imminent catastrophe in the late '90s, now became K'ang's model of reform. He urged the court

[3] *K'ang Nan-hai tzu-pien nien-p'u*, IV, 113–14, as translated by Richard Howard.

to follow the example of Meiji Japan and openly advocated a basic change from absolute monarchy to constitutional rule. Finally an opportunity to put his ideas into effect came when the Kuang-hsü emperor asked him to take charge of the government in June, 1898.

During K'ang's few months of tenure a stream of edicts issued forth from the court, aimed at transforming China into a modern state. The old bureaucracy was to be thoroughly revamped. Education and recruitment would be based on Western studies as well as Chinese; bureaucratic functions would be reorganized to serve modern needs. There would be a public school system and a public press. These, together with popularly elected local assemblies, would prepare the people to take part in eventual parliamentary government. In the economic sphere, too, K'ang had ambitious plans. Bureaus were set up to promote commerce, industry, modern banking, mining, and agricultural development. Lastly, and most importantly, K'ang attempted to reorganize and strengthen the armed forces. Here, however, he ran into serious difficulty trying to bring under central control armies which for decades had been virtually autonomous units loyal to their own commanders.

Had he not failed in this last respect, K'ang might have survived the bitter opposition which his reforms provoked from the entrenched bureaucracy. It was perhaps characteristic of his dogged adherence to principle, if not indeed of a self-righteous and egocentric character, that K'ang reckoned little with such hostility and even less with the surprise and bewilderment felt by many who were simply unaccustomed to rapid change and unable to cope with his radically new ideas. Before many of his plans could take effect, a coup d'etat restored the conservative empress dowager to active control of affairs and drove K'ang's group from power. Some died as martyrs to the cause of reform; others, like K'ang, escaped to become exiles.

Until the dynasty itself collapsed, K'ang continued to write and raise funds overseas in behalf of the movement. After the Revolution of 1911, however, K'ang's "cause" became more and more of a personal one. In a little more than a decade the trend of events and ideas had left him behind. As a constitutional monarchist who still protested his loyalty to the Manchu dynasty, K'ang was now swimming against a strong Republican tide; as a reformer who had always insisted on his fidelity to Confucius, he found himself suddenly surrounded by progressives—a generation that no longer needed to be won over to reform and could not now be won back to Confucius.

The significance of K'ang Yu-wei as a thinker lies in his attempt to provide a Confucian justification for basic institutional reforms. The so-called self-strengtheners had urged reform on the grounds of immediate utility, thinking that Western weapons and techniques could be adopted without proceeding further to any basic changes in Chinese government and society. They spoke of preserving the Confucian Way (Tao) through the use of Western "instruments" (ch'i) or "methods" (fa). Yet, as men like Wang T'ao came to appreciate, Western power and prosperity rested on something more than technology. To bring China abreast of the modern world, therefore, more radical changes would be needed. Thus reform began to take on a new meaning for them. Change would now extend to fa in the sense of institutions as well as fa in the sense of methods.

It was here that real trouble arose. According to a hallowed principle of Chinese dynastic rule, the life of a dynasty was bound up with its adherence to the constitution laid down by its founding father (the first emperor). Tampering with its institutions might bring the dynasty down, and supporters of the Manchus could be counted on to resist any such changes. For those more concerned over the Chinese way of life than the fate of the Manchus the problem was even more acute. How far could one go in changing basic institutions while still keeping the Way intact? Would not Confucianism be reduced to a mere set of pious platitudes once its social integument had been destroyed?

K'ang's resolution of this dilemma was a bold one. Rather than permit the sphere occupied by the Confucian Way in Chinese life to be further narrowed and displaced by Western "methods," he would redefine the Way and enlarge its scope so as virtually to include the latter. Instead of making more room for Western institutions alongside Confucianism, he would make room for them inside. This he did by exploiting to the fullest two ideas already put forth by Wang T'ao. The first of these was that the Way of the sages was precisely to meet change with change; Confucius himself had done so, and if alive today would do so again. K'ang provided this theory with an elaborate scriptural justification through his studies of the so-called "forged classics" and his sensational *Confucius As a Reformer*. In terms of its historical influence this was undoubtedly K'ang's main contribution—though not an original one—to the thinking of his times.

Implicit in his notion of reform, however, was a still more momentous idea, since it ran more directly counter to the age-old Confucian view of history and tradition: the idea of progress. It was one thing to assert that the Confucian sage, when faced by one of those cyclically-recurring cycles of degeneration spoken of by Mencius or the *Book of Changes,* took appropriate steps to reform the times, reassert the Way, and restore the institutions of the sage-kings. It was quite another to offer, in place of a return to the Golden Age, a utopia beckoning in the future.

Here again the idea was, among Chinese, originally Wang T'ao's. He had glimpsed a future stage in which the Way would make all things one, a natural result of the process going on around him by which the different nations in the world and their respective ways of life were being brought together by technological progress. He had even referred to it in terms taken from the Confucian *Book of Rites* as the age of Grand Unity or of the Great Commonwealth (*Ta t'ung*). What the *Book of Rites* had spoken of as a golden age at the dawn of history, however, Wang T'ao saw as a vision of the future. And K'ang Yu-wei, in his *Grand Unity,* made this vision the center of his whole world-view. Henceforth, "reform" would never again mean what it had in the past, an adaptation of laws and methods to cyclical change. It was now a wholesale launching of China into the modern world and, beyond that, into a glorious future.

Feng Kuei-fen and Hsüeh Fu-ch'eng, in their writings on reform, had shown deference to China's age-old pretensions to cultural superiority by reassuring their readers that she need not merely follow along behind the Western powers but could overtake and surpass' them. K'ang, in the *Grand Unity,* took the lead for China himself by pointing the way into the One World of the future. If China suffered humiliation now for her backwardness, looking ahead, he would be satisfied with nothing less for her than the ultimate in progress. In his world of the future there were to be no national and provincial barriers. Government would virtually cease to exist except in local units fixed arbitrarily on the basis of square degrees of longitude and latitude. Within these units life would be completely communal and completely egalitarian. All distinctions of race, class, clan, and family would also disappear, since they could no longer serve any valid social function. And in place of the differentiated loyalties which had bound men to their particular social group there would be only an undifferentiated feeling of human-kindness or love, which he identified with the Confucian virtue of humanity (*jen*).

Those who recall the layout of Mencius' well-fields, of which K'ang's square degrees of longitude and latitude are so reminiscent; or the neat symmetrical organization of society, set forth so early in the *Rites of Chou* and so late in the plans of the Taiping rebels; or the Chinese fondness for political geometry, reflected even in the plan of capital cities like Ch'ang-an and Peking, will recognize in K'ang's grand design, as even in the communes of Red China later, a quality by no means foreign to native tradition.

If in this respect, then, K'ang's vision of the future still strongly reflects the past, what can be said of his Confucianism? Does it too hold to tradition? Was K'ang either a staunch defender or a creative interpreter of Confucianism? The obvious grounds for placing him still within the Confucian tradition are his emphasis upon the cardinal virtue of *jen* and his efforts to preserve Confucianism as the national religion of the Chinese—as something completely inseparable from the Chinese way of life. Against this, most obviously, is his positive rejection of the Confucian family system along with other "divisive" elements in society.

Whatever abuses may have appeared in the family system, however, as it was formulated and practiced down through the centuries, it would still seem difficult to disassociate Confucius completely from it or to preserve Confucianism entirely without it. Without the family virtues and obligations, certainly, the concept of *jen* loses much of its tangible significance, and approaches more nearly—if it does not exactly coincide with—Mo Tzu's principle of undifferentiated universal love. Since Mo Tzu's social ideals resemble K'ang's so closely, the comparison is all the more pointed.

Furthermore, in K'ang's attempt to preserve Confucianism as a kind of national religion, there is something foreign to the spirit of Confucianism itself. The sage's teaching had been offered, and been accepted, as something universal. Its humanistic values were rooted in the nature of man and human society generally. K'ang's defense of it now as the basis of Chinese civilization and as the focus of a new nationalism, while testifying no doubt to his realization that China must have something comparable to the Christianity of the West or the Shinto cult in Japan, nevertheless sacrifices the substance of tradition for the trappings of nationalism. Henceforth Confucianism is to be valued, not on its own terms, but for its Chineseness.

What remains as unquestionably Confucian is K'ang's own sense of dedication to the service of society, his aim of "putting the world in order." Yet even this is not exclusively a Confucian concern (certainly Mo Tzu shared it), nor does his favorite expression for it, "saving the world," hark back only to the sage—there are overtones here, too, of the Buddhist saviors (*bodhisattvas*) and Jesus Christ.

In the light of history K'ang and the reform movement may well appear as the great turning point between old and new in Chinese thought. Confucianism, in his hands, was being launched on a perilous journey, in the course of which much baggage might have to be jettisoned if anything at all was to survive. Confucian traditionalists saw the dangers perhaps better than K'ang. Dropping him as pilot, however, was not the same thing as steering a safe course homeward. The storm now drove all before it, and there was no turning back.

K'ANG YU-WEI

Confucius As a Reformer

K'ang's *K'ung Tzu kai-chih k'ao* (lit., Study of Confucius' Reforms) was started in 1886 and finally published in 1897. It constitutes an extended analysis of the innovations which K'ang believed to have been advocated by Confucius. The following are taken from section introductions which present his general argumentation. As K'ang's subheadings indicate, they purport to show that Confucius' greatness derives from his having written the Six Classics to promote reform in his own time.

[From *K'ung Tzu kai-chih k'ao,* 9:1a; 10:1a-b]

HOW CONFUCIUS FOUNDED HIS TEACHING IN ORDER TO REFORM INSTITUTIONS

Every founder of doctrine in the world reformed institutions and established laws. This is true with Chinese philosophers in ancient times. Chinese principles and institutions were all laid down by Confucius. His disciples received his teachings and transmitted them so that they were carried out in the country and used to change the old customs. [9:1a]

THE SIX CLASSICS ALL WRITTEN BY CONFUCIUS TO REFORM INSTITUTIONS

Confucius was the founder of a doctrine. He was a godlike sage-king. He complements Heaven and earth and nurtures the myriad things. All men, things, and principles are embraced in the Great Way of Confucius. He is, therefore, the most accomplished and perfect sage since the history of mankind. And yet, concerning the Great Way of Confucius, one would search in vain for a single word [under the master's own name]. There are only the *Analects,* which was a record of the master's sayings taken down by his disciples, and the *Spring and Autumn Annals,* which was a kind of old-fashioned gazette copied from ancient documents relative to public events and ceremonies. As to the *Books of Odes, History, Rites, Music,* and *Changes,* they are regarded as the ancient records of Fu Hsi, the Hsia and Shang dynasties, King Wen and the Duke of Chou; thus they have nothing to do with Confucius. If this were true, Confucius would have been merely a wise scholar of later times, no better than Cheng K'ang-ch'eng [127–200] or Chu Hsi [1130–1200, who wrote commentaries on the Confucian classics]. How, then, could he have been called the only model of the human race and the perfect sage of all generations? . . . Before the Han dynasty it was known to all that Confucius was the founder of the doctrine and the reformer of institutions, and that he was the godlike sage-king. . . . Wherein lies the reason for this? It lies in the fact that scholars knew the Six Classics were written by Confucius. This was the opinion of all before the Han dynasty. Only when a scholar recognizes that the Six Classics were written by Confucius can he understand why Confucius was the great sage, the founder of the doctrine, and the model for all ages; and why he alone was called the supreme master. [10:1a–b]

The Three Ages

K'ang's theory of progress is set forth in terms of the Three Ages, a concept of the New Text School for which he derived classical sanction from the Kung-yang commentary on the *Spring and Autumn Annals,* the Li yün section of the *Book of Rites,* and commentaries by the Han scholars Tung Chung-shu and Ho Hsiu. Here we see the ancient cyclical view of history adapted to the modern evolutionary view.

[From *Lun yü chu,* 2:11a–12b]
The meaning of the *Spring and Autumn Annals* consists in the evolution of the Three Ages: the Age of Disorder, the Age of Order, and the Age of Great Peace. . . . The Way of Confucius embraces the evolution of the Three Sequences and the Three Ages. The Three Sequences were

used to illustrate the Three Ages, which could be extended to a hundred generations. The eras of Hsia, Shang, and Chou represent the succession of the Three Sequences, each with its modifications and accretions. By observing the changes in these three eras one can know the changes in a hundred generations to come. For as customs are handed down among the people later kings cannot but follow the practices of the preceding dynasty; yet since defects develop and have to be removed, each new dynasty must make modifications and additions to create a new system. The course of humanity progresses according to a fixed sequence. From the clans come tribes, which in time are transformed into nations. And from nations the Grand Unity comes about. Similarly, from the individual man the rule of tribal chieftains gradually becomes established, from which the relationship between ruler and subject is gradually defined. Autocracy gradually leads to constitutionalism, and constitutionalism gradually leads to republicanism. Likewise, from the individual man the relationship between husband and wife gradually comes into being, and from this the relationship between father and son is defined. This relationship of father and son leads to the loving care of the entire race, which in turn leads gradually to the Grand Unity, in which there is a reversion to individuality.

Thus there is an evolution from Disorder to Order, and from Order to Great Peace. Evolution proceeds gradually and changes have their origins. This is true with all nations. By observing the child, one can know the adult and old man; by observing the sprout, one can know the tree when it grows big and finally reaches the sky. Thus, by observing the modifications and additions of the three successive eras of Hsia, Shang, and Chou, one can by extension know the changes in a hundred generations to come.

When Confucius prepared the *Spring and Autumn Annals,* he extended it to embrace the Three Ages. Thus, during the Age of Disorder he considers his own state as the center, treating all other Chinese feudal states as on the outside. In the Age of Order he considers China as the center, while treating the outlying barbarian tribes as on the outside. And in the Age of Great Peace he considers everything, far or near, large or small, as if it were one. In doing this he is applying the principle of evolution.

Confucius was born in the Age of Disorder. Now that communications extend through the great earth and changes have taken place in Europe and America, the world is evolving toward the Age of Order. There will be a day when everything throughout the earth, large or small, far or near, will be like one. There will be no longer any nations, no more racial distinctions, and customs will be everywhere the same. With this uniformity will come the Age of Great Peace. Confucius knew all this in advance.

[From *Chung-yung chu,* 36b]

The methods and institutions of Confucius aim at meeting with the particular times. If, in the Age of Disorder, before the advent of civilization, one were to put into effect the institutions of Great Peace, this would certainly result in great harm. But if, in the Age of Order, one were to continue to cling to the institutions of the Age of Disorder, this too would result in great harm. The present time, for example, is the Age of Order. It is therefore necessary to propagate the doctrines of self-rule and independence, and to discuss publicly the matter of constitutional government. If the laws are not reformed, great disorder will result. . . .

The Need for Reforming Institutions

This memorial to the throne, submitted January 29, 1898, and entitled "Comprehensive Consideration of the Whole Situation," gives the arguments by which K'ang attempted to persuade the Kuang-hsü emperor to inaugurate reforms, which he did a few months later. Note K'ang's equivocal approach to the question of "ancestral institutions."

[From *Ying-ch'ao t'ung-ch'ou ch'üan-chü che,* in *Wu-hsü tsou-kao,* 1b–3b]

A survey of all states in the world will show that those states which undertook reforms became strong while those states which clung to the past perished. The consequences of clinging to the past and the effects of opening up new ways are thus obvious. If Your Majesty, with your discerning brilliance, observes the trends in other countries, you will see that if we can change, we can preserve ourselves; but if we cannot change, we shall perish. Indeed, if we can make a complete change, we shall become strong, but if we only make limited changes, we shall still perish. If Your Majesty and his ministers investigate the source of the disease, you will know that this is the right prescription.

Our present trouble lies in our clinging to old institutions without knowing how to change. In an age of competition between states, to put into effect methods appropriate to an era of universal unification and laissez-faire is like wearing heavy furs in summer or riding a high carriage across a river. This can only result in having a fever or getting oneself drowned. . . .

It is a principle of things that the new is strong but the old weak; that new things are fresh but old things rotten; that new things are active but old things static. If the institutions are old, defects will develop. Therefore there are no institutions that should remain unchanged for a hundred years. Moreover, our present institutions are but unworthy vestiges of the Han, T'ang, Yüan, and Ming dynasties; they are not even the institutions of the [Manchu] ancestors. In fact, they are the products of the fancy writing and corrupt dealing of the petty officials rather than the original ideas of the ancestors. To say that they are the ancestral institutions is an insult to the ancestors. Furthermore, institutions are for the purpose of preserving one's territories. Now that the ancestral territory cannot be preserved, what good is it to maintain the ancestral institutions? . . .

Although there is a desire to reform, yet if the national policy is not fixed and public opinion not united, it will be impossible for us to give up the old and adopt the new. The national policy is to the state just as the rudder is to the boat or the pointer is to the compass. It determines the direction of the state and shapes the public opinion of the country. [1b–2b]

Nowadays the court has been undertaking some reforms, but the action of the emperor is obstructed by the ministers, and the recommendations of the able scholars are attacked by old-fashioned bureaucrats. If the charge is not "using barbarian ways to change China," then it is "upsetting the ancestral institutions." Rumors and scandals are rampant, and people fight each other like fire and water. A reform in this way is as ineffective as attempting a forward march by walking backward. It will inevitably result in failure. Your Majesty knows that under the present circumstances reforms are imperative and old institutions must be abolished. I beg Your Majesty to make up your mind and to decide on the national policy. After the fundamental policy is determined, the methods of implementation must vary according to what is primary and what is secondary, what is important and what is insignificant, what is strong and what is weak, what is urgent and what can wait. . . . If anything goes wrong, no success can be achieved.

After studying ancient and modern institutions, Chinese and foreign, I have found that the institutions of the sage-kings and Three Dynasties [of Hsia, Shang, and Chou] were excellent, but that ancient times were different from today. I hope Your Majesty will daily read Mencius and follow his example of loving the people. The development of the Han, T'ang, Sung, and Ming dynasties may be learned, but it should be remembered that the age of universal unification is different from that of sovereign nations. I wish Your Majesty would study *Kuan Tzu* [4] and follow his idea of managing the country. As to the republican governments of the United States and France and the constitutional governments of Britain and Germany, these countries are far away and their customs are different from ours. Their changes occurred a long time ago and can no longer all be traced. Consequently I beg Your Majesty to adopt the purpose of Peter the Great of Russia as our purpose and to take the Meiji Reform of Japan as the model for our reform. The time and place of Japan's reform are not remote and her religion and customs are somewhat similar to ours. Her success is manifest; her example can be easily followed. [3a–b]

CONSERVATIVE REACTIONS

The great momentum attained by the reform movement after the Sino-Japanese War in 1894 also provoked strong conservative reactions. A stormy debate ensued in which the reformers were charged with subverting the established order and destroying Chinese culture. In Hunan province, where reformers like T'an Ssu-t'ung had organized an academy for the spreading of their ideas, the reaction was particularly forceful. Eminent scholars such as Wang Hsien-ch'ien (1842–1918), outstanding classicist and compiler of the monumental *Tung hua lu* (*Imperial Documents of the Ch'ing Dynasty*), and Yeh Te-hui (1864–1927), famous bibliophile, rallied to the defense of Chinese traditions and Confucianism. In Peking powerful figures led by Jung Lu (1836–1903) fought the reformers with logic and invective until, with the help of the empress dowager they succeeded in bringing the reform movement of 1898 to an abrupt end. Still another brand of opposition was encountered in the great

[4] Early book on political and economic institutions which foreshadows Legalist doctrines.

statesman Chang Chih-tung, who, though himself something of a reformer, wished to hold the line against drastic changes and tried to preserve intact the earlier distinction between traditional Confucian ethics and the Western techniques which should serve only as means for defending the Chinese Way.

Resistance to reform took three main lines. First, the conservatives argued that ancestral institutions should never be changed under any conditions. Said Tseng Lien, one of the conservative writers: "The country belongs to the ancestors; the emperor merely maintains the dynasty for them. He cannot change the permanent laws laid down by the ancestors." This argument, founded upon the tradition of filial piety, was in fact the most formidable obstacle to the reformers, and one which K'ang Yu-wei tried to overcome again and again in his memorials to the throne. It was this same argument which the Grand Councillor, Jung Lu, used so effectively against K'ang.

Secondly, the conservatives argued, on traditional Confucian lines, a good government depended upon men rather than upon laws. It was the moral state of the people that needed improvement, not legal or political institutions. Rather than try to change institutions, one should seek to change or win over the minds of the people. Without men exemplifying superior virtue in the government, this could never be achieved, and in default of it, institutional changes would only bring harm to the country.

Thirdly, as regards the cultivation of these virtues, the traditional teachings of China were definitely superior to those of the West. The Westerners, caring only for money, might build a strong and wealthy country, but would be unable to achieve harmony and unity. Western governments were based upon power; the Chinese government, upon humanity and righteousness. Calculating and self-centered, the Westerners neglected the ethical bases of government, and could offer no sound alternative for the establishment of a harmonious social order.

CH'U CH'ENG-PO
Reforming Men's Minds Comes Before Reforming Institutions

The memorial of the censor Ch'u Ch'eng-po, submitted in 1895 after China's disastrous defeat by Japan, analyzes that failure in a manner much different from the institutional reformers. It is not a failure to change laws and institutions which accounts for the defeat, but precisely that such changes were made without remedying the basic weakness—the incompetence and venality of officials. Since, in fact, graft and corruption among army and navy officers had rendered China's modern weapons useless in battle, Ch'u was on strong ground in arguing the need for official probity and integrity. The implication of this for him was that in the training and recruitment of officials traditional ethical values and moral character should be emphasized over technical qualifications and scientific training (which would have involved still further changes in methods and institutions). Thus, though not wholly opposed to change or to the reforms already undertaken, Ch'u resisted the reform movement's tendency toward progressive displacement of Chinese values—the Confucian Way—by Western methods and institutions.

[From *Chien-cheng t'ang che-kao*, 2:18a–22a]

In the present world our trouble is not that we lack good institutions but that we lack upright minds. If we seek to reform institutions, we must first reform men's minds. Unless all men of ability assist each other, good laws become mere paper documents; unless those who supervise them are fair and enlightened, the venal will end up occupying the places of the worthy. . . .

At the beginning of the T'ung-chih reign (1862–1874), Tseng Kuo-fan, Tso Tsung-t'ang, Shen Pao-chen, Li Hung-chang, and others, because the danger from abroad was becoming daily more serious, strongly emphasized Western learning. In order to effect large-scale manufacture, they built shipyards and machine factories; in order to protect our commercial rights, they organized the China Merchants' Steam Navigation Company and cotton mills; in order to educate persons of talent, they founded the Tung-wen College and other language schools; in order to strengthen training, they established naval and military academies. Countless other enterprises were inaugurated, and an annual expenditure amounting to millions was incurred. Truly no effort was spared in the attempt to establish new institutions after the pattern of the West.

When these enterprises were first undertaken, the regulations and systems were thoroughly considered so as to attain the best. It was asserted then that although China at the outset had to imitate the superior techniques of the West, eventually she would surpass the Western countries. But [in fact] perfunctory execution of these reforms has brought us to the point now where the island barbarians [the Japanese] have suddenly invaded us, and the whole situation of the nation has deteriorated. Was it because there were no reforms or because the reforms were no good? The real mistake was that we did not secure the right men to manage the new institutions. [18a–19a]

In some cases the authorities knew only how to indulge in empty talk; in other cases the officials succeeding those who originated the reforms gradually became lax and let the projects drop. Generally the initial effort was seldom maintained to the end; and while there was much talk, there was little action. . . . If the proposals had been carried out gradually and persistently, China would have long ago become invincible. But these far-reaching plans failed because we only put up an ostentatious façade behind which were concealed the avarice and selfishness [of the officials]. [19b]

In order to create a new impression in the country and to stimulate the lax morale of the people, it is necessary to distinguish between meritorious and unworthy men and to order rewards and punishments accordingly. . . . If this fundamental remedy is adopted, the raising of funds will bring in abundant revenues, and the training of troops will result in a strong army. Institutions that are good will achieve results day by day, while institutions that are not so good can be changed to bring out their maximum usefulness. Otherwise, profit-seeking opportunists will vie with each other in proposing novel theories . . . and there will be no limit to their evil doings. [20b–21a]

As to the present institutions and laws, although in name they adhere to past formulations "respectfully observed," in fact they have lost the essence of their original meaning. If we cling to the vestiges of the past, it will be conforming to externals while departing from the spirit. But if we get at the root, a single change can lead to complete fulfillment of the Way. . . . We should, therefore, make the necessary adjustments in accordance with the needs of the time. If we secure the right persons, all things can be transformed without a trace; but if we do not obtain the right persons, laws and institutions will only serve the nefarious designs of the wicked. [21a–22a]

CHU I-HSIN

Fourth Letter in Reply to K'ang Yu-wei

Chu I-hsin (1846–1894), an official who withdrew from the government to teach and pursue classical studies, prided himself on his Confucian orthodoxy

and made no compromises with Westernization. He opposed even the introduction of machines on the ground that, though useful in countries with vast
resources and a shortage of manpower, they would only create unemployment
in China and thus drive people to desperation and violence.

Chu correctly discerned that the effect of K'ang's ideas (as expressed in
Confucius As a Reformer) would be not only to change the outward forms
of Chinese life but ultimately to undermine traditional Confucian morality
itself. The "way" of the West could not be adopted piecemeal: its values and
institutions were inseparably related, as were those of China. On the other
hand, it was both impossible and undesirable for the Chinese to surrender
their own Way—the basis of their whole civilization—for that of the West.
The only solution was a return to fixed principles, rejecting expediency and
utilitarianism.

[From Su Yü, ed., *I-chiao ts'ung-pien*, 1:11a–13b]

Since ancient times there have been no institutions which might not develop defects. When a true king arises, he makes small changes if the
defects are small, and great changes if the defects are great. . . . Thus
Confucius said: "Let there be the [right] men and the government will
flourish; but without the [right] men, the government will decay and
cease." [5] The defects of a government are due to the failings of those who
manage the institutions rather than of those who establish them. Now by
referring to Confucius as a reformer, your real intention is to facilitate the
introduction of new institutions. The accounts of Confucius as a reformer
come from apocryphal texts and cannot be wholly believed. But even if
the sage had spoken thus, he was only taking a simple pattern and
elaborating upon it in order to return to the ancient institutions of the
Three Dynasties and sage-kings. How could he have intended to use
"barbarian ways to reform China"? [1:11a]

I have heard of "daily renovating one's virtue," [6] but I have never heard
of daily renovating one's moral principles. The scholars of the Ch'ien-lung
[1736–1795] and Chia-ch'ing [1796–1820] periods regarded moral principle as of great fundamental import. Now, in order to save them from
degeneration and loss you do not seek a return to fixed principles, but
instead, you talk about their being changed [i.e., of their having been
perverted and needing to be reformed]. The barbarians do not recognize
the moral obligations between ruler and minister, father and son, elder
brother and younger brother, husband and wife. There you have a per-

[5] *The Mean*, 20.
[6] *Book of Changes*, Ta-ch'u.

version of principles. Do you mean that the classics of our sages and the teachings of our philosophers are too jejune to follow, and that we must change them so as to have something new? Only if we first have principles can we then have institutions. Barbarian institutions are based on barbarian principles. Different principles make for different customs, and different customs give rise to different institutions. Now, instead of getting at the root of it all, you talk blithely of changing institutions. If the institutions are to be changed, are not the principles going to be changed along with them?

The manufacture of instruments by the workers involves techniques, not principles. As the minds of the people become more and more artful, clever contrivances will daily increase. Once started, there is no resistance to it. Why, therefore, need we fear that our techniques will not become sufficiently refined?

Now, because our techniques have not yet attained the highest level of skillfulness, it is proposed that we should seek to achieve this by changing our institutions as well as our principles. . . . Is this not like rescuing a person from being drowned by pushing him into a deep abyss? Is this not going much too far?

Men's minds are corrupted by utilitarianism. Those who run the institutions will utilize them for self-interest. One institution established only means one more evil added. Consequently, the path to good government is, above all, the rectification of the people's minds and the establishment of virtuous customs. The perfecting of institutions should come next.

Moreover, our institutions are by themselves clear and complete, and it is not necessary to borrow from foreign customs. How can we blame later mistakes on our ancestors and let the theory of utilitarianism be our guide?

Of course, the pitiably stupid people who only follow shadows and listen to echoes cannot be made to understand this. But even a few well-intentioned scholars, going to extremes and believing that the *Books of Odes, History, Rites,* and *Music,* which have been handed down to us by the sages, are not adequate to meet the changing circumstances, take to what is strange and novel and maintain that therein lies the path to wealth and power. But does the reason for the foreigners' being rich and powerful lie in this? Or does it not lie in their having a way which is the source and basis [of their institutions]? And is it not true that a way which

[78]

is basic and original with them can never be practiced in China, and furthermore that it should absolutely not be practiced by our descendants? [12b–13a]

Mencius said: "The superior man seeks simply to bring back the unchanging standard, and that being rectified, the masses are roused to virtue. When they are so roused, forthwith perversities and wickedness disappear."[7] A review of our history since ancient times will show that herein lies the key to order and disorder. [13b]

YEH TE-HUI
The Superiority of China and Confucianism

In his criticism of the reformers in the late '90s, Yeh Te-hui (1864–1927) attempted to defend not only Confucian ethical ideals but existing institutions. While acknowledging that the West had its points of excellence, worthy of selective emulation, for him they were few indeed compared to what China had to offer. Instead, therefore, of claiming for her simply moral superiority over the West, and thus seeming to retreat from vulnerable institutions into an unimpeachable tradition, Yeh tended to justify the whole existing order—the monarchy, rule by an elite, the civil service examination system, etc.—against democracy and Westernization. With regard to institutions, however, he claimed no more than China's right to keep her own because they were peculiarly suited to her, while in regard to Confucianism he did not hesitate to proclaim its universality and ultimate adoption by the West.

Conservatism of this type, which sanctified the status quo and identified Confucianism so closely with it, helped convince Chinese of the next generation that to overthrow the old dynastic order required the destruction of Confucianism too.

> [From Su Yü, ed., *I-chiao ts'ung-pien,* 3:32b–33a, 35b Ming chiao; 4:12a–13a Yu-hsien chin-yü, 31a Cheng chiai p'ien, 78b–79a Fei yu-hsüeh t'ung-i]

Of all countries in the five continents China is the most populous. It is situated in the north temperate zone, with a mild climate and abundant natural resources. Moreover, it became civilized earlier than all other nations, and its culture leads the world. The boundary between China and foreign countries, between Chinese and barbarians, admits of no argument and cannot be discussed in terms of their strength or our weakness.

Of the four classes of people the scholars are the finest. From the be-

[7] *Mencius,* VII B, 37.

ginning of the present dynasty until today there have been numerous great ministers and scholars who rose to eminence on the basis of their examination essays and poems. Although special examinations have been given and other channels of recruitment have been opened, it is mostly from the regular civil service examinations that men of abilities have risen up. The Western system of election has many defects. Under that system it is difficult to prevent favoritism and to uphold integrity. At any rate, each nation has its own governmental system, and one should not compel uniformity among them. [4:78b–79a]

An examination of the causes of success and failure in government reveals that in general the upholding of Confucianism leads to good government while the adoption of foreignism leads to disorder. If one keeps to kingly rule [relying on virtue], there will be order; if one follows the way of the overlord [relying on power], there will be disorder. . . .

Since the abdication of Yao and Shun the ruling of China under one family has become institutionalized. Because of China's vast territory and tremendous resources, even when it has been ruled under one monarch, still there have been more days of disorder than days of order. Now, if it is governed by the people, there will be different policies from many groups, and strife and contention will arise. [4:12a–13a]

[Mencius said:] "The people are the most important element in a nation," [8] not because the people consider themselves important, but because the sovereign regards them as important. And it is not people's rights that are important. Since the founding of the Ch'ing dynasty our revered rulers have loved the people as their own children. Whenever the nation has suffered from a calamity such as famine, flood, and war, the emperor has immediately given generous relief upon its being reported by the provincial officials. For instance, even though the treasury was short of funds recently, the government did not raise any money from the people except for the *likin* [9] tax. Sometimes new financial devices are proposed by ministers who like to discuss pecuniary matters, but even if they are approved and carried out by order of the department concerned, they are suspended as soon as it is learned that they are troubling the people. How vastly different is this from the practice of Western countries where taxes are levied in all places, on all persons, for all things, and at all times? [4:31a]

[8] *Mencius*, VII B, 14.   [9] Internal customs duties.

Confucianism represents the supreme expression of justice in the principles of Heaven and the hearts of men. In the future it will undoubtedly be adopted by civilized countries of both East and West. The essence of Confucianism will shine brightly as it renews itself from day to day.

Ethics is common to China and the West. The concept of blood relations and respect for parents prevails also among barbarians. To love life and hate killing is rooted in the human heart. The Confucian ideal is expressed in the *Spring and Autumn Annals,* which aims at saving the world from disorder and treason; proper conduct is defined in the *Book of Filial Piety,* which lays down the moral principles and obligations for all generations to come. And there is the *Analects,* which synthesizes the great laws of the ancient kings. Tseng Tzu, Tzu-hsia, Mencius, and others who transmitted the teaching all mastered the Six Arts and knew thoroughly the myriad changes of circumstances. All that the human heart desires to say was said several thousand years ago. [3:32b–33a]

Chinese scholars who attack Western religion err in false accusation, while those who admire it err in flattery. Indeed, only a superficial Confucianist would say that Westerners have no moral principles, and yet only fools would say that Western religion excels Confucianism. In so far as there is morality, there must be Confucianism. [3:35b]

CHANG CHIH-TUNG

Exhortation to Learn

Chang Chih-tung (1837–1909) was one of the leading figures in the empire during the last days of the Manchus. A brilliant scholar and official, widely esteemed for his personal integrity and patriotism, he was an early supporter of reform and as a provincial administrator promoted many industrial, railway, educational, and cultural projects. When his *Exhortation to Learn* (*Ch'üan-hsüeh p'ien*) was published in 1898, it was hailed by the reformers then in power and given official distribution by the emperor.

Basically, however, Chang was a moderate who coupled gradual reform with a stout adherence to Neo-Confucianism, defense of monarchical institutions, and loyalty to the dynasty. Avoiding extremes, he backed away from the radical measures of K'ang Yu-wei on the one hand, and on the other, from the reactionary policies that led to the Boxer catastrophe in 1900. A combination of moderation and shrewdness thus helped him survive politically to play an influential role at court in the first decade of the new century. During this period he was instrumental both in the enactment of educational and civil service reforms (including abolition of the famous eight-legged essay) and in the attempt to revive Confucianism as a state cult.

Chang's position is summed up in the catch-phrase "Chinese learning for substance, Western learning for function" (*Chung-hsüeh wei t'i, hsi-hsüeh wei yung*). The terms "substance" (*t'i*) and "function" (*yung*) Chang drew from the philosophical lexicon of Sung metaphysics, in which they stood for the ontological and functional aspects of the same reality. A similar distinction was expressed in the dichotomy between the Way or Principle (*tao*) and instruments (*ch'i*), wherein principle is the basis of the instrument and the instrument is the manifestation of the principle. Chang, following the example of earlier reformers who distinguished between the Chinese "Way" (or Chinese moral "principles") and Western instruments, used "substance" in reference to traditional Chinese values, and "function" (i.e., utility, practical application) in reference to the Western methods by which China and its traditional way of life were to be defended in the modern world. In this new formulation "substance" and "function" bore no intrinsic relationship to one another as they had for earlier Neo-Confucianists. Using the terms in an unphilosophic manner, Chang exploited their ambiguity in order to cover a compromise dictated by hard necessity.

There can be no doubt of Chang's genuine traditionalism, in the sense that he held fast to certain established Confucian traditions and sought as much to preserve these values intact as to provide a sanction for needed reforms. He was no K'ang Yu-wei, waving the banner of Confucius while marching off to destroy Confucianism. Nevertheless, his catch-phrases served only for the moment to hide the conflict between old and new. The compatability of "substance" and "function" was a problem now as it had not been for the Sung Neo-Confucianists. Chang, who was not wholly naive about the lengths to which Westernization would go (he insisted, for instance, that Western methods of administration were as essential as Western technology), nor wholly mistaken about the difficulties of establishing political democracy in China, still misjudged the frictions and tensions which modernization would create within the old order. To just such pressures conservative reformism soon fell a victim. As has been said, despotisms are never more endangered than when they begin to make concessions. Two years after the death of this venerable statesman in October, 1909, the Manchu dynasty itself collapsed.

[From *Ch-üan-hsüeh p'ien*, in *Chang Wen-hsiang kung ch-üan-chi*, ts'e 202:iab, iiiab, 2b–3a, 13a–14b, 23a–25a, 27ab; 203:9b, 19b, 22a]

The crisis of China today has no parallel either in the Spring and Autumn period [i.e., the time of Confucius] or in all the dynasties from the Ch'in and Han down through the Yüan and Ming. . . . Our imperial court has shown the utmost concern over the problem, living in anxiety and worry. It is ready to make changes and to provide special opportunities

[82]

for able ministers and generals. New schools are to be established and special examinations are to be held. All over the land men of serious purpose and sincere dedication have responded with enthusiasm and vigor. Those who seek to remedy the present situation talk of new learning; those who fear lest its acceptance should destroy the true Way hold fast to the teachings of the ancients. Both groups are unable to strike the mean. The conservatives resemble those who give up all eating because they have difficulty in swallowing, while the progressives are like a flock of sheep who have arrived at a road of many forks and do not know where to turn. The former do not know how to accommodate to special circumstances; the latter are ignorant of what is fundamental. Not knowing how to accommodate to special circumstances, the conservatives have no way to confront the enemy and deal with the crisis; not knowing the fundamental, the innovators look with contempt upon the teachings of the sages. Thus those who hold fast to the old order of things despise more and more the innovators and the latter in turn violently detest the conservatives. As the two groups are engaged in mutual recriminations, impostors and adventurers who do not hesitate to resort to falsification and distortion pour out their theories to confuse the people. Consequently students are in doubt as to which course to pursue, while perverse opinions spread all over the country. [202:ia–b]

United Hearts. I have learned of three things that are necessary for saving China in the present crisis. The first is to maintain the state. The second is to preserve the doctrine of Confucius; and the third is to protect the Chinese race. These three are inseparably related. We must protect the state, the doctrine, and the race with one heart, and this is what we mean by united hearts.

In order to protect the race we must first preserve the doctrine, and before the doctrine can be preserved, we must preserve the state and the race. How is the race to be preserved? If we have knowledge, it will be preserved; and by knowledge we mean the doctrine. How is the doctrine to be maintained? It is to be maintained by strength, and strength lies in armies. Thus, if the empire has no power and prestige, the doctrine will not be followed; and if the empire is not prosperous, the Chinese race will not be respected. [202:2b–3a]

The Three Bonds. The subject is bound to the sovereign, the son is bound to the father, and the wife is bound to the husband. . . . What makes a sage a sage, what makes China China, is just this set of bonds. Thus, if we recognize the bond of subject to sovereign, the theory of people's rights cannot stand. If we recognize the bond of son to father, then the theory that father and son are amenable to the same punishment and that funeral and sacrificial ceremonies should be abolished cannot stand. If we recognize the bond of wife to husband, then the theory of equal rights for men and women cannot stand. [202:13ab]

Our sage represented the highest ideal of human relationships. He established in detail and with clarity rules of decorum based on human feelings. Although Westerners have such rules only in abbreviated form, still foreigners have never abandoned the idea of decorum. For the norm of Heaven and the nature of man are about the same in China and in foreign countries. Without these rules of decorum no ruler could ever govern a state, and no teacher could ever establish his doctrine. [202:14b]

Rectifying Political Rights. Nowadays scholars who become vexed with the present order of things are angry at the foreigners for cheating and oppressing us, at the generals for being unable to fight, at the ministers for being unwilling to reform, at the educational authorities for not establishing modern schools, and at the various officials for not seeking to promote industry and commerce. They therefore advocate the theory of people's rights in order to get the people to unite and exert themselves. Alas, where did they find those words that would lead to disorder!

The theory of people's rights will bring us not a particle of good but a hundred evils. Are we going to establish a parliament? Among Chinese scholar-officials and among the people there are still many today who are obstinate and uneducated. They understand nothing about the general situation of the world, and they are ignorant of the affairs of state. They have never heard of important developments concerning the schools, political systems, military training, and manufacture of machinery. Suppose the confused and tumultuous people are assembled in one house, with one sensible man there out of a hundred who are witless, babbling aimlessly, and talking as if in a dream—what use would it be? Moreover, in foreign countries the matter of revenue is mainly handled by the lower house, while other matters of legislation are taken care of by the upper house. To be a member of parliament the candidate must possess a fairly good income. Nowadays Chinese merchants rarely have much capital, and the Chinese people are lacking in long range vision. If any important proposal for raising funds comes up for discussion, they will make excuses and keep silent; so their discussion is no different from nondiscussion. . . . This is the first reason why a parliament is of no use. . . .

At present China is indeed not imposing or powerful, but the people still get along well with their daily work, thanks to the dynastic institutions which hold them together. Once the theory of people's rights is adopted, foolish people will certainly be delighted, rebels will strike, order will not be maintained, and great disturbances will arise on all sides. Even those who advocate the theory of people's rights will not be able to live safely themselves. Furthermore, as the towns will be plundered and the Christian churches burned, I am afraid the foreigners, under the pretext of protecting [their nationals and interests], will send troops and warships to penetrate deeply and occupy our territories. The whole country will then be given to others without a fight. Thus the theory of people's rights is just what our enemies would like to hear spread about. [202:23a–24a]

Recently those who have picked up some Western theories have gone as far as to say that everybody has the right to be his own master. This is even more absurd. This phrase is derived from the foreign books of religion. It means that God bestows upon man his nature and soul and that every person has wisdom and intelligence which enable him to do useful work. When the translators interpret it to mean that every person has the right to be his own master, they indeed make a great mistake.

Western countries, whether they are monarchies, republics, or constitutional monarchies, all have a government, and a government has laws. Officials have administrative laws, soldiers have military laws, workers have labor laws, and merchants have commercial laws. The lawyers learn them; the judges administer them. Neither the ruler nor the people can violate the law. What the executive recommends can be debated by the parliament, but what the parliament decides can be vetoed by the throne. Thus it may be said that nobody is his own master. [202:24b–25a]

Following the Proper Order. If we wish to make China strong and preserve Chinese learning, we must promote Western learning. But unless we first use Chinese learning to consolidate the foundation and to give our purpose a right direction, the strong will become rebellious leaders and the weak, slaves. The consequence will be worse than not being versed in Western learning. . . .

Scholars today should master the Classics in order to understand the purpose of our early sages and teachers in establishing our doctrine. They must study history in order to know the succession of peace and disorder in our history and the customs of the land, read the philosophers and literary collections in order to become familiar with Chinese scholarship and fine writing. After this they can select and utilize that Western learning which can make up for our shortcomings and adopt those Western governmental methods which can cure our illness. In this way, China will derive benefit from Western learning without incurring any danger. [202:27a–b]

[*On Reform*]. It is the human relationships and moral principles that are immutable, but not legal systems; the Way of the sage, not instruments; the discipline of the mind, not technology.

Laws and institutions are what we meet changing situations with; they therefore need not all be the same. The Way is what we establish the foundation upon; it therefore must be uniform. . . . What we call the basis of the Way consists of the Three Bonds and the Four Cardinal Virtues.[10] If these are abandoned, great disorder will occur even before the new laws can be put into effect. But as long as they are preserved, even Confucius and Mencius, if they were to come back to life, could hardly condemn the reforms. [203:19b, 22a]

If we do not change our habits, we cannot change our methods [*fa*]; and if we cannot change our methods, we cannot change our instruments. . . . In Chinese learning the inquiry into antiquity is not important; what is important is knowledge of practical use. There are also different branches of Western learning: Western technology is not important, what is important is Western administration. [202:iiia]

There are five important factors in the administration of the new schools. First, both the old and the new must be studied. By the old we mean the *Four Books,* the five Classics, Chinese history, government, and geography; by the new we mean Western administration, Western technology, and Western history. The old learning is to be the substance; the new learning is to be for application [function]. Neither one should be neglected. Second, both administration and technology should be studied. Education, geography, budgeting, taxes, military preparations, laws and regulations, industry and commerce, belong to the category of Western administration. Mathematics, drawing, mining, medicine, acoustics, op-

[10] Decorum, righteousness, integrity, sense of shame.

tics, chemistry, and electricity belong to the category of Western technology. [203:9b]

REFORMISM AT THE EXTREME

In this final section on reform we take up two followers of K'ang Yu-wei who carried Chinese tradition over the brink to which K'ang had led it. They are T'an Ssu-t'ung (1865–1898) who, before his untimely death, sounded the knell of monarchism and Confucian ethics; and Liang Ch'i-ch'ao (1873–1929), the leading reformist-in-exile after 1898, who called for a complete renovation of Chinese life. As opposed to the conservative reformism of Chang Chih-tung, which prevailed in the last decade of Manchu rule, they represent the kind of radical reformism which prepared the ground for revolution in 1911.

T'AN SSU-T'UNG

T'an Ssu-t'ung is one of the most striking figures of the Reform Movement. The non-conformist son of a high official, he loved both independent study and the active life—now delving in books and writing poetry, now practicing swordsmanship, serving as a military officer in the Far West or traveling about as he pleased in search of historic sites and boon companions. He was disinclined toward an official career, and might never have sought office had he not, from his unorthodox studies (embracing Christianity and Buddhism as well as Confucianism and Taoism), developed a passionate interest in the Western world and the modernization of China. Active leadership in the reform movement and study under K'ang Yu-wei led eventually to participation at court in the Hundred Days of Reform. With its failure, he died a "martyr" at the age of thirty-three, risking death in hopes of rescuing the young Kuang-hsü emperor from his enemies.

Not only his martyrdom but his extremism made T'an a far greater hero to the new generation of Chinese than his master, K'ang. Accepting many of K'ang's basic ideas, he became an immediate and outspoken champion of some that K'ang foresaw only as future possibilities. He openly advocated republicanism against the monarchical system which K'ang would have retained and merely reformed. Here T'an cited Huang

Tsung-hsi as native authority for a view to which—not native tradition but—the West had led him. As against loyalty to the Manchus he proclaimed Chinese nationalism, pointing in this case to Wang Fu-chih as its exemplar in the past. T'an also attacked directly and unqualifiedly the traditional Confucian virtues based on specific human relationships which Chang Chih-tung had upheld as the essence of Confucianism and the Chinese way of life. It was these ideas—republicanism, nationalism, and opposition to the Chinese family system—that anticipated main trends in the early twentieth century.

T'AN SSU-T'UNG
On the Study of Humanity

T'an's chief work, *The Study of Humanity* (*Jen-hsüeh*, 1898), might more accurately be called *On Humanitarianism*. It offers an eclectic philosophy with elements drawn ostensibly from Confucianism, Buddhism, and Christianity. The central conception of *jen* differs little from that of K'ang: a generalized feeling of good will toward men which suggests most the "liberty, equality and fraternity" of the French Revolution, somewhat less Christian "charity" and Buddhist "compassion," and perhaps least of all, the Confucian virtue of "humanity" (*jen*). Though akin, in certain respects, to the Neo-Confucian concept of *jen* as a cosmic love which unites man to Heaven and earth, its ethical character is radically altered by T'an's repudiation of the obligations of human relationship, which in the past had given practical significance to *jen* for Confucianists and Neo-Confucianists alike.

[From *T'an Liu-yang ch'üan-chi, Jen-hsüeh*, A:37a–b, B:1a–10a]

When Confucius first set forth his teachings, he discarded the ancient learning, reformed existing institutions, rejected monarchism, advocated republicanism, and transformed inequality into equality. He indeed applied himself to many changes. Unfortunately, the scholars who followed Hsün Tzu forgot entirely the true meaning of Confucius' teaching, but clung to its superficial form. They allowed the ruler supreme, unlimited powers, and enabled him to make use of Confucianism in controlling the country. The school of Hsün Tzu insisted that duties based on human relationships were the essence of Confucianism, not knowing that this was a system applicable only to the Age of Disorder. Even for the Age of Disorder, any discussion of the human relationships [11] without reference to

---

[11] The relationships between ruler and minister, father and son, husband and wife, elder brother and younger brother, and friends.

Heaven would be prejudicial and incomplete, and the evil consequences would be immeasurable. How much worse, then, for them recklessly to have added the three bonds,[12] thus openly creating a system of inequality with its unnatural distinctions between high and low, and making men, the children of Heaven and earth, suffer a miserable life. . . .

For the past two thousand years the ruler-minister relationship has been especially dark and inhuman, and it has become worse in recent times. The ruler is not physically different or intellectually superior to man: on what does he rely to oppress 400 million people? He relies on the formulation long ago of the three bonds and five human relationships, so that, controling men's bodies, he can also control their minds. As Chuang Tzu said: "He who steals a sickle gets executed; he who steals a state becomes the prince." When T'ien Ch'eng-tzu stole the state of Ch'i, he also stole the [Confucian] system of humanity, righteousness and sage wisdom. When the thieves were Chinese and Confucianists, it was bad enough; but how could we have allowed the unworthy tribes of Mongolia and Manchuria, who knew nothing of China or Confucianism, to steal China by means of their barbarism and brutality! After stealing China, they controlled the Chinese by means of the system they had stolen, and shamelessly made use of Confucianism, with which they had been unfamiliar, to oppress China, to which they had been strangers. But China worshiped them as Heaven, and did not realize their guilt. Instead of burning the books in order to keep the people ignorant [as did the Ch'in], they more cleverly used the books to keep the people under control. Compared with them, the tyrannical emperor of the Ch'in dynasty was but a fool! [A:37a–38a]

At the beginning of the human race, there were no princes and subjects, for all were just people. As the people were unable to govern each other and did not have time to rule, they joined in raising up someone to be the prince. Now "joined in raising up" means, not that the prince selected the people [as for civil service],[13] but that the people selected the prince; it means that the prince was not far above the people, but rather on the same level with them. Again, by "joined in raising up" the prince, it means that there must be people before there can be a prince: the prince is therefore the "branch" [secondary] while the people are the

---

[12] Binding the minister to the ruler, the son to the father, the wife to the husband.
[13] The term "raised up" or "recommended" had been applied to candidates selected for office.

"root" [primary]. Since there is no such thing in the world as sacrificing the root for the branch, how can we sacrifice the people for the prince? When it is said that they "joined in raising up" the prince, it necessarily means that they could also dismiss him. The prince serves the people; the ministers assist the ruler to serve the people. Taxes are levied to provide the means for managing the public affairs of the people. If public affairs are not well managed, it is a universal principle that the ruler should be replaced. . . .

The ruler is also one of the people; in fact, he is of secondary importance as compared to ordinary people. If there is no reason for people to die for one another, there is certainly less reason for those of primary importance to die for one of secondary importance. Then, should those who died for the ruler in ancient times not have done so? Not necessarily. But I can say positively that there is reason only to die for a cause, definitely not reason to die for a prince. [B:1a–b]

In ancient times loyalty meant actually being loyal. If the subordinate actually serves his superior faithfully, why should not the superior actually wait upon his subordinate also? Loyalty signifies mutuality, the utmost fulfillment of a mutual relationship. How can we maintain that only ministers and subjects should live up to it? Confucius said: "The prince should behave as a prince, the minister as a minister." He also said: "The father should behave as a father, the son as a son, the elder brother as an elder brother, the younger brother as a younger brother, the husband as a husband, the wife as a wife." The founder of Confucianism never preached inequality. [B:2b]

As the evils of the ruler-minister relationship reached their highest development, it was considered natural that the relationships between father and son and between husband and wife should also be brought within the control of categorical morality.[14] This is all damage done by the categorizing of the three bonds. Whenever you have categorical obligations, not only are the mouths of the people sealed so that they are afraid to speak up, but their minds are also shackled so that they are afraid to think. Thus the favorite method for controlling the people is to multiply the categorical obligations. [B:7b–8a]

[14] Under the influence of Buddhism and perhaps utilitarianism, T'an viewed the traditional moral values as mere "names" or empty concepts (*ming*) in contrast to reality or actuality (*shih*).

As to the husband-wife relationship, on what basis does the husband extend his power and oppress the other party? Again it is the theory of the three bonds which is the source of the trouble. When the husband considers himself the master, he will not treat his wife as an equal human being. In ancient China the wife could ask for a divorce, and she therefore did not lose the right to be her own master. Since the inscription of the tyrannical law [against remarriage] on the tablet at K'uai-chi during the Ch'in dynasty, and particularly since its zealous propagation by the Confucianists of the Sung dynasty—who cooked up the absurd statement that "To die in starvation is a minor matter, but to lose one's chastity [by remarrying] is a serious matter"—the cruel system of the Legalists has been applied to the home, and the ladies' chambers have become locked-up prisons. [B:7–8]

Among the five human relationships, the one between friends is the most beneficial and least harmful to life. It yields tranquil happiness and causes not a trace of pain—so long as friends are made with the right persons. Why is this? Because the relationship between friends is founded on equality, liberty, and mutual feelings. In short, it is simply because friendship involves no loss of the right to be one's own master. Next comes the relationship between brothers, which is somewhat like the relationship between friends. The rest of the five relationships which have been darkened by the three bonds are like hell. [B:9a]

The world, misled by the conception of blood relations, makes erroneous distinctions between the nearly related and the remotely related, and relegates the relationship between friends to the end of the line. The relationship between friends, however, not only is superior to the other four relationships, but should be the model for them all. When these four relationships have been brought together and infused with the spirit of friendship, they can well be abolished. . . .

People in China and abroad are now talking of reforms, but no fundamental principles and systems can be introduced if the five relationships remain unchanged, let alone the three bonds. [B:9b–10a]

LIANG CH'I-CH'AO

Liang Ch'i-ch'ao, disciple of K'ang Yu-wei and his co-worker in the Reform Movement, escaped to Japan after the failure of K'ang's brief regime and there became perhaps the most influential advocate of reform in the years before the Revolution of 1911. His writings, in a lucid and forceful style, dealt with a wide range of political, social, and cultural issues. To thousands of young Chinese, studying abroad (most of them in Japan) or reading his books and pamphlets on the mainland, he became an inspiration and an idol—a patriotic hero, whose command of Chinese classical learning together with a remarkable sensitivity to ideas and trends in the West, gave him the appearance of an intellectual giant joining Occident and Orient, almost a universal man.

The fortnightly journal, *A People Made New* or *A New People* (*Hsin-min ts'ung-pao*), which Liang published in Yokohama from 1902 to 1905, showed a great change in his thinking. He was now exposed far more to Western influences, and enormously impressed by Japan's progress in contrast to China's repeated failures. Sensing the power of nationalism as the force which galvanized the Western peoples and the Japanese into action, realizing too the apathy and indifference of China's millions toward the abortive palace revolution of 1898 (as, indeed, toward all public affairs), Liang became fully convinced that popular education and the instillment of nationalism were China's greatest needs. Everything in her past culture which seemed an obstacle to national progress was to be cast aside.

Instead of reinterpreting Confucianism to find a sanction for progress, as he and K'ang had done earlier, Liang now put forward a new view of world history strongly colored by Social Darwinism: a struggle for survival among nations and races. Evolution of this fierce, competitive sort, rather than an optimistic view of inevitable progress to the Grand Unity, became the spur to drastic reform. In the 1890s he and K'ang had urged going beyond the mere adoption of Western "methods" and "instruments" to basic institutional reform; now he argued that institutional change itself could only be effected through a transformation of the whole Chinese way of life and particularly its morals, always considered the very essence of Confucianism. Morality was now to serve "the interest of the group," national survival.

But if so much were to be surrendered to the West, what would remain as distinctively Chinese in the new nationalism? Liang's equivocations on this point are evident in the selections which follow.[15] There must be

[15] They are also the subject of searching and detailed analysis by Joseph Levenson in his *Liang Ch'i-ch'ao and the Mind of Modern China* (Cambridge, 1953).

wholesale change, but what is good in China's past should still be preserved (there must, he insists, have been something of value in Chinese civilization which accounts for its survival, even if he cannot specify it here). Clearly, however, Liang's nationalism is now bound up very little with pride in the past and far more with a compulsive hope in China's future progress.

The frustration of Liang's, and China's, hopes is the story of the Republican era. Liang's distaste for violence and his refusal to turn Chinese nationalism against the Manchus made him less suited than Sun Yat-sen to become a great revolutionary leader, and his almost unfailing gift for misjudged compromises stood him in poor stead, after his return from exile, in the rough and tumble of Republican politics and warlordism. In the 1920s, while the revolutionary tide of Sun and the Nationalists rose, Liang withdrew to semi-retirement as a patriarch still revered but little heeded. Disillusioned with his own hopes, and viewing the West after the First World War as the victim of its own aggressiveness and acquistiveness, he took what consolation he could from the superiority of Chinese civilization as an expression of "Eastern spirituality" in contrast to the materialism of the West—an idea which he was neither the first to expound in the new Asia nor the last.

LIANG CH'I-CH'AO
A People Made New
[From *Hsin-min shuo*, in *Yin-ping shih wen-chi*, t'se 12:36b, 40a, 40b, 41a, 47a–b; 13:32b–33b]

Since the appearance of mankind on earth, thousands of countries have existed on the earth. Of these, however, only about a hundred still occupy a place on the map of the five continents. And among these hundred-odd countries there are only four or five great powers that are strong enough to dominate the world and to conquer nature. All countries have the same sun and moon, all have mountains and rivers, and all consist of people with feet and skulls; but some countries rise while others fall, and some become strong while others are weak. Why? Some attribute it to geographical advantages. But geographically, America today is the same as America in ancient times; why then do only the Anglo-Saxons enjoy the glory? Similarly, ancient Rome was the same as Rome today; why then have the Latin people declined in fame? Some attribute it to certain heroes. But Macedonia once had Alexander, and yet today it is no longer seen; Mongolia once had Chingis Khan, and yet today it can hardly maintain its existence. Ah! I know the reason. A state is formed by the assembling of people. The relationship of a nation to its people resembles that of the body to its four limbs, five viscera, muscles, veins, and corpuscles. It has never happened that the four limbs could be cut off, the five viscera wasted away, the muscles and veins injured, the corpuscles dried up, and yet the body still live. Similarly, it has never happened that a people could be foolish, timid, disorganized, and confused and yet the nation still stand. Therefore, if we wish the body to live for a long time, we must understand the methods of hygiene. If we wish the nation to be secure, rich, and honored, we must discuss the way for the people's being "made new." [13:36b]

The Meaning of "A People Made New." The term "people made new" does not mean that our people must give up entirely what is old in order to follow others. There are two meanings of "made new." One is to improve what is original in the people and so renew it; the other is to adopt what is originally lacking in the people and so make a new people. Without one of the two, there will be no success. . . .

A nation which can maintain itself in the world must have some peculiar characteristics on the part of its nationals. From morals and laws down to customs, habits, literature, and fine arts, all share an independent spirit which has been handed down from the forefathers to their descendants. Thus the group is formed and the nation develops. This is really the fundamental basis of nationalism. Our people have been established as a nation on the Asian continent for several thousand years, and we must have some special characteristics which are grand, noble, and perfect, and distinctly different from those of other races. We should preserve these characteristics and not let them be lost. What is called preserving, however, is not simply to let them exist and grow by themselves and then blithely say: "I am preserving them, I am preserving them." It is like a tree: unless some new buds come out every year, its withering away may soon be expected. Or like a well: unless there is always some new spring bubbling, its exhaustion is not far away. [12:40a]

If we wish to make our nation strong, we must investigate extensively the methods followed by other nations in becoming independent. We should select their superior points and appropriate them to make up our own shortcomings. Now with regard to politics, academic learning, and techniques, our critics know how to take the superior points of others to make up for our own weakness; but they do not know that the people's virtue, the people's wisdom, and the people's vitality are the great basis of politics, academic learning, and techniques. If they do not take the former but adopt the latter, neglect the roots but tend the branches, it will be no different from seeing the luxuriant growth of another tree and wishing to graft its branches onto our withered trunk, or seeing the bubbling flow of another well and wishing to draw its water to fill our dry well. Thus, how to adopt and make up for what we originally lacked so that our people may be made new, should be deeply and carefully considered. [12:40b]

All phenomena in the world are governed by no more than two principles: the conservative and the progressive. Those who are applying these two principles are inclined either to the one or to the other. Sometimes the two arise simultaneously and conflict with each other; sometimes the two exist simultaneously and compromise with each other. No one can exist if he is inclined only to one. Where there is conflict, there must be compromise. Conflict is the forerunner of compromise.

Those who excel at making compromises become a great people, such as the Anglo-Saxons, who, in a manner of speaking, make their way with one foot on the ground and one foot going forward, or who hold fast to things with one hand and pick up things with another. Thus, what I mean by "a people made new" is not those who are infatuated with Western ways and, in order to keep company with others, throw away our morals, learning, and customs of several thousand years' standing. Nor are they those who stick to old paper and say that merely embracing the morals, learning and customs of these thousands of years will be sufficient to enable us to stand upon the great earth. [12:41a]

On Public Morals. Among our people there is not one who looks on national affairs as if they were his own affairs. The significance of public morality has not dawned on us. Examining into it, however, we realize that the original basis for morality lies in its serving the interests of the group. As groups differ in their degree of barbarism or civilization, so do their appropriate morals vary. All of them, however, aim at consolidating, improving, and developing the group. . . . In ancient times some barbarians considered it moral to practice community of women, or to treat slaves as if they were not human beings. And modern philosophers do not call it immoral because under the particular situation at the time that was the proper thing to do in the interests of the group. Thus morality is founded on the interests of the group. If it is against this principle, even the perfect good can become an accursed evil. Public morality is therefore the basis of all morals. What is beneficial to the group is good; what is detrimental to the interests of the group is bad. This principle applies to all places and to all ages.

As to the external features of morality, they vary according to the degree of progress in each group. As groups differ in barbarism or civilization, so do their public interests and their morals. Morality cannot remain absolutely unchanged. It is not something that could be put into a fixed formula by the ancients several thousand years ago, to be followed by all generations to come. Hence, we who live in the present group should observe the main trends of the world, study what will suit our nation, and create a new morality in order to solidify, benefit, and develop our group. We should not impose upon ourselves a limit and refrain from going into what our sages had not prescribed. Search for public morality and there will appear a new morality, there will appear "a people made new." [12:47a–b]

On Progress. Generally, those who talk about a "renovation" may be divided into two groups. The lower group consists of those who pick up others' trite expressions and assume a bold look in order to climb up the official hierarchy. Their Western learning is stale stuff, their diplomacy relies on bribes, and their travels are moving in the dark. These people, of course, are not worth mentioning. The higher group consists of those who are worried about the situation and try hard to develop the nation and to promote well-being. But when asked about their methods, they would begin with diplomacy, training of troops, purchase of arms and manufacture of instruments; then they would proceed to commerce, mining and railways; and finally they would come, as they did recently, to officers' training, police, and education. Are these not the most important and necessary things for modern civilized nations? Yes. But can we attain the level of modern civilization and place our nation in an invincible position by adopting a little of this and that, or taking a small step now and then? I know we cannot. [13:32b]

Let me illustrate this by commerce. Economic competition is one of the big problems of the world today. It is the method whereby the powers attempt to conquer us. It is also the method whereby we should fight for our existence. The importance of improving our foreign trade has been recognized by all. But in order to promote foreign trade, it is necessary to protect the rights of our domestic trade and industry; and in order to protect these rights, it is necessary to issue a set of commercial laws. Commercial laws, however, cannot stand by themselves, and so it is necessary to complement them with other laws. A law which is not carried out is tantamount to no law; it is therefore necessary to define the powers of the judiciary. Bad legislation is worse than no legislation, and so it is necessary to decide where the legislative power should belong. If those who violate the law are not punished, laws will become void as soon as they are proclaimed; therefore, the duties of the judiciary must be defined. When all these are carried to the logical conclusion, it will be seen that foreign trade cannot be promoted without a constitution, a parliament, and a responsible government. Those who talk about foreign trade today blithely say, "I am promoting it, I am promoting it," and nothing more. I do not know how they are going to promote it. The above is one illustration, but it is true with all other cases. Thus I know why the so-called new methods nowadays are ineffectual. Why? Because without destruction there can be no construction. . . . What, then, is the way to effect our salvation and to achieve progress? The answer is that we must shatter at a blow the despotic and confused governmental system of some thousands of years; we must sweep away the corrupt and sycophantic learning of these thousands of years. [13:33a–b]

CHAPTER XXIII

THE NATIONALIST REVOLUTION

The Chinese revolution of 1911, which led to the overthrow of the Manchus the following year, was complex in its origins and confused as to its outcome. There is no single trend of thought or political action with which it can be identified. Nevertheless, amid the shifting currents of ideas and events in the two decades following, nationalism and republicanism emerged as perhaps the leading slogans in the political arena; and in the popular mind (if we may so speak of a people just awakening to political consciousness), it was Sun Yat-sen (1866–1925) and his Kuomintang followers who stood out as the most eloquent, though not always the most effective, spokesmen for these concepts. To express their basic aims and hopes is the purpose of the selections which follow. The next chapter will illustrate parallel developments in the intellectual sphere during this same republican era.

SUN YAT-SEN AND THE NATIONALIST REVOLUTION

The origins of the revolutionary movement may be traced back to 1895 when Sun, convinced that the Manchu regime was beyond hope of reforming, attempted his first abortive coup in Canton. As a practitioner of revolution Sun was never a great success, though this was his chosen profession; nor did he, on the other hand, stand out as a brilliant theoretician preparing the ground for revolution by the force and clarity of his ideas. It was rather as a visionary that Sun caught the imagination of Chinese youth—as a man of intense convictions and magnetic personality, who, through his crusading and somewhat quixotic career, dramatized ideas and catalyzed forces far more powerful than he. The first clear sign of this came just after the Russo-Japanese War, which gave great impetus to revolutionary nationalism throughout Asia. Japan was a hotbed of agitation among Chinese in exile and students sent abroad for study under official auspices. Sun, in 1905, joined his secret revolutionary society with other extremist groups to form the League of Common Alliance (*T'ung-meng hui*), out of which later grew the Kuomintang. Through its party organ, the *People's Report* (*Min pao*), this group published a manifesto which stated the aims of the movement, including three from which evolved the Three People's Principles.

One significant feature of this new movement is that it derived its inspiration very largely from Western sources. We have already seen how the thinking of the late nineteenth-century reformers was often decisively influenced by the West, either through its ideas or through the alternatives it confronted them with. In most cases, however, these reformers had been trained in the classical disciplines and prepared themselves for entry into the old elite. Even as reformers they felt a need somehow to reconcile the new with the old. Sun Yat-sen's case is different. His training was almost entirely in Western schools (including secondary education at a mission school in Hawaii). In contrast to generations of office seekers who had passed through the examination halls, this prospective leader of the new China aspired first to a military career and then went to medical school in Hongkong. Knowing little of classical studies, and inclined at first to think them useless, he inspired respect or enthusiasm more by what seemed his practical grasp of world trends than by any Chinese erudition. Moreover, his knowledge of China itself was limited, since his life was mostly spent in a few port cities, in Western outposts like Hongkong and Macao, or in exile abroad.

This is not to say that Sun was wholly Westernized. One whose early years had been spent in a peasant household, whose boyhood hero had been the Taiping leader Hung Hsiu-ch'üan, and whose associations in later life were for the most part with overseas Chinese, could be cut off from the official tradition and Confucian orthodoxy without ceasing in many ways to be Chinese. But it does mean that Sun's aims, primarily political in character and suggested by prevailing modes of thought in the West, were little adapted at the outset either to traditional Chinese attitudes or to the realities of Chinese life. They were inspired rather by a belief that, with the progress of civilization and the advance of science, Western ideas and institutions could be adopted quickly and easily by the Chinese, without regard to their past condition. Yet the bridging of this gap, between China's sluggish past and Sun's high-speed future, proved to be the great despair of the nationalist movement. China, as events after 1911 showed, could not be remade overnight. Sun's own program he was forced to modify, and others after him still faced an enormous task of assimilation and re-evaluation. This, however, is for our later readings to take up.

HU HAN-MIN
The Six Principles of the People's Report

The basic platform of the League of Common Alliance (*T'ung-meng hui*) was set forth in a manifesto issued in the fall of 1905. It reiterated Sun's early anti-Manchu and republican aims, as well as a third, "Equalization of Land Rights," which showed a developing interest in socialistic ideas. The manifesto also stated Sun's plan of revolution in three stages: 1) military government; 2) a provisional constitution granting local self-government; and 3) full constitutional government under a republican system.

A somewhat fuller statement of the League's basic principles was written for the third issue of the party organ, *People's Report,* in April, 1906, by its editor Hu Han-min (1879–1936). The statement carried Sun Yat-sen's endorsement. Three of the six principles set forth here—nationalism, republicanism, and land nationalization—correspond roughly to Sun's famous Three Principles. The other three, not reproduced below, dealt with problems of immediate concern to the revolutionists in Yokohama, as affecting their relations with others, especially the Japanese. The fourth principle asserts the indispensability of a strong, united China to the maintenance of world peace, since it is China's weakness which encourages the great powers to contend for special advantages and risk a catastrophic war. Here the influence of the Japanese statesman, Ōkuma Shigenobu, liberal leader whose support the revolutionists counted heavily upon, is evident. The fifth and sixth principles advocate close collaboration between the Chinese and Japanese, and urge other countries also to support the revolution. Nationalism, at this point, is thus not opposed to foreign intervention but in fact welcomes it—on the right side.

While the Manchu regime is the prime target of the revolutionists' indignation, their actual antagonists in the political struggle are not so much those in power at home as reformers in exile (like Liang Ch'i-ch'ao, then also active in Yokohama) who remain loyal to the dynasty and favor constitutional monarchy. During the first decade of the twentieth century the contest between these two groups, reformist and revolutionary, for the support of Chinese students in Japan was bitter and sometimes violent.

[From Tsou Lu (ed.), *Chung-kuo Kuomintang shih kao*, pp. 442–47]

1. *Overthrow of the Present Evil Government.* This is our first task. That a fine nation should be controlled by an evil one and that, instead of adopting our culture, the Manchus should force us to adopt theirs, is contrary to reason and cannot last for long. For the sake of our independence and salvation, we must overthrow the Manchu dynasty. The Manchus have hurt the Chinese people so much that there has arisen an inseparable barrier between them. Some have argued that the Manchus can be assimilated to Chinese culture as were the Ti, Ch'iang, and Hsien-pi tribes after their invasion of China. We need not discuss the incorrectness of this analogy, but let us ask this question: Were these tribes assimilated to Chinese culture during their rule of China, or were they assimilated after China's regeneration and their defeat and subjugation by the Chinese? Those who advocate assimilation of the Manchus without having them overthrown merely serve as tools of the tyrannical dynasty and are therefore shameless to the utmost. Our nationalism is not to be mixed with political opportunism. What distresses us sorely and hurts us unceasingly is the impossible position of subjugation we are in. If we recover our sovereignty and regain our position as ruler, it is not necessary to eliminate the evil race in order to satisfy our national aspirations. As an inferior minority, the Manchus rule the majority by means of political power. If their regime is overthrown, they will have nothing to maintain their existence. Whether they will flee to their old den [in the North] as did the defeated Mongols, or whether they will be assimilated to the Chinese as were the conquered Ti, Ch'iang and Hsien-pi tribes, we do not know. But unless their political power is overthrown, the Chinese nation will forever remain the conquered people without independence, and, being controlled by a backward nation, will finally perish with it in the struggle with the advanced foreign powers. That is why we say Manchu rule is contrary to reason and cannot last for long.

The Manchu government is evil because it is the evil race which usurped our government, and their evils are not confined to a few political measures but are rooted in the nature of the race and can neither be eliminated nor reformed. Therefore, even if there are a few ostensible reforms, the evils will remain just the same. The adoption of Western constitutional institutions and law will not change the situation . . . [contrary to the view of Liang Ch'i-ch'ao]. [pp. 442–43]

2. *Establishment of a Republic.* That absolute monarchy is unsuitable to the present age requires no argument. Political observers determine the level of a country's civilization by inquiring whether its political system is despotic or not. It is but natural therefore that those who propose new forms of government in the twentieth century should aim at rooting out the elements of absolutism. Revolutions broke out in China one after another in the past, but because the political system was not reformed, no good results ensued. Thus the Mongol dynasty was overthrown by the Ming, but within three hundred years the Chinese nation was again on the decline. For although the foreign rule was overthrown and a Chinese regime was installed in its place, the autocratic form of government remained unchanged, to the disappointment of the people.

According to the general theory of government, the opposite of autocracy is republican government, which, broadly speaking, may be divided into three kinds: first, aristocracy; second, democracy; and third, constitutional democracy. The latter is not only different from aristocracy but also from absolute democracy. People who depend on hearsay all argue that the Chinese nation lacks the tradition of democracy in its history, thus undermining the morale of our patriots. Alas! they are not only ignorant of political science but unqualified to discuss history. The greatest difficulty in establishing a constitutional government, as experienced by other countries, is the struggle of the common people against both the monarch and the nobility. The constitutional government was established without difficulty in America because after its independence there was no class other than the common people. One of the great features of Chinese politics is that since the Ch'in and Han dynasties there has existed no noble class (except for the Mongol and Manchu dynasties when a noble class was maintained according to then alien systems). After the overthrow of the Manchus, therefore, there will be no distinction between classes in China (even the United States has economic classes, but China has none). The establishment of constitutional government will be easier in China than in other countries. . . .

We agree with Herbert Spencer, who compared the difficulty of changing an established political system to that of changing the constitution of an organism after its main body has been formed. Since constitutional democracy can be esablished only after a revolution, it is imperative that following our revolution, only the best and the most public-spirited form of government should be adopted so that no defects will remain. Absolute government, be it monarchical or democratic, is government of injustice and inequality. As to constitutional monarchy, the demarcation between ruler and ruled is definite and distinct, and since their feelings toward each other are different, classes will arise. Constitutional democracy will have none of these defects, and equality will prevail. We can overthrow the Manchus and establish our state because Chinese nationalism and democratic thought are well developed. When we are able to do this, it is inconceivable that, knowing the general psychology of the people, we should abandon the government of equality and retain the distinction between ruler and ruled. [pp. 444–45]

Sun, during his exile in Europe, had been influenced by a variety of socialistic ideas as divergent as German state socialism and Henry George's single tax theories. While Sun's own thinking (and that of his associates) was still somewhat fluid and vague, the provision for "equalization of land rights" in the original *T'ung-meng hui* manifesto was clearly an adaptation of the ideas of Henry George and John Stuart Mill, calling for state appropriation of all future increases in land value but recognizing its present value as the property of the owner. Hu Han-min's version is more extreme (perhaps because of his own dire poverty as a youth). It represents a violent attack on landlordism and calls for complete socialization of the land. Hu also seems to be more conscious of the landlord-tenant problem in rural China than Sun was.

In the preceding section, however, Hu has already asserted that China, in contrast to the West, has no economic classes but only a ruling elite which must be overthrown. Therefore rural landlordism was not, presumably, the primary target in his mind. Whether as an accommodation to Sun or not, it is the urban landlordism attacked by Henry George in the West which appears to be Hu's major concern. In the port cities of China he sees a process developing like that in the West, and his object is to prevent its spread when China modernizes after the coming Revolution.[1]

Note in the following that Hu takes as his point of departure the economic evils of modern society, rather than age-old abuses in China. Note also the sanction for land nationalization which he finds in the ancient well-field system—a symbol for Hu of primitive communism.

[1] On this point, see further Harold Schiffrin, "Sun Yat-sen's Land Policy," in *Journal of Asian Studies*, Vol. XVI, No. 4 (August 1957), pp. 549–64.

3. *Land Nationalization.* The affliction of civilized countries in the modern age is not political classes but economic classes. Hence the rise of socialism. There are many socialist theories, but they all aim at leveling economic classes. Generally speaking, socialism may be divided into communism and collectivism, and nationalization of land is part of collectivism. Only constitutional democracies can adopt collectivism, for there the ruling authority resides in the state and the state machinery is controlled by a representative legislature. Thus there is no inequality involved if a democratic state, in reflecting social psychology, should adopt collectivism in order to promote the welfare of the people. Such, of course, cannot be said of a regime which allows of any political classes.

Not all collectivist theories can be applied to China at her present stage of development. But in the case of land nationalization we already have a model for it in the well-field system of the Three Dynasties, and it should not be difficult to introduce land nationalization as an adaptation of a past system to the present age of political reform. Nationalization of land is opposed to private ownership. It is based on the theory that since land is the essential element in production and is not man-made, any more than sunshine or air, it should not be privately owned.

The landlord system arises from many causes. At first land may be obtained as capital through accumulation of labor and used for productive purposes. Subsequently, as feudal domains develop, land is monopolized, and both capitalists and laborers become dependents of the feudal lords who are the first to receive the crops. The laborers borrow money from the capitalists, and the reason the latter are able to exploit the former is that the former cannot own land. Land values vary from age to age, but as civilization advances, the increase in land value is considerable —an increase not due to any effort on the part of the landlord, but nonetheless enjoyed by him alone. This is not just to harry men in society but completely to make servants of them.

The evil consequences of this system are that the landlord can acquire absolute power in society and thereby absorb and annex more land, that the farmers can be driven out of work, that people may be short of food and thus have to depend on outside supply, and that the entire country may be made poorer while capital and wealth all go to the landlords.

Land in China today, as affected by commercial development in the coastal ports, may in ten years have its value increased more than ten times what it was formerly. We can see from this that after the revolution with the progress of civilization, the same process would be accelerated in the interior. If a system of private monopoly is re-established, then the economic class will perpetuate itself as a political class, but if we make adequate provision against this at the beginning, we can easily plan so that the evil never arises.

There are various measures for carrying out land nationalization, but the main purpose is to deprive the people of the right of landownership while permitting them to retain other rights over land (such as superfices, emphyteusis, easement, etc.). And these rights must be obtained by permission of the state. There will be no private tenancy, nor will there be any permanent mortgage. In this way the power of the landlord will be wiped out from the Chinese continent. All land taxes levied by the state must have the approval of parliament; there will be no manipulations for private profit, nor heavy taxes detrimental to the farmers' interests. Profit from land will be high, but only self-cultivating farmers can obtain land from the state. In this way people will increasingly devote themselves to farming and no land will be wasted. Landlords who in the past have been nonproductive profiteers will now be just like the common people. They will turn to productive enterprises and this will produce striking results for the good of the whole national economy. [pp. 445–47]

SUN YAT-SEN
The Three People's Principles

After the revolution of 1911 Sun Yat-sen reluctantly allowed his secret revolutionary society to be converted into an open political party, the Kuomintang (National People's Party). It accomplished little through parliamentary politics, however, and even when Sun reverted to revolutionary tactics the lack of military support and his failure to obtain sufficient help from Japan or the West kept him from registering any substantial progress. Nevertheless, Sun was impressed and encouraged by the success of the Russian Revolution, and offers of Soviet help induced him in 1923 to reorganize the Kuomintang along Communist organizational lines and to enter upon a period of collaboration with the Soviets and the recently founded Chinese Communist Party. Even so, while making certain tactical adjustments in his propaganda line and adopting a more anti-Western tone, Sun was steadfast in his repudiation of Marxism as such.

[105]

The *Three People's Principles* (*San min chu-i*), which served as the basic text of the Nationalist movement, was given its final form in a series of lectures by Sun to party members in 1924, after the Kuomintang's reorganization with Soviet help the year before. It attempted to reformulate the principles put forward in 1905, modifying them in accordance with Sun's subsequent experience and the altered circumstances in which he was making a bid for military and political unification of the country.

Sun's nationalism, in 1905, had been directed mainly against the Manchus. Events after the revolution of 1911, however, proved that ridding China of foreign rule was not enough to assure her future as a nation. Even with the Manchus gone, China was as weak as ever, and still more disunited. Consequently, by 1924 foreign rule had been superseded in Sun's mind by two other issues. First was the Chinese people's need for national solidarity; though possessing all the other requisites of a great nation, they still lacked a capacity for cohesion. Second (and this was perhaps one means of generating the first), Sun found a new target of national indignation: foreign economic imperialism. This was an issue to which Sun acknowledged the Chinese people were not yet alive. Yet it had assumed new significance for him now as the basis for collaboration with the Communists in a national revolution against imperialism. And it reflected Sun's increasing bitterness toward the West for its failure to support him.

The lack of national solidarity Sun saw as in part the legacy of long foreign rule. It was aggravated, however, by a growing cosmopolitanism and internationalism resulting from the West's disenchantment with nationalism after the First World War. Sun, who had once represented the vanguard of nationalism from the West, now found himself fighting a rear guard action in defense of his old cause. He spoke more and more in deprecation of the modern West —its materialism especially—and increasingly sought in Chinese tradition the basis for a nationalism which it had never been made to serve before. In this Sun's political instinct was undoubtedly sound, whatever the deficiencies of his intellectual approach. For nationalism remained in fact a potent issue, in China as in the rest of Asia. Ironically, though, it was to be exploited most effectively by those whose "internationalism" Sun himself condemned—the Communists.

[From *Chung-shan ch'üan-shu*, I, 4-5, 15-16, 28-29, 51-52]

[*China as a Heap of Loose Sand*]. For the most part the four hundred million people of China can be spoken of as completely Han Chinese. With common customs and habits, we are completely of one race. But in the world today what position do we occupy? Compared to the other peoples of the world we have the greatest population and our civilization is four thousand years old; we should therefore be advancing in the front rank with the nations of Europe and America. But the Chinese people have only family and clan solidarity; they do not have national spirit. Therefore even though we have four hundred million people gathered together in one China, in reality they are just a heap of loose sand. Today we are the poorest and weakest nation in the world, and occupy the lowest position in international affairs. Other men are the carving knife and serving dish; we are the fish and the meat. Our position at this time is most perilous. If we do not earnestly espouse nationalism and weld together our four hundred million people into a strong nation, there is danger of China's being lost and our people being destroyed. If we wish to avert this catastrophe, we must espouse nationalism and bring this national spirit to the salvation of the country. [pp. 4–5, Lecture 1]

[*China as a "Hypo-colony"*]. Since the Chinese Revolution, the foreign powers have found that it was much less easy to use political force in carving up China. A people who had experienced Manchu oppression and learned to overthrow it, would now, if the powers used political force to oppress it, be certain to resist, and thus make things difficult for them. For this reason they are letting up in their efforts to control China by political force and instead are using economic pressure to keep us down. . . . As regards political oppression people are readily aware of their suffering, but when it comes to economic oppression most often they are hardly conscious of it. China has already experienced several decades of economic oppression by the foreign powers, and so far the nation has for the most part shown no sense of irritation. As a consequence China is being transformed everywhere into a colony of the foreign powers.

Our people keep thinking that China is only a "semi-colony"—a term by which they seek to comfort themselves. Yet in reality the economic oppression we have endured is not just that of a "semi-colony" but greater even than that of a full colony. . . . Of what nation then is China a colony? It is the colony of every nation with which it has concluded treaties; each of them is China's master. Therefore China is not just the colony of one country; it is the colony of many countries. We are not just the slaves of one country, but the slaves of many countries. In the event of natural disasters like flood and drought, a nation which is sole master appropriates funds for relief and distributes them, thinking this its own duty; and the people who are its slaves regard this relief work as something to which their masters are obligated. But when North China suffered drought several years ago, the foreign powers did not regard it as their responsibility to appropriate funds and distribute relief; only those foreigners resident in China raised funds for the drought victims, whereupon Chinese observers remarked on the great generosity of the foreigners who bore no responsibility to help. . . .

From this we can see that China is not so well off as Annam [under the French] and Korea [under the Japanese]. Being the slaves of one country represents a far higher status than being the slaves of many, and is far more advantageous. Therefore, to call China a "semi-colony" is quite incorrect. If I may coin a phrase, we should be called a "hypo-colony." This is a term that comes from chemistry, as in "hypo-phosphite." Among chemicals there are some belonging to the class of phosphorous compounds but of lower grade, which are called phosphites. Still another grade lower, and they are called hypo-phosphites. . . . The Chinese people, believing they were a semi-colony, thought it shame enough; they did not realize that they were lower even than Annam or Korea. Therefore we cannot call ourselves a "semi-colony" but only a "hypo-colony." [pp. 15–16, Lecture 2]

[*Nationalism and Cosmopolitanism*]. A new idea is emerging in England and Russia, proposed by the intellectuals, which opposes nationalism on the ground that it is narrow and illiberal. This is simply a doctrine of cosmopolitanism. England now and formerly Germany and Russia, together with the Chinese youth of today who preach the new civilization, support this doctrine and oppose nationalism. Often I hear young people say: "The Three Principles of the People do not fit in with the present world's new tendencies; the latest and best doctrine in the world is cosmopolitanism." But is cosmopolitanism really good or not? If that doctrine is good, why is it that as soon as China was conquered, her nationalism was destroyed? Cosmopolitanism is the same thing as China's theory of world empire two thousand years ago. Let us now examine that doctrine and see whether in fact it is good or not. Theoretically, we cannot say it is no good. Yet it is because formerly the Chinese intellectual class had cosmopolitan ideas that, when the Manchus crossed China's frontier, the whole country was lost to them. . . .

We cannot decide whether an idea is good or not without seeing it in practice. If the idea is of practical value to us, it is good; if it is impractical, it is bad. If it is useful to the world, it is good; if it is not, it is no good. The nations which are employing imperialism to conquer others and which are trying to retain their privileged positions as sovereign lords are advocating cosmopolitanism and want the whole world to follow them. [pp. 28–29, Lecture 3]

[*Nationalism and Traditional Morality*]. If today we want to restore the standing of our people, we must first restore our national spirit. . . . If in the past our people have survived despite the fall of the state [to foreign conquerors], and not only survived themselves but been able to assimilate these foreign conquerors, it is because of the high level of our traditional morality. Therefore, if we go to the root of the matter, besides arousing a sense of national solidarity uniting all our people, we must recover and restore our characteristic, traditional morality. Only thus can we hope to attain again the distinctive position of our people.

This characteristic morality the Chinese people today have still not forgotten. First comes loyalty and filial piety, then humanity and love, faithfulness and duty, harmony and peace. Of these traditional virtues, the Chinese people still speak, but now, under foreign oppression, we have been invaded by a new culture, the force of which is felt all across the nation. Men wholly intoxicated by this new culture have thus begun to attack the traditional morality, saying that with the adoption of the new culture, we no longer have need of the old morality.[2] . . . They say that when we formerly spoke of loyalty, it was loyalty to princes, but now in our democracy there are no princes, so loyalty is unnecessary and can be dispensed with. This kind of reasoning is certainly mistaken. In our country princes can be dispensed with, but not loyalty. If they say loyalty can be dispensed with, then I ask: "Do we, or do we not, have a nation? Can we, or can we not, make loyalty serve the nation? If indeed we can no longer speak of loyalty to princes, can we not, however, speak of loyalty to our people?" [pp. 51–52, Lecture 6]

The Principle of Democracy

In 1905 Sun had proclaimed the principle of democracy mainly against the advocates of constitutional monarchy whom he identified with "absolutism." In 1924 his notion of the forms this democracy should take is given more explicit expression, and against a background of personal experience which con-

---

[2] See Chapter XXIV.

firmed Sun's longstanding belief in the need for strong political leadership.
The result is a plan of government which he believed would insure popular
control through electoral processes, yet give a strong executive wide powers
to deal with the business of government. The emphasis is on leadership now,
not liberty. In fact, argues Sun (thinking again of the Chinese people as a
"heap of loose sand"), the struggle of the Chinese people is not for individual
liberty, of which they have had an excess, but for the "liberty of the nation."
Consequently, he attempts to distinguish between sovereignty, which the
people should retain, and the ability to rule, which should be vested in an elite
group of experts.

A distinctive feature of Sun's constitutional order is his five branches or
powers of the government. These would include the three associated with the
American government—executive, legislative and judicial—along with two
which were intended as a check on elected officials and their powers of appointment, and for which Sun believed Chinese political tradition provided a
unique precedent: a censorate or supervisory organ, and an independent civil
service system. These latter he spoke of as if they had indeed been independent
organs of the traditional Chinese state, thus enabling him as a nationalist not
only to offer a constitution which represented a unique Chinese synthesis but
also to redeem Chinese tradition and place it on at least a par with the West.
While it cannot be said that Sun's ideas were necessarily given a fair test in
Nationalist China, the net effect of this further separation of powers was probably to fragment the power of all but the executive.

The passages which follow illustrate Sun's fondness for analogies drawn
from the world of modern machines and applied to political situations.

[From *Chung-shan ch'üan-shu*, I, 117–18, 139–40, 141–42, 143–45,
adapted from Price, *San Min Chu I*, pp. 345–46, 350–58]

[*Separation of Sovereignty and Ability*]. How can a government be made
all-powerful? Once the government is all-powerful, how can it be made
responsive to the will of the people? . . . I have found a method to solve
the problem. The method which I have thought of is a new discovery
in political theory and is a fundamental solution of the whole problem.
. . . It is the theory of the distinction between sovereignty and ability.
[pp. 117–18, Lecture 5]

After China has established a powerful government, we must not be
afraid, as Western people are, that the government will become too strong
and that we will be unable to control it. For it is our plan that the political
power of the reconstructed state will be divided into two parts. One is
the power over the government; that great power will be placed entirely
in the hands of the people, who will have a full degree of sovereignty and

will be able to control directly the affairs of state—this political power is popular sovereignty. The other power is the governing power; that great power will be placed in the hands of the government organs, which will be powerful and will manage all the nation's business—this governing power is the power of the government. If the people have a full measure of political sovereignty and the methods for exercising popular control over the government are well worked out, we need not fear that the government will become too strong and uncontrollable. . . .

It is because Europe and America lacked compact and effective methods to control their government that their governmental machines have not, until the present day, been well-developed. Let us not follow in their tracks. Let the people in thinking about government distinguish between sovereignty and ability. Let the great political force of the state be divided into two: the power of the government and the power of the people. Such a division will make the government the machinery and the people the engineer. The attitude of the people toward the government will then resemble the attitude of the engineer toward his machine. The construction of machinery has made such advances nowadays that not only men with mechanical knowledge, but even children without any knowledge of machinery are able to control it. [pp. 139–40, Lecture 6]

[*The Four Powers of the People*]. What are the newest discoveries in the way of exercising popular sovereignty? First, there is suffrage, and it is the only method practiced throughout the so-called advanced democracies. Is this one form of popular sovereignty enough in government? This one power by itself may be compared to the earlier machines which could move forward only but not back.

The second of the newly discovered methods is the right of recall. When the people have this right, they possess the power of pulling the machine back.

These two rights give the people control over officials and enable them to put all government officials in their positions or to remove them from their positions. The coming and going of officials follows the free will of the people, just as the modern machines move to and fro by the free action of the engine. Besides officials, another important thing in a state is law; "with men to govern there must also be laws for governing." What powers must the people possess in order to control the laws? If the people think that a certain law would be of great advantage to them, they should have the power to decide upon this law and turn it over to the government for execution. This third kind of popular power is called the initiative.

If the people think that an old law is not beneficial to them, they should have the power to amend it and to ask the government to enforce the amended law and do away with the old law. This is called the referendum and is a fourth form of popular sovereignty.

Only when the people have these four rights can we say that democracy is complete, and only when these four powers are effectively applied can we say that there is a thorough-going, direct, and popular sovereignty. [pp. 141–42, Lecture 6]

[*The Five-Power Constitution*]. With the people exercising the four great powers to control the government, what methods will the government use in performing its work? In order that the government may have a complete organ through which to do its best work, there must be a five-power constitution. A government is not complete and cannot do its best work for the people unless it is based on the five-power constitution [i.e., a government composed of five branches: executive, legislative, judicial, civil service examination, and censorate]. . . .

All governmental powers were formerly monopolized by kings and emperors, but after the revolutions they were divided into three groups. Thus the United States, after securing its independence, established a government with three coordinate departments. The American system achieved such good results that it was adopted by other nations. But foreign governments have merely a triple-power separation. Why do we now want a separation of five powers? What is the source of the two new features in our five-power constitution?

The two new features come from old China. China long ago had the independent systems of civil service examination and censorate, and they were very effective. The imperial censors of the Manchu dynasty and the official advisers of the T'ang dynasty made a fine censoring system. The power of censorship includes the power to impeach. Foreign countries also have this power, only it is placed in the legislative body and is not a separate governmental power.

The selection of real talent and ability through examinations has been characteristic of China for thousands of years. Foreign scholars who have recently studied Chinese institutions highly praise China's old independent examination system. There have been imitations of the system for the selection of able men in the West. Great Britain's civil service examinations are modeled after the old Chinese system, but they are limited to ordinary officials. The British system does not yet possess the spirit of the independent examination of China.

In old China, only three governmental powers—judicial, legislative, and executive—were vested in the emperor. The other powers of civil service examination and the censorate were independent of the Throne. The old autocratic government of China can also be said to have had three separate departments and so it was very different from the autocratic governments of the West in which all power was monopolized by the king or emperor himself. During the period of autocratic government in China, the emperor did not monopolize the power of examination and the censorate.

Hence, as for the separation of governmental powers, we can say that China had three coordinate departments of government just as the modern democracies. China practiced the separation of autocratic, examination and censorate powers for thousands of years. Western countries have practiced the separation of legislative, judicial, and executive powers for only a little over a century. However, the three governmental powers in the West have been imperfectly applied and the three coordinate powers of old China led to many abuses. If we now want to combine the best from China and the best from other countries and guard against all kinds of abuse, we must take the three Western governmental powers —the executive, legislative and judicial—add to them the Chinese powers of examination and censorate and make a perfect government of five powers. Such a government will be the most complete and the finest in the world, and a state with such a government will indeed be of the people, by the people and for the people. [pp. 143-45, Lecture 6]

The People's Livelihood

The "People's Livelihood" (*min-sheng chu-i*) joined nationalism and democracy to make up Sun Yat-sen's Three People's Principles in 1906. It was meant to cover the economic side of Sun's program broadly enough so as to embrace a variety of social and economic theories which had attracted Sun's attention. Often he and his followers used *min-sheng chu-i* as an equivalent for socialism, drawing upon the popularity of this idea in general, while retaining the freedom to interpret it as they chose. For Sun in 1924 its most essential component was still Henry George's single tax. Though paying tribute to Marx as a "social scientist," Sun rejected entirely Marx's theory of class struggle and cited a work little known in the West, *The Social Interpretation of History,* by a Brooklyn dentist, Maurice William, as a conclusive refutation of Marx's economic determinism. Sun also disputed Marx's belief in the steady impoverishment of the worker under capitalism and the latter's imminent collapse. American experience (e.g., Henry Ford) showed that capitalist success and rising living standards for the worker were not mutually exclusive.

Sun exhibited great confidence in China's future, in her ability to catch up with the West and yet avoid its economic woes. China's problem was one of production, not of distribution; and the inequalty of wealth need never arise if economic development were based on his land tax program, which would prevent "unearned increments" from accruing to individuals at the same time that it provided revenues for state investment in industry. Sun envisaged a kind of state socialism, permitting small-scale capitalist enterprise to exist alongside nationalized industries and utilities. But the immediate need was to encourage China's infant industries. Here Sun stressed her emancipation from foreign economic imperialism, the main point of which was to gain customs autonomy, lost through the unequal treaties, and to erect protective tariffs. Foreign investment he was only too ready to promote. His program for agriculture involved mainly technological improvement.

Although Sun's analysis of China's economic problems correctly differentiated it as an undeveloped country from the more advanced industrial societies, his future program was conceived largely in terms of Western economic doctrines or experience. For a man who started life in a peasant household, he showed comparatively little awareness of the peasant's problems, and even less of their potential political significance.

[From *Chung-shan ch'üan-shu,* I, 166, 175–76, 177–79; adapted from Price, pp. 431–34, 437–41]

[*The Principle of Livelihood*]. The Kuomintang some time ago in its party platform adopted two methods by which the principle of livelihood is to be carried out. The first method is equalization of landownership; the second is regulation of capital. [p. 166]

Our first method consists in solving the land question. The methods for solution of the land problem are different in various countries, and each country has its own peculiar difficulties. The plan which we are following is simple and easy—equalization of landownership.

As soon as the landowners hear us talking about the land question and equalization of landownership, they are naturally alarmed as capitalists are alarmed when they hear people talking about socialism, and they want to rise up and fight it. If our landowners were like the great land-owners of Europe and had developed tremendous power, it would be very difficult for us to solve the land problem. But China does not have such big landowners, and the power of the small landowners is still rather weak. If we attack the problem now, we can solve it; but if we lose the present opportunity, we will have much more difficulty in the future. The discussion of the land problem naturally causes a feeling of fear among the landowners, but if the Kuomintang policy is followed, present land-owners can set their hearts at rest.

What is our policy? We propose that the government shall levy a tax proportionate to the price of the land and, if necessary, buy back the land according to its price.

But how will the price of the land be determined? I would let the landowner himself fix the price. . . . Many people think that if the landowners made their own assessment, they would undervalue the land and the government would lose out. . . . But suppose the government makes two regulations: first, that it will collect taxes according to the declared value of the land; second, that it can also buy back the land at the value declared. . . . According to this plan, if the landowner makes a low assessment, he will be afraid lest the government buy the land at the declared value and make him lose his property; if he makes too high an assessment, he will be afraid of the government taxes according to the value and his loss through heavy taxes. Comparing these two serious possibilities, he will certainly not want to report the value of his land too high or too low; he will strike the mean and report the true market price to the government. In this way neither the landowner nor the government will lose.

After land values have been fixed we should have a regulation by law that from that year all increase in land value, which in other countries means heavier taxation, shall revert to the community. This is because the increase in land value is due to improvement made by society and to the progress of industry and commerce. China's industry and commerce have made little progress for thousands of years, so land values have scarcely changed throughout these generations. But as soon as progress and improvement set in, as in the modern cities of China, land prices change every day, sometimes increasing a thousandfold and even ten thousandfold. The credit for the progress and improvement belongs to the energy and enterprise of all the people. Land increment resulting from that progress and improvement should therefore revert to the community rather than to private individuals. [pp. 175–76, Lecture 2]

[*Capital and the State*]. If we want to solve the livelihood problem in China and to "win eternal ease by one supreme effort," it will not be sufficient to depend only on the restriction of capital. The income tax levied in foreign countries is one method of regulating capital. But have these countries solved the problem of the people's livelihood?

China cannot be compared to foreign countries. It is not sufficient for us to regulate capital. Other countries are rich while China is poor; other countries have a surplus of production while China is not producing enough. So China must not only regulate private capital, but she must also develop state capital.

At present our state is split into pieces. How can we develop our state capital? It seems as if we could not find or anticipate a way. But our present disunion is only a temporary state of affairs; in the future we shall certainly achieve unity, and then to solve the livelihood problem we shall need to develop capital and promote industry.

First, we must build means of communication, railroads and waterways, on a large scale. Second, we must open up mines. China is rich in minerals, but alas, they are buried in the earth! Third, we must hasten to develop manufacturing. Although China has a multitude of workers, she has no machinery and so cannot compete with other countries. Goods used throughout China have to be manufactured and imported from other countries, with the result that our rights and interests are simply leaking away. If we want to recover these rights and interests, we must quickly employ state power to promote industry, use machinery in production, and see that all workers of the country are employed. When all the workers have employment and use machinery in production, we will have a great, new source of wealth. If we do not use state power to build up these enterprises but leave them in the hands of private Chinese or of foreign businessmen, the result will be the expansion of private capital and the emergence of a great wealthy class with the consequent inequalities in society. . . .

China is now suffering from poverty, not from unequal distribution of wealth. Where there are inequalities of wealth, the methods of Marx can, of course, be used; a class war can be advocated to destroy the inequalities. But in China, where industry is not yet developed, Marx's class war and dictatorship of the proletariat are impracticable. [pp. 177–79]

The Three Stages of Revolution

The significance of Sun's "Three Stages of Revolution" lies mainly in his doctrine of political tutelage, which represents perhaps the first conscious advocacy of "guided democracy" among the leaders of Asian nationalism. When first enunciated in 1905, it seems to have been Sun's answer to those who argued that the Chinese people, long accustomed to political absolutism and unaccustomed to participation in government, were unprepared for democracy. Sun acknowledged that a period of adjustment or transition would be required, but his early confidence in the people's ability to "learn" democracy is shown by the exact time schedule he had worked out for this process—political tutelage would last just six years.

The following explanation of the Three Stages is taken from *A Program of National Reconstruction,* prepared in 1918, and follows in the main his earlier ideas, though it stresses the difficulties of reconstruction encountered after the revolution. Sun's awareness of these difficulties led to increasing emphasis on the importance of strong leadership in the period of tutelage, somewhat less on the readiness of the people for democracy. In his *Outline of National Reconstruction,* written in 1924 just before his death, he omitted reference to a definite time schedule, as if to concede that the period of tutelage might extend beyond his original expectations.

[From *Chung-shan ch'üan-shu,* Vol. II, *Chien-kuo fang-lüeh,* Part I (also entitled *Sun Wen hsüeh-shuo*), Ch. 6, pp. 37–38, 39–49, 42]

[*The Three Phases of National Reconstruction*]. As for the work of revolutionary reconstruction, I have based my ideas on the current of world progress and followed the precedents in other countries. I have studied their respective advantages and disadvantages, their accomplishments and failures. It is only after mature deliberation and thorough preparation that I have decided upon the Program of Revolution and defined the procedure of the revolution in three stages. The first is the period of military government; the second, the period of political tutelage; and the third, the period of constitutional government.

The first stage is the period of destruction. During this period martial law is to be enforced. The revolutionary army undertakes to overthrow the Manchu tyranny, to eradicate the corruption of officialdom, to eliminate depraved customs, to exterminate the system of slave girls, to wipe out the scourge of opium, superstitious beliefs, and geomancy, to abolish the obstructive *likin* and so forth.

The second stage is a transitional period. It is planned that the provisional constitution will be promulgated and local self-government promoted to encourage the exercise of political rights by the people. The *hsien,* or district, will be made the basic unit of local self-government and is to be divided into villages and rural districts—all under the jurisdiction of the district government.

The moment the enemy forces have been cleared and military operations have ceased in a district, the provisional constitution will be promulgated in the district, defining the rights and duties of citizens and the governing powers of the revolutionary government. The constitution will be enforced for three years, after which period the people of the district will elect their district officers. However, if within the period of three years, the Self-Government Commission of a district can wipe out the evils enumerated above, get more than half of the population to understand the Three Principles of the People and pledge allegiance to the republic, complete the compilation of a census, determine the number of households and carry out constructive measures regarding police, sanitation, education, and highways in accordance with the minimum requirements prescribed in the provisional constitution, the district may also elect its own officials and become a full-fledged self-governing area.

In respect to such self-governing units the revolutionary government will exercise the right of political tutelage in accordance with the provisional constitution. When a period of six years expires after the attainment of political stability throughout the country, the districts which have become full-fledged self-governing units are each entitled to elect one representative to form the National Assembly. The task of the Assembly will be to adopt a five-power constitution and to organize a central government consisting of five branches, namely, the Executive Branch, the Legislative Branch, the Judicial Branch, the Examination Branch, and the Control Branch [Censorate].

When the constitution has been determined, the people of the various districts shall elect by ballot a President to organize the Executive Branch and representatives to organize the Legislative Branch. They are, however, not responsible to the President or to the Legislative Branch. All the five branches will be responsible to the National Assembly. Members of the various branches suspected of delinquency in duty will be impeached by the Control Branch before the National Assembly. Delinquent members of the Control Branch will be directly impeached by the National Assembly and dismissed when found guilty. The function of the National Assembly consists in amending the constitution and checking misconduct on the part of public functionaries. Qualifications of members of the National Assembly and of the five Branches and all other officials will be determined by the Examination Branch.

When the constitution is promulgated and the President and members of the National Assembly are elected, the Revolutionary Government will hand over its governing power to the President, and the period of political tutelage will come to an end.

The third phase is the period of the completion of reconstruction. During this period, constitutional government is to be introduced, and the self-governing body in a district will enable the people directly to exercise their political rights. In regard to the district government, the people are entitled to the rights of election, initiative, referendum, and recall. In regard to the national government, the people exercise the rights of suffrage, while the other rights are delegated to the representatives to the National Assembly. The period of constitutional government will mark the completion of reconstruction and the success of the revolution. This is the gist of the Revolutionary Program. [pp. 37–38]

[*The Necessity of Political Tutelage*]. What is meant by revolutionary reconstruction? It is extraordinary reconstruction and also rapid reconstruction. It differs from ordinary reconstruction which follows the natural course of society and is affected by the trend of circumstances. In a revolution extraordinary destruction is involved, such as the extermination of the monarchical system and the overthrow of absolutism. Such destruction naturally calls for extraordinary reconstruction.

Revolutionary destruction and revolutionary reconstruction complement each other like the two legs of a man or the two wings of a bird. The republic after its inauguration weathered the storm of extraordinary destruction. This, however, was not followed by extraordinary reconstruction. A vicious circle of civil wars has consequently arisen. The nation is on the descendent like a stream flowing downward. The tyranny of the warlords together with the sinister maneuvers of unscrupulous politicians is beyond control. In an extraordinary time, only extraordinary reconstruction can inspire the people with a new mind and make a new beginning of the nation. Hence the Program of Revolution is necessary. . . .

Before their independence the thirteen American colonies had been in an autonomous state and local self-government had developed to a remarkable degree. Consequently, since the founding of the republic, the country has been progressing notably well in the political field. This is because the political structure of the country was built on the foundation of a strongly developed autonomy. . . .

It is not so with France. Although France was an advanced and cultured country in Europe with an intelligent, energetic people, and although for a hundred years before the revolution she had been under the influence of democratic theories and, further, had the American precedent to follow, she was still unable to attain a republican constitutional government with one leap out of revolution. What is the reason? It lies in the fact that her political system had always been an absolute monarchy and that her government had long been centralized; she possessed no new world as an area for development and no self-government as a foundation.

China's defects are similar to those of France, but in addition the knowledge and political ability of our people are far below those of the French. And yet I have hoped to attain a republican constitutional government in one step after the revolution. How could this be brought about? It is to get out of this difficulty that I have devised a transitional period, during which a provisional constitutional government would be established to train the people for local self-government. [pp. 39–40]

It is not to be denied that the Chinese people are deficient in knowledge. Moreover, they have been soaked in the poison of absolute monarchy for several thousand years. . . . What shall we do now? Men of the Yuan Shih-k'ai type argue that the Chinese people, deficient in knowledge, are unfit for republicanism. Crude scholars have also maintained that monarchy is necessary.

Alas! Even an ox can be trained to plow the field and a horse to carry man. Are men not capable of being trained? Suppose that when a youngster was entering school, his father was told that the boy did not know the written characters and therefore could not go to school. Is such reasoning logical? It is just because he does not know the characters that the boy must immediately set about learning them. The world has now come to an age of enlightenment. Hence the growing popularity of the idea of freedom and equality, which has become the main current of the world and cannot be stemmed by any means. China therefore needs a republican government just as a boy needs school. As a schoolboy must have good teachers and helpful friends, so the Chinese people, being for the first time under republican rule, must have a far-sighted revolutionary government for their training. This calls for the period of political tutelage, which is a necessary transitional stage from monarchy to republicanism. Without this, disorder will be unavoidable. [p. 42]

General Theory of Knowledge and Action

Closely linked in Sun's mind to the concept of political tutelage was his theory of knowledge and action. By it Sun attempted to answer those "realists" who, in the years after the revolution, dismissed his grand schemes as impractical because they did not take into account the mentality of the average Chinese or the difficulties of wholesale reform. Curiously, the blame for China's past failure to put his program into effect Sun lays at the door of Wang Yang-ming and his doctrine of the unity of knowledge and action. According to Sun this doctrine had fostered a misconception among the Chinese that "to know is easy and to act is difficult"—an attitude which encouraged lethargy and inaction.

There would seem to be no logical grounds for thus interpreting Wang's teaching, and Sun himself certainly contributed nothing to a clarification of the philosophical issues involved. The points he really is anxious to make are these: 1) knowledge and action can be separated in the sense that some people (like himself) are thinkers, while others are just doers; and 2) the Chinese people as a whole only need faith or confidence in the effectiveness of action; they need not worry about the reasons for acting. The knowledge of a few, the Kuomintang elite, will provide direction for the efforts of the many.

In the passages which follow, note how conscious Sun is of Japan's example of successful modernization and how he assesses the applicability to China of the alleged reasons for this success. Wang Yang-ming's popularity among Japanese reformers is a circumstance which helps to account for his innocent involvement in Sun's controversy over knowledge and action.

[From *Chung-shan ch'üan-shu*, Vol. II, *Chien-kuo fang-lüeh*, Part I (also entitled *Sun Wen hsüeh-shuo*), Ch. 5, pp. 31–33, 36–37]

The doctrine of Wang Yang-ming, who taught the unity of knowledge and action, was intended to encourage men to do good. It may be inferred that Wang also considered it not difficult to know but difficult to act. . . . His efforts at encouraging people to do good are indeed admirable, but his teaching is incompatible with truth. What is difficult he considered easy, and what is easy, difficult. To encourage one to attempt the difficult is tantamount to asking one to act against human nature. . . .

It is said that the renovation of Japan was entirely inspired by the teaching of Wang Yang-ming. The Japanese themselves believe this and pay high tribute to Wang. It should be noted, however, that Japan was still in the feudalistic stage before the [Meiji] Renovation.[3] The people were not yet removed from the tradition of the past and the spirit of initiative and enterprise was not extinct. In the face of foreign aggression, while the official classes were floundering, patriotic citizens felt stirred to action. They advocated support of the emperor in order to resist the foreigners. . . . And when the Japanese failed to expel the foreigners, they immediately changed their course and turned to imitate the way of the foreigners. The Renovation owed its success to their learning from the foreigners. Thus the Japanese effected their reforms without knowing the principle involved. This obviously had nothing to do with Wang's doctrine of the unity of action and knowledge. . . .

While Japan carried out her reforms without seeking to know about them, China would not undertake reform measures until she understood them, and even so she hesitated to act for fear of difficulty. The Chinese have been misled by the teaching that to act is even more difficult than to know. Reformation or change of institutions is a great national event. It is not always possible to comprehend the various measures in advance. Their significance is understood only after they have been carried out. The enterprising and adventurous spirit was mainly responsible for the success of the Japanese Renovation. They did not know what reformation was until they had accomplished it. It was then that they called it the Renovation.

In the case of China, however, she first sought a comprehension of the reform and then made attempts to carry it out. As such knowledge could never be acquired, action was indefinitely postponed. Thus, while the philosophy of Wang Yang-ming failed to discourage enterprising

---

[3] The term Sun uses corresponds to the Japanese *ishin*, often rendered "Restoration." Sun has in mind, not the restoration of imperial rule, but the basic meaning of the term, renovation or reform.

Japan, it did not do anything toward encouraging her. But when such a teaching was advocated in lethargic China, it only did her harm.

In an age of scientific discoveries, Wang's doctrine of the unity of knowledge and action is sound when applied to a particular period or a particular undertaking, but when it is applied to an individual, it is certainly erroneous. With the growth of modern science one's knowledge and one's action are more and more set apart. One who knows does not have to act, and not only that, but one who acts does not have to know. . . .

I have spared no efforts in writing page after page with a view to proving that it is easy to act but difficult to know. It is my strong conviction that this is the necessary course through which China is to be saved. The accumulating weakness and the dying state of the country are due to the misleading effect of the theory that to know is not difficult but to act is difficult. . . . Thus the Chinese shun what is [actually] easy and take to the difficult. At first they seek to know before acting. Then finding that this cannot be accomplished, they feel helpless and give up all thoughts of attempting. Some, imbued with an undaunted spirit, devote their life-long effort to acquiring the knowledge of a certain undertaking. They may have acquired the knowledge and yet hesitate to apply it, being obsessed with the thought that to act is even more difficult. Hence those who do not have the knowledge, of course, fail to act, but even those who have acquired it do not dare to act. It develops that there is nothing that can be attempted in the world. . . .

The advance of civilization is achieved by three groups of persons: first, those who see and perceive ahead, or discoverers; second, those who see and perceive later, or promoters; and third, those who do not see or perceive, or practical workers. From this point of view, China does not lack practical workers, for the great masses of the people are of this kind. Some of my comrades, however, have the habit of saying that so-and-so is [merely] a theoretician, while so-and-so is a practical man. It is a grave fallacy indeed to entertain the idea that a few practical men could reform the nation.

Look at the huge factories, busy boulevards, and imposing buildings of the foreigners in Shanghai. The men of action who performed the work of construction were the Chinese workmen, while the foreigners were the thinkers or planners, who never personally undertook the construction. Hence in the construction of a country it is not the practical workers but the idealists and planners that are difficult to find. . . .

This is the reason for the lack of progress in our national reconstruction after the revolution. I therefore feel the necessity for this thorough refutation, hoping that those who see and perceive late can eventually awake from their error and change their course. In this way they will no longer mislead the world with a theory seemingly right but actually wrong, and no longer hinder the great multitude of practical workers. Herein lies the great hope for the future of our reconstruction.

DEMOCRACY OR ABSOLUTISM: THE DEBATE OVER POLITICAL TUTELAGE

Sun Yat-sen's concept of political tutelage, a key doctrine of the Kuomintang after his death, also remained a continuing issue in Chinese politics. With all the talk about a constitution and preparation for the adoption of democratic institutions, party tutelage still provided the working basis of the new regime and the rationale for Chiang Kai-shek's increasingly strong role as Sun's heir to Kuomintang leadership. The party itself, however, was by no means unanimous in support of this idea. The middle-class and considerably Westernized Chinese which it represented, especially in the commercial ports, included numerous individuals educated abroad or exposed to Western ideas of political democracy. Many of them were poorly reconciled to what seemed a reactionary and dictatorial system of party leadership. Others not identified with the party itself, but active in educational institutions or in journalism, did not hesitate to attack this fundamental premise of the Nanking regime.

The debate which ensued on this issue in the 1930s illustrates a basic dilemma of Kuomintang rule. Though committed to a kind of limited democracy on the theory that the building of national unity must take priority over the extension of political freedom, the party nevertheless allowed its critics just enough freedom to defeat its own purposes— enough so that they could effectively impair the party's authority, not enough so that they felt any indebtedness to the Kuomintang for this privilege.

[124]

LO LUNG-CHI
What Kind of Political System Do We Want?

Lo Lung-chi (1896—) was a Western-trained educator and journalist, who wrote this criticism of Sun Yat-sen's doctrine of political tutelage shortly after his return to China, following studies at Wisconsin, at the London School of Economics under Harold Laski, and for the doctorate at Columbia (1928). He later served as editor of influential newspapers in North China, became a leader of the left-wing Democratic League, and was active politically under the Communists. He suffered condemnation as a "rightist," however, during the "Hundred Flowers" campaign in 1957.

By the time Lo wrote this article Communism already offered an important political alternative to the Kuomintang, and Marxist doctrines, such as the withering away of the state, had become a part of his intellectual frame of reference.

[From "Wo-men yao shen-mo yang ti cheng-chih chih-tu," in *Hsin yüeh,* Vol. II, No. 12 (1930), pp. 4–13]

We may sincerely say that we do not advocate any high-sounding theory of eliminating the state. We recognize that "to abolish the state through the party" is a blind alley in the twentieth century. In the present world the only road we can take is to maintain the state. *But in taking this road, we want to have the kind of state we cherish and the kind of governmental system we can support.*

On hearing this, the Kuomintang leaders must be delighted and say, "Why, come and join us!"

We admit that the Kuomintang also wants the state. The President of the Kuomintang began his first lecture on the Three Principles of the People by saying: "Gentlemen: I have come here today to speak to you about the Three Principles of the People. What are the Three Principles of the People? They are, by the simplest definition, the principles for our nation's salvation." Whether the Three Principles of the People are the principles for our nation's salvation, or whether the principles for our nation's salvation are necessarily the Three Principles, is a problem outside the scope of the present article. But it is undeniable that those who want to save the state must first recognize the existence of the state. The Kuomintang slogan of "reconstructing the state through the party" is clearly different from the Communist slogan of "abolishing the state through the party." What we cannot lightly lose sight of, however, is the kind of political system the Kuomintang adopts in its reconstructed state.

Let us first discuss with those who talk of "saving" and "reconstructing" the state the following problems: 1) What is the nature of the state? 2) What is the purpose of the state? 3) What should be the strategy for the reconstruction of the state?

Frankly, in the entire *Complete Works of Sun Yat-sen,* no mention has ever been made about such fundamental problems of political philosophy as the nature of the state and the purpose of the state. What concerned Dr. Sun most was the strategy for "national salvation" and "national reconstruction." [4] His weakness—which at the same time was his strength —lay in the fact that in the selection of a strategy his main concern was the attainment of his objectives, not the evaluation of the means. Because he paid no attention to the purpose of the state, he often took "national salvation" or "national reconstruction" for that purpose. Because he was concerned with the end rather than the means, often in the matter of strategy he took a road that was opposed to the nature and purpose of the state. *The strategy of "party above the state" is an illustration.*

To our mind, only when we have a full realization of problems (1) and (2) above can we decide on the strategy. Let us discuss these three problems in the following order:

First, the state is an instrument, and in this respect we are agreed with the Communists. But while the Communists consider the state an instrument of the capitalist class for the oppression of the proletariat, we believe that it is the instrument of the *people as a whole* for the achievement of a certain common purpose through mutual constraints and mutual cooperation.

This seemingly unimportant point should be clearly recognized as the point of departure by all those who talk about political systems. The great trouble of China today is that, on the one hand, the Communists consider the state an instrument of class war and, on the other, those who cry for "national salvation" and "national reconstruction" regard

---

[4] The character for state and nation being the same in Chinese, these slogans also had the meaning of "the state's salvation" and "the state's reconstruction." The emotional appeal of nationalism was used, in this case, for the glorification of the state.

the state as the ultimate purpose itself. For those who consider the state as an end, the people exist for the sake of the state rather than the state for the sake of the people. They do not ask what benefits the state offers the people, but maintain that "national salvation" and "love for the state" are the unconditional duties of the people. And they do not hesitate to employ those weighty words of "national salvation" and "national reconstruction" to silence the people. Thus the people may not be aided in time of famine and calamity, but burdensome taxes must be collected; local peace may not be maintained, but civil war must be fought. Because the state is an end, people become the means for "national salvation" and "national reconstruction." And so the state need not protect the life and property of the people, who become the slaves of the "principle of national salvation"; nor need it support freedom of thought, for schools should become propaganda agencies for the "principle of national salvation." In short, as soon as the banner of "national salvation" and "national reconstruction" is hoisted, all burdensome taxes and levies and all fighting and wars receive new significance. The people can only surrender unconditionally. . . .

When the party is placed above the state, the state becomes the instrument of the party rather than the instrument of the entire people for the attainment of the common purpose. This, of course, is contrary to the nature of the state. Perhaps the Kuomintang people will say that what concerns a revolutionary party is the end rather than the means, and that although the system of "party above the state" may be contrary to the nature of the state, it is this strategy that will achieve the purpose of the state. Let us then examine whether or not the system of "party above the state" can achieve the purpose of the state.

The political systems of other countries today are founded on two different principles: dictatorship and democracy. Dictatorship refers to the political system under which the political power of the state is held by one person, one party, or one class. Democracy refers to the political system under which political power resides in the people as a whole and *all citizens of age can participate directly or indirectly in politics on an equal basis.* The system of "party above the state" or "party authority above state authority" is certainly a dictatorship rather than a democracy.

We must emphatically declare here that we are *absolutely opposed to dictatorship, whether it be dictatorship by one person, one party, or one class. Our reason is very simple: dictatorship is not the method whereby the purpose of the state can be achieved.* Let us explain briefly as follows:

First, the state is the instrument of the people for the attainment of their common purpose through mutual constraint and cooperation. Its function is to protect the rights of the people. We believe that the rights of the people are secure only to the extent that the people themselves have the opportunity to protect them. In the present society, man's public spirit has not developed to such a perfection that we can entrust entirely our political rights to a person, a group, or a class and depend upon him or it to be the guardian of our rights. In practical politics, *he who loses political power will lose all protection of his rights.* . . .

Secondly, . . . The function of the state is to tend and develop the people. In a dictatorship the function of tending and developing is lost. Take, for instance, the cultivation and development of the thought of the people. A dictatorship, whether enlightened or dark, will consider freedom of thought its greatest enemy. The first task it sets itself is to reshape the mind of the people in a single mold by a so-called thought-unification movement. . . . After oppression and persecution under a dictatorship, the people's thought necessarily becomes timid, passive, dependent, senile, and the people themselves may even become pieces of thoughtless machinery.

Thirdly, the state is the instrument of the entire people for the attainment of the common purpose of happiness for all through mutual restraint and cooperation. In order to achieve this purpose the state must furnish the people with an environment of peace, tranquillity, order, and justice. A dictator, be it an individual, a party, or a class, occupies a special position in national politics. This fundamentally rejects political equality as well as justice. The special position of the dictator inevitably incurs the indignation and hatred of the people for their governors, and indignation and hatred are the source of all revolutions. In a society of recurrent revolutions, peace, tranquillity, and order are naturally not to be found. . . .

The Kuomintang itself recognized the inherent evils of dictatorship, but it uses such words as "temporary" and "transitional" to cover the system. The word "temporary" or "transitional" often designates the so-called period of political tutelage. . . .

We believe that the saying, "the more you learn, the more there is to learn," applies equally to politics as to other callings. Man seeks experience and progress in politics unceasingly because there is no limit to them. If the people must have reached a certain ideal stage before they can participate in political activities, then the British and the Americans should also be under political tutelage now. To obtain experience from trial and error, to effect progress from experience—this is the political method of the British and Americans, and this also is the reason why we are opposed to political tutelage. If political tutelage is ever necessary, we believe the rulers—the present tutors—are more urgently in need of training than the people. . . .

Whether during the period of tutelage we should or should not adopt dictatorship with its doctrine of "party above the state" or "party authority above state authority" is another problem. It is our view that because of its inherent evils, dictatorship itself is an unworthy system. To adopt an unworthy system to be our model during the period of political tutelage is diametrically opposed to the purpose of national reconstruction. . . .

TSIANG T'ING-FU

Revolution and Absolutism

The Kuomintang system of one-party rule under a strong leader found a defender, rather than a critic, in another Western-trained (Oberlin and Columbia) scholar, Tsiang T'ing-fu (1895—). A college professor and an authority on political and diplomatic history at the time he wrote this essay, Tsiang became increasingly active as a Nationalist official, as ambassador to the USSR, and later as the Nationalists' permanent representative on the United Nations Security Council (known there as T. F. Tsiang).

[From "K'ai-ming yü chuan-chih," in *Tu-li p'ing-lun*, No. 80 (December 1933), pp. 2–5]

When the news of the Fukien incident [5] broke out, people throughout the country felt gloomy over the prospects of the nation. China seemed to have reached the stage where neither revolution nor nonrevolution was a solution.

You might say it would be better not to have any revolution, but then

[5] The revolt of the left-wing Kuomintang leaders and the 19th Route Army in Fukien province at the end of 1933.

the government would definitely fail to satisfy the wishes of the people. If the government is to satisfy the wishes of the people, you cannot rely on arguments alone. If you are unarmed, no matter how reasonable your arguments are, the government—from the central government above to the district governments below—will at most feel disturbed, but will not pay any attention to you. For if the government does pay attention, either some people within the government or some people outside of it will suffer some loss to their private interests.

Mr. Hu Han-min has recently said that not a single good thing has been done by the government during the past two years. His statement is both overdrawn and inadequate. It is overdrawn because the government did do some good things, but they were of no avail and probably did not outweigh the bad things it had done. The statement is inadequate because the situation described applies not only to the government in the past two years but to the government in the past twenty years. Actually, while China did not have a very good government in the past twenty years, there was no extremely evil government either. Extremely good or extremely bad governments existed at the local level, but not at the national. For even if the central government had intended to do something good, it did not have the capacity to do anything very good. Similarly, even if it had intended to do something bad, it did not have the capacity to do anything bad. This is generally true with the past twenty years during which groups and individuals of various kinds, including Yüan Shih-k'ai and Chiang Kai-shek, assumed control of the government. In my opinion, even northern warlords such as Yüan Shih-k'ai, Tuan Ch'i-jui, Wu P'ei-fu, and Chang Tso-lin were all desirous of doing good, but no good results came out of them. This is because all their energy was spent in dealing with their political enemies. When engaged in dealing with their enemies, they had to sacrifice reconstruction to maintain an army and resort to any dubious means in order to win. The problem is therefore not that of personality but that of circumstances. Given the circumstances, no one could achieve good results. The basic situation of China may be summarized in one sentence: Without a unified political power, there can be no good government. . . .

Viewed from the standpoint of history, this phenomenon is quite natural, and no nation is an exception to it. Advanced Western countries such as England, France, and Russia resembled China in their early stages of development when there was only internal order but not revolution. In England the Wars of the Roses raged in the fifteenth century but no results were achieved. It was toward the end of the fifteenth century that Henry VII unified England and began a century of absolutism under the name of the Tudor dynasty. During these hundred years the British people had a good rest and rehabilitation; as a result, the national state was formed. The seventeenth century saw the culmination of political conflicts in a genuine revolution. Historians are agreed that had there not been any Tudor autocracy in the sixteenth century there could not have been any revolution in the seventeenth century. . . . [Tsiang goes on to cite the Bourbons and the French Revolution, the Romanovs and the Russian Revolution as illustrations of the same point.]

The present situation in China is similar to that of England before the Tudor absolutism, or that of France before the Bourbon absolutism, or that of Russia before the Romanov absolutism. The Chinese too can have only internal disturbance but not genuine revolution. Although we had several thousand years of absolute government, unfortunately, our absolute monarchs, because of environmental peculiarities, did not fulfill their historic duty. The heritage left to the republic by the Manchu dynasty was too poor to be revolutionary capital. In the first place, our state is still a dynastic state, not a national one. Chinese citizens are generally loyal to individuals, families, or localities rather than to the state. Secondly, our absolute monarchs did not leave us a class that could serve as the nucleus of a new regime. In fact, the historic task of the Chinese monarchies was to destroy all the classes and institutions outside the royal family which could possibly become the center of political power. As a result, when the royal family was overthrown, the state became a "heap of loose sand." Thirdly, under the absolutist regime our material civilization lagged far behind. Consequently, when the foreigners took advantage of our trouble after the outbreak of the revolution, we were unable to offer any effective resistance.

In sum, the political history of all countries is divided into two phases: first, the building of a state; and second, the promotion of national welfare by means of the state. Since we have not completed the first phase, it is idle to talk of the second. As a Western saying goes, "the better is often the enemy of the good." The so-called revolution of China today is a great obstacle to our national reconstruction. The Chinese people should adopt an objective attitude and view the civil war as an historical process, just as physicians study physiology. We should foster the unifying force, because it is the vital power of our state organism. We should eliminate the anti-unification force, because it is the virus in our state organism. Our present problem is the existence of our state, not what type of state we should have.

HU SHIH
National Reconstruction and Absolutism

A direct rejoinder to T. F. Tsiang's defense of Kuomintang party dictatorship came from one of the intellectual leaders of republican China, Hu Shih (1891—). Like Lo and Tsiang, he had been educated in the United States (Cornell and Columbia) and become a thoroughgoing exponent of Westernization or modernization in many fields. As such he was often critical of the Kuomintang and of attitudes expressed by Sun Yat-sen or Chiang Kai-shek. Nevertheless, his personal standing as a scholar and thinker was so high both in China and the West that the Nanking government entrusted important diplomatic and educational assignments to him, including (most recently) the presidency of its top academic institution, the Academia Sinica.

[From "Chien-kuo yü chuan-chih," in *Tu-li p'ing-lun*, No. 81 (December 1933), pp. 3–5]

1. Is Absolutism a Necessary Stage for National Reconstruction?

In regard to this problem, there is a basic difference between Mr. Tsiang T'ing-fu's views and mine. As I see it, the history of England, France, and Russia as cited by Mr. Tsiang is only the history of national reconstruction in the three countries. But the scope of national reconstruction is very broad and the factors involved are complex. We cannot single out "absolutism" as the only cause or condition. We may say that the three dynasties (the Tudors of England, the Bourbons of France, and the Romanovs of Russia) were the periods during which their respective states were built, but we cannot prove that the formation of the state in these three countries was due to absolute rule. . . . The birth and propagation of the new English language and literature, the circulation of the English Bible and the Prayer Book, the influence of Oxford and Cambridge universities, the impact of London as England's political, economic, and cultural center, the rapid development of the textile industry, the rise of the middle class—all of these were important factors in the formation of the English national state. Most of these factors did not first appear under the Tudor dynasty; their origins may be traced to the time before the Tudors, although their development was particularly rapid in that century of unity and peace.

What Mr. Tsiang probably means to say is that a unified political power is indispensable to the building of the state. However, his use of the term absolutism to describe the unity of political power easily leads the people to think of a dictatorship with unlimited power. The reign of Henry VIII was the period in which parliamentary power began to rise: members of Parliament were secure from arrest and the king established the new church upon the support of Parliament. Therefore, instead of asserting that absolutism is an indispensable stage for the building of the state, we had better say that unity of political power is the condition. And unity of political power does not depend on completely following the dictatorship of the Romanov dynasty.

2. Why Did Centuries of Absolute Government Fail to Create a National State in China?

Concerning this question, my views are again different from those of Mr. Tsiang. Generally speaking, China had long since become a national state. What we now find defective is that the solidarity and unity of the Chinese national state has proved inadequate for a modern national state. In national consciousness, in unity of language, in unity of history and culture, in unity and continuity of governmental system (including examination, civil service, law, etc.)—in all these, China in the past two thousand years was qualified to be a national state. It is true that there were periods of foreign rule, but during those periods national consciousness became more vigorous and enduring so that eventually there arose national heroes such as Liu Yü, Chu Yüan-chang, Hung Hsiu-ch'üan, and Sun Yat-sen, who led the national revolutions. Indeed, all of the capital for national reconstruction which we have today is the national consciousness passed on to us by our forebears through two thousand years. . . .

As to the three defects pointed out by Mr. Tsiang, they prove only the evil consequences of the former social and political order, but not the lack of a national state in China. First, Mr. Tsiang said: "Chinese citizens are generally loyal to individuals, families, or localities rather than to the state." This is because in the old days the power of the state did not extend directly to the people. When "the emperor was as remote as the sky [from the people]," how could anyone by-pass his family, which exerts an immediate influence on his life, and profess loyalty to the state in the abstract, unless he was highly educated? The famous Burke of eighteenth-century England said: "In order that the people love the state, the state must first be lovable." Can we then say that England in the eighteenth century had not become a national state? The reason the masses of the people today do not love the nation is partly that they are inadequately educated and therefore unable to imagine a state, and partly that the state has not bestowed any benefits upon the people.

CHIANG KAI-SHEK: NATIONALISM AND TRADITIONALISM

Chiang Kai-shek (1887—), who took over leadership after Sun Yat-sen's death, was a devoted follower and admirer of Dr. Sun. He was also a very different man from his mentor. For one thing, Chiang had virtually no Western education, and, knowing no foreign language well, was dependent upon others to interpret the West for him. Consequently his ideas were formed much more within the Chinese tradition, and found their most typical expression in the language and formulas of the past. His experience of foreign lands was also much more limited. The net effect even of his relatively brief travel and study in Japan and later in Soviet Russia was only to increase his consciousness of being a Chinese. Throughout life this consciousness deepened as a result of intensive and prolonged study of Chinese classical literature.

Understandably then, it was the first of Sun's Three Principles, Nationalism, which had the most significance for Chiang. Others of his contemporaries, however, no less intensely nationalistic than he and no less limited in their experience of the outside world, still showed by their eager acceptance of Western standards that the new nationalism could be quite divorced from any real attachment to the values of the past. The contact zone of East and West, in which such a cultural hybrid as Dr. Sun had been produced just a generation before, had moved from Honolulu, Hongkong, Macao, and Yokohama, into the very classrooms of provincial China where Western-style education now prevailed. Chiang himself, in a certain sense, had moved with it. He had, for instance, become a devout Methodist, married a Wellesley-educated girl, attempted to learn English, adopted Western standards of personal hygiene, and made considerable use of Western advisers. All this notwithstanding, his own philosophy of life drew more and more upon Chinese sources of inspiration, and in offering it to the Chinese people as a national way of life, he cut more and more directly across the Westernizing trend of the times.

What Chiang found so essential in Chinese tradition—Confucian ethics —actually represented an important link between him and Dr. Sun. The latter, in his long struggle to organize and lead a national revolution, had come to a new appreciation of the traditional Confucian virtues for which earlier he had found little use. They could serve as a means of achieving social discipline and national cohesion among a people who were otherwise just a "heap of loose sand." Sun thereby found a political value in a system of ethics which had hitherto meant little to him personally. Chiang himself had no less reason, politically, to adopt the same view. He confronted all the same problems of leadership as Sun, and felt the same need for disciplined loyalty among his followers. Moreover, as a military man he must have possessed even keener a sense of the importance of discipline in general.

With Chiang, however, it was more than a question of simply exploiting traditional attitudes which could serve present purposes. It had become a deep personal conviction of his (as it never seems to have been of Sun's) that moral values were the ultimate basis of human life. His own experience of life seems to have taught him the value of self-discipline to the individual, as much as of social discipline to the nation. There is one account, of uncertain reliability, which speaks of his life in Shanghai just after the Revolution as "a period of rather riotous living. . . . With a comfortable income such as he was receiving, there was much chance for moral degeneration. His friends, knowing his temper, and that persuasion would be futile, deplored this; and he would have gone from bad to worse, had it not been for the fact that the second revolutionary war started and kindled again the smoldering ashes of patriotism." [6] Whatever the truth of this may be, there is something intriguing in the idea that Chiang, after a period of youthful dissipation, underwent a process of self-reformation and discovered, on throwing himself again into the

[6] Cf. Emily Hahn, *Chiang Kai-shek,* p. 48.

revolutionary struggle, that he had a personal need for dedication to something greater than himself. For it was this combination of self-discipline and service to the nation, which had perhaps been the means of rescuing him from himself earlier, that Chiang constantly urged upon Chinese youth.

These convictions manifested themselves early in Chiang's public career, and he has never abandoned them. In 1924, as superintendent of the Kuomintang military academy at Whampoa, where Soviet influence was strong and the revolutionary fever ran high, Chiang did not hesitate to base military indoctrination on a text compiled from the moral teachings of the nineteenth-century Neo-Confucianist and Restoration hero, Tseng Kuo-fan. Thus, in contrast to Sun's glorification of the Taiping leader, Hung Hsiu-ch'üan, as a national revolutionary figure, Chiang acclaimed the very suppressor of the Taipings (and a servant of the Manchus) as the finest exemplar of national tradition. In this way the cultivation of personal virtue and nobility of character was stressed over revolutionary fervor.

Ten years later, when Chiang launched his New Life movement as a program for the strengthening of national morale, the Confucian virtues of decorum, righteousness, integrity, and a sense of shame, provided the chief catchwords and main content of this campaign of mass indoctrination. Significantly, the first of these virtues, *li,* implied an acceptance of social discipline, of law and authority, in opposition to the trend from the West toward unfettered individualism. Again, in 1943 when Chiang published his *China's Destiny* to serve as a primer for the party and its Youth Corps, he declared that, with the approaching end of foreign rule and exploitation in China, the great task would be one of internal reconstruction through moral rearmament, Confucian-style. Even in the '50s, after the retreat to Formosa, courses in Neo-Confucian ethical philosophy were compulsory for all students under the Kuomintang regime.

It would be a distortion of Chiang's social philosophy and program to sum it up in terms only of nationalism and Neo-Confucian ethics. He remained committed to all of Dr. Sun's Three Principles, including a large measure of economic planning and state socialism. And if he did not pursue with equal vigor these other aspects of Sun's original program, his justification for the delay in achieving the objectives of People's Rule and People's Livelihood was one provided by Sun himself in the doctrine of political tutelage. Military unification must come first.

Nevertheless, it was here that the incongruity of Chiang's program became apparent. Party tutelage and Chiang's role as near-dictator were premised on the fact that the revolution had not yet been brought to an end. In a revolutionary situation, strong leadership and a quasi-military organization were still indispensable. Yet Chiang, as a revolutionary leader, tried to rally his forces with a conservative ideology. Where messianic zeal was called for, he offered austerity and restraint.

It must be allowed that Chiang's traditionalism was more than a personal idosyncrasy, a quixotic gesture. As our next chapter will show, there were other Chinese at this time—including erstwhile advocates of Westernization, now disillusioned—who joined him in attacking Western individualism and materialism as a threat to the spiritual and moral values of Chinese civilization. Nor was this a purely Chinese phenomenon. Nationalists in India and Japan often shared a revulsion for those aspects of Western life which Chiang found so distasteful in treaty ports like Shanghai. Commercialism, cynicism, soft-living, and self-indulgence seemed to typify the bourgeois culture of the West as transplanted to the soil of Asia. Was this all the West had to offer in place of the traditional values it was destroying? On this point, Chiang's rejection of extreme Western liberalism linked him in spirit with an Indian nationalist like Gandhi, while his *Essentials of the New Life Movement* (from which excerpts are given below), showed at the same time his close kinship with the authors of *Fundamentals of Japan's National Polity* (*Kokutai no hongi*), the official credo of Japanese nationalism in the '30s, who decried as he did the individualism and class antagonism of the West, while extolling the social virtues of Confucianism.[7]

Chiang's traditionalism, it is true, was never conceived as a total opposition to Westernization. The Three People's Principles—nationalism, democracy, and socialism—were basically Western in inspiration, and however much he or Dr. Sun adapted them to their own tastes, the use of such slogans constituted a recognition on their part that Western ideals had an irresistible attraction for twentieth-century Asia. Yet in the face

[7] This is not to say, of course, that the three did not differ considerably in other respects.

of this dominant trend, traditionalism, even when it took the form of an attempted synthesis of East and West and made generous acknowledgement of China's debt to the latter, suffered serious drawbacks as the basis for a national ideology. Quite apart from Chiang's own role as a "revolutionary" leader, the rising demand for material improvement, the great expectations aroused for social progress, and the promise of a freer and easier life for all which Westernization seemed to offer, created a profound dissatisfaction with things as they were, a revolutionary atmosphere in which the response to traditional values and virtues was most often one of impatience.

Nowhere could this be seen more clearly than among the younger generation, and especially the educated. Chiang's own attempts at economic and military modernization created a need for men with training along Western lines, and yet few such men would take Chiang's Confucianism seriously, while many openly resisted it. As our next chapter will show, a considerable gulf had already opened up in the early years of the republic between its intellectual and political leaders. Under Chiang this gulf widened, and while he was by no means wholly responsible for the estrangement, it had become clear that his brand of traditionalism, far from providing a common ground among Chinese, was now itself a source of disunity.

CHIANG KAI-SHEK
Essentials of the New Life Movement

The New Life Movement was inaugurated by Chiang in a speech at Nanchang in September, 1934. Its immediate purpose was to rally the Chinese people for a campaign against the Communists in that region, but a more general aim was to tighten discipline and build up morale in the Kuomintang and nation as a whole. Laxity in public life, official corruption, indiscipline in the ranks of party and army, and apathy among the people were among the weaknesses Chiang tried to overcome by a great moral reformation emphasizing Confucian self-cultivation, a life of frugality, and dedication to the nation. There were exhortations too in behalf of personal hygiene and physical training, as well as injunctions against tobacco and opium-smoking, dancing, spitting on the floor, and leaving coats unbuttoned. In these respects, however, Chiang thought of himself as promoting progress—cleaning up and dressing up China in answer to the type of Westerner who complained about her untidiness and lack of sanitation.

An important influence on the New Life ideology was exerted by Chiang's close adviser and Minister of Education, Ch'en Li-fu (1890—), Western-educated exponent of a modernized Neo-Confucianism. He has been reputed as the "ghost writer" of this text, but has personally denied any part in it.

[From *Hsin sheng-huo yün-tung kang-yao*, in *Tsung-ts'ai yen-lun hsüan-chi*, III, 403-14]

THE OBJECT OF THE NEW LIFE MOVEMENT

Why Is a New Life Needed?

The general psychology of our people today can be described as spiritless. What manifests itself in behavior is this: lack of discrimination between good and evil, between what is public and what is private, and between what is primary and what is secondary. Because there is no discrimination between good and evil, right and wrong are confused; because there is no discrimination between public and private, improper taking and giving [of public funds] occur; and because there is no distinction between primary and secondary, first and last are not placed in the proper order. As a result, officials tend to be dishonest and avaricious, the masses are undisciplined and calloused, the youth become degraded and intemperate, the adults are corrupt and ignorant, the rich become extravagant and luxurious, and the poor become mean and disorderly. Naturally it has resulted in disorganization of the social order and national life, and we are in no position either to prevent or to remedy natural calamities, disasters caused from within, or invasions from without. The individual, society and the whole country are now suffering. If the situation should remain unchanged, it would be impossible even to continue living under such miserable conditions. In order to develop the life of our nation, protect the existence of our society, and improve the livelihood of our people, it is absolutely necessary to wipe out these unwholesome conditions and to start to lead a new and rational life.

THE CONTENT OF THE NEW LIFE MOVEMENT

1. The Principles of the New Life Movement.

The New Life Movement aims at the promotion of a regular life guided by the four virtues, namely, *li, i, lien,* and *ch'ih*.[8] These virtues

[8] Standard translations for these terms are: *li*, decorum or rites; *i*, righteousness or duty; *lien*, integrity or honesty; *ch'ih*, sense of shame. Since Chiang defines the terms in what follows, we have kept the romanized forms here.

must be applied to ordinary life in the matter of food, clothing, shelter, and action. The four virtues are the essential principles for the promotion of morality. They form the major rules for dealing with men and human affairs, for cultivating oneself, and for adjustment to one's surroundings. Whoever violates these rules is bound to fail; and a nation which neglects them will not survive.

There are two kinds of skeptics:

First, some hold that the four virtues are merely rules of good conduct. No matter how good they may be, they are not sufficient to save a nation whose knowledge and technique are inferior to others.

Those who hold this view do not seem to understand the distinction between matters of primary and secondary importance. People need knowledge and technique because they want to do good. Otherwise, knowledge and technique can only be instruments of dishonorable deeds. *Li, i, lien,* and *ch'ih* are the principal rules alike for the community, the group, or the entire nation. Those who do not observe these rules will probably utilize their knowledge and ability to the detriment of society and ultimately to their own disadvantage. Therefore, these virtues not only can save the nation, but also can rebuild the nation.

Secondly, there is another group of people who argue that these virtues are merely formal refinements which are useless in dealing with hunger and cold. The argument is probably due to a misunderstanding of the famous teaching of Kuan Tzu,[9] who said: "When one does not have to worry about one's food and clothing, then one cares for personal honor; when the granary is full, then people learn good manners." These skeptics fail to realize that the four virtues are the basic elements of man. If one cannot be a man, what is the use of having abundance of food and clothing? Moreover, Kuan Tzu did not intend to make a general statement; he merely referred to a particular aspect of the subject. In fact, the essence of his statesmanship lay in the pre-eminence given to the four virtues, which he called the four pillars of the nation. When these virtues prevail, even if food and clothing are insufficient, they can be produced by manpower; or, if the granary is empty, it can be filled through human effort. On the other hand, when these virtues are not observed, if food and clothing are insufficient, they will not be made sufficient by fighting and

---

[9] Reputed author of an early text in which these four virtues are spoken of as the pillars of the nation.

robbing; or, if the granary is empty, it will not be filled by stealing and begging. The four virtues, which rectify the misconduct of men, are the proper methods of achieving abundance. Without them, there will be fighting, robbing, stealing, and begging among men. In that event, even if food and clothing are sufficient, even if grain fills the granaries, they cannot be enjoyed by the people. Robbers are usually most numerous in the wealthiest cities of the world. This is an obvious illustration of disorder caused by nonobservance of virtues. People become traitors, Communists and corrupt officials, not because they are driven by hunger and cold, but because they have neglected the cultivation of virtue. The four virtues are so important that they must be adopted as the guiding principles of our life.

2. The Meaning of *Li, I, Lien*, and *Ch'ih*.

Although *li, i, lien*, and *ch'ih* have always been regarded as the foundations of the nation, yet the changing times and circumstances may require that these principles be given a new interpretation. As applied to our life today, they may be interpreted as follows:

Li means regulated attitude.
I means right conduct.
Lien means clear discrimination.
Ch'ih means real self-consciousness.

The word *li* (decorum) means *li* (reason). It becomes natural law, when applied to nature; it becomes a rule, when applied to social affairs; and it signifies discipline, when used in reference to national affairs. A man's conduct is considered regular if it conforms with the above law, rule, and discipline. When one conducts oneself in accordance with the regular manner, one is said to have the regulated attitude.

The word *i* means proper. Any conduct which is in accordance with *li* —i.e., natural law, social rule, and national discipline—is considered proper. To act improperly, or to refrain from acting when one knows it is proper to act, cannot be called *i*.

The word *lien* means clear. It denotes distinction between right and wrong. What agrees with *li* and *i* is right, and what does not agree is wrong. To take what we recognize as right and to forego what we recognize as wrong constitute clear discrimination.

The word *ch'ih* means consciousness. When one is conscious of the fact that his own actions are not in accordance with *li, i, lien,* and *ch'ih,* one feels ashamed. When one is conscious of the fact that others are wrong, one feels disgusted. But the consciousness must be real and thorough so that one will strive to improve what one feels to be a shame and to eliminate what one feels to be disgusting. This is called real self-consciousness.

From the above explanations, it is clear that *ch'ih* governs the motive of action, that *lien* gives the guidance for it, that *i* relates to the carrying out of an action, and that *li* regulates its outward form. The four are interrelated. They are interdependent upon each other in the perfecting of virtue.

THE APPLICATION OF LI, I, LIEN AND CH'IH TO FOOD, CLOTHING, SHELTER AND ACTION

The means of maintaining our livelihood may be divided into three phases: first, the obtaining of materials; second, the selection of quality; and third, the manner in which these materials are used. Let me explain each separately.

1. The obtaining of materials should be in conformity with the principle of *lien.* Clear discrimination should be exercised between what is ours and what is not. If something does not belong to us, we should not take it. In other words, the materials for our daily life should be acquired through our own labor or through other proper means. Strife should not be encouraged. A parasite is not a good example. Even giving and taking improperly should be avoided. "What really matters is the loss of integrity, not dying from hunger." This famous Confucian saying illustrates the point.

2. The selection of quality should be in conformity with the principle of *i.* Do the proper thing with due regard to special circumstances arising from persons, times, places, and positions. For instance, it is proper for an old man to use silk and to take meat, to be excused from carrying heavy burdens on the road, and to have some leisure; but a young man should be satisfied with moderate food and clothing and be ready to endure hardships. What is proper in winter is not necessarily proper in summer. What is proper in the north is not necessarily proper in the south. Similarly, different positions may influence a situation differently. A ruler, or a military commander, must have authority and rights that are becoming

to his dignity and necessary for his work—authority and rights which should neither be excessive nor inadequate but should be proper to his position and rank.

3. The manner in which materials are used should be in conformity with the principle of *li,* which includes natural law, social rules, and national discipline.

CONCLUSION

In short, the main object of the New Life Movement is to substitute a rational life for the irrational, and to achieve this we must observe *li, i, lien,* and *ch'ih* in our daily life.

1. By observing these virtues, it is hoped that rudeness and vulgarity will be got rid of, and that the life of our people will conform to the standard of art. By art we are not referring to the special enjoyment of the gentry. We mean the cultural standard of all the people, irrespective of sex, age, wealth, and class. It is the boundary line between civilized life and barbarism. It is the only way by which one can achieve the purpose of man, for only by artistically controlling oneself and dealing with others can one fulfill the duty of mutual assistance. . . . A lack of artistic training is the cause of suspicion, jealousy, hatred, and strife that are prevalent in our society today. . . . To investigate things so as to extend our knowledge; to distinguish between the fundamental and the secondary; to seek the invention of instruments; to excel in our techniques—these are the essentials of an artistic life, the practice of which will enable us to wipe out the defects of vulgarity, confusion, crudity, and baseness.

2. By observing these virtues, it is hoped that beggary and robbery will be eliminated, and that the life of our people will be productive. The poverty of China is primarily caused by the fact that there are too many consumers and too few producers. Those who consume without producing usually live as parasites or as robbers. They behave thus because they are ignorant of the four virtues. To remedy this we must make them produce more and spend less. They must understand that luxury is improper and that living as a parasite is a shame.

3. By observing these virtues, it is hoped that social disorder and individual weakness will be remedied and that people will become more military-minded. If a country cannot defend itself, it has every chance of losing its existence. . . . Therefore our people must have military train-

ing. As a preliminary, we must acquire the habits of orderliness, cleanliness, simplicity, frugality, promptness, and exactness. We must preserve order, emphasize organization, responsibility, and discipline, and be ready to die for the country at any moment.

In conclusion, the life of our people will be elevated if we live artistically; we will become wealthy if we live productively; and we will be safe if we lead a military way of life. When we do this, we will have a rational life. This rational life is founded on *li, i, lien,* and *ch'ih.* The four virtues, in turn, can be applied to food, clothing, shelter, and action. If we can achieve this, we will have revolutionized the daily life of our people and laid the foundation for the rehabilitation of our nation.

China's Destiny

China's Destiny appeared in March, 1943, during the darkest period of the war with Japan, when Chinese morale badly needed boosting. Chiang explained at length how his country's difficulties in the past arose from foreign oppression and the consequent deterioration of national life. The recent abrogation of the unequal treaties by Britain and the United States, however, heralded a new era of independence and self-respect for China once the Japanese were defeated. Chiang's great goal was still political and military unification. To achieve this he outlined a five-point program of national reconstruction emphasizing pride in China's past, a return to Confucian virtues, restoration of the traditional system of group-responsibility and mutual aid, and a long-range program of economic development along lines laid down by Sun—industrialization, land "equalization," and state capitalism in a planned and closely controlled economy.

A prime target of Chiang's indignation was the prevalence of foreign ideologies and attitudes among intellectuals, who were accused of yielding and pandering to popular trends. Extreme Western liberalism, almost as much as Communism, came under his fire for encouraging moral anarchy, the pursuit of selfish ambitions, and the quest for private profit or class domination. True enough, Chiang insisted that these tendencies represented not Western civilization itself, properly understood, but only a superficial imitation of the West by shallow-minded Chinese. Nevertheless, exoneration of the West to this extent could only sharpen the indictment of his own countrymen.

As a result, his views tended not only to antagonize Westernized intellectuals in China but even to discourage businessmen, who found private enterprise discredited and offered little place in a planned economy dominated by bureaucratic capitalism. (By contrast, Mao Tse-tung, after 1941, was wooing businessmen with talk of a mixed economy.) Moreover, Chiang's identification of the West with imperialism, exploitation, and profit-seeking helped create a popular image which persisted long after his tributes to his allies and his acknowledgements of Western contributions to China had been forgotten. Thus the Nanking regime itself was embarrassed when, in the postwar struggle with the Communists, it had nowhere else to turn for help but to the West.

[Adapted from *China's Destiny,* tr. by Wang Chung-hui, pp. 72–84, 212–21]

SOCIAL EFFECTS [OF THE UNEQUAL TREATIES]

During the last hundred years, under the oppression of unequal treaties, the life of the Chinese people became more and more degenerate. Everyone took self-interest as the standard of right and wrong, and personal desires as the criterion of good and evil; a thing was considered as right if it conformed to one's self-interest or good if it conformed to one's personal desires. Rascals became influential in the villages, rogues were active in the cities, sacrificing public safety and the welfare of others to satisfy their own interest and desires. In the meantime, extravagant and irresponsible ideologies and political doctrines were freely advanced, either to rationalize self-interest and personal desires or to exploit them for ulterior motives. The rationalizers idolized them as an expression of the self; and the exploiters utilized them as a means of fomenting disturbances in the community, in order to fish in troubled waters. The practice of following in the footsteps of the sages, of emulating the heroes and of being "friends with the ancients" not only tended to disappear, but was even considered mean and despicable. [p. 72]

MORAL EFFECTS

For five thousand years China had always stressed the importance of honest work and frugality. Her people were noted for their simplicity in food and clothing; women occupied themselves with their looms and men with their plows. These good habits, however, were swept clean by the prevalence in the [foreign] concessions of the vices of opium-smoking, gambling, prostitution, and robbery.

China's ancient ethical teachings and philosophies contained detailed and carefully worked out principles and rules for the regulation and maintenance of the social life of man. The structure of our society underwent many changes, but our social life never deviated from the principles governing the relationship between father and son, husband and wife, brother and brother, friend and friend, superior and inferior, man and

[145]

woman, old and young, as well as principles enjoining mutual help among neighbors and care of the sick and weak.

During the past hundred years, wherever the influence of the concessions was felt, these principles were not only neglected but also despised. Between father and son, husband and wife, brothers and friends, superiors and inferiors, old and young, and among neighbors, the old sentiments of respect and affection and the spirit of mutual help and cooperation were disappearing. Only material interests were taken into consideration and everywhere there was a general lack of moral standards by which to judge oneself. Whenever duty called, people tried to shirk it; whenever there was material profit to be gained, they struggled for it. Truth was concealed between superiors and inferiors, and mutual deception was practiced among friends. The aged and the weak could find no protection, the poor and the sick no relief. Members of the same family were often considered as strangers and fellow countrymen as enemies. In some extreme cases, people even went so far as to "regard rascals as their fathers," and shamelessly served their enemies, thereby violating all principles of family and social relationships without even being aware of their own moral degeneracy. A country which had hitherto attached the greatest importance to decorum and righteousness was now in danger of losing its sense of integrity and honor. What harm these unequal treaties had caused!

The deterioration of national morality also tended to affect the physique of our people. The physical strength of the numberless unemployed in the cities was easily impaired. The health of those merchants who abandoned themselves to a life of extravagance and dissoluteness could not but break down. The most serious thing, however, was the effect upon the health of the youth in the schools. Physical training was not popularized in most of the schools; moral education was also neglected by school masters and teachers. In the meantime, the extravagant and dissolute life outside the school attracted the students, caused them to indulge in evil habits and resulted in the deterioration of their moral character. Infectious and venereal diseases, too, which were rampant in the cities, further undermined their physical constitution. How could these young men, who were unsound in body and mind, help to advance learning, reform social customs, render service to the state and promote enterprises after their graduation? The inevitable result of such a state of affairs was the steady disintegration of our country and the further demoralization of the Chinese nation. [pp. 75–77]

PSYCHOLOGICAL EFFECTS

After the Student Movement of May 4, 1919, two currents of thought, ultra-individualistic liberalism and class-struggle communism, found their way into Chinese academic circles, and later became widespread in the country. On the whole, Chinese academic circles desired to effect a change in our culture, forgetting that it had certain elements which are immutable. With respect to different Western theories they imitated only their superficial aspects and never sought to understand their true significance in order to improve China's national life. The result was that a large number of our scholars and students adopted the superficialities and nonessentials of Western culture and lost their respect for and confidence in our own culture. [pp. 81–82]

Under these circumstances Chinese scholars and politicians who misinterpreted liberalism and abused communism were disposed, openly or indirectly, intentionally or unintentionally, to take a foreign power's stand as their own and to identify a foreign power's interests with theirs. Nay, they even went to the length of putting a favorable color on imperialism and of becoming the tools of aggression. They almost forgot who they were, why they were studying, and what they were doing. Their propaganda and educational activities among the masses were conducted in this mental atmosphere, causing the people to regard as a matter of course the impairment of our state sovereignty and the endangering of our national life. And what is worse, they were unaware that such impairment and endangering were furthered by their blindly following foreign "isms." This truly constituted the greatest crisis in the history of our culture and the most serious menace to the spirit of our people. It is high time for us to wake up and reform ourselves thoroughly. Only thus can we save the nation and ourselves; only thus can we become a self-invigorating people, and build up an independent and free China. [pp. 83–84]

THE DECISIVE FACTOR IN CHINA'S DESTINY

The work of reforming social life and carrying out the program of national reconstruction is one of paramount importance in the process of national revival—a task which requires persistent effort. Individuals, striving singly, will not achieve great results, nor lasting accomplishments. Consequently, all adult citizens and promising youths whether in a town, a district, a province, or in the country at large, should have a common organization with a systematic plan for binding the members together and headquarters to promote joint reconstruction activities and also personal accomplishments. Only by working with such a central organization can individuals live up to Dr. Sun Yat-sen's words: "To dedicate the few score years of our perishable life to the laying of an imperishable foundation for our nation."

In the past our adult citizens have been unable to unite on a large scale or for a long period. They have been derisively compared to "a heap of loose sand" or spoken of as having "only five-minutes' enthusiasm." Now, incapacity to unite is a result of selfishness, and the best antidote for selfishness is public spirit. That unity does not last is due to hypocrisy and the best antidote for hypocrisy is sincerity. With a public spirit, one can take "all men as one's kin and all things as one's company." With sincerity, one can persevere and succeed in the end. Since the Three Principles of the People are based on public good and absolute sincerity, the Kuomintang is all-embracing in spirit while in action it can "abide by the good once it has been chosen"—a fact I have clearly pointed out in my account of the Kuomintang's reorganization.

The principal fault of our youth today, and the cause of their failure and ineffectual living lie essentially in the unsound education they have received. Since they do not follow the guidance of their teachers, or realize the importance of organization as a factor in the success or failure of their life, and since they do not understand what freedom and discipline mean, they are irresponsible in their conduct and unrealistic in their thinking. As soon as they enter society, they feel the lack of ability and confidence to take up any practical work, let alone the task of social and national reconstruction. To make themselves fit for hardships and responsibilities, for social reforms and national reconstruction, it is necessary that their thinking should be scientifically trained and their behavior strictly disciplined. For this reason, immediately after the outbreak of the war of resistance I organized the San Min Chu I [Three People's Principles] Youth Corps to meet the imperative needs of young men and women throughout the country, to give a new life to the Kuomintang, and to furnish a new driving force for the [Chinese] nation. [pp. 212–14]

Given this rare opportunity at the threshold of their life, our youth should calmly plan for their life work in the light of the needs of a modern state. To avoid the mistake of living a misguided and regrettable life, they should never again allow themselves to be led astray by blind and impulsive following of others as in the past. We must realize that the Three Principles represent not only the crystallization of China's time-honored civilization and of her people's highest virtues, but also the inevitable trend of world affairs in this modern age. The San Min Chu I Youth Corps is the central organization of all Chinese youths who are faithful adherents of the Three Principles. All young men and women must therefore place themselves under the guidance of the Corps in order to keep their aims true and to avoid doing harm to themselves and to the nation. It is only by working within the framework of the Corps' program that they can make decisions about their life work in the right direction. Members of the Corps will receive strict training and observe strict discipline. They will promote all phases of the life of the people, and protect the interests of the entire nation. It will be their mission to save the country from decline and disorganization, to wipe out national humiliation, to restore national strength, and to show loyalty to the state and filial devotion to the nation. They should emulate the sages and heroes of history and be the life blood of the people and the backbone of the nation. The youths of the whole nation should not only join the Corps as the starting point of their careers, but should also consider it an honor to be thus enrolled. They should understand that the orders issued by the Corps are aimed at sustaining the collective life of the youth of the whole nation, and that the strong organization of the Corps will enable them to achieve their common objective, namely, the success of our National Revolution in the realization of the Three Principles of the People.

To sum up, the Kuomintang and the San Min Chu I Youth Corps are organic parts of the nation—a fact which need not be dwelt upon at length. But there is one point which should be repeated to my fellow countrymen, namely: that the Kuomintang is the headquarters of our national reconstruction, open to all and to be enjoyed by all. The independence of our nation hinges upon the success of the Kuomintang

Revolution. Without the Kuomintang, there would be no China. In a word, China's destiny is entrusted to the Kuomintang. If the Kuomintang Revolution should fail, China as a nation would have nothing to rely upon. Should this happen, not only would China cease to rank as one of the Four Powers of the world, but she would be at the mercy of other countries. The name of the Chinese Republic would disappear altogether from the map of the world. We should all realize this: Considering the state as an organism as far as its life is concerned, we may say that the Three Principles constitute the soul of our nation, because without these Principles our national reconstruction would be deprived of its guiding spirit. And, considering the state as an organism as far as its functions are concerned, we may say that the Kuomintang is the life blood of our nation and the members of the San Min Chu I Youth Corps may be likened to new blood corpuscles. Without the Kuomintang, China would be deprived of its pivot. If all the revolutionary elements and promising youths in the country really want to throw in their lot with the fate of the country, if they regard national undertakings as their own undertakings and the national life as their own life—then, they should all enlist in the Kuomintang or in the Youth Corps. By so doing, they can discharge the highest duties of citizenship and attain the highest ideal in life. Then and only then can our great mission of national reconstruction be completed. [pp. 219–21]

初胡　　秀獨陳

CHAPTER XXIV

THE NEW CULTURE
MOVEMENT

The New Culture Movement, as its name implies, was an attempt to destroy what remained of traditional Confucian culture in the Republican era and to replace it with something new. The collapse of the old dynastic system in 1911 and the failure of Yüan Shih-k'ai's Confucian-garbed monarchical restoration in 1916 meant that, politically, Confucianism was almost dead. It had, however, been much more than a political philosophy. It had been a complete way of life, which nationalism and republicanism only supplanted in part. There were some even among republicans who felt that certain aspects of the old culture, Confucian ethics especially, should be preserved and strengthened, lest the whole fabric of Chinese life come apart and the new regime itself be seriously weakened. Others, with far more influence on the younger generation, drew precisely the opposite conclusion. For them nothing in Confucianism was worth salvaging from the debris of the Manchu dynasty. On the contrary, whatever vestiges of the past remained in the daily life and thinking of the people should be rooted out; otherwise the young republic would rest on shaky foundations and its progress would be retarded by a backward citizenry. The new order required a whole new culture. The political revolution had to be followed by a cultural revolution.

During and just after the First World War the intellectual spearhead of this second revolution went on the offensive, launching a movement that reached out in many directions and touched many aspects of Chinese society. Roughly it may be divided into six major phases, presented below in more or less chronological order. They are 1) the attack on Confucianism; 2) the Literary Revolution; 3) the proclaiming of a new philosophy of life; 4) the debate on science and the philosophy of life;

5) the "doubting of antiquity" movement; and 6) the debate on Chinese and Western cultural values. Needless to say, these phases overlapped each other considerably, and certain leading writers figured prominently in more than one phase of the movement.

From its anti-traditionalist character one may infer that the leaders of the movement looked very much to the West. Positivism was their great inspiration, science and materialism were their great slogans, and—in the early years especially—John Dewey and Bertrand Russell were their great idols. The leaders themselves were in many cases Western educated, though not necessarily schooled in the West, since Western-style education was by now established in the East, in Japan, and in the new national and missionary colleges of China. Often college professors themselves, they now had the lecture platform to make use of, as well as the new organs of public journalism and the intellectual and literary reviews which were a novel feature of the modern age. Above all, they had a new audience, young, intense, frustrated by China's failures in the past, and full of eager hopes for the future.

THE ATTACK ON CONFUCIANISM

The open assault on Confucianism, which began in 1916, was led by Ch'en Tu-hsiu (1879–1942), editor of a magazine entitled *The New Youth*. Earlier reformers had attacked at most certain of the concepts of Confucianism, often indeed in the name of a purified and revitalized Confucian belief, or, with less obvious partisanship, combining criticism of certain aspects with praise of others. Ch'en, by contrast, challenged Confucianism from beginning to end, realizing as he did so that he struck at the very heart of the traditional culture. For him, a partisan of "science" and "democracy," Confucianism stood simply for reaction and obscurantism. He identified it with the old regime, with Yüan Shih-k'ai's attempt to restore the·monarchy, with everything from the past that, to his mind, had smothered progress and creativity.

Such an uncompromising attack was bound to shock many—those who had taken Confucianism as much for granted as the good earth of China, or those who still held to it consciously, and with some pride, as an expression of cultural nationalism. But there were others upon whom

Ch'en's bold denunciations had an electrifying effect—those, particularly young teachers and students, for whom Confucianism had come to hold little positive meaning as their own education became more Westernized; for whom, in fact, it was now more likely to be felt in their own lives simply as a form of unwanted parental or societal restraint. Young people of this group, with Peking as their center, *The New Youth* as their mouthpiece, and Ch'en as their literary champion, were glad to throw themselves into a crusade against this bugbear from the past, and to proclaim their own coming of age in the modern world by shouting: "Destroy the old curiosity shop of Confucius!"

CH'EN TU-HSIU
The Way of Confucius and Modern Life

Through articles such as this, which appeared in December, 1916, Ch'en Tu-hsiu established himself as perhaps the most influential writer of his time. His popular review, *Hsin ch'ing-nien* (*The New Youth*), had for its Western title "La Jeunesse Nouvelle," reflecting the avant-garde character of its editor, whose higher education had been obtained in a Japanese normal college and later in France. Here the Westernized and "liberated" Ch'en directs his fire at social customs and abuses which seemed to have Confucian sanction but had no place in the modern age. Already the man who was to found the Chinese Communist Party five years later speaks as an economic determinist and moral relativist, but still very much of an individualist.

[From "K'ung Tzu chih tao yü hsien-tai sheng-huo," *Hsin ch'ing-nien*, Vol. II, No. 4 (December 1916), pp. 3–5]

The pulse of modern life is economic and the fundamental principle of economic production is individual independence. Its effect has penetrated ethics. Consequently the independence of the individual in the ethical field and the independence of property in the economic field bear witness to each other, thus reaffirming the theory [of such interaction]. Because of this [interaction], social mores and material culture have taken a great step forward.

In China, the Confucianists have based their teachings on their ethical norms. Sons and wives possess neither personal individuality nor personal property. Fathers and elder brothers bring up their sons and younger brothers and are in turn supported by them. It is said in chapter thirty of the *Book of Rites* that "While parents are living, the son dares not regard his person or property as his own." [27:14] This is absolutely not the way to personal independence. . . .

In all modern constitutional states, whether monarchies or republics, there are political parties. Those who engage in party activities all express their spirit of independent conviction. They go their own way and need not agree with their fathers or husbands. When people are bound by the Confucian teachings of filial piety and obedience to the point of the son not deviating from the father's way even three years after his death [1] and the woman obeying not only her father and husband but also her son,[2] how can they form their own political party and make their own choice? The movement of women's participation in politics is also an aspect of women's life in modern civilization. When they are bound by the Confucian teaching that "To be a women means to submit," [3] that "The wife's words should not travel beyond her own apartment," and that "A woman does not discuss affairs outside the home," [4] would it not be unusual if they participated in politics?

In the West some widows choose to remain single because they are strongly attached to their late husbands and sometimes because they prefer a single life; they have nothing to do with what is called the chastity of widowhood. Widows who remarry are not despised by society at all. On the other hand, in the Chinese teaching of decorum, there is the doctrine of "no remarriage after the husband's death." [5] It is considered to be extremely shameful and unchaste for a woman to serve two husbands or a man to serve two rulers. The *Book of Rites* also prohibits widows from wailing at night [XXVII:21] and people from being friends with sons of widows. [IX:21] For the sake of their family reputation, people have forced their daughters-in-law to remain widows. These women have had no freedom and have endured a most miserable life. Year after year these many promising young women have lived a physically and spiritually abnormal life. All this is the result of Confucian teachings of decorum [or rites].

In today's civilized society, social intercourse between men and women is a common practice. Some even say that because women have a tender nature and can temper the crudeness of man, they are necessary in public

---

[1] Referring to *Analects*, I:11.
[2] *Book of Rites*, IX:24.
[3] *Book of Rites*, IX:24.
[4] *Book of Rites*, I:24.
[5] *Book of Rites*, IX:24.

or private gatherings. It is not considered improper even for strangers to sit or dance together once they have been introduced by the host. In the way of Confucian teaching, however, "Men and women do not sit on the same mat," "Brothers- and sisters-in-law do not exchange inquiries about each other," "Married sisters do not sit on the same mat with brothers or eat from the same dish," "Men and women do not know each other's name except through a matchmaker and should have no social relations or show affection until after marriage presents have been exchanged," [6] "Women must cover their faces when they go out," [7] "Boys and girls seven years or older do not sit or eat together," "Men and women have no social relations except through a matchmaker and do not meet until after marriage presents have been exchanged," [8] and "Except in religious sacrifices, men and women do not exchange wine cups." [9] Such rules of decorum are not only inconsistent with the mode of life in Western society; they cannot even be observed in today's China.

Western women make their own living in various professions such as that of lawyer, physician, and store employee. But in the Confucian way, "In giving or receiving anything, a man or woman should not touch the other's hand," [10] "A man does not talk about affairs inside [the household] and a woman does not talk about affairs outside [the household]," and "They do not exchange cups except in sacrificial rites and funerals." [11] "A married woman is to obey" and the husband is the standard of the wife.[12] Thus the wife is naturally supported by the husband and needs no independent livelihood.

A married woman is at first a stranger to her parents-in-law. She has only affection but no obligation toward them. In the West parents and children usually do not live together, and daughters-in-law, particularly, have no obligation to serve parents-in-law. But in the way of Confucius, a woman is to "revere and respect them and never to disobey day or night," [13] "A woman obeys, that is, obeys her parents-in-law," [14] "A woman serves her parent-in-law as she serves her own parents," [15] she "never should disobey or be lazy in carrying out the orders of parents and parents-in-law." "If a man is very fond of his wife, but his parents

[6] *Book of Rites*, I:24.
[8] *Book of Rites*, X:51.
[10] *Book of Rites*, XXVII:20.
[12] *Book of Rites*, IX:24.
[14] *Book of Rites*, XLI:6.

[7] *Book of Rites*, X:12.
[9] *Book of Rites*, XXVII:17.
[11] *Book of Rites*, X:12.
[13] *I-li*, ch. 2; Steele, Vol. I, p. 39.
[15] *Book of Rites*, X:3.

do not like her, she should be divorced." [16] (In ancient times there were many such cases, like that of Lu Yü [1125–1210].) "Unless told to retire to her own apartment, a woman does not do so, and if she has an errand to do, she must get permission from her parents-in-law." [17] This is the reason why the tragedy of cruelty to daughters-in-law has never ceased in Chinese society.

According to Western customs, fathers do not discipline grown-up sons but leave them to the law of the country and the control of society. But in the way of Confucius, "When one's parents are angry and not pleased and beat him until he bleeds, he does not complain but instead arouses in himself the feelings of reverence and filial piety." [18] This is the reason why in China there is the saying, "One has to die if his father wants him to, and the minister has to perish if his ruler wants him to". . . .

Confucius lived in a feudal age. The ethics he promoted is the ethics of the feudal age. The social mores he taught and even his own mode of living were teachings and modes of a feudal age. The political institutions he advocated were those of a feudal age. The objectives, ethics, social norms, mode of living, and political institutions did not go beyond the privilege and prestige of a few rulers and aristocrats and had nothing to do with the happiness of the great masses. How can this be shown? In the teachings of Confucius, the most important element in social ethics and social life is the rules of decorum and the most serious thing in government is punishment. In chapter one of the *Book of Rites*, it is said that "The rules of decorum do not go down to the common people and the penal statutes do not go up to great officers." [I:35] Is this not solid proof of the [true] spirit of the way of Confucius and the spirit of the feudal age?

THE LITERARY REVOLUTION

Paralleling the attack on Confucianism was the attack on the classical literary language—the language of Confucian tradition and of the old-style scholar-official. With the abandonment of the "eight-legged essay"

[16] *Book of Rites*, X:12.   [17] *Book of Rites*, X:13.
[18] *Book of Rites*, X:12.

examinations for the civil service in 1905, the discarding too of the official language, so far removed from ordinary speech, might seem to have been inevitable. This was a time of rising nationalism, which in the West had been linked to the rise of vernacular literatures; an era of expanding education, which would be greatly facilitated by a written language simpler and easier to learn; a period of strong Westernization in thought and scholarship, which would require a more flexible instrument for the expression of new concepts. No doubt each of these factors contributed to the rapid spread of the literary revolution after its launching by Hu Shih, with the support of Ch'en Tu-hsiu, in 1917. And yet it is a sign of the strong hold which the classical language had on educated men, and of its great prestige as a mark of learning, that until Hu appeared on the scene with his novel ideas, even the manifestos of reformers and revolutionaries had kept to the classical style of writing as if there could be no other.

Hu Shih (1891—) had studied agriculture at Cornell on a Boxer Idemnity grant and philosophy at Columbia under John Dewey, of whom he became the leading Chinese disciple. Even before his return home he had begun advocating a new written language for China, along with a complete re-examination and re-evaluation of the classical tradition in thought and literature. Ch'en Tu-hsiu's position as head of the department of literature at Peking National University, and his new political organ, *The New Youth,* represented strong backing for Hu's revolutionary program—a program all the more commanding of attention because its aim was not merely destructive of traditional usage but, ambitiously enough, directed to the stimulation of a new literature and new ideas. Instead of dwelling solely upon the deficiencies of the past, Hu's writings were full of concrete and constructive suggestions for the future. There was hope here, as well as indignation.

Hu's program thus looked beyond the immediate literary revolution, stressing the vernacular as a means of communication, to what came to be known as the literary renaissance. There can be no doubt that this movement stimulated literary activity along new lines, especially in the adoption of forms and genres then popular in the West. Yet there is real doubt that this new literary output was able to fulfill the positive hopes of Hu. It excelled in social criticism, and so contributed further to the processes of social and political disintegration. Also—and this is particularly true of Hu's own work—it rendered great service in the rehabilitation of popular literature from earlier centuries, above all the great Chinese novels. But whether it produced in its own right a contemporary literature of great literary distinction and creative imagination remains a question, a question for historians and critics of the future with a better perspective on these times and on the political movements in which this new generation of writers became so easily caught up.

HU SHIH

A Preliminary Discussion of Literary Reform
[From *Wen-hsüeh kai-liang ch'u-i*, in *Hu Shih wen-ts'un*, Collection I, Ch. 1, pp. 5–16; original version in *Hsin ch'ing-nien*, Vol. II, No. 5 (January 1917), pp. 1–11]

Many people have been discussing literary reform. Who am I, unlearned and unlettered, to offer an opinion? Nevertheless, for some years I have studied the matter and thought it over many times, helped by my deliberations with friends; and the conclusions I have come to are perhaps not unworthy of discussion. Therefore I shall summarize my views under eight points and elaborate on them separately to invite the study and comments of those interested in literary reform.

I believe that literary reform at the present time must begin with these eight items: 1) Write with substance; 2) Do not imitate the ancients; 3) Emphasize grammar; 4) Reject melancholy; 5) Eliminate old clichés; 6) Do not use allusions; 7) Do not use couplets and parallelisms; and 8) Do not avoid popular expressions or popular forms of characters.

1. *Write with substance.* By "substance" I mean: (a) Feeling. . . . Feeling is the soul of literature. Literature without feeling is like a man without a soul. . . . (b) Thought. By thought I mean insight, knowledge, and ideals. Thought does not necessarily depend on literature for transmission but literature becomes more valuable if it contains thought, and thought is more valuable if it possesses literary value. This is the reason why the essays of Chuang Tzu, the poems of T'ao Ch'ien [365–427], Li Po [689–762], and Tu Fu [712–770], the *tz'u* of Hsin Chiahsüan [1140–1207], and the novel of Shih Nai-an [that is, the *Shui-hu chuan* or *Water Margin*] are matchless for all times. . . . In recent years literary men have satisfied themselves with tones, rhythm, words,

and phrases, and have had neither lofty thoughts nor genuine feeling. This is the chief cause of the deterioration of literature. This is the bad effect of superficiality over substantiality, that is to say, writing without substance. To remedy this bad situation, we must resort to substance. And what is substance? Nothing but feeling and thought.

2. *Do not imitate the ancients.* Literature changes with time. Each period from Chou and Ch'in to Sung, Yüan, and Ming has it own literature. This is not my private opinion but the universal law of the advancement of civilization. Take prose, for example. There is the prose of the *Book of History,* the prose of the ancient philosophers, the prose of [the historians] Ssu-ma Ch'ien and Pan Ku, the prose of the [T'ang and Sung masters] Han Yü, Liu Tsung-yüan, Ou-yang Hsiu, and Su Hsün, the prose of the *Recorded Conversations* of the Neo-Confucianists, and the prose of Shih Nai-an and Ts'ao Hsüeh-ch'in [d. c.1765, author of *The Dream of the Red Chamber*]. This is the development of prose. . . . Each period has changed in accordance with its situation and circumstance, each with its own characteristic merits. From the point of view of historical evolution, we cannot say that the writings of the ancients are all superior to those of modern writers. The prose of Tso Ch'iu-ming [sixth century B.C., author of the *Tso chuan*] and Ssu-ma Ch'ien are wonderful, but compared to the *Tso chuan* and *Records of the Historian,* wherein is Shih Nai-an's *Shui-hu chuan* inferior? . . .

I have always held that colloquial stories alone in modern Chinese literature can proudly be compared with the first class literature of the world. Because they do not imitate the past but only describe the society of the day, they have become genuine literature. . . .

3. *Emphasize grammar.* Many writers of prose and poetry today neglect grammatical construction. Examples are too numerous to mention, especially in parallel prose and the four-line and eight-line verses.

4. *Reject melancholy.* This is not an easy task. Nowadays young writers often show passion. They choose such names as "Cold Ash," "No Birth," and "Dead Ash" as pen names, and in their prose and poetry, they think of declining years when they face the setting sun, and of destitution when they meet the autumn wind. . . . I am not unaware of the fact that our country is facing many troubles. But can salvation be achieved through tears? I hope all writers become Fichtes and Mazzinis and not like Chia I [201–169 B.C.], Wang Ts'an [177–217], Ch'ü Yüan

[343–277 B.C.], Hsieh Kao-yü [1249–1295], etc. [who moaned and complained]. . . .

5. *Eliminate old clichés.* By this I merely mean that writers should describe in their own words what they personally experience. So long as they achieve the goal of describing the things and expressing the mood without sacrificing realism, that is literary achievement. Those who employ old clichés are lazy people who refuse to coin their own terms of description.

6. *Do not use allusions.* I do not mean allusion in the broad sense. These are of five kinds: (a) Analogies employed by ancient writers, which have a universal meaning . . . ; (b) Idioms; (c) References to historical events . . . ; (d) Quoting from or referring to people in the past for comparison . . . ; and (e) Quotations. . . . Allusions such as these may or may not be used.

But I do not approve of the use of allusions in the narrow sense. By using allusions I mean that writers are incapable of creating their own expressions to portray the scene before them or the concepts in their minds, and instead muddle along by borrowing old stories or expressions which are partly or wholly inapplicable. . . .

7. *Do not use couplets and parallelisms.* Parallelism is a special characteristic of human language. This is why in ancient writings such as those of Lao Tzu and Confucius, there are occasionally couplets. The first chapter of the *Tao-te ching* consists of three couplets. *Analects* I:14, I:15 and III:17 are all couplets. But these are fairly natural expressions and have no indication of being forced or artificial, especially because there is no rigid requirement about the number of words, tones, or parts of speech. Writers in the age of literary decadence, however, who had nothing to say, emphasized superficiality, the extreme of which led to the development of the parallel prose, regulated *tz'u,* and the long regulated verse. It is not that there are no good products in these forms, but they are, in the final analysis, few. Why? Is it not because they restrict to the highest degree the free expression of man? (Not a single good piece can be mentioned among the long regulated verse.) To talk about literary reform today, we must "first establish the fundamental" [19] and not waste our useful energy in the nonessentials of subtlety and delicacy. This is why I advocate giving up couplets and rhymes. Even

[19] *Mencius,* VI A:15.

[160]

if they cannot be abolished, they should be regarded as merely literary stunts and nothing to be pursued seriously.

There are still people today who deprecate colloquial novels as tri-fling literature, without realizing that Shih Nai-an, Ts'ao Hsüeh-ch'in, and Wu Chien-jen [1867–1910] [20] all represent the main line of literature while parallel and regulated verse are really trifling matters. I know some will keep clear of me when they hear this.

8. *Do not avoid popular expressions or popular forms of characters.* When Buddhist scriptures were introduced into China, because classical expressions could not express their meanings, translators used clear and simple expressions. Their style already approached the colloquial. Later, many Buddhist lectures and dialogues were in the colloquial style, thus giving rise to the "conversation" style. When the Neo-Confucianists of the Sung dynasty used the colloquial in their *Recorded Conversations,* this style became the orthodox style of scholarly discussion. (This was followed by scholars of the Ming.) By that time, colloquial expressions had already penetrated rhymed prose, as can be seen in the colloquial poems of T'ang and Sung poets. From the third century to the end of the Yüan, North China had been under foreign races and popular literature developed. In prose there were such novels as the *Shui-hu chuan* and *Hsi yu chi (Journey to the West).* In drama the products were innumerable. From the modern point of view, the Yüan period should be considered as a high point of literary development; unquestionably it produced the greatest number of immortal works. At that time writing and colloquial speech were the closest to each other and the latter almost became the language of literature. Had the tendency not been checked, living literature would have emerged in China, and the great work of Dante and Luther [who inaugurated the substitution of a living language for dead Latin] would have taken place in China. Unfortunately, the tendency was checked in the Ming when the government selected officials on the basis of the rigid "eight-legged" prose style and at the same time literary men like the "seven scholars" including Li [Meng-yang, 1472–1529] considered "returning to the past" as highbrow. Thus the once-in-a-millenium chance of uniting writing and speech was killed prematurely, midway in the process. But from the modern viewpoint

[20] Author of the *Erh-shih nien mu-tu chih kuai hsien-chuang (Strange Phenomena Seen in Two Decades).*

of historical evolution, we can definitely say that the colloquial literature is the main line of Chinese literature and that it should be the medium employed in the literature of the future. (This is my own opinion; not many will agree with me today.) For this reason, I hold that we should use popular expressions and words in prose and poetry. Rather than using dead expressions of 3,000 years ago, it is better to employ living expressions of the twentieth century, and rather than using the language of the Ch'in, Han, and the Six Dynasties, which cannot reach many people and cannot be universally understood, it is better to use the language of the *Shui-hu* and *Hsi yu chi* which is understood in every household.

CH'EN TU-HSIU

On Literary Revolution
[From "Wen-hsüeh ko-ming lun," *Hsin ch'ing-nien,* Vol. II, No. 6 (February 1917), pp. 1–4]

The movement of literary revolution has been in the making for some time. My friend Hu Shih is the one who started the revolution of which he is the vanguard. I do not mind being an enemy of all old-fashioned scholars in the country and raising to great heights the banner of "the Army of Literary Revolution" to support my friend. On this banner shall be written these three fundamental principles of our revolutionary army: 1) Destroy the aristocratic literature which is nothing but literary chiseling and flattery, and construct a simple, expressive literature of the people; 2) Destroy the outmoded, showy, classical literature and construct a fresh and sincere literature of realism; 3) Destroy the obscure and abstruse "forest" literature [21] and construct a clear and popular literature of society. . . .

At this time of literary reform, aristocratic literature, classical literature, and forest literature should all be rejected. What are the reasons for attacking these three kinds of literature? The answer is that aristocratic literature employs embellishments and depends on previous writers and therefore has lost the qualities of independence and self-respect; that classical literature exaggerates and piles word after word and has lost the fundamental objective of expressing emotions and realistic descriptions; and that forest literature is difficult and obscure and is claimed to be

---

[21] An expression of Ch'en's for esoteric literature.

lofty writing but is actually of no benefit to the masses. The form of such literatures is continuous repetition of previous models. It has flesh but no bones, body but no spirit. It is an ornament and is of no actual use. With respect to their contents, their horizon does not go beyond kings and aristocrats, spiritual beings and ghosts, and personal fortunes and misfortunes. The universe, life, and society are all beyond their conception. These defects are common to all three forms of literature. These types of literature are both causes and effects of our national character of flattery, boasting, insincerity, and flagrant disregard of truth and facts. Now that we want political reform, we must regenerate the literature of those who are entrenched in political life. If we do not open our eyes and see the literary tendencies of the world society and the spirit of the time but instead bury our heads in old books day and night and confine our attention to kings and aristocrats, spiritual beings and ghosts and immortals, and personal fortunes and misfortunes, and in so doing hope to reform literature and politics, it is like binding our four limbs to fight Meng Pen [an ancient strong man].

HU SHIH

Constructive Literary Revolution: A Literature of National
Speech—A National Speech of Literary Quality
[From "Chien-she ti wen-hsüeh ko-ming lun," *Hsin ch'ing-nien*, Vol. IV, No. 4 (April 1918), pp. 290–306; *Hu Shih wen-ts'un*. Collection I, pp. 56–73]

Since I returned to China last year, in my speeches on literary revolution in various places, I have changed my "eight points" [in the previous selection] into something positive and shall summarize them under four items:

1. Speak only when you have something to say. (A different version of the first of the eight points.)

2. Speak what you want to say and say it in the way you want to say it. (Different version of points 2–6.)

3. Speak what is your own and not that of someone else. (Different version of point 7.)

4. Speak in the language of the time in which you live. (Different version of point 8.)

The literary revolution we are promoting aims merely at the creation of a Chinese literature of national speech. Only when there is such a literature can there be a national speech of literary quality. And only when there is a national speech of literary quality can our national speech be considered a real national speech. A national speech without literary quality will be devoid of life and value and can be neither established nor developed. This is the main point of this essay.

I have carefully gone into the reasons why in the past 2,000 years China has had no truly valuable and living classical-style literature. My own answer is that what writers in this period have written is dead stuff, written in a dead language. A dead language can never produce a living literature. . . .

Why is it that a dead language cannot produce a living literature? It is because of the nature of literature. The function of language and literature lies in expressing ideas and showing feelings. When these are well done, we have literature. Those who use a dead classical style will translate their own ideas into allusions of several thousand years ago and convert their own feelings into literary expressions of centuries past. . . . If China wants to have a living literature, we must use the plain speech that is the natural speech, and we must devote ourselves to a literature of national speech. . . .

Someone says: "If we want to use the national speech in literature, we must first have a national speech. At present we do not have a standard national speech. How can we have a literature of national speech?" I will say, this sounds plausible but is really not true. A national language is not to be created by a few linguistic experts or a few texts and dictionaries of national speech. To create a national speech, we must first create a literature of national speech. Once we have a literature of national speech, we shall automatically have a national speech. This sounds absurd at first but my readers will understand if they think carefully. Who in the world will be willing to learn a national speech from texts and dictionaries? While these are important, they are definitely not the effective means of creating a national speech. The truly effective and powerful text of national speech is the literature of national speech—novels, prose, poems, and plays written in the national speech. The time when these works prevail is the day when the Chinese national speech will have been established. Let us ask why we are now able simply to pick up the brush and write essays in the plain speech style and use several hundred colloquial terms. Did we learn this from some textbook of plain speech? Was it not that we learned from such novels as the *Shui-hu chuan, Hsi yu chi, Hung-lou meng,* and *Ju-lin wai-shi* (*Unofficial History of Officialdom*)? This type of plain speech literature is several hundred times as powerful as textbooks and dictionaries. . . . If we want to establish anew a standard national speech, we must first of all produce numerous works like these novels in the national speech style. . . .

A literature of national speech and a national speech of literary quality are our basic programs. Let us now discuss what should be done to carry them out.

I believe that the procedure in creating a new literature consists of three steps: 1) acquiring tools, 2) developing methods, and 3) creating. The first two are preparatory. The third is the real step to create a new literature.

1. *The tools.* Our tool is plain speech. Those of us who wish to create a literature of national speech should prepare this indispensable tool right away. There are two ways to do so:

(a) Read extensively literary works written in the plain speech that can serve as models, such as the works mentioned above, the *Recorded Conversations* of the Sung Neo-Confucianists and their letters written in the plain speech, the plays of the Yüan period, and the stories and monologues of the Ming and Ch'ing times. T'ang and Sung poems and *tz'u* written in the plain speech should also be selected to read.

(b) In all forms of literature, write in the plain speech style. . . . Not only those of us who promote the literature of plain speech should do this. I also advise those opposing this literature to do the same. Why? Because if they are not capable of writing in the plain speech style, it means that they are not qualified to oppose this type of literature. . . . I therefore advise them to do a little more writing in this style, write a few more songs and poems in the plain speech, and try to see whether the plain speech has any literary value. If, after trying for several years, they still feel that the plain speech style is not so good as the classical style, it will not be too late for them to attack us. . . .

2. *Methods.* I believe that the greatest defect of the literary men who have recently emerged in our country is the lack of a good literary method. . . . The "new novel" of today is completely devoid of a literary method.

Writers do not have the technique of plot, construction, or description of people and things. They merely write many long and repulsive pieces which are qualified only to fill the space of the second section of a newspaper, but not qualified to have a place in a new literature. Comparatively speaking, the novel is the most developed genre of literature in China in recent years. If even it is in such a poor state, then nothing can be said about other genres like poetry and drama. . . .

Generally speaking, literary methods are of three kinds:

(a) The method of collecting material. . . . I believe that for future literary men the method of collecting material should be about as follows:

(*i*) Enlarge the area from which material is to be collected. The three sources of material, namely, officialdom, houses of prostitution, and dirty society [from which present novelists draw their material] are definitely not enough. At present, the poor man's society, male and female factory workers, ricksha pullers, farmers in the interior districts, small shop owners and peddlers everywhere, and all conditions of suffering have no place in literature [as they should]. Moreover, now that new and old civilizations have come into contact, problems like family catastrophes, tragedies in marriage, the position of women, the unfitness of present education, etc., can all supply literature with material.

(*ii*) Stress actual observation and personal experience. . . .

(*iii*) Use broad and keen imagination to supplement observation and experience. . . .

(b) The method of construction. . . . This may be separated into two steps, namely, tailoring and laying the plot. . . . First, one must find out whether the material should be used for a short or long poem, or for a long novel or a short story, or for a play. . . . While tailoring is to determine what to do, laying the plot is to determine how to do it. . . .

(c) The method of description. . . .

3. *Creation*. The two items, tools and methods, discussed above are only preparations for the creation of a new literature. Only when we have mastered the tools and know the methods can we create a new Chinese literature. As to what constitutes the creation of a new literature, I had better not say a word. In my opinion we in China today have not reached the point where we can take concrete steps to create a new literature, and there is no need of talking theoretically about the tech-

niques of creation. Let us first devote our efforts to the first two steps of preparatory work.

A NEW PHILOSOPHY OF LIFE

The energetic assault on traditional thought and literature focused attention on what should replace Confucianism as a way of looking at the world and at life. Here again, during the years 1918–1919, Ch'en Tu-hsiu and Hu Shih manifested their role as leaders of the whole New Culture Movement. At a time which saw the introduction and lively discussion of the philosophies of Kant, Haeckel, Marx, Nietzsche, Bergson, James, Dewey, Russell, and others, Ch'en and Hu bespoke the dominant belief in science and social progress. In these days Ch'en, reacting strongly against what he conceived to be the social conformism and authoritarianism of Confucian thought, emphasized individualism as the basis of his philosophy. Yet his belief in science and materialism also inclined him strongly to the study of Marxism—an inclination checked to some degree by his interest in the ideas of John Dewey, who lectured widely in China in 1919 and 1920. Hu Shih, for his part, identified himself unequivocally with pragmatism. Nevertheless, in the movement as a whole philosophical allegiances were less clear-cut. It was a period of fermentation and transition, producing also strong counter-currents to trends from the West (as shown in succeeding sections) We can say, however, that the prevailing trend was toward popular acceptance of such slogans as individualism, freedom, progress, democracy, and science.

CH'EN TU-HSIU

The True Meaning of Life
[From "Jen-sheng chen i," in *Hsin ch'ing-nien*, Vol. IV, No. 2 (February 1918), pp. 90–93]

What is the ultimate purpose in life? What should it be, after all? . . . From ancient times not a few people have offered explanations. . . . In my opinion, what the Buddha said is vague. Although the individual's birth and death are illusory, can we say that humanity as a whole is not really existent? . . . The teachings of Christianity, especially, are fabrications out of nothing and cannot be proved. If God can create the human race, who created Him? Since God's existence or nonexistence cannot be proved, the Christian philosophy of life cannot be completely believed in. The rectification of the heart, cultivation of the person, family harmony, national order, and world peace that Confucius and Mencius talked about are but some activities and enterprises in life and cannot cover the total meaning of life. If we are totally to sacrifice ourselves to benefit others, then we exist for others and not for ourselves. This is definitely not the fundamental reason for man's existence. The idea [of altruism] of Mo Tzu is also not free from one-sidedness. The doctrines of Yang Chu [fourth century B.C.?] and Nietzsche fully reveal the true nature of life, and yet if we follow them to their extremes, how can this complex, organized, and civilized society continue? . . .

Because we Chinese have accepted the teachings [of contentment and laissez faire] of Lao Tzu and Chuang Tzu, we have to that extent been backward. Scientists say that there is no soul after a man's death. . . . It is difficult to refute these words. But although we as individuals will inevitably die, it is not easy for the whole race or humanity to die off. The civilization created by the race or humanity will remain. It is recorded in history and will be transmitted to later generations. Is this not the consciousness or memory of our continuation after death?

From the above, the meaning of life as seen by the modern man can be readily understood. Let me state it briefly as follows:

1. With reference to human existence, the individual's birth and death are transitory but society really exists.

2. The civilization and happiness of society are created by individuals and should be enjoyed by individuals.

3. Society is an organization of individuals—there can be no society without individuals. . . . The will and the happiness of the individual should be respected.

4. Society is the collective life of individuals. If society is dissolved, there will be no memory or consciousness of the continuation of the individual after he dies. Therefore social organization and order should be respected.

5. To carry out one's will and to satisfy his desires (everything from food and sex to moral reputation is "desire") are the basic reasons for

the individual's existence. These goals never change. (Here we can say that Heaven does not change and the Way does not change either.)

6. All religions, laws, moral and political systems are but necessary means to preserve social order. They are not the individual's original purpose of enjoyment in life and can be changed in accordance with the circumstances of the time.

7. Man's happiness in life is the result of man's own effort and is neither the gift of God nor a spontaneous natural product. If it were the gift of God, how is it that He was so generous with people today and so stingy with people in the past? If it is a spontaneous, natural product, why is it that the happiness of the various peoples in the world is not uniform?

8. The individual in society is comparable to the cell in the body. Its birth and death are transitory. New ones replace the old. This is as it should be and need not be feared at all.

9. To enjoy happiness, do not fear suffering. Personal suffering at the moment sometimes contributes to personal happiness in the future. For example, the blood shed in righteous wars often wipes out the bad spots of a nation or mankind. Severe epidemics often hasten the development of science.

In a word, what is the ultimate purpose in life? What should it be, after all? I dare say:

During his lifetime, an individual should devote his efforts to create happiness and to enjoy it, and also to keep it in store in society so that individuals of the future may also enjoy it, one generation doing the same for the next and so on unto infinity.

HU SHIH

Pragmatism
[From *Shih-yen chu-i*, in *Hu Shih wen-ts'un*. Collection I, ch. 2, pp. 291–320; originally published in *Hsin ch'ing-nien*, Vol. VI, No. 4 (April 1919), pp. 342–58]

There are two fundamental changes in basic scientific concepts which have had the most important bearings on pragmatism. The first is the change of the scientific attitude toward scientific laws. Hitherto worshipers of science generally had a superstition that scientific laws were unalterable universal principles. They thought that there was an eternal, unchanging "natural law" immanent in all things in the universe and that when this law was discovered, it became scientific law. However, this attitude toward the universal principle has gradually changed in the last several decades. Scientists have come to feel that such a superstitious attitude toward a universal principle could hinder scientific progress. Furthermore, in studying the history of science they have learned that many discoveries in science are the results of hypotheses. Consequently, they have gradually realized that the scientific laws of today are no more than the hypotheses which are the most applicable, most convenient, and most generally accepted as explanations of natural phenomena. . . . Such changes of attitude involve three ideas: 1) Scientific laws are formulated by men; 2) They are hypotheses—whether they can be determined to be applicable or not entirely depends on whether they can satisfactorily explain facts; 3) They are not the eternal, unchanging natural law. There may be such a natural law in the universe, but we ,cannot say that our hypothecated principles are this law. They are no more than a shorthand to record the natural changes known to us. [pp. 291–94]

Besides this, there was in the nineteenth century another important change which also had an extremely important bearing on pragmatism. This is Darwin's theory of evolution. . . . When it came to Darwin, he boldly declared that the species were not immutable but all had their origins and developed into the present species only after many changes. From the present onward, there can still be changes in species, such as the grafting of trees and crossing of fowls, whereby special species can be obtained. Not only do the species change, but truth also changes. The change of species is the result of adaptation to environment and truth is but an instrument with which to deal with environment. As the environment changes, so does truth accordingly. The concept of loyalty to the emperor during the Hsüan-t'ung era [1909–1911] was no longer the concept of loyalty to the emperor during the Yung-cheng and Ch'ien-lung eras [1723–1795]. Since the founding of the republic, such concepts have been completely cast aside and are useless. Only when we realize that there is no eternal, unchanging truth or absolute truth can we arouse in ourselves a sense of intellectual responsibility. The knowledge that mankind needs is not the way or principle which has an absolute existence but the particular truths for here and now and for particular individuals. Absolute truth is imaginary, abstract, vague, without evidence, and cannot be demonstrated. [pp. 294–95]

THE PRAGMATISM OF JAMES

What we call truth is actually no more than an instrument, comparable to this piece of paper in my hand, this chalk, this blackboard, or this teapot. They are all our instruments. Because this concept produced results, people in the past therefore called it truth and because its utility still remains, we therefore still call it truth. If by any chance some event takes place for which the old concept is not applicable, it will no longer be truth. We will search for a new truth to take its place. . . .

Truth is recognized to be truth because it has helped us ferry the river or make a match. If the ferry is broken down, build another one. If the sailboat is too slow, replace it with a steam launch. If this marriage broker won't do, give him a good punch, chase him out, and ask a dependable friend to make a match.

This is the theory of truth in pragmatism. [pp. 309–10]

THE FUNDAMENTAL CONCEPTS OF DEWEY'S PHILOSOPHY

Dewey is a great revolutionist in the history of philosophy. . . . He said that the basic error of modern philosophy is that modern philosophers do not understand what experience really is. All quarrels between rationalists and empiricists and between idealists and realists are due to their ignorance of what experience is. [p. 316]

Dewey was greatly influenced by the modern theory of biological evolution. Consequently, his philosophy is completely colored by bio-evolutionism. He said that "experiencing means living; and that living goes on in and because of an environing medium, not in a vacuum. . . . The human being has upon his hands the problem of responding to what is going on around him so that these changes will take one turn rather than another, namely, that required by his own further functioning. . . . He is obliged to struggle—that is to say, to employ the direct support given by the environment in order indirectly to effect changes that would not otherwise occur. In this sense, life goes on by means of controlling the environment. Its activities must change the changes going on around it; they must neutralize hostile occurrences; they must transform neutral events into cooperative factors or into an efflorescence of new features." [22]

This is what Dewey explained as experience. [p. 318]

The foregoing are the basic concepts of Dewey's philosophy. Summarized, they are: 1) Experience is life and life is dealing with environment; 2) In the act of dealing with environment, the function of thought is the most important. All conscious actions involve the function of thought. Thought is an instrument to deal with environment; 3) True philosophy must throw overboard the previous toying with "philosophers' problems" and turn itself into a method for solving human problems.

What is the philosophical method for solving human problems? It goes without saying that it must enable people to have creative intelligence, must enable them to envisage a bright future on the basis of present needs, and must be able to create new methods and tools to realize that future. [p. 320]

THE DEBATE ON SCIENCE AND THE PHILOSOPHY OF LIFE

The prevailing glorification of science prompted a reaction in some quarters, which pointed to the inadequacy of science when conceived as a philosophy for dealing with some of the fundamental questions of human life. The debate was touched off by a lecture at Tsing-hua College, near Peking, by Dr. Chang Chün-mai (Carsun Chang, 1886—) who insisted upon the need for a metaphysics as the basis for a genuine philosophy of life. In the controversy which followed (also known as the controversy between metaphysics and science), Chang drew some support from his teacher Liang Ch'i-ch'ao, now much disillusioned with Western materialism and scientism, and from the professional philosopher and translator of Bergson, Chang Tung-sun (1886—). A far larger number of writers, however, immediately rose to attack metaphysics and defend science. Chang's chief opponent was Ting Wen-chiang (1888–1936), a geologist by profession, who stigmatized metaphysics as mere superstition and insisted that there were no genuine problems of philosophy or psychology which lay outside the domain of science or to which science, with the progress of civilization, would not eventually find

[22] John Dewey, *Creative Intelligence* (New York, Henry Holt, 1917), pp. 8–9.

an answer. Many others with a basically materialistic view, from Ch'en Tu-hsiu (now a Marxian and Communist) to Hu Shih and Wu Chih-hui (1865–1953), a writer closely identified with the Kuomintang, joined in the battle. Altogether the writings which dealt with this issue, later compiled in book form, amounted to over 250,000 words. In the end, as far as majority opinion was concerned, the "anti-metaphysics, pro-science" group carried the day. The controversy thus served only to underscore the overwhelming acceptance of pragmatism and materialism among the younger generation of writers and students.

CHANG CHÜN-MAI
The Philosophy of Life

Chang Chün-mai (known in the West as Carsun Chang) was a young professor of philosophy when he delivered this controversial lecture on February 14, 1923. Like so many others of his generation, he had received his higher education in Japan (Waseda University) and Europe. A follower of Liang Ch'i-ch'ao and a believer in the "spiritual" civilization of China, he combined Bergsonian intuitionism with the Neo-Confucian School of the Mind (especially the teachings of Wang Yang-ming). In later years Chang was also politically active as the leader of a "third-force" advocating nationalism and socialism, which had some influence among intellectuals but little mass following.

[From *Jen-sheng kuan* in Chang Chün-mai et al., *K'o-hsüeh yü jen-sheng kuan*, I, 4–9]

The central focus of a philosophy of life is the self. What is relative to it is the nonself. . . . But all problems of the nonself are related to human life. Now human life is a living thing and cannot so easily be governed by formulae as can dead matter. The unique character of a philosophy of life becomes especially clear when we compare it with science.

First of all, science is objective whereas a philosophy of life is subjective. The highest standard of science consists in its objective efficacy. Mr. A says so, Mr. B says so, and C, D, E, F all say so. In other words, a general law is applicable to the entire world. . . . A philosophy of life is different. Confucius' doctrine of firm action and Lao Tzu's doctrine of nonaction represent different views. . . . Darwin's theory of struggle and survival and Kropotkin's theory of mutual aid represent different

[173]

views. All these have their pros and cons and no experiment can be conducted to determine who is right and who is wrong. Why? Because they are philosophies of life; because they are subjective.

Secondly, science is controlled by the logical method whereas a philosophy of life arises from intuition. . . . Science is restricted by method and by system. On the other hand, philosophies of life—whether the pessimism of Schopenhauer and Hartmann or the optimism of Lambert, Nietzsche, and Hegel; whether Confucius' doctrine of personal perfection and family harmony or Buddha's doctrine of renunciation; and whether the Confucian doctrine of love with distinctions or the teaching of universal love of Mo Tzu and Jesus—are not restricted by any logical formula. They are not governed by definitions or methods. They are views held according to one's conscience for the sake of setting a norm for the world and for posterity. This is the reason why they are intuitive.

Thirdly, science proceeds from an analytical method whereas a philosophy of life proceeds from synthesis. The key to science is analysis. . . . A philosophy of life, on the other hand, is synthetic. It includes everything. If subjected to analysis, it will lose its true meaning. For example, the Buddha's philosophy of life is to save all living beings. If one seeks his motive and says that it is due to the Indian love of meditation or to India's climate, to some extent such analysis is reasonable. But it would be a mistake to conclude that Buddhism and all it contains can be explained in terms only of the motives just analyzed. Why? Motives and a philosophy of life are different things. A philosophy of life is a whole and cannot be discovered in what has been divided or mutilated. . . .

Fourthly, science follows the law of cause and effect whereas a philosophy of life is based on free will. The first general law governing material phenomena is that where there is cause, there is effect. . . . Even the relation between body and mind . . . is also the result of cause and effect. But purely psychological phenomena are different, and a philosophy of life is much more so. Why is it that Confucius did not even sit long enough to warm his mat [before hurrying off to serve society] or that Mo Tzu's stove did not have a chance to burn black [before he did likewise]? Why was Jesus crucified, and why did Shakyamuni devote his life to asceticism? All these issued from the free action of conscience and were not determined by something else. Even in an ordinary person, such things as repentance, self-reform, and a sense of responsibility cannot be explained by the law of cause and effect. The master agent is none other than the person himself. This is all there is to it, whether in the case of great men like Confucius, Mo Tzu, the Buddha, and Jesus, or in the case of an ordinary man.

Fifthly, science arises from the phenomenon of uniformity among objects whereas a philosophy of life arises from the unity of personality. The greatest principle in science is the uniformity of the course of nature. Plants, animals, and even inorganic matter can all be classified. Because of the possibility of classification, there is a principle running through all changes and phenomena of a particular class of objects, and therefore a scientific formula for it can be discovered. But in human society some people are intelligent while others are stupid, some are good and some are bad, and some are healthy while others are not. . . . The distinction of natural phenomena is their similarity, while that of mankind is its variety. Because of this variety there have been the "first to be enlightened" and the "hero" as they are called in traditional Chinese terminology and the "creator" and "genius" as they are called in Western terminology. All these are merely intended to show the unique character of human personality.

From the above we can see that the distinguishing points of a philosophy of life are subjectivity, intuitiveness, synthesizing power, free will, and personal unity. Because of these five qualities, the solution of problems pertaining to a philosophy of life cannot be achieved by science, however advanced it may be, but can only be achieved by man himself. . . .

TING WEN-CHIANG
Metaphysics and Science

Ting Wen-chiang (V. K. Ting) was a professor of geology at the University of Peking when he responded to Chang Chün-mai with this article published in April, 1923. Trained at Cambridge and Glasgow universities, he was widely respected for his writings in the fields of geology, mining, geography, etc., but became known also as a leading political pamphleteer. In 1919, a few years before this controversy arose, he had accompanied Liang Ch'i-ch'ao, Carsun Chang, and others on an inspection trip to Europe, from which the latter returned much disillusioned with the materialism of the West. Though Ting's basic outlook was not altered by this experience, from it developed his interest in a wider range of questions—political and philosophical—than his scientific studies had embraced earlier.

[From *Hsüan-hsüeh yü k'o-hsüeh*, in Chang Chün-mai et al., *K'o-hsüeh yü jen-sheng kuan*, I, 1–19]

Metaphysics is a bewildered specter which has been haunting Europe for twenty centuries. Of late it has gradually lost its treacherous occupation and all of a sudden come to China, its body swinging, with all its banners and slogans, to lure and fool the Chinese people. If you don't believe me, look at Chang Chün-mai's "Philosophy of Life." Chang is my friend, but metaphysics is an enemy of science. . . .

Can a philosophy of life and science be separated? . . . Chang's explanation is that philosophies of life are "most diversified" and therefore science is not applicable to them. But it is one thing to say that at present philosophies of life are not unified and quite another thing to say that they can never be unified. Unless you can advance a reason to prove why they can never be unified, we are obliged to find the unity. Furthermore, granted that at present "there are no standards of right and wrong, truth or falsity," [as Chang said], how can we tell that right and wrong and truth and falsity cannot be discovered? Unless we discover them, how are we going to have standards? To find right and wrong and truth and falsity, what other method is there aside from the scientific? . . .

Among those who study biology, who does not know that the problem of the good or evil nature of man and Darwin's theories of struggle and survival are all scientific problems and are problems already solved? But Chang claims that these are subjective and are philosophies of life and cannot be subjected to experiment to show which is right and which is wrong. By merely looking at his inability to separate a philosophy of life from science, we know that they are basically inseparable. [p. 6]

Chang says that a philosophy of life is not controlled by the logical method. Science replies: Whatever cannot be studied and criticized by logic is not true knowledge. He claims that "purely psychological phenomena" lie outside the law of cause and effect. Science replies: Psychological phenomena are at bottom materials of science. If the phenomena you are talking about are real, they cannot go beyond the sphere of science. He has repeatedly emphasized individuality and intuition, but he has placed these outside the logical method and definition. It is not that science attaches no importance to individuality and intuition. But

[176]

the individuality and intuition recognized by science are those that "emerge from living experience and are based on evidences of experience," [as Hu Shih has said]. Chang has said that a philosophy of life is a synthesis—"It is a whole and cannot be discovered in what has been divided and mutilated." Science replies: We do not admit that there is such a confused, undifferentiated thing. Furthermore, he himself has distinguished the self and the nonself and listed nine items under the latter. Thus he has already analyzed it. He says that "the solution of problems pertaining to a philosophy of life cannot be achieved by science." Science replies: Anything with a psychological content and all true concepts and inferences are materials for science. [pp. 14–15]

Whether we like it or not, truth is truth and falsity is falsity. As truth is revealed, metaphysics becomes helpless. Consequently, the universe that used to belong to metaphysics has been taken over by science. . . . Biology has become a science. . . . Psychology has also declared [its] independence. Thereupon metaphysics has retreated from First Philosophy to ontology but it is still without regret and brags before science, saying: "You cannot study intuition; you cannot study reality outside of sensation. You are corporeal, I am metaphysical. You are dead; I am living." Science does not care to quarrel with it, realizing that the scientific method is all-mighty in the realm of knowledge. There is no fear that metaphysics will not finally surrender. [p. 16]

Metaphysicians only talk about their ontology. We do not want to waste our valuable time attacking them. But young people at large are fooled by them and consider all problems relating to religion, society, government, and ethics to be really beyond the control of the logical method. They think there is really no right or wrong, no truth or falsity. They believe that these problems must be solved by what they call a philosophy of life which they say is subjective, synthesizing, and consisting of free will.

If so, what kind of society will ours be? If so, there will be no need to read or learn, and experience will be useless. We will need only to "hold views according to our conscience," for philosophies of life "all issue from the free action of conscience and are not dictated by something else." In that case, aren't study, learning, knowledge, and experience all a waste of time? Furthermore, there will be no room for discussing any problem, for discussion requires logical formulae, definitions, and methods, and all these are unacceptable to Chang Chün-mai. . . . Moreover, everyone has his own conscience. What need is there for anyone to "enlighten" or "set an example" for us? If everyone can "hold his view" according to his irrational philosophy of life, why should he regard the philosophies of life of Confucius, the Buddha, Mo Tzu, or Jesus as superior to his own? And there is no standard of right and wrong or truth and falsity. Thus a person's philosophy of life may be self-contradictory, and he may be preaching the doctrine of equality of the sexes and practicing polygamy at the same time. All he needs to say is that it is "the free action of his conscience," and he does not have to bother whether it is logical or not. Whenever it is the free action of conscience, naturally other people must not interfere. Could we live in such a society for a single day? [pp. 18–19]

WU CHIH-HUI

A New Concept of the Universe and Life
Based on a New Belief

These excerpts are from a long essay by Wu Chih-hui (1865–1953), which Hu Shih hailed as "the most significant event" in the controversy over science and metaphysics. "With one stroke of the pen he ruled out God, banished the soul, and punctured the metaphysical idea that man is the most spiritual of all things." Wu, an iconoclast who had a reputation as something of a wit and satirist, is remembered for his declaration, which became a virtual battle-cry among the anti-Confucianists: "All thread-bound [old-style] books should be dumped in the lavatory."

After taking the first steps up the old civil service ladder under the Manchus, Wu had become involved in the reform movement, and then had studied for many years in Japan, England and France, where he espoused anarchism. Acquaintance with Sun Yat-sen led him eventually into the revolutionary movement. He became a confidant of Sun and Chiang Kai-shek, and in his later years a sort of elder statesman among the Nationalists.

[From *I-ko hsin hsin-yang ti yü-chou kuan chi jen-sheng kuan*, in Chang Chün-mai *et al.*, *K'o-hsüeh yü jen-sheng kuan*, II, 24–137]

Chang Chün-mai has mobilized his soldiers of science to protect his specter of metaphysics and engage in warfare with Ting Wen-chiang. Liang Ch'i-ch'ao has formulated for them "laws of the war of words" in preparation for stepped up mobilization on both sides and for a prolonged struggle. . . . To some extent I feel that even if the struggle lasted for a hundred years, there would be no conclusion. [pp. 24–25]

What philosophy of life have you, oldster? Well, friends, let me tell you. . . .

We need only say that "the universe is a greater life." Its substance involves energy at the same time. To use another term, it may also be called power. From this power the will is produced. . . . When the will comes into contact with the external world, sensations ensue, and when these sensations are welcomed or resisted, feelings arise. To make sure that the feelings are correct, thought arises to constitute the intellect. When the intellect examines again and again a certain feeling to see to it that it is natural and proper or to correct the intellect's own ignorance, this is intuition. [pp. 28–30]

What is the need of any spiritual element or the so-called soul, which never meets any real need anyway? [p. 32]

I strongly believe 1) that the spirit cannot be separated from matter. . . . 2) that the universe is a temporary thing. . . . 3) that people today are superior to people in the past and that people in the future will be superior to people today. . . . 4) that they are so in both good and evil. . . . 5) that the more advanced material civilization becomes, the more plentiful will material goods be, the human race will tend more and more to unity, and complicated problems will be more and more easily solved. . . . 6) that morality is the crystallization of civilization and that there has never been a low morality when civilization reached a higher state. . . . and 7) that all things in the universe can be explained by science. [pp. 112–37]

HU SHIH

Science and Philosophy of Life
   [From *Hu Shih wen-ts'un,* Collection II, Ch. 1, pp. 121–39]

The Chinese people's philosophy of life has not yet been brought face to face with science. At this moment we painfully feel that science has not been sufficiently promoted, that scientific education has not been developed, and that the power of science has not been able to wipe out the black smoke that covers the whole country. To our amazement there are still prominent scholars [like Liang Ch'i-ch'ao] who shout, "European science is bankrupt," blame the cultural bankruptcy of Europe on science, deprecate it, score the sins of the scientists' philosophy of life, and do not want science to exert any influence on a philosophy of life. Seeing this, how can those who believe in science not worry? How can they help crying out loud to defend science? This is the motive which has given rise to this big battle of "science versus philosophy of life." We must understand this motive before we can see the position the controversy occupies in the history of Chinese thought. . . .

Chang Chün-mai's chief point is that "the solution of problems pertaining to a philosophy of life cannot be achieved by science." In reply to him, we should make clear what kind of philosophy of life has been produced when science was applied to problems pertaining to a philosophy of life. In other words, we should first describe what a scientific philosophy of life is and then discuss whether such a philosophy of life can be established, whether it can solve the problems pertaining to a philosophy of life, and whether it is a plague on Europe and poison to the human race, as Liang Ch'i-ch'ao has said it is. I cannot help feeling that in this discussion consisting of a quarter of a million words, those who fight for science, excepting Mr. Wu Chih-hui, share a common error, namely, that of not stating in concrete terms what a scientific philosophy of life is, but merely defending in an abstract way the assertion that science *can* solve the problems of a philosophy of life. . . . They have not been willing publicly to admit that the concrete, purely materialistic, and purely mechanistic philosophy of life is the scientific philosophy of life. We say they have not been willing; we do not say they have not dared. We merely say that with regard to the scientific philosophy of life, the defenders of science do not believe in it as clearly and firmly as does Mr. Wu Chih-hui and therefore they cannot publicly defend their view. . . .

In a word, our future war plan should be to publicize our new belief, to publicize what we believe to be the new philosophy of life. The basic ideas of this new philosophy of life have been declared by Mr. Wu. We shall now summarize these general ideas, elaborate and supplement them to some extent, and present here an outline of this new philosophy of life:

1. On the basis of our knowledge of astronomy and physics, we should recognize that the world of space is infinitely large.

2. On the basis of our geological and paleontological knowledge, we should recognize that the universe extends over infinite time.

3. On the basis of all our verifiable scientific knowledge, we should recognize that the universe and everything in it follow natural laws of movement and change—"natural" in the Chinese sense of "being so of themselves"—and that there is no need for the concept of a supernatural Ruler or Creator.

4. On the basis of the biological sciences, we should recognize the terrific wastefulness and brutality in the struggle for existence in the biological world, and consequently the untenability of the hypothesis of a benevolent Ruler who "possesses the character of loving life."

5. On the basis of the biological, physiological, and psychological sciences, we should recognize that man is only one species in the animal kingdom and differs from the other species only in degree but not in kind.

6. On the basis of the knowledge derived from anthropology, sociology, and the biological sciences, we should understand the history and causes of the evolution of living organisms and of human society.

7. On the basis of the biological and psychological sciences, we should recognize that all psychological phenomena are explainable through the law of causality.

8. On the basis of biological and historical knowledge, we should recognize that morality and religion are subject to change, and that the causes of such change can be scientifically discovered.

9. On the basis of our newer knowledge of physics and chemistry, we should recognize that matter is not dead or static but living and dynamic.

10. On the basis of biological and sociological knowledge, we should recognize that the individual—the "small self"—is subject to death and extinction, but mankind—the "Large Self"—does not die and is immortal, and should recognize that to live for the sake of the species and posterity is religion of the highest kind; and that those religions which seek a future life either in Heaven or the Pure Land, are selfish religions.

This new philosophy of life is a hypothesis founded on the commonly accepted scientific knowledge of the last two or three hundred years. We may confer on it the honorable title of "scientific philosophy of life." But to avoid unnecessary controversy, I propose to call it merely "the naturalistic philosophy of life."

"THE DOUBTING OF ANTIQUITY"

Another significant trend of the New Culture Movement which owes its inception to Hu Shih is the new historical and critical approach to the study of Chinese philosophy and literature begun by Hu with his doctoral studies at Columbia. His *Outline of the History of Chinese Philosophy* (*Chung-kuo che-hsüeh shih ta-kang*), published in 1919, is permeated with a spirit of doubt which led him to reject tradition and to study Chinese thought historically and critically. This spirit soon penetrated the whole New Culture Movement. Hu's friend Ch'ien Hsüan-t'ung (1887–1938) and pupil Ku Chieh-kang (1893—) took it up as a concerted "debunking" movement in the early 1920s, which resulted in an almost complete rejection of traditional beliefs in regard to ancient Chinese history, as well as to the loss by the Confucian Classics of whatever sacredness, prestige or authority they still retained.

The attacks of reformers in recent decades had already undermined belief in the political and social ethics of Confucianism among young Chinese. As Nationalists, however, these same reformers had often felt a pride in Chinese antiquity which inclined them to spare it the devastating scrutiny to which they subjected the recent past. Now ancient history too—a domain in which Confucianists had always excelled and which was so vital to their whole world view—was invaded and occupied by modern skepticism.

KU CHIEH-KANG

Preface to Debates on Ancient History (1926)
[From *Ku-shih pien,* Vol, I, Pt. I, pp. 40–66]

In those years [1918 ff.] Dr. Hu Shih published many articles. Those articles often provided me with the methods for the study of history. . . . If I can do what Dr. Hu has done in his investigations of the novel *Shui-hu chuan,* discovering the stages through which the story developed and going through the story systematically to show how these stages changed, wouldn't it be interesting! At the same time I recalled that this past spring Dr. Hu published an article on the "well-field" system in the periodical *Construction* [*Chien-she*], using the same critical method of investigation. It shows that ancient history can be investigated by the same method as the investigation of the novel. [p. 40]

As is well known, the history of China is generally considered to be 5,000 years old (or 2,276,000 years according to the apocryphal books!). Actually it is only 2,000 years old if we deduct the history recorded in spurious works and also unauthenticated history based on spurious works. Then we have only what is left after a big discount! At this point I could not help arousing in my mind an ambition to overthrow unauthentic history. At first I wanted only to overthrow unauthentic history recorded in unauthentic books. Now I wanted also to overthrow unauthentic history recorded in authentic works. Since I read the first section of [K'ang Yu-wei's] *Confucius As a Reformer* [*K'ung Tzu kai-chih k'ao*] my thought had been germinating for five or six years, and now for the first time I had a clear conception and a definite plan to overthrow ancient history. What is this plan? Its procedure involves three things to be done. First, the origin and the development of the events recorded in unauthentic histories must be investigated one by one. Secondly, every event in the authentic histories must be investigated to see what this and that person said about it, list what they said and compare them, like a judge examining evidence so that no lie can escape detection. Thirdly, although the words of liars differ, they follow a certain common pattern, just as the rules governing plots in plays are uniform although the stories themselves differ. We can detect the patterns in their ways of telling falsehood. [pp. 42–43]

My only objective is to explain the ancient history transmitted in the tradition of a certain period by the circumstances of that period. . . . Take Po-i [c.1122 B.C.?, who according to tradition preferred starving to death to serving another king]. What was the man really like? Was he the son of the Lord of Ku-chu? We have no way of knowing. But we do know that in the Spring and Autumn period people liked to talk about moral cultivation and upheld the "gentleman" as the standard of molding personal character. Consequently, when Po-i was talked about in the *Analects,* he was described as "not keeping in mind other people's former wickedness" [V:22] and "refusing to surrender his will or degrade himself." [XVIII:8] We also know that in the Contending States period, rulers and prime ministers liked to keep scholars in their service and scholars desperately looked for rulers to serve. For this reason, *The Book of Mencius* says of Po-i that, having heard King Wen was in power, his hopes were aroused and he declared: "Why should I not go and follow him? I hear King Wen is hospitable to the old." [IV A:13, VII A:22] We also know that after the Ch'in united the empire, the concept of absolute loyalty to the ruler became very strong and no one could escape from the mutual obligation between ruler and minister. For this reason, in the *Historical Records* he is recorded as one who bowed before King Wu of Chou to admonish him [not to overthrow King Chou of Shang], and having failed in this mission, chose to follow what he believed to be right, refusing to eat the food produced under the Chou and starving to death in the Shou-yang Mountain.[23] After the Han dynasty the story which had undergone many changes before became stabilized; books had become common, and as a result the personality of Po-i no longer changed in accordance with the varying circumstances of time. We therefore should treat ancient history in the same way as we treat the stories of our own day, for they have all passed from mouth to mouth.

THE CONTROVERSY OVER CHINESE AND WESTERN CULTURES

Intimately related to the debate on science and metaphysics was the controversy over Chinese and Western cultures, which arose from the apparent disillusionment with the West of some who had been the strongest champions of Westernization not long before. In 1919 Liang Ch'i-ch'ao returned from Europe, where he had observed the aftermath of the First World War. The picture he proceeded to give of the West was much in contrast to his earlier view of it as the vanguard of social progress and enlightened civilization. Now he saw it as sick and declining, the victim of its own obsession with science, materialism, and mechanization. The notion of inevitable progress, which had once inspired his belief that China could cut loose from its past and move forward to new greatness, was now bankrupt. Its bankruptcy, however, was all the West's, not Liang's. If Europe fell victim to its own shattered illusions, neither he nor China need suffer in the catastrophe. For the failure of science and

[23] *Shih chi*, ch. 61.

materialism served only to vindicate China and its "spiritual" civilization.

Liang was by no means ready to forego completely the benefits of science and material progress. The failure of the West he saw as resulting from its proclivity toward extremes, its overemphasis on materialism today being an excessive reaction to the exaggerated idealism and spirituality of medieval Europe. China's historical mission had been to preserve a balance between the two, and in the modern world she was specially equipped to reconcile these divergent forces in a new humanistic civilization. Thus Liang arrived at a new syncretism. Whatever was of value in Western science and material progress China could claim for herself and blend with her own spiritual traditions. The latter Liang identified selectively —and here revealed his growing anti-intellectualism—with the idealistic and intuitionist strains of Buddhism and Neo-Confucianism. Clearly Liang wanted the best of both worlds for China, and the better part was clearly Chinese.

Strong support for this view came from Liang Shu-ming (1893—), who likewise saw the superiority of Chinese civilization as lying in its capacity for harmonizing opposing extremes. As in the debate over science and metaphysics, however, the voices of those who spoke for progress and modernism—with Hu Shih again among the leaders—prevailed against the neo-traditionalists. The latter might appeal to national pride or self-respect, and thus swell a growing sense of nationalism, but they could not arrest the steady disintegration of traditional Chinese civilization, which Liang himself had done much to hasten.

LIANG CH'I-CH'AO

Travel Impressions of Europe
[From Lin Chih-chun (comp.), *Yin-ping shih ho-chi*, Vol. V, chuan-chi No. 23, Pt. i, sec. 13, pp. 35–37]

What is our duty? It is to develop our civilization with that of the West and to supplement Western civilization with ours so as to synthesize and transform them to make a new civilization. . . .

Recently many Western scholars have wanted to import Asia civilization as a corrective to their own. Having thought the matter over carefully, I believe we are qualified for that purpose. Why? In the past, the ideal and the practical in Western civilization have been sharply divided.

[185]

Idealism and materialism have both gone to the extreme. Religionists have onesidedly emphasized the future life. Idealistic philosophers have engaged in lofty talk about the metaphysical and mysterious, far, far removed from human problems. The reaction came from science. Materialism swept over the world and threw overboard all lofty ideals. Therefore I once said, "Socialism, which is so fashionable, amounts to no more than fighting for bread." Is this the highest goal of mankind?

Now pragmatism and evolutionism are being promoted, the aim being to embrace the ideal in the practical and to harmonize mind and matter. In my opinion, this is precisely the line of development in our ancient systems of thought. Although the schools of the sages—Confucius, Lao Tzu, and Mo Tzu—are different, their common goal is to unify the ideal and the practical. . . . Also, although Buddhism was founded in India, it really flourished in China. . . . Take Chinese Meditation Buddhism [Ch'an, Zen]. It can truly be considered as practical Buddhism and worldly Buddhism. Certainly it could have developed only outside India, and certainly it can reveal the special characteristics of the Chinese people. It enables the way of renouncing the world and the way of remaining in the world to go hand in hand without conflict. At present philosophers like Bergson and Eucken want to follow this path but have not been able to do so. I have often thought that if they could have studied the works of the Buddhist Idealistic School, their accomplishments would surely have been greater, and if they could have understood Meditation Buddhism, their accomplishments would have been still greater.

Just think. Weren't the pre-Ch'in philosophers and the great masters of the Sui and the T'ang eras our loving and sagely ancestors who have left us a great heritage? We, being corrupted, do not know how to enjoy them and, today we suffer intellectual starvation. Even in literature, art, and the rest, should we yield to others? Of course we may laugh at those old folks among us who block their own road of advancement and claim that we Chinese have all that is found in Western learning. But should we not laugh even more at those who are drunk with Western ways and regard everything Chinese as worthless, as though we in the last several hundred years have remained primitive and have achieved nothing? We should realize that any system of thought must have its own period as the background. What we need to learn is the essential spirit of that system and not the conditions under which it was produced, for once we come

[186]

to the conditions, we shall not be free from the restrictions of time. For example, Confucius said a great deal about ethics of an aristocratic nature which is certainly not suitable today. But we should not take Confucius lightly simply because of this. Shall we cast Plato aside simply because he said that the slavery system should be preserved? If we understand this point, we can study traditional Chinese subjects with impartial judgment and accept or reject them judiciously.

There is another very important matter. If we want to expand our civilization, we must borrow the methods of other civilizations because their methods of study are highly refined. [As Confucius said]: "If one wants a job well done, he must first sharpen his tools." [24] For what other reason was it [than the failure to do this] that while everyone in the past read Confucius and Li Po, no one got anywhere? I therefore hope that our dear young people will, first of all, have a sincere purpose of respecting and protecting our civilization; secondly, that they will apply Western methods to the study of our civilization and discover its true character; thirdly, that they will put our own civilization in order and supplement it with others' so that it will be transformed and become a new civilization; and fourthly, that they will extend this new civilization to the outside world so that it can benefit the whole human race.

LIANG SHU-MING
Eastern and Western Civilizations and Their Philosophies

At a time when Confucianism was being decried everywhere as decadent and outmoded, Liang Shu-ming, originally a Buddhist scholar, caused a stir by his conversion to Confucianism (as represented by the school of Wang Yang-ming). After examining Indian and Western philiosophies, he boldly declared that the future world civilization would be a reconstructed Chinese civilization. Though not unappreciative of certain Western values, such as individualism and science, which he hoped China might some day embrace in a synthesis with her own humanistic values, Liang condemned wholesale imitation of the West as impractical and undesirable. Moreover, unlike conservatives who were tempted to think that modern methods might be employed to defend traditional society, Liang was a genuine traditionalist, ready to dispense with both modernity and the status quo in Chinese society, where these proved incompatible with his Confucian ideals.

[24] *Analects*, XV:9.

According to Liang, the underlying bases of Western democracy—material, social, and spiritual—were totally lacking in China and quite foreign to the Chinese spirit. Consequently political democracy of the Western type could not possibly succeed there. Reformers and revolutionaries who tried arbitrarily to superimpose Western institutions on China failed to recognize the essentially rural and agrarian character of Chinese society. A sound program of reconstruction, Liang believed, could start only at the grass roots and slowly evolve a new socialist society, avoiding the excesses of both capitalism and communism.

To promote such reconstruction of agriculture and rural life, Liang founded an Institute of Rural Reconstruction and a political party, the National Socialists. He became an outspoken critic of the Nationalist regime, and equally so of the Communists later, being one of the few intellectuals who refused to confess his ideological errors.

[From *Tung-hsi wen-hua chi ch'i che-hsüeh*, pp. 54–202]

There are three ways in human life: 1) to go forward; 2) to modify and to achieve harmony, synthesis, and the mean in the self; and 3) to go backward. . . . The fundamental spirit of Chinese culture is the harmony and moderation of ideas and desires, whereas that of Indian civilization is to go backward in ideas and desires [and that of the West is to go forward]. [pp. 54–55]

Generally speaking, Westerners have been too strong and too vigorous in their minds and intellect. Because of this they have suffered spiritually. This is an undeniable fact since the nineteenth century. [p. 63]

Let us first compare Western culture with Chinese culture. First, there is the conquest of nature on the material side of Western culture—this China has none of. Second, there is the scientific method on the intellectual side of Western culture—this also China has none of. And thirdly, there is democracy on the social side of Western culture—this, too, China has none of. . . . This shows negatively that the way of Chinese culture is not that of the West but the second way [mentioned above, namely: achieving the mean]. . . . As to Indian culture . . . religion alone has flourished, subordinating to it philosophy, literature, science, and art. The three aspects of life [material, intellectual, and social] have become an abnormal spiritual development, and spiritual life itself has been an almost purely religious development. This is really most extraordinary. Indian culture has traveled its own way, different from that of the West. Needless to say, it is not the same as that of Chinese culture. [pp. 64–66]

In this respect Chinese culture is different from that of India, because of the weakness of religion as we have already said. For this reason, there is not much to be said about Chinese religions. The most important thing in Chinese culture is its metaphysics, which is applicable everywhere. . . . Chinese metaphysics is different from that of the West and India. It is different in its problems. . . . The problems discussed in the ancient West and ancient India have in fact not existed in China. While the problems of the West and India are not really identical, still they are the same in so far as the search for the reality of the universe is concerned. Where they are the same is exactly where they are decidedly different from China. Have you heard of Chinese philosophers debating monism, dualism, or pluralism, or idealism and materialism? The Chinese do not discuss such static problems of tranquil reality. The metaphysics handed down from the greatest antiquity in China, which constituted the fundamental concept of all learning—great and small, high and low—is that completely devoted to the discussion of change, which is entirely nontranquil in reality. [pp. 114–15]

The first point of the Confucian philosophy of life arising out of this type of Chinese metaphysics is that life is right and good. Basically, this metaphysics speaks in terms of "the life of the universe." Hence it is said that "Change means reproduction and reproduction." [25] Confucius said many things to glorify life, like "The great characteristic of Heaven and earth is to give life," [26] and "Does Heaven speak? All the four seasons pursue their course and all things are continually being produced" [27] . . . . Human life is the reality of a great current. It naturally tends toward the most suitable and the most satisfactory. It responds to things as they come. This is change. It spontaneously arrives at centrality, harmony, and synthesis. Hence its response is always right. This is the reason why the Confucian school said: "What Heaven has conferred is what we call human nature. To fulfill the law of human nature is what we call the Way." [28] As long as one fulfills his nature, it will be all right. This is why it is said that it can be understood and put into practice even by men and women of the simplest intelligence. This knowledge and ability are what Mencius called the knowledge possessed by man without deliberation and

[25] *Book of Changes, Hsi tz'u* I, ch. 5; Legge, *Yi King,* p. 356.
[26] *Book of Changes, Hsi tz'u* II, ch. 1; Legge, p. 381.
[27] *Analects,* XVII:19.   [28] *The Mean,* ch. 1.

the ability possessed by him without having been acquired by learning.[29] Today we call it intuition. [pp. 121–25]

This sharp intuition is what Confucius called *jen* [humanity]. . . . Therefore Confucius taught people to "seek *jen*."[30] All human virtues come out of this intuition. . . . Only sharp intuition can enable man to be just right and good in his conduct, and *jen* can produce such a sharp intuition in the highest degree. *Jen* is the substance (*t'i*) and sharp intuition is the function (*yung*). . . . All that Confucianists have sought is a life that is just right. A life that is just right does not consist in rigidly following one particular objective law but in being natural and always achieving the right measure and degree [that is, the mean]. To be rigid surely cannot be just right, and its greatest harm is to hamper the inward springs of life and to violate the law of nature. The Confucianists have believed that a life that is just right is the most natural and most consonant with the changes of the universe—what Confucius called the "operation of the natural law." In this natural change, there is always centrality and harmony. [pp. 126–29]

Clearly, contemporary Western thinkers demand a change in the traditional Western view of life. The tendency they seek is precisely the path of China, the path of Confucianism [namely, intuition or the Confucian *jen*]. . . . The forward path of the West has been entirely devoted to the search for the external, completely casting aside the self and destroying the spirit, so that while the external life is rich and beautiful, the internal life is empty to the point of zero. Therefore Westerners now unanimously make a strenuous effort to rid themselves of the narrow and oppressive world which reason and intellection have imposed on them. . . . In the present world, intuition will rise to replace intellection. [pp. 177–78]

What attitude should we Chinese hold now? What should we select from the three cultures? We may say:

1. We must reject the Indian attitude absolutely and completely.

2. We must accept Western culture as a whole [including conquest of nature, science, and democracy] but make some fundamental changes. That is to say, we must change the Western attitude somewhat [from intellection to intuition].

3. We must renew our Chinese attitude and bring it to the fore, but do so critically. [p. 202]

[29] *Mencius*, VII A:15.   [30] *Analects*, VII:14.

The attitude I want to recommend is what Confucius called "strength." . . . What I ask now is nothing more than our going forward to act, and that activity at its best should issue directly from our feelings. . . . When Confucius said that "to be strong, resolute, simple, and slow in speech is near to humanity," [31] he revealed the nobility of the will of the individual and the richness of our feelings. [pp. 211–13]

HU SHIH
Our Attitude Toward Modern Western Civilization

The most surprising rejoinder to the critics of the West came from Hu Shih, who defended the "materialistic" West on the ground that it was indeed more spiritual than China.
[From *Hu Shih wen-ts'un*, Collection III, Ch. 1, pp. 1–13]

At present the most unfounded and most harmful distortion is to ridicule Western civilization as materialistic and worship Eastern civilization as spiritual. . . . Modern civilization of the West, built on the foundation of the search for human happiness, not only has definitely increased material enjoyment to no small degree, but can also definitely satisfy the spiritual demands of mankind. In philosophy it has applied highly refined methods unceasingly to the search for truth and to investigation into the vast secrets of nature. In religion and ethics, it has overthrown the religion of superstitions and established a rational belief, has destroyed divine power and established a humanistic religion, has discarded the unknowable Heaven or Paradise and directed its efforts to building a paradise among men and Heaven on earth. It has cast aside the arbitrarily asserted transcendence of the individual soul, has utilized to the highest degree the power of man's new imagination and new intellect to promote a new religion and new ethics that is fully socialized, and has endeavored to work for the greatest amount of happiness for the greatest number of people.

The most outstanding characteristic of Eastern civilization is to know contentment, whereas that of Western civilization is not to know contentment.

Contented Easterners are satisfied with their simple life and therefore

[31] *Analects*, XVII:23.

do not seek to increase their material enjoyment. They are satisfied with ignorance and with "not understanding and not knowing" [32] and therefore have devoted no attention to the discovery of truth and the invention of techniques and machinery. They are satisfied with their present lot and environment and therefore do not want to conquer nature but merely be at home with nature and at peace with their lot. They do not want to change systems but rather to mind their own business. They do not want a revolution, but rather to remain obedient subjects.

The civilization under which people are restricted and controlled by a material environment from which they cannot escape, and under which they cannot utilize human thought and intellectual power to change environment and improve conditions, is the civilization of a lazy and nonprogressive people. It is truly a materialistic civilization. Such civilization can only obstruct but cannot satisfy the spiritual demands of mankind.

SA MENG-WU, HO PING-SUNG, AND OTHERS
Declaration for Cultural Construction on a Chinese Basis (1935)

The increasing pace of Westernization in the early '30s, especially in the universities, prompted further expressions of fear that Chinese culture might be wholly submerged. This declaration by ten university professors in the magazine *Cultural Construction* deplored the prevailing trend and, in the general vein of Liang Ch'i-ch'ao and Liang Shu-ming, called for a synthesis of Chinese and Western cultures which would nevertheless be distinctively Chinese. Vague though this syncretism was, it attracted enough attention throughout the country so that Hu Shih felt compelled to protest, as he did in the piece which follows the declaration here, this kind of "conservatism . . . hiding under the smoke-screen of compromise."

[From "Chung-kuo pen-wei ti wen-hua chien-she hsüan-yen," in *Wenhua chien-she*, Vol. 1, No. 4 (January 1935), pp. 3–5]

Some people think we should return to the past. But ancient China is already history, and history cannot and need not be repeated. Others believe that China should completely imitate England and the United States. These viewpoints have their special merits. But China, which is neither England nor the United States, should have her own distinctive characteristics. Furthermore, China is now passing from an agricultural feudal society to an industrial society, and is in a different situation from

[32] *Book of Odes,* Ta ya, Wen wang 7.

England and the United States, which have been completely industrialized. We therefore definitely oppose complete imitation of them. Besides the proponents of imitating England and the United States, there are two other schools of thought, one advocating imitation of Soviet Russia, the other, of Italy and Germany. But they make the same mistake as those promoting the imitation of England and the United States; they likewise ignore the special spatial and temporal characteristics of China. . . .

We demand a cultural construction on the Chinese basis. In the process of reconstruction, we should realize that:

1. China is China, not just any geographical area, and therefore has her own spatial characteristics. At the same time, China is the China of today, not the China of the past, and has her own temporal characteristics. We therefore pay special attention to the needs of here and now. The necessity to do so is the foundation of the Chinese basis.

2. It is useless merely to glorify ancient Chinese systems and thought. It is equally useless to curse them. We must examine our heritage, weed out what should be weeded out, and preserve what should be preserved. Those good systems and great doctrines which are worthy of praise should be brought to greater light with all our might and be presented to the whole world, while evil systems and inferior thoughts which are worthy of condemnation should be totally eliminated without the slightest regret.

3. It is right and necessary to absorb Western culture. But we should absorb what is worth absorbing and not, with the attitude of total acceptance, absorb its dregs also.

4. Cultural construction on the Chinese basis is a creative endeavor, one that is pushing ahead. Its objective is to enable China and the Chinese, who are backward and have lost their unique qualities in the cultural sphere, not only to keep pace with other countries and peoples, but also to make valuable contributions to a world culture.

5. To construct China in the cultural sphere is not to abandon the idea of the world as a Grand Unity. Rather, it is first to reconstruct China and make her a strong and complete unit so that she may have adequate strength to push forward the Grand Unity of the world.

Essentially speaking, China must have both self-recognition and a world perspective, and must have neither any idea of seclusion nor any determination to imitate blindly. Such recognition is profound and precise recognition. Proceeding on such recognition, our cultural reconstruction should be: Not to adhere to the past, nor to imitate blindly, but to stand on the Chinese basis, keep a critical attitude, apply the scientific method, examine the past, hold on to the present, and create the future.

HU SHIH

Criticism of the "Declaration for Cultural Construction on a Chinese Basis" (1935)
[From *Hu Shih wen-ts'un,* Collection IV, Ch. 4, pp. 535–40]

At the beginning of the year ten professors, Sa Meng-wu, Ho Ping-sung, et al., issued a declaration on "cultural construction on a Chinese basis." Considerable popular attention in the country has been attracted to it in the last several months. . . . I can't help pointing out that while the ten professors repeatedly uttered the phrase "Chinese basis" and while they declared in so many words that they were "not conservatives," in reality it is their conservative thinking that has been fooling them. The declaration is a most fashionable expression of a reactionary mood prevalent today. Of course, it is out of fashion for people conscientiously to advocate returning to the past and therefore their conservative thinking takes refuge under the smoke-screen of compromise. With respect to indigenous culture, the professors advocated discarding the dregs and preserving the essence, and with respect to the new culture of the world they advocated accepting the good and rejecting the bad and selecting what is best. This is the most fashionable tune of compromise. . . .

The fundamental error of Professors Sa, Ho, and others lies in their failure to understand the nature of cultural change. . . . Culture itself is conservative. . . . When two different cultures come into contact, the force of competition and comparison can partially destroy the resistance and conservatism of a certain culture. . . . In this process of survival of the fittest, there is no absolutely reliable standard by which to direct the selection from the various aspects of a culture. In this gigantic cultural movement, the "scientific method" the ten professors dream of does not work. . . . There is always a limit to violent change in the various spheres of culture, namely, that it can never completely wipe out the conservative nature of an indigenous culture. This is the "Chinese basis" the destruction of which has been feared by numerous cautious people of the past as well as the present. This indigenous basis is found in the life and habits produced by a certain indigenous environment and history. Simply stated, it is the people—all the people. This *is* the "basis." There is no danger that this basis will be destroyed. No matter how radically the material existence has changed, how much intellectual systems have altered, and how much political systems have been transformed, the Japanese are still Japanese and the Chinese are still Chinese. . . . The ten professors need not worry about the "Chinese basis". . . . Those of us who are forward looking should humbly accept the scientific and technological world culture and the spiritual civilization behind it. . . . There is no doubt that in the future the crystallization of this great change will, of course, be a culture on the "Chinese basis."

CHAPTER XXV

CHINESE COMMUNISM

On the surface Chinese Communism would seem to have little to do with Chinese tradition. From the outset—from the Party's founding in 1921 under the leadership of the iconoclast Ch'en Tu-hsiu—it has been blatantly hostile to Confucian tradition and unashamedly committed to violent overthrow of the old order. Mao Tse-tung too, though he has recognized a kind of native tradition in the peasant rebellions and popular "revolutionary" literature of earlier dynasties, has not thereby acknowledged any debt to the past. For him, recurrent rebellions showed only how the Chinese masses had suffered and protested. They did not show a way out of the historical impasse: the constant re-establishment of dynasticism and warlordism after futile outbursts of popular discontent.

For such an abortive revolutionary tradition Mao could feel pity, but if any lesson was to be learned—and this was Mao's real point—it was the uniqueness of Marxism-Leninism and of the victory which the Communist Party alone had been able to achieve over such an oppressive past. Where earlier failures demonstrated only the need for something totally new to break a deadlock which had spelled frustration and stagnation for all, the ideology and organization of Communism had for the first time given China a revolution worthy of the name.

Yet if, in Communist eyes, the successful Chinese revolution has been so peculiarly a product of superior Marxist science and leadership, Chinese Communism has been also, in the perspective of history, an unmistakable product of the Chinese revolution. For almost a century this revolution had been in the making—perhaps even for longer, if it is taken as part of a much older process, as the latest issue from the ancient womb of dynastic change. But conjoined to the familiar processes of dynastic decay, which might have led to a rebellion typical of the past, was a world revolution of which Communism itself must be considered only one manifestation, a world revolution which, long before Ch'en Tu-hsiu and a handful of intellectuals met to launch the Communist Revolution, had already effected far-reaching and fundamental changes in the Chinese way of life.

It is not our purpose here to assess the forces and factors which contributed to the triumph of Communism in China. The circumstances in which the Party took its rise, however, have a bearing on the relation between Communism and the Chinese tradition. By 1921 the course of revolutionary change was already well advanced. Not only had the Manchu dynasty fallen, but every attempt to restore the old monarchical and dynastic system had met with insuperable resistance. If, therefore, the republican era still looked much like earlier periods of warlordism and decentralization, the possibility had nevertheless vanished of this phase yielding eventually and inexorably to another period of dynastic rule.

With it, however, had not vanished the need for a government strong enough to serve the same purposes—and more: to cope with the enormous problems of China's adjustment to the modern world. In the answers to that need proposed by Sun Yat-sen, anti-Marxist though he was, it is not difficult to discern tendencies with a close affinity to Communism. Whatever Dr. Sun's own intentions, the popularity of his People's Principles (which went almost unchallenged from either Left or Right long after his death) helped create an atmosphere conducive to the acceptance of Communist aims: the People's Livelihood or Socialism, of a state-controlled economy; the People's Rule or Democracy as Sun interpreted it, of rule by a party elite under a strong leader; and Nationalism as adapted by Sun to the Leninist struggle against colonialism, of hostility to and suspicion of the West.

While republican politics floundered in a sea of warlordism and economic dislocation, the estrangement of Chinese intellectuals from traditional ideals and institutions deepened. This process, which began with concessions to Westernization by even would-be defenders of Confucianism, had reached a climax well before the republican revolution with the abandonment of the traditional curriculum for the civil service, long the institutional stronghold of Confucian ideology. If a new political elite were ever to regain the power of the old centralized bureaucracy, it was as unlikely to consist of Confucian scholar-officials as the regime itself was to take the form of monarchy. Instead now of intellectuals serving as defenders of tradition, they had become its most implacable critics. Thus Confucianism had not only lost its bureaucratic function, but even the basis of its intellectual life.

As we have seen in the preceding chapter, the dominant trend of thought in the New Culture Movement was toward Westernization. This was expressed in certain general attitudes which won increasing acceptance among the educated and especially among the younger generation: 1) positivism, as a belief in the value and universal applicability of methods of inquiry developed for the natural sciences; 2) pragmatism, in the sense that the validity of an idea was to be judged primarily by its effectiveness; and 3) materialism, especially as a denial of traditional religious and ethical systems. While each of these attitudes might be held by as liberal a scholar and as eloquent an anti-Communist as Hu Shih, for many others they represented transitional stages on a road that led naturally and easily to Communism—to an acceptance of Marxism as the science of society, of Leninism as the effective method for achieving social revolution, and of dialectical materialism as a philosophy of life.

More than any such intellectual trends, however, what created a receptivity to revolutionary change among the Chinese people as a whole were attitudes of a more general and pervasive character. First among these was the desire for and expectation of a better life, which the material progress of the West had seemed to bring within hope of realization. Second was a new view of history as dominated by forces which would either crush those who fell behind or guarantee a bright future to those who understood and utilized them. Third was the prevailing frustration over China's failure to keep pace with these forces and to fulfill the high expectations of her modern political prophets.

Each of these attitudes contributed to a climate of opinion which called for wholesale change, and in which nothing that was not "revolutionary" could hope to arouse popular enthusiasm. Of this the revolutionary aims of the Kuomintang itself are an eloquent example. But more instructive for present purposes is the inability of the Kuomintang to win support for its brand of revolution from precisely those intellectuals who helped form the minds of the educated elite. We have already seen how quick Western-educated and "liberal-minded" Chinese were to find fault with the Nationalist regime for its failure to exemplify liberal principles and establish political democracy. Yet toward the Communists, whose political aims were still more authoritarian and totalitarian, these same "liberals" sometimes showed far more indulgence. In the revolutionary context of the times it was not difficult for the Communists to gain acceptance as fellow "progressives"—a little extreme perhaps, but nonetheless devoted to the cause of social and economic revolution, to science and technological progress, and above all to the total destruction of the old order.

Yet it was in a more fundamental sense than this that Westernized intellectuals and the exponents of modern Western philosophies helped prepare the way for Communism. Hu Shih had joined hands with Ch'en Tu-hsiu in the attack on traditional values, but nothing pragmatism had to offer in the way of scientific analyses or solutions to the specific problems of modern Chinese society proved intelligible or acceptable to the great masses of Chinese as a substitute for the old value system. Thus if the weakening of traditional ethics did not leave an actual vacuum for Communist doctrine to fill, still the materialistic and utilitarian tendencies of the time offered little resistance to, and could easily be exploited by, the new dogmatism.

Having considered, in an admittedly cursory and no doubt too sweeping fashion, some points in the development of modern Chinese thought from which Chinese Communism took its departure, we shall defer an assessment of its relation to Chinese tradition until the general aims and principles of the movement have been examined. In the selections which follow the presentation of these aims and principles is guided by two basic criteria, which it would be well to keep in mind. First, since this is not intended as a documentary history of Chinese Communism, questions of primarily historical significance are not emphasized. These include questions of strategy and tactics which, though of fundamental importance to an understanding of the Communists' actual rise to power, cannot properly be evaluated except through a more detailed analysis of historical factors than is possible within the scope of this study. Second, this survey centers upon the most important pronouncements of Mao Tse-tung, as the chief exponent of Chinese Communism today. Past leaders and lower-ranking spokesmen are included only where they give expression to ideas that have a significance beyond the importance of their expositors.

Within these limitations the readings attempt to answer the following basic questions:

1. What have been the overall aims of the Chinese Communists, aims for which they have succeeded in gaining the support of both Party members and Chinese outside the Party?

2. In what light have Chinese Communists interpreted their own relation to China's past history and traditions?

3. What are the philosophical premises upon which Communist doctrine claims to be based?

4. What are the ideological factors most vital to the actual practice of Chinese Communism; in other words, what are the basic elements of Communist discipline?

THE NATURE OF THE COMMUNIST REVOLUTION

In this section are presented readings which attempt to answer the first two questions above. They are meant to suggest the overall character and significance of the Communist revolution as its leaders have interpreted them to the Chinese people as a whole. In a second section the theoretical bases of party indoctrination and discipline, directed primarily to the party elite, will be set forth.

LI TA-CHAO
The Victory of Bolshevism

Li Ta-chao (1888–1927) was a Peking University professor and librarian who joined in the intellectual ferment which found expression in Ch'en Tu-hsiu's *New Youth* magazine. He exerted an especially profound influence on his student and library assistant, the youthful Mao Tse-tung. Marxism had attracted comparatively little attention among Chinese, until the success of the October revolution inspired Li to hail it enthusiastically in this article for the November 15 issue of the *New Youth* in 1918. Thereafter he launched a Marxist study club from which recruits were drawn for the founding of the Communist Party in 1921. One of the co-founders of the Party, along with Ch'en Tu-hsiu, Li later was captured in a raid on the Soviet Embassy compound in Peking and executed. Since Ch'en, the original chairman of the

Party, was subsequently expelled and disowned by it, Li came to be honored in his place and to be revered posthumously as the Party's founding father.

Although not yet a convinced Marxist at this time, in this article Li bespeaks a widespread feeling of hope and expectation aroused by the Bolshevik revolution among Chinese bitterly disappointed in the outcome of the Chinese revolution of 1911. Note how he specifically acclaims it as a new and potent religion offering messianic hope for the future.

[From Teng and Fairbank, *China's Response to the West*, pp. 246–49]

"Victory! Victory! The Allies have been victorious! Surrender! Surrender! Germany has surrendered!" These words are on the national flag bedecking every doorway, they can be seen in color and can be indistinctly heard in the intonation of every voice. . . .

But let us think carefully as small citizens of the world, to whom exactly does the present victory belong? Who has really surrendered? Whose is the achievement this time? And for whom do we celebrate? . . .

For the real cause of the ending of the war was not the vanquishing of the German military power by the Allied military power, but the vanquishing of German militarism by German socialism. . . . The victory over German militarism does not belong to the Allied nations; even less does it belong to our factious military men who used participation in the war only as an excuse [for engaging in civil war], or to our opportunistic, cunningly manipulative politicians. It is the victory of humanitarianism, of pacifism; it is the victory of justice and liberty; it is the victory of democracy; it is the victory of socialism; it is the victory of Bolshevism [Chinese text inserts "Hohenzollern" by error]; it is the victory of the red flag; it is the victory of the labor class of the world; and it is the victory of the twentieth century's new tide. Rather than give Wilson and others the credit for this achievement, we should give the credit to Lenin [these names are inserted in English], Trotsky, Collontay [Alexandra Kollontai], to Liebknecht, Scheidemann, and to Marx . . .

Bolshevism is the ideology of the Russian Bolsheviki. What kind of ideology is it? It is very difficult to explain it clearly in one sentence. If we look for the origin of the word, we see that it means "majority." An English reporter once asked Collontay, a heroine in that [Bolshevik] party, what the meaning of "Bolsheviki" was. The heroine answered . . . "Its meaning will be clear only if one looks at what they are doing." According to the explanation given by this heroine, then, "Bolsheviki means only what they are doing." But from the fact that this heroine had called herself a Revolutionary Socialist in western Europe, and a Bolshevika in eastern Europe, and from the things they have done, it is clear that their ideology is revolutionary socialism; their party is a revolutionary socialist party; and they follow the German socialist economist Marx as the founder of their doctrine. Their aim is to destroy the national boundaries which are obstacles to socialism at present, and to destroy the system of production in which profit is monopolized by the capitalist. Indeed, the real cause of this war was also the destruction of national boundaries. Since the present national boundaries cannot contain the expansion of the system of production brought about by capitalism, and since the resources within each nation are inadequate for the expansion of its productive power, the capitalist nations all began depending on war to break down these boundaries, hoping to make of all parts of the globe one single, coordinated economic organ.

So far as the breaking down of national boundaries is concerned, the socialists are of the same opinion with them. But the purpose of the capitalist governments in this matter is to enable the middle class in their countries to gain benefits; they rely on world economic development by one class in the victor nations, and not on mutual cooperation among humanitarian, reasonable organizations of the producers of the world. This war will cause such a victor nation to advance from the position of a great power to that of a world empire. The Bolsheviki saw through this point; therefore they vigorously protested and proclaimed that the present war is a war of the tsar, of the kaiser, of kings and emperors, that it is a war of capitalist governments, but it is not their war. Theirs is the war of classes, a war of all the world's proletariat and common people against the capitalists of the world. While they are opposed to war itself, they are at the same time not afraid of it. They hold that all men and women should work. All those who work should join a union, and there should be a central administrative soviet in each union. Such soviets then should organize all the governments of the world. There will be no congress, no parliament, no president, no prime minister, no cabinet, no legislature, and no ruler. There will be only the joint soviets of labor, which will decide all matters. All enterprises will belong to those who work therein, and aside from this no other possessions will be allowed. They will unite the proletariat of the world, and create global freedom with their greatest, strongest power of resistance: first they will create a federation of European democracies, to serve as the foundation of a world federation. This is the ideology of the Bolsheviki. This is the new doctrine of the twentieth-century revolution.

In a report by Harold Williams in the London *Times,* Bolshevism is considered a mass movement. He compares it with early Christianity, and finds two points of similarity: one is enthusiastic partisanship, the other is a tendency to revelation. He says, "Bolshevism is really a kind of mass movement, with characteristics of religion". . . . Not only the Russia of today, but the whole world of the twentieth century probably cannot avoid being controlled by such religious power and swayed by such a mass movement. . . .

Whenever a disturbance in this worldwide social force occurs among the people, it will produce repercussions all over the earth, like storm clouds gathering before the wind and valleys echoing the mountains. In the course of such a world mass movement, all those dregs of history which can impede the progress of the new movement—such as emperors, nobles, warlords, bureaucrats, militarism, capitalism—will certainly be destroyed as though struck by a thunderbolt. Encountering this irresistible tide, these things will be swept away one by one. . . . Henceforth, all that one sees around him will be the triumphant banner of Bolshevism, and all that one hears around him will be Bolshevism's song of victory. The bell is rung for humanitarianism! The dawn of freedom has arrived! See the world of tomorrow; it assuredly will belong to the red flag! . . . The revolution in Russia is but the first fallen leaf warning the world of the approach of autumn. Although the word "Bolshevism" was created by the Russians, the spirit it embodies can be regarded as that of a common awakening in the heart of each individual among mankind of the twentieth century. The victory of Bolshevism, therefore, is the victory of the spirit of common awakening in the heart of each individual among mankind in the twentieth century.

MAO TSE-TUNG
Report on an Investigation of the Hunan Peasant Movement

Under the early leadership of Ch'en Tu-hsiu the Chinese Communist Party followed a policy of collaboration with the Kuomintang dictated by the

Comintern. Since this ended in near-disaster for the Party in 1927 and brought about Ch'en's fall from leadership, Ch'en's writings and ideas do not figure prominently today in the orthodox tradition of Chinese Communist doctrine. By contrast this report on the Hunan Peasant movement by Mao Tse-tung (1893—), who was then of much less importance in the Party hierarchy, has, since his rise to supremacy, come to be regarded as a document of the greatest significance to the development of the revolution.

After taking part in the formation of the Communist Party, Mao had been assigned in 1925 to the organizing of peasants in his native Hunan, where he became convinced of the enormous revolutionary potential of the peasantry. In this report, prepared early in 1927, Mao describes the methods used by the peasant associations, and reveals with undisguised satisfaction the campaign of terror waged against local landlords and officials. These terror tactics became an essential feature of Mao's systematic program of class warfare in areas taken over by the Red Army. Such a condoning of extremism is contrary to the dominant strain in Chinese thought, which favors moderation, compromise, and harmony, but has ample precedent in Chinese political practice and in peasant revolutions like the Taiping Movement. Curiously enough, among the great deeds of the peasants which Mao lists (including the organizing of peasants' associations and cooperatives, tax reduction, price control, etc.) we find prohibitions on gambling, opium smoking, feasting, and wine-drinking, which reflect the strain of native puritanism already encountered in the Taipings.

More significant, in view of the later importance attached to the land problem, is Mao's failure to say anything about the confiscation and redistribution of land among the poor peasants. This period he describes was one of collaboration with the Kuomintang, and the tactics pursued were limited by the Comintern's desire not to offend Kuomintang sensibilities on the question of land expropriation. Mao, concurrently a Kuomintang party official (for a time chief of its Agitprop department and candidate for the Kuomintang Central Committee), was also careful to avoid such offense in writing this report. On the other hand, there is ample evidence, in the passages which follow, of Mao's remarkable capacity to see things through the eyes of the peasant.

[From *Selected Works of Mao Tse-tung*, I, 21–57]

THE IMPORTANCE OF THE PEASANT PROBLEM

During my recent visit to Hunan [1] I conducted an investigation on the spot into the conditions in the five counties of Siangtan, Siangsiang, Hengshan, Liling, and Changsha. In the thirty-two days from January 4 to February 5, in villages and in county towns, I called together for fact-finding conferences experienced peasants and comrades working for the

---

[1] Hunan was then the storm-center of the peasant movement in China. Unless otherwise noted, footnotes in these selections are from the official text. [Ed.]

peasant movement, listened attentively to their reports, and collected a lot of material. Many of the hows and whys of the peasant movement were quite the reverse of what I had heard from the gentry in Hankow and Changsha. And many strange things there were that I had never seen or heard before. I think these conditions exist in many other places.

All kinds of arguments against the peasant movement must be speedily set right. The erroneous measures taken by the revolutionary authorities concerning the peasant movement must be speedily changed. Only thus can any good be done for the future of the revolution. For the rise of the present peasant movement is a colossal event. In a very short time, in China's central, southern, and northern provinces, several hundred million peasants will rise like a tornado or tempest, a force so extraordinarily swift and violent that no power, however great, will be able to suppress it. They will break all trammels that now bind them and rush forward along the road to liberation. They will send all imperialists, warlords, corrupt officials, local bullies, and bad gentry to their graves. All revolutionary parties and all revolutionary comrades will stand before them to be tested, and to be accepted or rejected as they decide.

To march at their head and lead them? Or to follow at their rear, gesticulating at them and criticising them? Or to face them as opponents?

Every Chinese is free to choose among the three alternatives, but circumstances demand that a quick choice be made. [pp. 21–22]

DOWN WITH THE LOCAL BULLIES AND BAD GENTRY!

All Power to the Peasant Association!

The peasants attack as their main targets the local bullies and bad gentry and the lawless landlords, hitting in passing against patriarchal ideologies and institutions, corrupt officials in the cities, and evil customs in the rural areas. In force and momentum, the attack is like a tempest or hurricane; those who submit to it survive and those who resist it perish. As a result, the privileges which the feudal landlords have enjoyed for thousands of years are being shattered to pieces. The dignity and prestige of the landlords are dashed to the ground. With the fall of the authority of the landlords, the peasant association becomes the sole organ of authority, and what people call "All power to the peasant association" has come to pass. Even such a trifle as a quarrel between man and wife has to be settled at the peasant association. Nothing can be settled in the absence of people from the association. The association is actually dictating in all matters in the countryside, and it is literally true that "whatever it says, goes." The public can only praise the association and must not condemn it. The local bullies and bad gentry and the lawless landlords have been totally deprived of the right to have their say, and no one dares mutter the word "No." To be safe from the power and pressure of the peasant association, the first-rank local bullies and bad gentry fled to Shanghai, the second-rank ones to Hankow, the third-rank ones to Changsha, and the fourth-rank ones and even lesser fry can only remain in the countryside and surrender to the peasant association.

"I'll donate ten dollars, please admit me to the peasant association," one of the smaller gentry would say.

"Pshaw! Who wants your filthy money!" the peasants would reply.

Many middle and small landlords, rich peasants and middle peasants, formerly opposed to the peasant association, now seek admission in vain. Visiting various places, I often came across such people, who solicited my help. "I beg," they would say, "the committeeman from the provincial capital to be my guarantor."

The census book compiled by the local authorities under the Manchu regime consisted of a regular register and a special register; in the former honest people were entered, and in the latter burglars, bandits, and other undesirables. The peasants in some places now use the same method to threaten people formerly opposed to the association: "Enter them in the special register!"

Such people, afraid of being entered in the special register, try various means to seek admission to the association and do not feel at ease until, as they eagerly desire, their names are entered in its register. But they are as a rule sternly turned down, and so spend their days in a constant state of suspense; barred from the doors of the association, they are like homeless people. In short, what was generally sneered at four months ago as the "peasants' gang" has now become something most honorable. Those who prostrated themselves before the power of the gentry now prostrate themselves before the power of the peasants. Everyone admits that the world has changed since last October.

"AN AWFUL MESS!" AND "VERY GOOD INDEED!"

The revolt of the peasants in the countryside disturbed the sweet dreams of the gentry. When news about the countryside reached the cities, the gentry there immediately burst into an uproar. When I first arrived in Changsha, I met people from various circles and picked up a good deal of street gossip. From the middle strata upwards to the right-wingers of the Kuomintang, there was not a single person who did not summarize the whole thing in one phrase: "An awful mess!" Even quite revolutionary people, carried away by the opinion of the "awful mess" school which prevailed like a storm over the whole city, became downhearted at the very thought of the conditions in the countryside, and could not deny the word "mess." Even very progressive people could only remark: "Indeed a mess, but inevitable in the course of the revolution." In a word, nobody could categorically deny the word "mess."

But the fact is, as stated above, that the broad peasant masses have risen to fulfill their historic mission, that the democratic forces in the rural areas have risen to overthrow the rural feudal power. The patriarchal-feudal class of local bullies, bad gentry, and lawless landlords has formed the basis of autocratic government for thousands of years, the cornerstone of imperialism, warlordism and corrupt officialdom. To overthrow this feudal power is the real objective of the national revolution. What Dr. Sun Yat-sen wanted to do in the forty years he devoted to the national revolution but failed to accomplish, the peasants have accomplished in a few months. This is a marvelous feat which has never been achieved in the last forty or even thousands of years. It is very good indeed. It is not "a mess" at all. It is anything but "an awful mess." [pp. 23–25]

THE QUESTION OF "GOING TOO FAR"

There is another section of people who say: "Although the peasant association ought to be formed, it has gone rather too far in its present actions." This is the opinion of the middle-of-the-roaders. But how do matters stand in reality? True, the peasants do in some ways "act unreasonably" in the countryside. The peasant association, supreme in authority, does not allow the landlords to have their say and makes a clean sweep of all their prestige. This is tantamount to trampling the landlords underfoot after knocking them down. The peasants threaten: "Put you in the special register"; they impose fines on the local bullies and bad gentry and demand contributions; they smash their sedan-chairs. Crowds of people swarm into the homes of the local bullies and bad gentry who oppose the peasant association, slaughtering their pigs and consuming their grain. They may even loll for a minute or two on the ivory beds of the young mesdames and mademoiselles in the families of the bullies and gentry. At the slightest provocation they make arrests, crown the arrested with tall paper-hats, and parade them through the villages: "You bad gentry, now you know who we are!" Doing whatever they like and turning everything upside down, they have even created a kind of terror in the countryside. This is what some people call "going too far," or "going beyond the proper limit to right a wrong," or "really too outrageous."

The opinion of this group, reasonable on the surface, is erroneous at bottom.

First, the things described above have all been the inevitable results of the doings of the local bullies and bad gentry and lawless landlords themselves. For ages these people, with power in their hands, tyrannized over the peasants and trampled them underfoot; that is why the peasants have now risen in such a great revolt. The most formidable revolts and the most serious troubles invariably occur at places where the local bullies and bad gentry and the lawless landlords were the most ruthless in their evil deeds. The peasants' eyes are perfectly discerning. As to who is bad and who is not, who is the most ruthless and who is less so, and who is to be severely punished and who is to be dealt with lightly, the peasants keep perfectly clear accounts and very seldom has there been any discrepancy between the punishment and the crime.

Secondly, a revolution is not the same as inviting people to dinner, or writing an essay, or painting a picture, or doing fancy needlework; it cannot be anything so refined, so calm and gentle, or so mild, kind, courteous, restrained, and magnanimous.[2] A revolution is an uprising, an act of violence whereby one class overthrows another. A rural revolution is a revolution by which the peasantry overthrows the authority of the feudal landlord class. If the peasants do not use the maximum of their strength, they can never overthrow the authority of the landlords which has been deeply rooted for thousands of years. In the rural areas, there must be a great fervent revolutionary upsurge, which alone can arouse hundreds and thousands of the people to form a great force. All the actions mentioned above, labeled as "going too far," are caused by the power of the peasants, generated by a great, fervent, revolutionary upsurge in the countryside. Such actions were quite necessary in the second period of the peasant movement (the period of revolutionary action). In this pe-

[2] These were the virtues of Confucius, as described by one of his disciples.

[208]

riod, it was necessary to establish the absolute authority of the peasants. It was necessary to stop malicious criticisms against the peasant association. It was necessary to overthrow all the authority of the gentry, to knock them down and even trample them underfoot. All actions labeled as "going too far" had a revolutionary significance in the second period. To put it bluntly, it was necessary to bring about a brief reign of terror in every rural area; otherwise one could never suppress the activities of the counter-revolutionaries in the countryside or overthrow the authority of the gentry. To right a wrong it is necessary to exceed the proper limits, and the wrong cannot be righted without the proper limits being exceeded.[3] [pp. 26–27]

VANGUARD OF THE REVOLUTION

The main force in the countryside which has always put up the bitterest fight is the poor peasants. Throughout both the period of underground organization and that of open organization, the poor peasants have fought militantly all along. They accept most willingly the leadership of the Communist Party. They are the deadliest enemies of the local bullies and bad gentry and attack their strongholds without the slightest hesitation. [p. 31]

Without the poor peasants (the "riffraff" as the gentry call them) it would never have been possible to bring about in the countryside the present state of revolution, to overthrow the local bullies and bad gentry, or to complete the democratic revolution. Being the most revolutionary, the poor peasants have won the leadership in the peasant association. . . . This leadership of the poor peasants is absolutely necessary. Without the poor peasants there can be no revolution. To reject them is to reject the revolution. To attack them is to attack the revolution. Their general direction of the revolution has never been wrong. [p. 32]

[3] "Going beyond the proper limit to right a wrong" is an old Chinese phrase. It means that, though the wrong is righted, the proper limit has been exceeded in righting it. This phrase has often been used as a pretext to prevent thorough-going measures and to justify mere patching and tinkering. It implies that the established order of things should not be utterly destroyed, but only certain remedial measures need be introduced for its betterment. Thus it provides a convenient formula for the reformists and the opportunists within the revolutionary ranks. Here Comrade Mao Tse-tung is refuting such people. When he says in the text "To right a wrong, we must go beyond the proper limit; otherwise the wrong cannot be righted," he means that mass revolutionary measures, not reformist-revisionist measures, must be taken to end the old feudal order.

A man in China is usually subjected to the domination of three systems of
authority: 1) the system of the state (political authority), ranging from
the national, provincial, and county government to the township government; 2) the system of the clan (clan authority), ranging from the central and branch ancestral temples to the head of the household; and 3) the
system of gods and spirits (theocratic authority), including the system of
the nether world ranging from the King of Hell to the city gods and local
deities, and that of supernatural beings ranging from the Emperor of
Heaven to all kinds of gods and spirits. As to women, apart from being
dominated by the three systems mentioned above, they are further dominated by men (the authority of the husband). These four kinds of authority—political authority, clan authority, theocratic authority, and the
authority of the husband—represent the whole ideology and institution
of feudalism and patriarchy, and are the four great cords that have bound
the Chinese people and particularly the peasants. We have already seen
how the peasants are overthrowing the political authority of the landlords in the countryside. The political authority of the landlords is the
backbone of all other systems of authority. Where it has already been
overthrown, clan authority, theocratic authority, and the authority of the
husband are all beginning to totter. Where the peasant association is
powerful, the clan elders and administrators of temple funds no longer
dare oppress members of the clan or embezzle the funds. The bad clan
elders and administrators have been overthrown as local bullies and bad
gentry. No ancestral temple dare any longer, as it used to do, inflict cruel
corporal and capital punishments like "beating," "drowning," and "bury-
ing alive." The old rule that forbids women and poor people to attend
banquets in the ancestral temple has also been broken. On one occasion the
women of Paikwo, Hengshan, marched into their ancestral temple, sat
down on the seats and ate and drank, while the grand patriarchs could
only look on. At another place the poor peasants, not admitted to the
banquets in the temples, swarmed in and ate and drank their fill, while
the frightened local bullies, bad gentry, and gentlemen in long gowns
all took to their heels.

Theocratic authority begins to totter everywhere as the peasant movement develops. In many places the peasant associations have taken over the temples of the gods as their offices. Everywhere they advocate the appropriation of temple properties to maintain peasant schools and to defray association expenses, calling this "public revenue from superstition." Forbidding superstition and smashing idols has become quite the vogue in Liling. In its northern districts the peasants forbade the festival processions in honor of the god of pestilence. There were many idols in the Taoist temple on Fupo hill, Lukow, but they were all piled up in a corner to make room for the district headquarters of the Kuomintang, and no peasant raised any objection. When a death occurs in a family, such practices as sacrifice to the gods, performance of Taoist or Buddhist rites, and offering of sacred lamps are becoming rare. It was Sun Hsiaoshan, the chairman of the peasant association, who proposed all this, so the local Taoist priests bear him quite a grudge. In the Lungfeng Nunnery in the North Third district, the peasants and school teachers chopped up the wooden idols to cook meat. More than thirty idols in the Tungfu Temple in the South district were burnt by the students together with the peasants; only two small idols, generally known as "His Excellency Pao," [4] were rescued by an old peasant who said, "Don't commit a sin!" In places where the power of the peasants is predominant, only the older peasants and the women still believe in gods, while the young and middle-aged peasants no longer do so. Since it is the young and middle-aged peasants who are in control of the peasant association, the movement to overthrow theocratic authority and eradicate superstition is going on everywhere.

As to the authority of the husband, it has always been comparatively weak among the poor peasants, because the poor peasant women, compelled for financial reasons to take more part in manual work than women of the wealthier classes, have obtained more right to speak and more power to make decisions in family affairs. In recent years rural economy has become even more bankrupt and the basic condition for men's domination over women has already been undermined. And now, with

---

[4] Pao Cheng, commonly known as "His Excellency Pao," was once prefect of Kaifeng, capital of the North Sung dynasty (A.D. 960–1127). He was famous in popular legend as an upright official and a fearless, impartial judge who had a knack for passing true judgments on all the cases he tried.

the rise of the peasant movement, women in many places have set out immediately to organize the rural women's association; the opportunity has come for them to lift up their heads, and the authority of the husband is tottering more and more every day. In a word, all feudal and patriarchal ideologies and institutions are tottering as the power of the peasants rises. In the present period, however, the peasants' efforts are concentrated on the destruction of the landlords' political authority. Where the political authority of the landlords is already completely destroyed, the peasants are beginning their attacks in the other three spheres, namely, the clan, the gods, and the relationship between men and women. At present, however, such attacks have only just "begun" and there can be no complete overthrow of the three until after the complete victory of the peasants' economic struggle. Hence at present our task is to guide the peasants to wage political struggles with their utmost strength, so that the authority of the landlords may be thoroughly uprooted. An economic struggle should also be started immediately in order that the land problem and other economic problems of the poor peasants can be completely solved.[5]

The abolition of the clan system, of superstitions, and of inequality between men and women will follow as a natural consequence of victory in political and economic struggles. If we crudely and arbitrarily devote excessive efforts to the abolition of such things, we shall give the local bullies and bad gentry a pretext for undermining the peasant movement by raising such slogans of counter-revolutionary propaganda as "The peasant association does not show piety towards ancestors," "The peasant association abuses the gods and destroys religion," and "The peasant association advocates the community of women." Clear proof has been forthcoming recently at both Siangsiang in Hunan and Yangsin in Hupeh, where the landlords were able to take advantage of peasant opposition to the smashing of idols. The idols were set up by the peasants, and in time they will pull them down with their own hands; there is no need for anybody else prematurely to pull down the idols for them. The agitational line of the Communist Party in such matters should be: "Draw the bow to the full without letting go the arrow, and be on the alert."[6]

---

[5] This one reference to the land problem is missing from the original version and has apparently been added retrospectively to enhance Mao's stature as a prophet of the peasant revolution who early recognized the importance of this problem. [Ed.]

[6] This metaphor of archery is from Mencius. Here it means that while Communists

The idols should be removed by the peasants themselves, and the temples for martyred virgins and the arches for chaste and filial widowed daughters-in-law should likewise be demolished by the peasants themselves; it is wrong for anyone else to do these things for them.

In the countryside I, too, agitated among the peasants for abolishing superstitions. What I said was:

"One who believes in the Eight Characters[7] hopes for good luck; one who believes in geomancy hopes for the beneficial influence of the burial ground.[8] This year the local bullies, bad gentry, and corrupt officials all collapsed within a few months. Is it possible that till a few months ago they were all in good luck and all under the beneficial influence of their burial grounds, while in the last few months they have all of a sudden been in bad luck and their burial grounds all ceased to exert any beneficial influence on them?

"The local bullies and bad gentry jeer at your peasant association, and say: 'How strange! It has become a world of committeemen; look, you can't even go to the latrines without meeting one of them!' Quite true, in the towns and in the villages, the trade unions, the peasant association, the Kuomintang, and the Communist Party all have their committee members—it is indeed a world of committeemen. But is this due to the Eight Characters and the burial grounds? What a strange thing! The Eight Characters of all the poor wretches in the countryside have suddenly changed for the better! And their burial grounds have suddenly started to exert a beneficial influence!

"The gods? They may quite deserve our worship. But if we had no peasant association but only the Emperor Kuan[9] and the Goddess of Mercy, could we have knocked down the local bullies and bad gentry? The gods and goddesses are indeed pitiful; worshiped for hundreds of years, they have not knocked down for you a single local bully or a single one of the bad gentry!

---

hould develop the political consciousness of the peasants to the fullest extent, they hould leave it to the peasants' own initiative to abolish superstitious and other bad practices.

[7] A method of fortune-telling in China by studying the two cyclic characters respectively for the year, month, day, and hour of the birth of a person.

[8] This refers to the superstitious belief that the location of the ancestors' graves exerts influence on the fortunes of the descendants. The geomancer claims that he can tell whether the site and its surroundings are auspicious.

[9] Kuan Yu, a warrior in the epoch of the Three Kingdoms (A.D. 196–264), was widely worshiped by the Chinese as the God of Loyalty and War.

"Now you want to have your rent reduced. I would like to ask: How will you go about it? Believe in the gods, or believe in the peasant association?" These words of mine made the peasants roar with laughter. [pp. 45-49]

CULTURAL MOVEMENT

With the downfall of the power of the landlords in the rural areas, the peasants' cultural movement has begun. And so the peasants, who hitherto bitterly hated the schools, are now zealously organizing evening classes. The "foreign-style schools" were always unpopular with the peasants. In my student days I used to stand up for the "foreign-style schools" when, upon returning to my native place, I found the peasants objecting to them. I was myself identified with the "foreign-style students" and "foreign-style teachers," and always felt that the peasants were somehow wrong. It was during my six months in the countryside in 1925, when I was already a Communist and had adopted the Marxist viewpoint, that I realized I was mistaken and that the peasants' views were right. The teaching materials used in the rural primary schools all dealt with city matters and were in no way adapted to the needs of the rural areas. Besides, the primary school teachers behaved badly towards the peasants, who, far from finding them helpful, grew to dislike them. As a result, the peasants wanted old-style rather than modern schools— "Chinese classes," as they call them, rather than "foreign classes"—and they preferred the masters of the old-style school to the teachers in the primary schools.

Now the peasants are energetically organizing evening classes, which they call peasant schools. Many such schools have been opened and others are being established; on the average there is one school to every township. The peasants are very enthusiastic about establishing such schools, and regard only such schools as their own. The funds for evening classes come from the "public revenue from superstitious practices," the funds of ancestral temples and other kinds of public funds or public property that have been lying idle. The county education boards wanted to use these public funds for establishing primary schools, that is, "foreign-style schools" not adapted to the needs of the peasants, while the peasants wanted to use them for peasant schools; as a result of the dispute, both sides got part of the funds, though in certain places the peasants got the whole. As a result of the growth of the peasant movement, the cultural level of the peasants has risen rapidly. Before long there will be tens of thousands of schools sprouting up in the rural areas throughout the whole province, and that will be something quite different from the futile clamor of the intelligentsia and so-called "educators" for "popular education," which for all their hullabaloo has remained an idle phrase. [pp. 56–57]

The Chinese Revolution and the Chinese Communist Party

Along with *On New Democracy* which appeared soon after it (January, 1940), *The Chinese Revolution and the Chinese Communist Party* (December, 1939) is one of two basic texts prepared by Mao to provide a definitive interpretation of the nature and aims of the revolution. Together they represent an adroit analysis of the Party's situation and the strategy to be pursued in the achievement of its objectives, presented in the simple catechetical style, the vigorous and unadorned prose, which are so characteristic of Mao's direct approach to mass indoctrination.

Much had happened since Mao's early days as a peasant organizer in Hunan, when he had become fired with enthusiasm for the revolutionary potentialities of the peasant masses. The lesson of early defeats and disappointments in Hunan and long experience as a practicing revolutionary leader, both in the Kiangsi Soviet and on the Long March to Yenan, are reflected in Mao's analysis of revolutionary strategy. He had devoted much attention to military matters in the early years at Yenan, and had expressed himself at great length on problems of guerilla warfare, military tactics, revolutionary objectives, mass organization and discipline, etc. Some of his main points are summarized in the selections which follow.

At the same time, Mao had been devoting himself to intensive study of Marxism-Leninism and the writings of Stalin. He had prepared texts setting forth the chief theoretical tenets of Communist orthodoxy (excerpts from which are presented in section two of this chapter) and he had given much attention to the proper interpretation of Chinese history and the nature of the Chinese revolution in "orthodox" terms. Indications of this, including Mao's acceptance of Stalin's periodization of Chinese history according to the classical Western pattern (from primitive communism, to slavery, to feudalism, to capitalism) rather than Marx's differentiation of it as a peculiarly Asiatic or Oriental society, are found in the writings below. They present first Mao's view of Chinese history, his characterization of the revolution, and his analysis of revolutionary strategy. Following them are passages from *On New Democracy,* stating the political and economic program Mao had formulated for this stage in the revolution.

[215]

It should be remembered that these two works were written in the middle phase of the second United Front period, supposedly based on collaboration with the Kuomintang against the Japanese. With the conclusion of the Moscow-Berlin Pact, signalizing Stalin's accommodation of the Axis powers, the struggle against Japan no longer rated such a high priority. Mao, though still eager to exploit anti-Japanese feeling, felt less of a need to work closely with the Nationalists in the "anti-imperialist" struggle. Accordingly he placed greater stress on the revolution within China and on the Communist Party's leadership of it, as over against the Kuomintang.

[From *Selected Works*, III, 73–86]

THE CHINESE NATION

Developing along the same lines as many other nations of the world, the Chinese nation (chiefly the Hans) first went through some tens of thousands of years of life in classless primitive communes. Up to now approximately 4,000 years have passed since the collapse of the primitive communes and the transition to class society, first slave society and then feudalism. In the history of Chinese civilization, agriculture and handicraft have always been known as highly developed; many great thinkers, scientists, inventors, statesmen, military experts, men of letters, and artists have flourished, and there is a rich store of classical works. The compass was invented in China very long ago. The art of paper-making was discovered as early as 1,800 years ago. Block-printing was invented 1,300 years ago. In addition, movable types were invented 800 years ago. Gunpowder was used in China earlier than in Europe. China, with a recorded history of almost 4,000 years, is therefore one of the oldest civilized countries in the world.

The Chinese nation is not only famous throughout the world for its stamina and industriousness, but also as a freedom-loving people with a rich revolutionary tradition. The history of the Hans, for instance, shows that the Chinese people would never submit to rule by the dark forces and that in every case they succeeded in overthrowing or changing such a rule by revolutionary means. In thousands of years of the history of the Hans, there have been hundreds of peasant insurrections, great or small, against the régime of darkness imposed by the landlords and nobility. And it was the peasant uprisings that brought about most dynastic changes. All the nationalities of China have always rebelled

[216]

against the foreign yoke and striven to shake it off by means of resistance. They accept a union on the basis of equality, not the oppression of one nationality by another. In thousands of years of history of the Chinese nation many national heroes and revolutionary leaders have emerged. So the Chinese nation is also a nation with a glorious revolutionary tradition and a splendid historical heritage. [pp. 73–74]

ANCIENT FEUDAL SOCIETY

Although China is a great nation with a vast territory, an immense population, a long history, a rich revolutionary tradition, and a splendid historical heritage, yet she remained sluggish in her economic, political, and cultural development after her transition from the slave system into the feudal system. This feudal system, beginning from the Chou and Ch'in dynasties, lasted about 3,000 years. [p. 74]

It was under this feudal system of economic exploitation and political oppression that the Chinese peasants throughout the ages led a slave-like life in dire poverty and suffering. Under the yoke of feudalism they had no freedom of person. The landlords had the right to beat and insult them and even to put them to death at will, while the peasants had no political rights whatever. The extreme poverty and backwardness of the peasants resulting from such ruthless exploitation and oppression by the landlord class is the basic reason why China's economy and social life has remained stagnant for thousands of years. . . .

The ruthless economic exploitation and political oppression of the peasantry by the landlord class forced the peasants to rise repeatedly in revolt against its rule. . . . However, since neither new productive forces, nor new relations of production, nor a new class force, nor an advanced political party existed in those days, and consequently peasant uprisings and wars lacked correct leadership as is given by the proletariat and the Communist Party today, the peasant revolutions invariably failed, and the peasants were utilized during or after each revolution by the landlords and the nobility as a tool for bringing about a dynastic change. Thus, although some social progress was made after each great peasant revolutionary struggle, the feudal economic relations and feudal political system remained basically unchanged.

Only in the last hundred years did fresh changes take place. [pp. 75–76]

As mentioned in Section 2, Chinese feudal society lasted for about 3,000 years. It was not until the middle of the nineteenth century that great internal changes took place in China as a result of the penetration of foreign capitalism.

As China's feudal society developed its commodity economy and so carried within itself the embryo of capitalism, China would of herself have developed slowly into a capitalist society even if there had been no influence of foreign capitalism. The penetration of foreign capitalism accelerated this development. [pp. 76–77]

Yet this fresh change represented by the emergence and development of capitalism constitutes only one aspect of the change that has taken place since imperialistic penetration into China. There is another aspect which co-exists with it as well as hampers it, namely, the collusion of foreign imperialism with China's feudal forces to arrest the development of Chinese capitalism. [p. 78]

The contradiction between imperialism and the Chinese nation, and the contradiction between feudalism and the great masses of the people, are the principal contradictions in modern Chinese society. . . . The struggles arising from these contradictions and their intensification inevitably result in the daily-developing revolutionary movements. The great revolutions of modern and contemporary China have emerged and developed on the basis of these fundamental contradictions. [pp. 81–82]

THE CHINESE REVOLUTION

The national revolutionary struggle of the Chinese people has a history of exactly one hundred years dating from the Opium War of 1840, and of thirty years dating from the revolution of 1911. As this revolution has not yet run its full course and there has not yet been any signal achievement with regard to the revolutionary tasks, it is still necessary for all the Chinese people, and above all the Chinese Communist Party, to assume the responsibility for a resolute fight. [pp. 82–83]

Since the character of present-day Chinese society is colonial, semi-colonial and semi-feudal, then what after all are our chief targets or enemies at this stage of the Chinese revolution?

They are none other than imperialism and feudalism, namely, the bourgeoisie of the imperialist countries and the landlord class at home. For these and none other are the principal agents that carry out oppression in Chinese society at the present stage and obstruct its advance. These agents conspire to oppress the Chinese people and, since national oppression by imperialism is the heaviest oppression, imperialism has become the foremost and fiercest enemy of the Chinese people.

Since Japan's armed invasion of China, the principal enemies of the Chinese revolution have been Japanese imperialism and all the collaborators and reactionaries who are in collusion with it, who have either openly capitulated or are prepared to capitulate.

The Chinese bourgeoisie, also actually oppressed by imperialism, once led revolutionary struggles; it played a principal leading role, for instance, in the revolution of 1911, and also joined such revolutionary struggles as the Northern Expedition and the present Anti-Japanese War. In the long period from 1927 to 1937, however, the upper stratum of the bourgeoisie, as represented by the reactionary bloc of the Kuomintang, was in league with imperialism and formed a reactionary alliance with the landlord class, turning against the friends who had helped it—the Communist Party, the proletariat, the peasantry and other sections of the petty bourgeoisie, betraying the Chinese revolution and thereby causing its defeat. [pp. 83–84]

Confronted with such enemies, the Chinese revolution becomes protracted and ruthless in nature. Since the enemies are extremely powerful, the revolutionary forces, unless allowed a long period of time, cannot be massed and steeled into a power that will finally crush them. Since the enemy's suppression of the Chinese revolution is exceedingly ruthless, the revolutionary forces cannot hold their own positions and take over the enemy's unless they steel themselves and develop their tenacity. The view that the forces of the Chinese revolution can be built up in the twinkling of an eye and the Chinese revolutionary struggle can triumph overnight is therefore incorrect.

Confronted with such enemies, the Chinese revolution must, so far as its principal means or the principal form is concerned be an armed rather than a peaceful one. This is because our enemy makes it impossible for the Chinese people, deprived of all political freedoms and rights, to take any peaceful political action. Stalin said, "In China, armed revolution is fighting against armed counter-revolution. This is one of the peculiarities and one of the advantages of the Chinese revolution." [10] This statement is a perfectly correct formulation. The view which belittles armed struggle, revolutionary war, guerrilla war and army work is therefore incorrect.

Confronted with such enemies, the Chinese revolution has also to tackle the question of revolutionary base areas. Since powerful imperialism and its allies, the reactionary forces in China, have occupied China's key cities for a long time, if the revolutionary forces do not wish to compromise with them but want to carry on the struggle staunchly, and if they intend to accumulate strength and steel themselves and avoid decisive battles with their powerful enemy before they have mustered enough strength, then they must build the backward villages into advanced, consolidated base areas, into great military, political, economic, and cultural revolutionary bastions, so that they can fight the fierce enemy who utilizes the cities to attack the rural districts and, through a protracted struggle, gradually win an overall victory for the revolution. In these circumstances, owing to the unevenness in China's economic development (not a unified capitalist economy), to the immensity of China's territory (which gives the revolutionary forces sufficient room to maneuver in), to the disunity inside China's counter-revolutionary camp which is fraught with contradictions, and to the fact that the struggle of the peasants, the main force in the Chinese revolution, is led by the party of the proletariat, the Communist Party, a situation arises in which, on the one hand, the Chinese revolution can triumph first in the rural districts and, on the other hand, a state of unevenness is created in the revolution and the task of winning complete victory in the revolution becomes a protracted and arduous one. It is thus clear that the protracted revolutionary struggle conducted in such revolutionary base areas is chiefly a peasant guerrilla war led by the Chinese Communist Party. To neglect building up revolutionary base areas in the rural districts, to neglect performing arduous work among the peasants, and to neglect guerrilla war, are therefore all incorrect views.

However, to emphasize armed struggle does not mean giving up other

[10] J. V. Stalin, *On the Perspective of the Revolution in China,* as translated in *Political Affairs* (New York, December, 1950), p. 29.

forms of struggle; on the contrary, armed struggle will not succeed unless coordinated with other forms of struggle. And to emphasize the work in rural base areas does not mean giving up our work in the cities and in the vast rural districts under the enemy's rule; on the contrary, without the work in the cities and in other rural districts, the rural base areas will be isolated and the revolution will suffer defeat. Moreover, the capture of the cities now serving as the enemy's main bases is the final objective of the revolution, an objective which cannot be achieved without adequate work in the cities.

This shows clearly that it is impossible for the revolution to triumph in both the cities and the countryside unless the enemy's principal instrument for fighting the people—his armed forces—is destroyed. Thus besides annihilating enemy troops in war, it is important to work for their disintegration.

This shows clearly that, in the Communist Party's propaganda and organizational work in the cities and the countryside long occupied by the enemy and dominated by the forces of reaction and darkness, we must adopt, instead of an impetuous and adventurist line, a line of hiding the crack forces, accumulating strength, and biding our time. In leading the people's struggle against the enemy we must adopt the tactics of advancing slowly but surely, by making the fullest possible use of all forms of open and legal activities permitted by laws and decrees and social customs and basing ourselves on the principles of justifiability, expediency and restraint; vociferous cries and rash actions can never lead to success.
[pp. 84–86]

On New Democracy

According to the established Communist (Stalinist) view, China was following in the main the path of other societies from feudalism through a bourgeois-democratic revolution to a socialist revolution led by the proletariat. During the earlier period of Kuomintang-Communist collaboration, the latter acknowledged the "bourgeois" Nationalists as the main force of the so-called democratic revolution. In 1940, however, Mao was unwilling to grant such leadership to the Kuomintang, even though he conceded that the "democratic" revolution had not yet been completed and the socialist revolution still waited upon it. His *On New Democracy*—based on Leninist and Stalinist doctrines concerning the nature of the bourgeois-democratic revolution in colonial and semi-colonial countries, and its relation to the anti-imperialist struggle led by the Soviet Union—was Mao's way of insuring Communist (proletarian) leadership for a new type of democratic revolution.

Politically the New Democracy bears little resemblance to Western democracy but conforms rather to Leninist "democratic centralism," which insures Communist domination of a multi-class coalition. Economically it involves a moderate program of land reform and nationalization of key industries. It was this moderate program which led some Western observers to think of the Communists as simply "agrarian reformers." Yet Mao's writings make it abundantly clear that Communists had no intention of sharing real power and every intention of pushing on to full socialism.

[From *Selected Works,* III, 109–55]

THE CHINESE REVOLUTION IS PART OF THE WORLD REVOLUTION

The historical feature of the Chinese revolution consists in the two steps to be taken, democracy and socialism, and the first step is now no longer democracy in a general sense, but democracy of the Chinese type, a new and special type—New Democracy. How, then, is this historical feature formed? Has it been in existence for the past hundred years, or is it only of recent birth?

If we only make a brief study of the historical development of China and of the world we shall understand that this historical feature did not emerge as a consequence of the Opium War, but began to take shape only after the first imperialist world war and the Russian October Revolution. [pp. 109–10]

Before these events, the Chinese bourgeois-democratic revolution belonged to the category of the old bourgeois-democratic world revolution, and was part of that revolution.

After these events, the Chinese bourgeois-democratic revolution changes its character and belongs to the category of the new bourgeois-democratic revolution and, so far as the revolutionary front is concerned, forms part of the proletarian-socialist world revolution.

Why? Because the first imperialist world war and the first victorious socialist revolution, the October Revolution, have changed the historical direction of the whole world and marked a new historical era of the whole world. [pp. 110–11]

This "world revolution" refers no longer to the old world revolution —for the old bourgeois world revolution has long become a thing of the past—but to a new world revolution, the socialist world revolution. Similarly, to form "part" of the world revolution means to form no longer a part of the old bourgeois revolution but of the new socialist revolution. This is an exceedingly great change unparalleled in the history of China and of the world.

This correct thesis propounded by the Chinese Communists is based on Stalin's theory.

As early as 1918, Stalin wrote in an article commemorating the first anniversary of the October Revolution:

The great world-wide significance of the October Revolution chiefly consists in the fact that:

(1) It has widened the scope of the national question and converted it from the particular question of combating national oppression in Europe into the general question of emancipating the oppressed peoples, colonies, and semi-colonies from imperialism.

(2) It has opened up wide possibilities for their emancipation and the right paths towards it, has thereby greatly facilitated the cause of the emancipation of the oppressed peoples of the West and the East, and has drawn them into the common current of the victorious struggle against imperialism.

(3) It has thereby erected a bridge between the socialist West and the enslaved East, having created a new front of revolutions against world imperialism, extending from the proletarians of the West, through the Russian revolution to the oppressed peoples of the East.[11]

Since writing this article, Stalin has again and again expounded the theoretical proposition that revolutions in colonies and semi-colonies have already departed from the old category and become part of the proletarian-socialist revolution. [pp. 112–13]

The first stage of the Chinese revolution (itself subdivided into many minor stages) belongs, so far as its social character is concerned, to a new type of bourgeois-democratic revolution, and is not yet a proletarian-socialist revolution; but it has long become part of the proletarian-socialist world revolution and is now even an important part of such a world revolution and its great ally. The first step in, or the first stage of, this revolution is certainly not, and cannot be, the establishment of a capitalist society under the dictatorship of the Chinese bourgeoisie; on the contrary, the first stage is to end with the establishment of a new-democratic society under the joint dictatorship of all Chinese revolutionary classes headed by the Chinese proletariat. Then, the revolution will develop into

[11] J. V. Stalin, *Works*, Eng. ed. (Moscow, 1953), IV, 169–70.

the second stage so that a socialist society can be established in China. [p. 115]

NEW-DEMOCRATIC POLITICS

As to the question of "political structure" [in the New Democracy], it is the question of the form of structure of political power, the form adopted by certain social classes in establishing their organs of political power to oppose their enemy and protect themselves. Without an adequate form of political power there would be nothing to represent the state. China can now adopt a system of people's congresses—the people's national congress, the people's provincial congresses, the people's county congresses, the people's district congresses, down to the people's township congresses—and let these congresses at various levels elect the organs of government. But a system of really universal and equal suffrage, irrespective of sex, creed, property, or education, must be put into practice so that the organs of government elected can properly represent each revolutionary class according to its status in the state, express the people's will and direct revolutionary struggles, and embody the spirit of New Democracy. Such a system is democratic centralism.[12] Only a government of democratic centralism can fully express the will of all the revolutionary people and most powerfully fight the enemies of the revolution. The spirit of "not to be monopolized by a few" must be embodied in the organizations of the government and the army; without a genuinely democratic system such an aim can never be attained, and that would mean a discrepancy between the political structure and the state system.

The state system—joint dictatorship of all revolutionary classes. The political structure—democratic centralism. This is new-democratic government; this is a republic of New Democracy, the republic of the anti-

[12] According to an earlier definition of Mao's, in his report on "The Role of the Chinese Communist Party in the National War," democratic centralism in the Party consists in the following principles: 1) that individuals must subordinate themselves to the organization; 2) that the minority must subordinate itself to the majority; 3) that the lower level must subordinate itself to the higher level; and 4) that the entire membership must subordinate itself to the Central Committee. "Whether in the army or in the local organizations, democracy within the Party is meant to strengthen discipline and raise fighting capacity, not to weaken them" (*Selected Works*, II, 254–55). [Ed.]

Japanese united front, the republic of the new Three People's Principles with the three cardinal policies, and the Republic of China true to its name. Today we have a Republic of China in name, but not one in reality; the task today is to bring about the reality that would fit its name. [p. 121]

NEW-DEMOCRATIC ECONOMY

We must establish in China a republic that is politically new-democratic as well as economically new-democratic.

Big banks and big industrial and commercial enterprises shall be owned by this republic.

Enterprises, whether Chinese-owned or foreign-owned, which are monopolistic in character or which are on too large a scale for private management, such as banks, railways, and air lines, shall be operated by the state so that private capital cannot dominate the livelihood of the people: This is the main principle of the control of capital.

This was also a solemn statement contained in the Manifesto of the First National Congress of the Kuomintang during the period of the Kuomintang-Communist cooperation; this is the correct objective for the economic structure of the new-democratic republic. The state-operated enterprises of the new-democratic republic under the leadership of the proletariat are socialist in character and constitute the leading force in the national economy as a whole; but this republic does not take over other forms of capitalist private property, or forbid the development of capitalist production that "cannot dominate the livelihood of the people," for China's economy is still very backward.

This republic will adopt certain necessary measures to confiscate the land of landlords and distribute it to those peasants having no land or only a little land, carry out Dr. Sun Yat-sen's slogan of "land to the tillers," abolish the feudal relations in the rural areas, and turn the land into the private property of the peasants. In the rural areas, rich peasant economic activities will be tolerated. This is the line of "equalization of land ownership." The correct slogan for this line is "land to the tillers." In this stage, socialist agriculture is in general not yet to be established, though the various types of cooperative enterprises developed on the basis of "land to the tillers" will contain elements of socialism. [p. 122]

[225]

A given culture is the ideological reflection of the politics and economy of a given society. There is in China an imperialist culture which is a reflection of the control or partial control of imperialism over China politically and economically. This part of culture is advocated not only by the cultural organizations run directly by the imperialists in China but also by a number of shameless Chinese. All culture that contains a slave ideology belongs to this category. There is also in China a semi-feudal culture which is a reflection of semi-feudal politics and economy and has as its representatives all those who, while opposing the new culture and new ideologies, advocate the worship of Confucius, the study of the Confucian canon, the old ethical code, and the old ideologies. Imperialist culture and semi-feudal culture are affectionate brothers, who have formed a reactionary cultural alliance to oppose China's new culture. This reactionary culture serves the imperialists and the feudal class, and must be swept away. Unless it is swept away, no new culture of any kind can be built up. [p. 141]

SOME ERRORS ON THE QUESTION OF THE NATURE OF CULTURE

So far as national culture is concerned, the guiding role is fulfilled by Communist ideology, and efforts should be made to disseminate socialism and communism among the working class and to educate, properly and methodically, the peasantry and other sections of the masses in socialism. But national culture as a whole is at present not yet socialist.

New-democratic politics, economy, and culture all contain a socialist element, and not an ordinary but a decisive one at that, because they are under the leadership of the proletariat. But taken as a whole, the political, economic and cultural conditions are as yet not socialist but new-democratic. [p. 152]

A NATIONAL, SCIENTIFIC, AND MASS CULTURE

New-democratic culture is national. It opposes imperialist oppression and upholds the dignity and independence of the Chinese nation. It belongs to our own nation, and bears our national characteristics. It unites with the socialist and new-democratic cultures of all other nations and establishes with them the relations whereby they can absorb something from each other and help each other to develop, and form together the new culture of the world; but it can never unite with the reactionary imperialist culture of any nation, for it is a revolutionary national culture. China should absorb on a large scale the progressive cultures of foreign countries as an ingredient for her own culture; in the past we did not do enough work of this kind. We must absorb whatever we today find useful, not only from the present socialist or new-democratic cultures of other nations, but also from the older cultures of foreign countries, such as those of the various capitalist countries in the age of enlightenment. However, we must treat these foreign materials as we do our food, which should be chewed in the mouth, submitted to the working of the stomach and intestines, mixed with saliva, gastric juice, and intestinal secretions, and then separated into essence to be absorbed and waste matter to be discarded—only thus can food benefit our body; we should never swallow anything raw or absorb it uncritically. So-called "wholesale Westernization" [13] is a mistaken viewpoint. China has suffered a great deal in the past from the formalist absorption of foreign things. Likewise, in applying Marxism to China, Chinese Communists must fully and properly unite the universal truth of Marxism with the specific practice of the Chinese revolution; that is to say, the truth of Marxism must be integrated with the characteristics of the nation and given a definite national form before it can be useful; it must not be applied subjectively as a mere formula. Formula-Marxists are only fooling with Marxism and the Chinese revolution, and there is no place for them in the ranks of the Chinese revolution. China's culture should have its own form, namely, a national form. National in form, new-democratic in content—such is our new culture today

New-democratic culture is scientific. It is opposed to all feudal and superstitious ideas; it stands for seeking truth from facts, it stands for objective truth and for the unity between theory and practice. On this point, the scientific thought of the Chinese proletariat can form an anti-imperialist, anti-feudal and anti-superstition united front with the still progressive bourgeois materialists and natural scientists, but it can never

[13] A view advanced by a number of the Chinese bourgeois scholars completely enslaved by antiquated individualist bourgeois Western culture. They recommended so-called "wholesale Westernization," which means imitating the capitalist countries of Europe and America in everything.

form a united front with any reactionary idealism. Communists may form an anti-imperialist and anti-feudal united front for political action with certain idealists and even with religious followers, but we can never approve of their idealism or religious doctrines. A splendid ancient culture was created during the long period of China's feudal society. To clarify the process of development of this ancient culture, to throw away its feudal dross, and to absorb its democratic essence is a necessary condition for the development of our new national culture and for the increase of our national self-confidence; but we should never absorb anything and everything uncritically. We must separate all the rotten things of the ancient feudal ruling class from the fine ancient popular culture that is more or less democratic and revolutionary in character. As China's present new politics and new economy have developed out of her old politics and old economy, and China's new culture has also developed out of her old culture, we must respect our own history and should not cut ourselves adrift from it. However, this respect for history means only giving history a definite place among the sciences, respecting its dialectical development, but not eulogizing the ancient while disparaging the modern, or praising any noxious feudal element. As to the masses of the people and the young students, the essential thing is to direct them not to look backward, but to look forward. [pp. 153–55]

THE TWOFOLD TASK OF THE CHINESE REVOLUTION AND THE CHINESE
COMMUNIST PARTY
[From *Selected Works*, "The Chinese Revolution and the Chinese Communist Party," III, 100–1]

To complete China's bourgeois-democratic revolution (the new-democratic revolution) and to prepare to transform it into a socialist revolution when all the necessary conditions are present—that is the sum total of the great and glorious revolutionary task of the Communist Party of China. All members of the Party should strive for its accomplishment and should never give up half-way. Some immature Communists think that we have only the task of the democratic revolution at the present stage, but not that of the socialist revolution at the future stage; or that the present revolution or the agrarian revolution is in fact the socialist revolution. It must be emphatically pointed out that both views are erroneous. Every Communist must know that the whole Chinese revolutionary movement led by the Chinese Communist Party is a complete revolutionary movement embracing the two revolutionary stages, democratic and socialist, which are two revolutionary processes differing in character, and that the socialist stage can be reached only after the democratic stage is completed. The democratic revolution is the necessary preparation for the socialist revolution, and the socialist revolution is the inevitable trend of the democratic revolution. And the ultimate aim of all Communists is to strive for the final building of socialist society and communist society.

The Dictatorship of the People's Democracy

The Dictatorship of the People's Democracy was written for the Twenty-eighth Anniversary of the Communist Party, July 1, 1949, on the eve of the complete conquest of mainland China. In the main it conforms to the principles laid down in *On New Democracy*, affirming that the new government would continue to represent a coalition of classes under the proletarian leadership of the Communist Party. The present text is noteworthy, however, for its clear definition of what democracy and dictatorship were to represent under the new regime—a definition based on concepts set forth by Lenin much earlier.

After an historical résumé demonstrating the indispensability of Marxism-Leninism and Communist leadership to the Chinese revolution, Mao takes up hypothetical objections to Communism and answers them in his typical catechetical fashion. The key question here concerns its dictatorial character, which Mao does not deny, and the key distinction he draws is a political one, subsuming economic class distinctions, between the "people" (those who accept Communist leadership) and the "reactionaries" (those who do not).

[From Brandt *et al., A Documentary History of Chinese Communism,* pp. 456–58]

PEOPLE'S DEMOCRATIC DICTATORSHIP

"You are dictatorial." Dear sirs, you are right; that is exactly what we are. The experience of several decades, amassed by the Chinese people, tells us to carry out the people's democratic dictatorship. That is, the right of reactionaries to voice their opinions must be abolished and only the people are allowed to have the right of voicing their opinions.

Who are the "people"? At the present stage in China, they are the working class, the peasant class, the petty bourgeoisie, and national bourgeoisie. Under the leadership of the working class and the Communist

Party, these classes unite together to form their own state and elect their own government (so as to) carry out a dictatorship over the lackeys of imperialism—the landlord class, the bureaucratic capitalist class, and the Kuomintang reactionaries and their henchmen representing these classes —to suppress them, allowing them only to behave properly and not to talk and act wildly. If they talk and act wildly their (action) will be prohibited and punished immediately. The democratic system is to be carried out within the ranks of the people, giving them freedom of speech, assembly, and association. The right to vote is given only to the people and not to the reactionaries. These two aspects, namely, democracy among the people and dictatorship over the reactionaries, combine to form the people's democratic dictatorship.

Why should it be done this way? Everybody clearly knows that otherwise the revolution would fail, and the people would meet with woe and the State would perish.

"Don't you want to eliminate state authority?" Yes, but we do not want it at present, we cannot want it at present. Why? Because imperialism still exists, the domestic reactionaries still exist, and classes in the country still exist. Our present task is to strengthen the apparatus of the people's state, which refers mainly to the people's army, people's police, and people's courts, for the defense of the country, and the protection of the people's interests; and with this as a condition, to enable China to advance steadily, under the leadership of the working class and the Communist Party, from an agricultural to an industrial country, and from a new democratic to a socialist and communist society, to eliminate classes and to realize the state of universal fraternity. The army, police, and courts of the state are instruments by which classes oppress classes. To the hostile classes the state apparatus is the instrument of oppression. It is violent, and not "benevolent." "You are not benevolent." Just so. We decidedly will not exercise benevolence towards the reactionary acts of the reactionaries and reactionary classes. Our benevolence applies only to the people, and not to the reactionary acts of the reactionaries and reactionary classes outside the people.

The (function of the) people's state is to protect the people. Only when there is the people's state, is it possible for the people to use democratic methods on a nationwide and all-round scale to educate and reform themselves, to free themselves from the influence of reactionaries at home and abroad (this influence is at present still very great and will exist for a long time and cannot be eliminated quickly), to unlearn the bad habits and ideas acquired from the old society and not to let themselves travel on the erroneous path pointed out by the reactionaries, but to continue to advance and develop towards a socialist and communist society accomplishing the historic mission of completely eliminating classes and advancing towards a universal fraternity.

The methods we use in this field are democratic; that is, methods of persuasion and not coercion. When people break the law they will be punished, imprisoned, or even sentenced to death. But these are individual cases and are different in principle from the dictatorship over the reactionary class as a class.

FUTURE OF THE REACTIONARIES

After their political regime is overthrown the reactionary classes and the reactionary clique will also be given land and work and a means of living; they will be allowed to re-educate themselves into new persons through work, provided they do not rebel, disrupt, or sabotage. If they are unwilling to work, the people's state will compel them to work. Propaganda and educational work will also be carried out among them, and, moreover, with care and adequacy, as we did among captured officers. This can also be called "benevolent administration," but we shall never forgive their reactionary acts and will never let their reactionary activity have the possibility of a free development.

Such re-education of the reactionary classes can only be carried out in the state of the people's democratic dictatorship. If this work is well done the main exploiting classes of China—the landlord and bureaucratic capitalist classes—will be finally eliminated. (Of the exploiting classes) there remain the national bourgeoisie among many of whom appropriate educational work can be carried out at the present stage. When socialism is realized, that is, when the nationalization of private enterprises has been carried out, they can be further educated and reformed. The people have in their hands a powerful state apparatus and are not afraid of the rebellion of the national bourgeois class.

The grave problem is that of educating the peasants. The peasants' economy is scattered. Judging by the experience of the Soviet Union, it requires a very long time and careful work to attain the socialization of agriculture. Without the socialization of agriculture, there will be no complete and consolidated socialism. And to carry out the socialization of agriculture a powerful industry with state-owned enterprises as the main component must be developed. The state of the people's democratic dictatorship must step by step solve this problem (of the industrialization of the country).

THE THEORY AND PRACTICE OF CHINESE COMMUNISM

This second group of readings is designed to show the theoretical bases of Communist indoctrination and discipline. Since they are intended by their authors for a more specialized audience, the party elite, some of these documents are quite technical and employ a vocabulary that is often abstract and artificial. The ordinary student of Chinese thought may find such treatises almost as forbidding and esoteric as Buddist psychology or Neo-Confucian metaphysics. Nevertheless, the great importance attached to theory by the Chinese Communists cannot be overlooked out of too great a preoccupation with their historical accomplishments. Mao Tse-tung has always been much impressed with Lenin's statement: "Without a revolutionary theory, there can be no revolutionary movement." However contrived that theory may be as an explanation of the revolution itself, there can be no doubt that its acceptance by the Chinese Communists gave them an ideological unity and dynamism that their opponents—Chinese and even Western—sometimes lacked.

MAO TSE-TUNG
On Contradiction

This essay is one of two basic theoretical works by Mao, the other being *On Practice* (which follows it here). Though actually written shortly after the latter, *On Contradiction* is of a more general nature and therefore appears here in logical rather than in chronological order. It was produced by Mao Tse-tung in the early Yenan period and delivered in the form of lectures to the Anti-Japanese Military and Political College in Yenan.

Mao's intensive study at this time of the Communist tradition—from Marx and Engels down through Lenin and Stalin—derives from at least two important considerations. One is the necessity, after years devoted to the practical revolutionary struggle in Hunan and Kiangsi, for improving his own knowledge of basic Communist doctrine in order to present his ideas and policies in orthodox terms. No doubt he suffered some disadvantage in party debates with those who had studied Communist literature more carefully than he— who, while Mao was heavily engaged in the countryside, had given full time in Shanghai or Moscow to mastery of the formal theory and jargon of Marxism-Leninism. Mao's contempt for such "doctrinaires" and "formalists," and their ignorance of revolutionary practice, is manifest in these writings.

Yet Mao's answer to formalism in the Party is not to belittle theory. On the contrary he rises to the challenge with his own formulation of orthodox doctrine deriving from the patristic tradition of Communism, constantly acknowledging his debt to Marx, Engels, Lenin, and Stalin. Mao is far from the defiant rebel, the free-wheeling independent, and far more the prudent practitioner of a science in which he has full faith, the dedicated leader whose practical grasp of disciplined action confirms the importance of ideological orthodoxy. Accordingly, Mao's essay, *On Contradiction,* gives a closely-reasoned and concise summation of those principles which he considers fundamental to Marxism-Leninism, stressing on the one hand their universality, and on the other the particular forms which they must take according to the needs of time and place. For, not to admit the variety of forms which the class struggle must take, would be to limit the universal significance of Communist doctrine—something Mao could never allow.

[From *Selected Works,* II, 17–52]

THE TWO WORLD OUTLOOKS

The dialectical world outlook had already emerged in ancient times both in China and in Europe. But ancient dialectics has something spontaneous and naive about it; being based upon the social and historical conditions of those times, it was not formulated into an adequate theory, hence it could not fully explain the world, and was later supplanted by metaphysics. The famous German philosopher Hegel, who lived from the late eighteenth century to the early nineteenth, made very important contributions to dialectics, but his is idealist dialectics. It was not until Marx and Engels, the great men of action of the proletarian movement, made a synthesis of the positive achievements in the history of human knowledge and, in particular, critically absorbed the rational elements of Hegelian dialectics and created the great theory of dialectical materialism and historical materialism, that a great, unprecedented revolution took place in the history of human knowledge. Later Lenin and Stalin have further developed this great theory. Introduced into China, this theory immediately brought about tremendous changes in the world of Chinese thought.

This dialectical world outlook teaches man chiefly how to observe and analyze skilfully the movement of opposites in various things, and, on the basis of such analysis, to find out the methods of solving the contradictions. Consequently, it is of paramount importance for us to understand concretely the law of contradiction in things.

THE UNIVERSALITY OF CONTRADICTION

For convenience in exposition, I shall deal here first with the universality of contradiction, and then with the particularity of contradiction. Only a brief remark is needed to explain the former, because many people have accepted the universality of contradiction ever since the great creators and continuers of Marxism—Marx, Engels, Lenin, and Stalin—established the materialist-dialectical world outlook and applied materialist dialectics with very great success to many aspects of the analysis of human history and of natural history, to many aspects of changes in society and in nature (as in the Soviet Union); but there are still many comrades, especially the doctrinaires, who are not clear about the problem of the particularity of contradiction. They do not understand that the universality of contradiction resides precisely in the particularity of contradiction. Nor do they understand how very significant it is for our further guidance in revolutionary practice to study the particularity of contradiction in the concrete things confronting us. Therefore, the problem of the particularity of contradiction should be studied with special attention and explained at sufficient length. For this reason, when we analyze the law of contradiction in things, we should first analyze the universality of contradiction, then analyze with special attention the particularity of contradiction, and finally return to the universality of contradiction.

The universality or absoluteness of contradiction has a twofold meaning. One is that contradiction exists in the process of development of all things and the other is that in the process of development of each thing a movement of opposites exists from beginning to end. [pp. 17–19]

Even under the social conditions of the Soviet Union a difference exists between the workers and the peasants; the difference is a contradiction, though, unlike that between labor and capital, it will not become intensified into antagonism or assume the form of class struggle: in the course of socialist construction the workers and the peasants have formed a firm alliance and will gradually solve this contradiction in the process of development from socialism to communism. This is a question of distinction in the character of contradictions, not a matter of the presence or absence of them. Contradiction is universal, absolute, existing in all processes of the development of things, and running through all processes from beginning to end. [p. 21]

THE PARTICULARITY OF CONTRADICTION

It is not only necessary to study the particular contradiction and the quality determined thereby in every great system of forms of motion of matter, but also to study the particular contradiction and the quality of every form of motion of matter at each stage of its long course of development. In all forms of motion, each process of development that is real and not imaginary is qualitatively different. In our study we must emphasise and start from this point.

Qualitatively different contradictions can only be solved by qualitatively different methods. For example: the contradiction between the proletariat and the bourgeoisie is solved by the method of socialist revolution; the contradiction between the great masses of the people and the feudal system is solved by the method of democratic revolution; the contradiction between colonies and imperialism is solved by the method of national revolutionary war; the contradiction between the working class and the peasantry in socialist society is solved by the method of collectivization and mechanization of agriculture; the contradiction within the Communist Party is solved by the method of criticism and self-criticism; the contradiction between society and nature is solved by the method of developing the productive forces. Processes change, old processes and old contradictions disappear, new processes and new contradictions emerge, and the methods of solving contradictions differ accordingly. There is a basic difference between the contradictions solved by the February Revolution and the October Revolution in Russia, as well as between the methods used to solve them. The use of different methods to solve different contradictions is a principle which Marxist-Leninists must strictly observe. The doctrinaires do not observe this principle: they do not understand the differences between the various revolutionary situations, and consequently do not understand that different methods should be used to solve different contradictions; on the contrary, they uniformly adopt a formula which they fancy to be unalterable and inflexibly apply it everywhere, a procedure which can only bring setbacks to the revolution or make a great mess of what could have been done well.

In order to reveal the particularity of contradictions in their totality as well as their interconnection in the process of development of things, that is, to reveal the quality of the process of development of things, we must reveal the particularity of each aspect of the contradiction in the process, otherwise it is impossible to reveal the quality of the process; this is also a matter to which we must pay the utmost attention in our study.

A great thing or event contains many contradictions in the process of its development. For instance, in the process of China's bourgeois-democratic revolution there are the contradiction between the various oppressed classes in Chinese society and imperialism, the contradiction between the great masses of the people and feudalism, the contradiction between the proletariat and the bourgeoisie, the contradiction between the peasantry together with the urban petty bourgeoisie on the one hand, and the bourgeoisie on the other, the contradiction between various reactionary ruling blocs, etc.; the situation is exceedingly complex. Not only do all these contradictions each have their own particularity and cannot be treated uniformly, but the two aspects of every contradiction also have each their own characteristics and cannot be treated uniformly. Not only should we who work for the Chinese revolution understand the particularity of each of the contradictions in the light of their totality, that is, from the interconnection of those contradictions, but we can understand the totality of the contradictions only by a study of each of their aspects. To understand each of the aspects of a contradiction is to understand the definite position each aspect occupies, the concrete form in which it comes into interdependence as well as conflict with its opposite, and the concrete means by which it struggles with its opposite when the two are interdependent and yet contradictory, as well as when the interdependence breaks up. The study of these problems is a matter of the utmost importance. Lenin was expressing this very idea when he said that the most essential thing in Marxism, the living soul of Marxism, is the concrete analysis of concrete conditions.[14] Contrary to Lenin's teaching, our doctrinaires never use their brains to analyze anything concretely; in their writings and speeches they always strike the keynote of the "eight-legged essay" which is void of any content, and have thus brought about in our Party a very bad style in work. [pp. 24–26]

From this it can be seen that in studying the specific nature of any contradiction—contradiction in various forms of motion of matter, contradiction in various forms of motion in every process of development, each aspect of the contradiction in every process of development, contradiction at the various stages of every process of development and each aspect of the contradiction at the various stages of development—in studying the specific nature of all these contradictions, we should be free from any taint of subjective arbitrariness and must make a concrete analysis of them. Apart from a concrete analysis there can be no knowledge of the specific nature of any contradiction. We must all the time bear in mind Lenin's words: the concrete analysis of concrete conditions.

Marx and Engels were the first to supply us with an excellent model of such concrete analysis.

When Marx and Engels applied the law of contradiction in things to the study of the process of social history, they saw the contradiction between the productive forces and the relations of production; they saw the contradiction between the exploiting class and the exploited class, as well as the contradiction produced thereby between the economic foundation and its superstructures, such as politics and ideology; and they saw how these contradictions inevitably lead to different social revolutions in different class societies.

When Marx applied this law to the study of the economic structure of capitalist society, he saw that the basic contradiction of this society is the contradiction between the social character of production and the private character of ownership. It is manifested in the contradiction between the organized character of production in individual enterprises and the unorganized character of production in society as a whole. The class manifestation of this contradiction is the contradiction between the bourgeoisie and the proletariat.

Because of the vastness of the scope of things and the limitlessness of

[14] V. I. Lenin, *Collected Works,* Russian ed. (Moscow, 1950), XXXI, 143.

[237]

their development, what in one case is universality is in another changed into particularity. On the other hand, what in one case is particularity is in another changed into universality. The contradiction contained in the capitalist system between the socialization of production and the private ownership of the means of production is something common to all countries where capitalism exists and develops; for capitalism, this constitutes the universality of contradiction. However, this contradiction in capitalism is something pertaining to a certain historical stage in the development of class society in general; as far as the contradiction between the productive forces and the relations of production in class society in general is concerned, this constitutes the particularity of contradiction. But while revealing by analysis the particularity of every contradiction in capitalist society, Marx expounded even more profoundly, more adequately and more completely the universality of the contradiction between the productive forces and the relations of production in class society in general. . . .

When Stalin explained the historical roots of Leninism in his famous work, *The Foundations of Leninism,* he analyzed the international situation in which Leninism was born, together with various contradictions in capitalism which had reached their extreme under the conditions of imperialism, and analyzed how these contradictions made the proletarian revolution a question of immediate action and how they created favorable conditions for a direct onslaught upon capitalism. Besides all these, he analyzed the reasons why Russia became the home of Leninism, how Tsarist Russia represented the focus of all the contradictions of imperialism, and why the Russian proletariat could become the vanguard of the international revolutionary proletariat. In this way, Stalin analyzed the universality of the contradiction in imperialism, showing how Leninism is Marxism of the era of imperialism and the proletarian revolution, and analyzed the particularity of the imperialism of Tsarist Russia in the contradiction of imperialism in general, showing how Russia became the birth-place of the theory and tactics of the proletarian revolution and how in such a particularity is contained the universality of contradiction. This kind of analysis made by Stalin serves us as a model in understanding the particularity and the universality of contradiction and their interconnection. [pp.32–34]

As regards the problem of the particularity of contradiction, there are
still two sides which must be specially singled out for analysis, that is, the
principal contradiction and the principal aspect of a contradiction.

In the process of development of a complex thing, many contradictions
exist; among these, one is necessarily the principal contradiction whose
existence and development determine or influence the existence and development of other contradictions. [p. 35]

So in studying any process—if it is a complicated process in which more
than two contradictions exist—we must do our utmost to discover its
principal contradiction. Once the principal contradiction is grasped, any
problem can be readily solved. This is the method Marx taught us when
he studied capitalist society. When Lenin and Stalin studied imperialism and the general crisis of capitalism, and when they studied Soviet
economy, they also taught us this method. [p. 37]

Some people think that this is not the case with certain contradictions.
For example: in the contradiction between the productive forces and
the relations of production, the productive forces are the principal aspect;
in the contradiction between theory and practice, practice is the principal
aspect; in the contradiction between the economic foundation and its
superstructure, the economic foundation is the principal aspect: and
there is no change in their respective positions. This is the view of mechanistic materialism, and not of dialectical materialism. True, the productive forces, practice, and the economic foundation generally manifest
themselves in the principal and decisive role; whoever denies this is not
a materialist. But under certain conditions, such aspects as the relations
of production, theory and the superstructure in turn manifest themselves
in the principal and decisive role; this must also be admitted. When
the productive forces cannot be developed unless the relations of production are changed, the change in the relations of production plays the
principal and decisive role. When, as Lenin put it, "Without a revolutionary theory, there can be no revolutionary movement," [15] the creation
and advocacy of the revolutionary theory plays the principal and deci-

[15] V. I. Lenin, *What Is To Be Done?*

sive role. When a certain job (this applies to any job) is to be done but there is as yet no directive, method, plan or policy defining how to do it, the directive, method, plan or policy is the principal and decisive factor. When the superstructure (politics, culture and so on), hinders the development of the economic foundation, political and cultural reforms become the principal and decisive factors. In saying this, are we running counter to materialism? No. The reason is that while we recognize that in the development of history as a whole it is material things that determine spiritual things and social existence that determines social consciousness, at the same time we also recognise and must recognise the reaction of spiritual things and social consciousness on social existence, and the reaction of the superstructure on the economic foundation. This is not running counter to materialism; this is precisely avoiding mechanistic materialism and firmly upholding dialectical materialism. [pp. 40–41]

THE IDENTITY AND STRUGGLE OF THE ASPECTS OF A CONTRADICTION

Having understood the problem of the universality and particularity of contradiction, we must proceed to study the problem of the identity and struggle of the aspects of a contradiction.

Identity, unity, coincidence, interpermeation, interpenetration, interdependence (or interdependence for existence), interconnection or co-operation—all these different terms mean the same thing and refer to the following two conditions: first, each of the two aspects of every contradiction in the process of development of a thing finds the presupposition of its existence in the other aspect and both aspects coexist in an entity; second, each of the two contradictory aspects, according to given conditions, tends to transform itself into the other. This is what is meant by identity. [p. 42]

The agrarian revolution we have carried out is already and will be such a process in which the land-owning landlord class becomes a class deprived of its land, while the peasants, once deprived of their land, become small holders of land. The haves and the have-nots, gain and loss, are interconnected because of certain conditions; there is identity of the two sides. Under socialism, the system of the peasants' private ownership will in turn become the public ownership of socialist agriculture; this has already taken place in the Soviet Union and will take place throughout the world. Between private property and public property there is a bridge leading from the one to the other, which in philosophy is called identity, or transformation into each other, or interpermeation.

To consolidate the dictatorship of the proletariat or the people's dictatorship is precisely to prepare the conditions for liquidating such a dictatorship and advancing to the higher stage of abolishing all state systems. To establish and develop the Communist Party is precisely to prepare the condition for abolishing the Communist Party and all party systems. To establish the revolutionary army under the leadership of the Communist Party and to carry on the revolutionary war is precisely to prepare the condition for abolishing war for ever. These contradictory things are at the same time complementary. [p. 45]

THE ROLE OF ANTAGONISM IN CONTRADICTION

"What is antagonism?" is one of the questions concerning the struggle within a contradiction. Our answer is: antagonism is a form of struggle within a contradiction, but not the universal form.

In human history, antagonism between classes exists as a particular manifestation of the struggle within a contradiction. The contradiction between the exploiting class and the exploited class: the two contradictory classes coexist for a long time in one society, be it a slave society, or a feudal or a capitalist society, and struggle with each other; but it is not until the contradiction between the two classes has developed to a certain stage that the two sides adopt the form of open antagonism which develops into a revolution. In a class society, the transformation of peace into war is also like that. [pp. 49–50]

As we have pointed out above, the contradiction between correct ideology and erroneous ideologies within the Communist Party reflects in the Party the class contradictions when classes exist. In the beginning, or with regard to certain matters, such a contradiction need not immediately manifest itself as antagonistic. But with the development of the class struggle, it can also develop and become antagonistic. The history of the Communist Party of the Soviet Union shows us that the contradiction between the correct ideology of Lenin and Stalin and the erroneous ideologies of Trotsky, Bukharin, and others, was in the beginning not yet manifested in an antagonistic form, but subsequently developed into antagonism. A similar case occurred in the history of the Chinese Communist Party. The contradiction between the correct ideology of many of our comrades in the Party and the erroneous ideologies of Ch'en Tu-hsiu, Chang Kuo-t'ao, and others was also in the beginning not manifested in an antagonistic form, but subsequently developed into antagonism. At present the contradiction between the correct ideology and the erroneous ideologies in our Party is not manifested in an antagonistic form and, if comrades who have committed mistakes can correct them, it will not develop into antagonism. Therefore the Party on the one hand must carry on a serious struggle against erroneous ideologies, and on the other hand, must give the comrades who have committed mistakes sufficient opportunity to become aware of them. Under such conditions, struggles pushed to excess are obviously not appropriate. But if those people who have commited mistakes persist in them and increase the gravity of their mistakes, then it is possible that such contradictions will develop into antagonism. [pp. 50–51]

Lenin said: "Antagonism and contradiction are utterly different. Under socialism, antagonism disappears, but contradiction exists." [16] That is to say, antagonism is only a form of struggle within a contradiction but not its universal form; we cannot impose the formula everywhere. [p. 52]

On Practice

Despite its title, which might lead one to expect a discussion of the practical aspects of waging revolution, this essay is actually a highly theoretical discussion of the problem of knowledge and practice in Marxist-Leninist terms. Though not claiming or revealing any originality on Mao's part, it shows again the importance which he attached to the formulation of fundamental philosophical principles as a basis for the preservation of ideological unity. In this case, by emphasizing the inseparability of theory and practice and by condemning any tendency which leaned toward one side or the other, Mao had a formula which could be applied unfailingly to the criticism of opposing policies in any situation. The proper balance between the two was a precarious thing to maintain and only Party leadership could, in the final analysis, judge "objective truth" in such matters. Obedience to it was therefore the only sure means of avoiding the twin heresies of doctrinairism and empiricism.

On Practice, though it deals with a somewhat narrower problem than *On Contradiction,* was actually written before the latter and probably indicates Mao's particular angle of approach to the study of Marxism-Leninism in this period. It has been described as a period of intense Bolshevization or Leninization of the Chinese Communist Party during the years at Yenan, dictated

[16] V. I. Lenin's critical notes on Bukharin's *Economics of the Transitional Period.*

by the necessity of preserving Party orthodoxy against the twofold dangers which arose from collaboration with the Kuomintang and the constant adaptation of policy and strategy to a rapidly changing situation. The official commentary provides some insight into the ideological significance attached to this statement in the context of the times:

"There used to be a group of doctrinaires in the Chinese Communist Party who, disregarding the experience of the Chinese revolution and denying the truth that Marxism is not a dogma but a guide to action, for a long time bluffed people with words and phrases torn out of their context from Marxist works. There was also a group of empiricists who, for a long time clinging to their own fragmentary experience, could neither understand the importance of theory for revolutionary practice nor see the whole of the revolutionary situation, and thus worked blindly, though industriously. The Chinese revolution of 1931–1934 was greatly damaged by the incorrect ideas of these two groups of comrades, particularly by those of the doctrinaires who, wearing the cloak of Marxism, misled large numbers of comrades. This article was written to expose from the viewpoint of Marxist theory of knowledge such subjectivist mistakes in the Party as doctrinairism and empiricism, especially doctrinairism. As its stress is laid on exposing doctrinaire subjectivism which belittles practice, this article is entitled 'On Practice.' These views were originally presented in a lecture at the Anti-Japanese Military and Political College in Yenan." [17]

[From *Selected Works*, I, 283–97]

The Marxists holds that man's social practice alone is the criterion of the truth of his knowledge of the external world. In reality, man's knowledge becomes verified only when, in the process of social practice (in the process of material production, of class struggle, and of scientific experiment), he achieves the anticipated results. If man wants to achieve success in his work, that is, to achieve the anticipated results, he must make his thoughts correspond to the laws of the objective world surrounding him; if they do not correspond, he will fail in practice. If he fails he will derive lessons from his failure, alter his ideas, so as to make them correspond to the laws of the objective world, and thus turn failure into success; this is what is meant by "failure is the mother of success," and "a fall into the pit, a gain in your wit."

The theory of knowledge of dialectical materialism raises practice to the first place, holds that human knowledge cannot be separated the least bit from practice, and repudiates all incorrect theories which deny the im-

---

[17] *Selected Works*, I, 282.

portance of practice or separate knowledge from practice. Thus Lenin said, "Practice is higher than (theoretical) knowledge because it has not only the virtue of universality, but also the virtue of immediate reality." [18] [pp. 283–84]

Apart from their genius, the reason why Marx, Engels, Lenin, and Stalin could work out their theories is mainly their personal participation in the practice of the contemporary class struggle and scientific experimentation; without this no amount of genius could bring success. The saying "a scholar does not step outside his gate, yet knows all the happenings under the sun" was mere empty talk in the technologically undeveloped old times; and although this saying can be realized in the present age of technological development, yet the people with real firsthand knowledge are those engaged in practice, and only when they have obtained "knowledge" through their practice, and when their knowledge, through the medium of writing and technology, reaches the hands of the "scholar," can the "scholar" know indirectly "the happenings under the sun."

If a man wants to know certain things or certain kinds of things directly, it is only through personal participation in the practical struggle to change reality, to change those things or those kinds of things, that he can come into contact with the phenomena of those things or those kinds of things; and it is only during the practical struggle to change reality, in which he personally participates, that he can disclose the essence of those things or those kinds of things and understand them. [p. 287]

Thus the first step in the process of knowledge is contact with the things of the external world; this belongs to the stage of perception. The second step is a synthesis of the data of perception by making a rearrangement or a reconstruction; this belongs to the stage of conception, judgment, and inference. It is only when the perceptual data are extremely rich (not fragmentary or incomplete) and are in correspondence to reality (not illusory) that we can, on the basis of such data, form valid concepts and carry out correct reasoning.

Here two important points must be emphasized. The first, a point which has been mentioned before, but should be repeated here, is the question of the dependence of rational knowledge upon perceptual knowledge. The person is an idealist who thinks that rational knowledge need not be

[18] V. I. Lenin, *Philosophical Notebooks*, Russian ed. (Moscow, 1947), p. 185.

derived from perceptual knowledge. In the history of philosophy there is the so-called "rationalist" school which admits only the validity of reason, but not the validity of experience, regarding reason alone as reliable and perceptual experience as unreliable; the mistake of this school consists in turning things upside down. The rational is reliable precisely because it has its source in the perceptual, otherwise it would be like water without a source or a tree without roots, something subjective, spontaneous, and unreliable. As to the sequence in the process of knowledge, perceptual experience comes first; we emphasize the significance of social practice in the process of knowledge precisely because social practice alone can give rise to man's knowledge and start him on the acquisition of perceptual experience from the objective world surrounding him. For a person who shuts his eyes, stops his ears, and totally cuts himself off from the objective world, there can be no knowledge to speak of. Knowledge starts with experience—this is the materialism of the theory of knowledge.

The second point is that knowledge has yet to be deepened, the perceptual stage of knowledge has yet to be developed to the rational stage —this is the dialectics of the theory of knowledge.[19] It would be a repetition of the mistake of "empiricism" in history to hold that knowledge can stop at the lower stage of perception and that perceptual knowledge alone is reliable while rational knowledge is not. This theory errs in failing to recognize that, although the data of perception reflect certain real things of the objective world (I am not speaking here of idealist empiricism which limits experience to so-called introspection), yet they are merely fragmentary and superficial, reflecting things incompletely instead of representing their essence. To reflect a thing fully in its totality, to reflect its essence and its inherent laws, it is necessary, through thinking, to build up a system of concepts and theories by subjecting the abundant perceptual data to a process of remodeling and reconstructing—discarding the crude and selecting the refined, eliminating the false and retaining the true, proceeding from one point to another, and going through the outside into the inside; it is necessary to leap from perceptual knowledge to rational knowledge. Knowledge which is such a reconstruction does not become emptier or less reliable; on the contrary, whatever has been

---

[19] Cf. Lenin, *Philosophical Notebooks,* p. 146: "For the sake of knowing, one must start to know, to study, on the basis of experience and rise from experience to general knowledge."

scientifically reconstructed on the basis of practice in the process of knowledge is something which, as Lenin said, reflects objective things more deeply, more truly, more fully. As against this, the vulgar plodders, respecting experience yet despising theory, cannot take a comprehensive view of the entire objective process, lack clear direction and long-range perspective, and are self-complacent with occasional successes and peep-hole views. Were those persons to direct a revolution, they would lead it up a blind alley.

The dialectical-materialist theory of knowledge is that rational knowledge depends upon perceptual knowledge and perceptual knowledge has yet to be developed into rational knowledge. Neither "rationalism" nor "empiricism" in philosophy recognizes the historical or dialectical nature of knowledge, and although each contains an aspect of truth (here I am referring to materialist rationalism and empiricism, not to idealist rationalism and empiricism), both are erroneous in the theory of knowledge as a whole. The dialectical-materialist process of knowledge from the perceptual to the rational applies to a minor process of knowledge (e.g., knowing a single thing or task) as well as to a major one (e.g., knowing a whole society or a revolution).

But the process of knowledge does not end here. The statement that the dialectical-materialist process of knowledge stops at rational knowledge, covers only half the problem. And so far as Marxist philosophy is concerned, it covers only the half that is not particularly important. What Marxist philosophy regards as the most important problem does not lie in understanding the laws of the objective world and thereby becoming capable of explaining it, but in actively changing the world by applying the knowledge of its objective laws. From the Marxist viewpoint, theory is important, and its importance is fully shown in Lenin's statement: "Without a revolutionary theory there can be no revolutionary movement." [20] But Marxism emphasizes the importance of theory precisely and only because it can guide action. If we have a correct theory, but merely prate about it, pigeon-hole it, and do not put it into practice, then that theory, however good, has no significance.

Knowledge starts with practice, reaches the theoretical plane via practice, and then has to return to practice. The active function of knowledge

[20] V. I. Lenin, *What Is To Be Done?*

[246]

not only manifests itself in the active leap from perceptual knowledge to rational knowledge, but also—and this is the more important—in the leap from rational knowledge to revolutionary practice. The knowledge which enables us to grasp the laws of the world must be redirected to the practice of changing the world, that is, it must again be applied in the practice of production, in the practice of the revolutionary class struggle and revolutionary national struggle, as well as in the practice of scientific experimentation. This is the process of testing and developing theory, the continuation of the whole process of knowledge. [pp. 290–93]

But generally speaking, whether in the practice of changing nature or of changing society, people's original ideas, theories, plans, or programs are seldom realized without any change whatever. This is because people engaged in changing reality often suffer from many limitations: they are limited not only by the scientific and technological conditions, but also by the degree of development and revelation of the objective process itself (by the fact that the aspects and essence of the objective process have not yet been fully disclosed). In such a situation, ideas, theories, plans, or programs are often altered partially and sometimes even wholly along with the discovery of unforeseen circumstances during practice. That is to say, it does happen that the original ideas, theories, plans, or programs fail partially or wholly to correspond to reality and are partially or entirely incorrect. In many instances, failures have to be repeated several times before erroneous knowledge can be rectified and made to correspond to the laws of the objective process, so that subjective things can be transformed into objective things, viz., the anticipated results can be achieved in practice. But in any case, at such a point, the process of man's knowledge of a certain objective process at a certain stage of its development is regarded as completed. . . .

It often happens, however, that ideas lag behind actual events; this is because man's knowledge is limited by a great many social conditions. We oppose the die-hards in the revolutionary ranks whose ideas, failing to advance with the changing objective circumstances, manifest themselves historically as "right" opportunism. These people do not see that the struggles arising from contradictions have already pushed the objective process forward, while their knowledge has stopped at the old stage. This characterizes the ideas of all die-hards. With their ideas divorced from social practice, they cannot serve to guide the chariot-wheels of society; they can only trail behind the chariot grumbling that it goes too fast, and endeavor to drag it back and make it go in the opposite direction.

We also oppose the phrase-mongering of the "leftists." Their ideas are ahead of a given stage of development of the objective process: some of them regard their fantasies as truth; others, straining to realize at present an ideal which can only be realized in the future, divorce themselves from the practice of the majority of the people at the moment and from the realities of the day and show themselves as adventurist in their actions. Idealism and mechanistic materialism, opportunism, and adventurism, are all characterized by a breach between the subjective and the objective, by the separation of knowledge from practice. The Marxist-Leninist theory of knowledge, which is distinguished by its emphasis on social practice as the criterion of scientific truth, cannot but resolutely oppose these incorrect ideologies. The Marxist recognizes that in the absolute, total process of the development of the universe, the development of each concrete process is relative; hence, in the great stream of absolute truth, man's knowledge of the concrete process at each given stage of development is only relatively true. The sum total of innumerable relative truths is the absolute truth.[21] [pp. 294-96]

To discover truth through practice, and through practice to verify and develop truth. To start from perceptual knowledge and actively develop it into rational knowledge, and then, starting from rational knowledge, actively direct revolutionary practice so as to remold the subjective and the objective world. Practice, knowledge, more practice, more knowledge; the cyclical repetition of this pattern to infinity, and with each cycle, the elevation of the content of practice and knowledge to a higher level. Such is the whole of the dialectical materialist theory of knowledge, and such is the dialectical materialist theory of the unity of knowing and doing. July, 1937 [p. 297]

LIU SHAO-CH'I
How To Be a Good Communist

Liu Shao-ch'i (1905–   ), a veteran Communist who joined the Party in 1921, the year of its founding, has been one of Mao's closest co-workers and speaks

[21] Cf. V. I. Lenin, *Materialism and Empirio-Criticism*, Chapter II, Section 5.

as a theoretician with an authority second only to Mao. When the People's Republic was established in 1949, he became vice-chairman of the Central People's Government, and after Mao relinquished the chairmanship in 1959, Liu succeeded to it.

How To Be a Good Communist is a basic text of indoctrination for party members, delivered first as a series of lectures in July, 1939, at the Institute of Marxism-Leninism in Yenan. It represents one more aspect of the campaign for tightening Party discipline and strengthening orthodoxy which was pressed in the late '30s and early '40s in order to insure the proper assimilation of new recruits, growing rapidly in number, and the maintenance of Party unity along orthodox Leninist lines.

The original Chinese title of this work is literally *The Cultivation of Communist Party Members*. Both the title and Liu's frequent reference to earlier Chinese concepts of self-cultivation suggest a link with Chinese tradition, though perhaps only a tenuous one. In any case, the crucial factor in Communist cultivation is Party authority and guidance. Though the Party does not conceal its readiness to apply the most stringent sanctions against recalcitrance and deviation, it is highly conscious of the limits to which coercion may be employed in maintaining order and discipline. Wherever possible, it encourages Party members to discipline themselves, and prefers persuasion quietly backed by overwhelming force to outright dictation and naked oppression. A further inducement for Party cadres is the hope of joining the new elite. The prospect of rising to some power and authority in the system encourages them to stomach indoctrination and discipline which otherwise might be quite unpalatable for those who were merely subject to it.

In this, again, there is nothing unique or peculiar to Chinese Communism, but the extension of these methods to the nation as a whole has been a significant element in maintaining ideological unity under the Communist regime.

[From *How To Be a Good Communist,* pp. 15–34]

Comrades! In order to become the most faithful and best pupils of Marx, Engels, Lenin, and Stalin, we need to carry on cultivation in all aspects in the course of the long and great revolutionary struggle of the proletariat and the masses of the people. We need to carry on cultivation in the theories of Marxism-Leninism and in applying such theories in practice; cultivation in revolutionary strategy and tactics; cultivation in studying and dealing with various problems according to the standpoint and methods of Marxism-Leninism; cultivation in ideology and moral character; cultivation in Party unity, inner-Party struggle, and discipline; cultivation in hard work and in the style of work; cultivation in being skillful in dealing with different kinds of people and in associating with the masses of the people; and cultivation in various kinds of scientific knowledge, etc. We are all Communist Party members and so we have a general cultivation in common. But there exists a wide discrepancy today between our Party members. Wide discrepancy exists among us in the level of political consciousness, in work, in position, in cultural level, in experience of struggle, and in social origin. Therefore, in addition to cultivation in general we also need special cultivation for different groups and for individual comrades.

Accordingly, there should be different kinds of methods and forms of cultivation. For example, many of our comrades keep a diary in order to have a daily check on their work and thoughts or they write down on small posters their personal defects and what they hope to achieve and paste them up where they work or live, together with the photographs of persons they look up to, and ask comrades for criticism and supervision. In ancient China, there were many methods of cultivation. There was Tseng Tze [22] who said: "I reflect on myself three times a day." The *Book of Odes* has it that one should cultivate oneself "as a lapidary cuts and files, carves and polishes." Another method was "to examine oneself by self-reflection" and to "write down some mottoes on the right hand side of one's desk" or "on one's girdle" as daily reminders of rules of personal conduct. The Chinese scholars of the Confucian school had a number of methods for the cultivation of their body and mind. Every religion has various methods and forms of cultivation of its own. The "investigation of things, the extension of knowledge, sincerity of thought, the rectification of the heart, the cultivation of the person, the regulation of the family, the ordering well of the state and the making tranquil of the whole kingdom" as set forth in *The Great Learning* [23] also means the same. All this shows that in achieving one's progress one must make serious and energetic efforts to carry on self-cultivation and study. However, many of these methods and forms cannot be adopted by us because most of them are idealistic, formalistic, abstract, and divorced from social practice. These scholars and religious believers exaggerate the function of subjective initiative, thinking that so long as they keep their general "good intentions" and are devoted

[22] A disciple of Confucius.
[23] *The Great Learning* is said to be "a Book handed down by the Confucian school, which forms the gate by which beginners enter into virtue."

to silent prayer they will be able to change the existing state of affairs, change society, and change themselves under conditions separated from social and revolutionary practice. This is, of course, absurd. We cannot cultivate ourselves in this way. We are materialists and our cultivation cannot be separated from practice.

What is important to us is that we must not under any circumstances isolate ourselves from the revolutionary struggles of different kinds of people and in different forms at a given moment and that we must, moreover, sum up historical revolutionary experience and learn humbly from this and put it into practice. That is to say, we must undertake self-cultivation and steel ourselves in the course of our own practice, basing ourselves on the experiences of past revolutionary practice, on the present concrete situation and on new experiences. Our self-cultivation and steeling are for no other purpose than that of revolutionary practice. That is to say, we must modestly try to understand the standpoint, the method and the spirit of Marxism-Leninism, and understand how Marx, Engels, Lenin and Stalin dealt with people. And having understood these, we should immediately apply them to our own practice, i.e., in our own lives, words, deeds, and work. Moreover, we should stick to them and unreservedly correct and purge everything in our ideology that runs counter to them, thereby strengthening our own proletarian and Communist ideology and qualities. That is to say, we must modestly listen to the opinions and criticisms of our comrades and of the masses, carefully study the practical problems in our lives and in our work and carefully sum up our experiences and the lessons we have learned so as to find an orientation for our own work. In addition, on the basis of all these, we must judge whether we have a correct understanding of Marxism-Leninism and whether we have correctly applied the method of Marxism-Leninism, found out our own shortcomings and mistakes and corrected them. At the same time, we must find out in what respects specific conclusions of Marxism-Leninism need to be supplemented, enriched and developed on the basis of well-digested new experiences. That is to say, we must combine the universal truth of Marxism-Leninism with the concrete practice of the revolution.

These should be the methods of self-cultivation of us Communist Party members. That is to say, we must use the methods of Marxism-Leninism to cultivate ourselves. This kind of cultivation is entirely different from other kinds of cultivation which are idealistic and are divorced from social practice.

In this connection, we cannot but oppose certain idle talk and mechanicalism on the question of cultivation and steeling.

First of all, we must oppose and resolutely eliminate one of the biggest evils bequeathed to us by the education and learning in the old society—the separation of theory from practice. In the course of education and study in the old society many people thought that it was unnecessary or even impossible to act upon what they had learned. Despite the fact that they read over and over again books by ancient sages they did things the sages would have been loath to do. Despite the fact that in everything they wrote or said they preached righteousness and morality they acted like out-and-out robbers and harlots in everything they did. Some "high-ranking officials" issued orders for the reading of the Four Books and the Five Classics,[24] yet in their everyday administrative work they ruthlessly extorted exorbitant requisitions, ran amuck with corruption and killing, and did everything against righteousness and morality. Some people read the Three People's Principles over and over again and could recite the Will of Dr. Sun Yat-sen, yet they oppressed the people, opposed the nations who treated us on an equal footing, and went so far as to compromise with or surrender to the national enemy. Once a scholar of the old school told me himself that the only maxim of Confucius that he could observe was: "To him food can never be too dainty; minced meat can never be too fine," adding that all the rest of the teachings of Confucius he could not observe and had never proposed to observe. Then why did they still want to carry on educational work and study the teachings of the sages? Apart from utilizing them for window-dressing purposes, their objects were: 1) to make use of these teachings to oppress the exploited and to make use of righteousness and morality for the purpose of hoodwinking and suppressing the culturally backward people; 2) to attempt thereby to secure better government jobs, make money and achieve fame, and reflect credit on their parents. Apart from these objects, their actions were not restricted by the sages' teachings. This was the attitude and return of the "men of letters" and "scholars" of the old society to the

[24] The Four Books and Five Classics are nine ancient Chinese classics of philosophy, history, poetry, etc., of the Confucian Canon.

sages they "worshiped." Of course we Communist Party members cannot adopt such an attitude in studying Marxism-Leninism and the excellent and useful teachings bequeathed to us by our ancient sages. We must live up to what we say. We are honest and pure and we cannot deceive ourselves, the people, or our forefathers. This is an outstanding characteristic as well as a great merit of us Communist Party members. [pp. 15-18]

What is the most fundamental and common duty of us Communist Party members? As everybody knows, it is to establish Communism, to transform the present world into a Communist world. Is a Communist world good or not? We all know that it is very good. In such a world there will be no exploiters, oppressors, landlords, capitalists, imperialists, or fascists. There will be no oppressed and exploited people, no darkness, ignorance, backwardness, etc. In such a society all human beings will become unselfish and intelligent Communists with a high level of culture and technique. The spirit of mutual assistance and mutual love will prevail among mankind. There will be no such irrational things as mutual deception, mutual antagonism, mutual slaughter and war, etc. Such a society will, of course, be the best, the most beautiful, and the most advanced society in the history of mankind. Who will say that such a society is not good? Here the question arises: Can Communist society be brought about? Our answer is "yes." About this the whole theory of Marxism-Leninism offers a scientific explanation that leaves no room for doubt. It further explains that as the ultimate result of the class struggle of mankind, such a society will inevitably be brought about. The victory of Socialism in the U.S.S.R. has also given us factual proof. Our duty is, therefore, to bring about at an early date this Communist society, the realization of which is inevitable in the history of mankind.

This is one aspect. This is our ideal.

But we should understand the other aspect, that is, in spite of the fact that Communism can and must be realized it is still confronted by powerful enemies that must be thoroughly and finally defeated in every respect before Communism can be realized. Thus, the cause of Communism is a long, bitter, arduous but victorious process of struggle. Without such a struggle there can be no Communism. [p. 24]

Comrades! If you only possess great and lofty ideals but not the spirit of "searching for the truth from concrete facts" and do not carry on genuinely practical work, you are not a good Communist Party member. You can only be a dreamer, a prattler, or a pedant. If on the contrary, you only do practical work but do not possess the great and lofty ideals of Communism, you are not a good Communist, but a common careerist. A good Communist Party member is one who combines the great and lofty ideals of Communism with practical work and the spirit of searching for the truth from concrete facts.

The Communist ideal is beautiful while the existing capitalist world is ugly. It is precisely because of its ugliness that the overwhelming majority of the people want to change it and cannot but change it. In changing the world we cannot divorce ourselves from reality, or disregard reality; nor can we escape from reality or surrender to the ugly reality. We must adapt ourselves to reality, understand reality, seek to live and develop in reality, struggle against the ugly reality and transform reality in order to realize our ideals. [pp. 29–30]

At all times and on all questions, a Communist Party member should take into account the interests of the Party as a whole, and place the Party's interests above his personal problems and interests. It is the highest principle of our Party members that the Party's interests are supreme. [p. 31]

If a Party member has only the interests and aims of the Party and Communism in his ideology, if he has no personal aims and considerations independent of the Party's interests, and if he is really unbiased and unselfish, then he will be capable of the following:

1. He will be capable of possessing very good Communist ethics. Because he has a firm outlook he "can both love and hate people." He can show loyalty to and ardent love for all his comrades, revolutionaries, and working people, help them unconditionally, treat them with equality, and never harm any one of them for the sake of his own interests. He can deal with them in a "faithful and forgiving" spirit and "put himself in the position of others." He can consider others' problems from their points of view and be considerate to them. "He will never do to others anything he would not like others to do to him." He can deal with the most vicious enemies of mankind in a most resolute manner and conduct a persistent struggle against the enemy for the purpose of defending the interests of the Party, the class, and the emancipation of mankind. As the Chinese saying goes: "He will worry long before the rest of the world begins to

worry and he will rejoice only after the rest of the world has rejoiced." Both in the Party and among the people he will be the first to suffer hardship and the last to enjoy himself. He never minds whether his conditions are better or worse than others, but he does mind as to whether he has done more revolutionary work than others, or whether he has fought harder. In times of adversity, he will stand out courageously and unflinchingly, and in the face of difficulties he will demonstrate the greatest sense of responsibility. Therefore, he is capable of possessing the greatest firmness and moral courage to resist corruption by riches or honors, to resist tendencies to vacillate in spite of poverty and lowly status, and to refuse to yield in spite of threats or force.

2. He will also be capable of possessing the greatest courage. Since he is free from any selfishness whatever and has never done "anything against his conscience," he can expose his mistakes and shortcomings and boldly correct them in the same way as the sun and the moon emerge bright and full following a brief eclipse. He is "courageous because his is a just cause." He is never afraid of truth. He courageously upholds truth, expounds truth to others, and fights for truth. Even if it is temporarily to his disadvantage to do so, even if he will be subjected to various attacks for the sake of upholding truth, even if the opposition and rebuff of the great majority of the people forces him into temporary isolation (glorious isolation) and even if on this account his life may be endangered he will still be able to stem the tide and uphold truth and will never resign himself to drifting with the tide. So far as he himself is concerned, he has nothing to fear.

3. He will be best capable of acquiring the theory and method of Marxism-Leninism, viewing problems and perceiving the real nature of the situation keenly and aptly. Because he has a firm and clear-cut class standpoint, he is free from personal worries and personal desires which may blur or distort his observation of things and understanding of truth. He has an objective attitude. He tests all theories, truths, and falsehoods in the course of revolutionary practice and is no respecter of persons.

4. He will also be capable of being the most sincere, most candid, and happiest of men. Since he has no selfish desires and since he has nothing to conceal from the Party, "there is nothing which he is afraid of telling others" as the Chinese saying goes. Apart from the interests of the Party

and of the revolution, he has no personal losses or gains or other things to worry about. He can "look after himself when he is on his own." He takes care not to do wrong things when he works independently and without supervision and when there is ample opportunity for him to do all kinds of wrong things. His work will be found in no way incompatible with the Party's interests no matter how many years later it is reviewed. He does not fear criticism from others and he can courageously and sincerely criticize others. That is why he can be sincere, candid and happy.

5. He will be capable of possessing the highest self-respect and self-esteem. For the interests of the Party and of the revolution, he can also be the most lenient, most tolerant, and most ready to compromise, and he will even endure, if necessary, various forms of humiliation and injustice without feeling hurt or bearing grudges. As he has no personal aims or designs, he has no need to flatter others and does not want others to flatter him, either. He has no personal favors to ask of others, so he has no need to humble himself in order to ask help from others. For the interests of the Party and the revolution he can also take care of himself, protect his life and health, raise his theoretical level and enhance his ability. But if for the sake of certain important aims of the Party and of the revolution he is required to endure insults, shoulder heavy burdens and do work which he is reluctant to do, he will take up the most difficult and important work without the slightest hesitation and will not pass the buck.

A Communist Party member should possess all the greatest and noblest virtues of mankind. He should also possess the strict and clear-cut standpoint of the Party and of the proletariat (that is, Party spirit and class character). Our ethics are great precisely because they are the ethics of Communism and of the proletariat. Such ethics are not built upon the backward basis of safeguarding the interests of individuals or a small number of exploiters. They are built, on the contrary, upon the progressive basis of the interests of the proletariat, of the ultimate emancipation of mankind as a whole, of saving the world from destruction and of building a happy and beautiful Communist world. [pp. 32–34]

On Inner-Party Struggle

This essay, delivered by Liu Shao-ch'i as a series of lectures to a Party school in July, 1941, is a kind of sequel to *How To Be a Good Communist* in the series of basic indoctrination texts used for tightening Party organization and morale during the reform campaigns of the early '40s. Where the earlier work focused upon the individual Party member and his self-discipline, attention here is more on the relations among Party members and their conduct within the organization. It is a question then of inner struggle for self-purification of the Party, not of outward struggle for supremacy over others.

The tremendous dynamism of Chinese Communism, especially in this early period, owes no less to its concept of struggle both within and without the Party than to its messianic promises for the future. As a means of keeping Party members in a constant state of alertness, sensitive to the larger interests of the Party rather than to their own, and as a method for overcoming the traditional weakness of hierarchical, bureaucratic organizations—factionalism and favoritism—this kind of ceaseless internal struggle has probably been highly effective. One of its most essential Leninist features is the insistence upon differences in principle as the only valid issues for such struggles. This emphasis on the precise definition of principle and uncompromising adherence to it may seem quite un-Chinese, if we accept the stereotype of the Chinese as having a traditional distaste for rigid dogma and doctrine. Actually, however, Communist principles are far from immutable, and here, as in so many other instances, the Party leadership retains considerable freedom to reinterpret and redefine as it deems necessary.

[From *On Inner-Party Struggle,* pp. 2–69]

INTRODUCTORY REMARKS

Right from the day of its birth, our Party has never for a single moment lived in any environment but that of serious struggle. The Party and the proletariat have constantly lived inside the encirclement of various non-proletarian classes—the big bourgeoisie, the petty bourgeoisie, the peasantry, and even the remnants of feudal forces. All these classes, when they are struggling against the proletariat or when they are cooperating with it, utilize the unstable elements within the Party and the proletariat to penetrate into the heart of the Party and the proletariat and constantly influence the Party and the proletariat in ideology, in living habits, in theory and in action. This is the origin of all kinds of erroneous and undesirable tendencies within the Party. It is the social basis of all kinds of opportunism within the Party, and it is also the source of inner-Party struggles.

Inner-Party struggles are a reflection of the class struggles outside the Party.

From the very day of its inception, our Party has struggled not only against the enemies outside the Party but also against all kinds of hostile and nonproletarian influences inside the Party. These two kinds of struggle are different, but both are necessary and have a common class substance. If our Party did not carry on the latter type of struggle, if it did not struggle constantly within the Party against all undesirable tendencies, if it did not constantly purge the Party of every type of nonproletarian ideology and overcome both "left" and "right" opportunism, then such nonproletarian ideology and such "left" and "right" opportunism might gain ground in the Party and influence or even dominate our Party. This would make it impossible for the Party to consolidate and develop itself or to preserve its independence. This would endanger the Party and lead to its degeneration. Such nonproletarian ideology and "left" or "right" opportunism can corrupt our Party, or certain sections of it, and can even transform the character of our Party or sections of it into that of a nonproletarian organization. For example, it was in this manner that the Social-Democratic parties in Europe were corrupted by bourgeois ideology and transformed into political parties of a bourgeois type, thus becoming the main social pillars of the bourgeoisie.

Therefore, such inner-Party struggle is absolutely necessary and cannot be avoided. Any idea of trying to avoid inner-Party struggle, or of refraining from criticizing others' mistakes so that they will not criticize one's own errors, is totally wrong.

Inner-Party struggles consist principally of ideological struggles. Their content is made up of the divergencies and antagonisms arising in matters of ideology and principle. The divergencies and antagonisms among our comrades on matters of ideology and principle can develop into political splits within the Party, and, under certain circumstances, even into inevitable organizational splits; but, in character and content, such divergencies and antagonisms are basically ideological struggles.

Consequently, any inner-Party struggle not involving divergencies in matters of ideology and principle and any conflict among Party members not based on divergencies in matters of principle is a type of unprincipled struggle, a struggle without content. This kind of struggle without principle or content is utterly unnecessary within the Party. It is detrimental and not beneficial to the Party. Every Party member should strictly avoid such struggles. [pp. 2–4]

Comrade Stalin said:

The question here is that contradictions can be overcome only by means of struggle for this or that principle, for defining the goal of this or that struggle,

[258]

for choosing this or that method of struggle that may lead to the goal. We can and we must come to agreement with those within the Party who differ with us on questions of current policy, on questions of a purely practical character. But if these questions involve differences over principle, then no agreement, no "middle" line can save the cause. There is and there can be no "middle" line on questions of principle. The work of the Party must be based either on these or those principles. The "middle" line on questions of principle is a "line" that muddles up one's head, a "line" that covers up differences, a "line" of ideological degeneration of the Party, a "line" of ideological death of the Party. It is not our policy to pursue such a "middle" line. It is the policy of a party that is declining and degenerating from day to day. Such a policy cannot but transform the Party into an empty bureaucratic organ, standing isolated from the working people and becoming a puppet unable to do anything. Such a road cannot be our road.

He added:

Our Party has been strengthened on the basis of overcoming the contradictions within the Party.

This explains the essential nature of inner-Party struggle. [p. 5]

Many comrades did not understand that our inner-Party struggle is a struggle over principle, a struggle for this or that principle, for defining the goal of this or that struggle, for choosing this or that method of struggle that may lead to the goal.

These comrades did not understand that on questions of current policy, on questions of purely practical character, we can and must come to agreement with those within the Party who differ with us. They did not know or understand that on issues involving principle, on questions of defining the goal of our struggles and of choosing the methods of struggle needed to reach such goal they should wage an uncompromising struggle against those in the Party who hold divergent opinions; but on questions of current policy, on questions of a purely practical character, they should come to agreement with those within the Party who hold divergent opinions instead of carrying on an irreconcilable struggle against them, so long as such questions do not involve any difference over principle. [p. 17]

HOW TO CONDUCT INNER-PARTY STRUGGLE

Comrades! Now the question is very clear. It is how to conduct inner-Party struggle correctly and appropriately.

On this question, the Communist Parties of the U.S.S.R. and many other countries have much experience and so has the Chinese Party. Lenin and Stalin have issued many instructions and so has the Central Committee of our Party. Our comrades must make a careful study of these experiences and instructions, which will also be discussed when we come to the question of Party-building. Today I will not touch upon them. I will bring up for the reference of our comrades only the following points, on the basis of the experience of the inner-Party struggle of the Chinese Party.

First of all, comrades must understand that inner-Party struggle is a matter of the greatest seriousness and responsibility. We must conduct it with the strictest and most responsible attitude and should never conduct it carelessly. In carrying out inner-Party struggle we must first fully adopt the correct stand of the Party, the unselfish stand of serving the interests of the Party, of doing better work, and of helping other comrades to correct their mistakes and to gain a better understanding of the problems. We ourselves must be clear about the facts and problems by making a systematic investigation and study. At the same time, we must carry on systematic, well-prepared, and well-led inner-Party struggles.

Comrades must understand that only by first taking the correct stand oneself can one rectify the incorrect stand of others. Only by behaving properly oneself can one correct the misbehavior of others. The old saying has it: "One must first correct oneself before one can correct others." [pp. 55–56]

Secondly, . . . In conducting inner-Party struggle comrades must try their best to assume a sincere, frank, and positive educational attitude in order to achieve unity in ideology and principle. Only in cases where we have no alternative, when it is deemed imperative, may we adopt militant forms of struggle and apply organizational measures. All Party organizations, within appropriate limits, have full right to draw organizational conclusions in regard to any Party member who persists in his errors. The application of Party disciplinary measures and the adoption of organizational measures are entirely necessary under certain circumstances. Such measures, however, cannot be used casually or indiscriminately. Party discipline cannot be upheld simply by the excessive punishment of comrades by Party organizations. The upholding of Party discipline and Party unity does not in the main depend on the punishment of comrades (if they have to be upheld in such a manner it signifies a crisis in the Party), but rather on the actual unity of the Party in ideology and principle, and on the consciousness of the vast majority of the Party members. When we are eventually fully clear regarding ideology and principle, it is very easy for us to draw organizational conclusions, if necessary. It does not take us a minute to expel Party members or announce voluntary withdrawal from the Party. [pp. 58–59]

Thirdly, criticisms directed against Party organizations or against comrades and their work must be appropriate and well-regulated. Bolshevik self-criticism is conducted according to the Bolshevik yardstick. Excessive criticism, the exaggeration of others' errors, and indiscriminate name-calling are all incorrect. The case is not that the more bitter the inner-Party struggle, the better; but that inner-Party struggle should be conducted within proper limits and that appropriateness should be observed. Both over-shooting the target or falling short of it are undesirable. [p. 60]

Fourthly, the holding of struggle meetings, either inside or outside the Party, should in general be stopped. The various defects and errors should be pointed out in the course of summing up and reviewing work. We should first deal with "the case" and then with "the person." We must first make clear the facts, the points at issue, the nature, the seriousness, and the cause of the errors and defects, and only then point out who are responsible for these defects and errors, and whose is the major responsibility and whose is the minor responsibility. [p. 61]

Fifthly, every opportunity to appeal must be given to comrades who have been criticized or punished. As a rule, a comrade should be personally notified of all records or organizational conclusions that may be made about him, and these should be made in his presence. If he does not agree, then after discussion, the case may be referred to a higher authority. (In the case of anyone who expresses dissatisfaction after having been punished the Party organization concerned must refer the case to a higher authority even if the comrade himself does not want to make an appeal.) No Party organization can prevent any comrade who has been punished from appealing to a higher authority. No Party member can be deprived of his right to appeal. No Party organization can withhold any appeal. [p. 62]

On questions of ideology or principle, if agreement cannot be finally reached within the Party organization after discussion, the matter may be settled by a majority decision. After that, the minority who still hold different opinions may have the right to reserve their opinions on condition that they absolutely abide by the decision of the majority in respect to organizational matters and in their activities. [p. 63]

Sixthly, a clear line should be drawn and a proper link should be established between struggles waged inside the Party and those waged outside the Party. [p. 63]

Seventhly, in order to prevent unprincipled disputes within the Party, it is necessary to lay down the following measures:

1. Party members who disagree with the Party's leading body or any Party organization should submit their views and criticisms to the appropriate Party organization and should not talk about it casually among the masses.

2. Party members who disagree with other Party members, or certain responsible Party members, may criticize them in their presence or in certain specific Party organizations and should not talk about it casually.

3. Party members or Party committees of a lower level who disagree with a Party committee of a higher level, may bring the issue to the Party committee of a higher level, or ask it to call a meeting to study the matter, or should refer the matter to a Party committee of a still higher level, but they should not talk about it casually or inform Party committees of a still lower level about the matter.

4. When Party members discover any other Party member doing something wrong and acting in a manner detrimental to the interests of the Party they must report such activities to the appropriate Party organization and should not attempt to cover up the matter or attempt to mutually shield each other.

5. Party members should promote an upright style of work and oppose anything of a deceitful nature, oppose any kind of deceitful talk and actions, and should severely condemn all those who indulge in idle talk, gossiping, prying into others' secrets, and the spreading of rumors. The leading bodies of the Party must from time to time issue instructions forbidding Party members to talk about certain specific matters.

6. The leading bodies at all levels must from time to time summon those comrades who indulge in idle talk and unprincipled disputes and talk with them, correct them and warn them, or subject them to discipline in other ways.

7. Party committees at all levels must respect the opinions set forth by Party members. They should frequently convene meetings to discuss questions and review their work, and provide Party members with ample opportunity to express their opinions.

Unprincipled disputes should in general be forbidden and no judgment should be passed on them, because it is impossible to judge who is right and who is wrong in such unprincipled disputes. [pp. 64–66]

All in all, inner-Party struggle is fundamentally a form of struggle and controversy over ideology and principles. Inside the Party everything must submit to reason, everything must be reasoned out, and everything must have some reason for it, otherwise it will not do. We can do anything without difficulty if we have reasoned it out.

Inside the Party we must cultivate the practice of submitting to reason. The yardstick for determining whether this or that reason is sound is: the interests of the Party and the interests of the proletarian struggle; the subordination of the interests of the part to those of the whole, and the subordination of the immediate interests to long-range interests. All reasons and viewpoints are sound when they are beneficial to the interests of the Party, to the interests of the proletarian struggle, to the long-range interests of the Party as a whole, and to the long-range interests of the proletarian struggle as a whole, otherwise they are not sound. Any struggle that does not submit to reason or that has no reason for it is an unprincipled struggle. [pp. 67–68]

Everything must submit to reason! It would not do if it didn't! It would not do either if we reason incorrectly! It would be even more undesirable if we indulge in empty talk! Of course this is a rather difficult job. But only in this way can we become qualified as Bolsheviks. [p. 69]

MAO TSE-TUNG
Combat Liberalism

If to Liu Shao-ch'i the essence of Marxism-Leninism lay in "principled struggle," to Mao Tse-tung the essence of liberalism lay in indifference to principle. The latter he sees not as a political philosophy but as the want of one, a moral infection which arises from bourgeois individualism and produces selfishness, self-indulgence, slackness, a noncommittal attitude, avoidance of struggle, and a desire for peace-at-any-price. In this respect his views resemble those of Chiang Kai-shek in *China's Destiny* (Mao's piece was actually written earlier, in September, 1937), but they represent a much more severe and sweeping critique. Missing is Chiang's recognition that not all of Western liberalism conformed to this caricature of its weaknesses.

Ironically, Mao's position was enunciated during the early phase of the second United Front period. No doubt one of his purposes was to insure that Party members would not be contaminated and corrupted in the midst of collaboration with Westernized "liberals."

[From *Selected Works,* II, 74–76]

We advocate an active ideological struggle, because it is the weapon for achieving solidarity within the Party and the revolutionary organizations and making them fit to fight. Every Communist and revolutionary should take up this weapon.

But liberalism negates ideological struggle and advocates unprincipled peace, with the result that a decadent, philistine style in work has appeared and certain units and individuals in the Party and the revolutionary organizations have begun to degenerate politically.

Liberalism manifests itself in various ways.

Although the person concerned is clearly known to be in the wrong, yet because he is an old acquaintance, a fellow townsman, a school-friend, a bosom companion, a loved one, an old colleague, or a former subordinate, one does not argue with him on the basis of principle but lets things slide in order to maintain peace and friendship. Or one touches lightly upon the matter without finding a thorough solution, so as to maintain harmony all around. As a result, harm is done to the organization as well as to the individual concerned. This is the first type of liberalism.

To indulge in irresponsible criticism in private, without making positive suggestions to the organization. To say nothing to people's faces, but to gossip behind their backs; or to say nothing at a meeting, but to gossip after it. Not to care for the principle of collective life but only for unrestrained self-indulgence. This is the second type.

Things of no personal concern are put on the shelf; the less said the better about things that are clearly known to be wrong; to be cautious in order to save one's own skin, and anxious only to avoid reprimands. This is the third type.

To disobey orders and place personal opinions above everything. To demand special dispensation from the organization, but to reject its discipline. This is the fourth type.

To engage in struggles and disputes against incorrect views, not for the sake of solidarity, progress, or improving the work, but for personal attacks, letting off steam, venting personal grievances, or seeking revenge. This is the fifth type.

Not to dispute incorrect opinions on hearing them, and not even to report counter-revolutionary opinions on hearing them, but to tolerate them calmly as if nothing had happened. This is the sixth type.

Not to engage in propaganda and agitation, to make speeches or carry on investigations and inquiries among the masses, but to leave the masses alone, without any concern for their weal and woe; to forget that one is a Communist, and to behave as if a Communist were merely an ordinary person. This is the seventh type.

Not to feel indignant at actions detrimental to the interests of the masses, not to dissuade or to stop the person responsible for them or to explain things to him, but to allow him to continue. This is the eighth type.

To work half-heartedly without any definite plan or direction; to work perfunctorily and let things drift. "So long as I remain a bonze, I go on tolling the bell." This is the ninth type.

To regard oneself as having performed meritorious service in the revolution and to put on the airs of a veteran; to be incapable of doing great things, yet to disdain minor tasks; to be careless in work and slack in study. This is the tenth type.

To be aware of one's own mistakes yet make no attempt to rectify them, and to adopt a liberal attitude towards oneself. This is the eleventh type.

We can name several more. But these eleven are the principal types.

All these are manifestations of liberalism.

In revolutionary organizations liberalism is extremely harmful. It is a corrosive which disrupts unity, undermines solidarity, induces inactivity, and creates dissension. It deprives the revolutionary ranks of compact organization and strict discipline, prevents policies from being thoroughly carried out, and divorces the organizations of the Party from the masses under their leadership. It is an extremely bad tendency.

Liberalism stems from the selfishness of the petty bourgeoisie, which puts personal interests foremost and the interests of the revolution in the second place, thus giving rise to ideological, political, and organizational liberalism.

Liberals look upon the principles of Marxism as abstract dogmas. They approve of Marxism, but are not prepared to practice it or to practice it in full; they are not prepared to replace their own liberalism with Marxism. Such people have got Marxism, but they have also got liberalism: they talk Marxism but practice liberalism; they apply Marxism to others but liberalism to themselves. Both kinds of goods are in stock and each has its particular use. That is how the minds of certain people work.

Liberalism is a manifestation of opportunism and conflicts fundamentally with Marxism. It has a passive character and objectively has the effect of helping the enemy; thus the enemy welcomes its preservation in our midst. Such being its nature, there should be no place for it in the revolutionary ranks.

We must use the active spirit of Marxism to overcome liberalism with its passivity. A Communist should be frank, faithful and active, looking upon the interests of the revolution as his very life and subordinating his personal interests to those of the revolution; he should, always and everywhere, adhere to correct principles and wage a tireless struggle against all incorrect ideas and actions, so as to consolidate the collective life of the Party and strengthen the ties between the Party and the masses; and he should be more concerned about the Party and the masses than about the individual, and more concerned about others than about himself. Only thus can he be considered a Communist.

All loyal, honest, active and staunch Communists must unite to oppose the liberal tendencies shown by certain people among us, and turn them in the right direction. This is one of the tasks on our ideological front.

On Art and Literature

The so-called *Cheng-feng* movement of Party reform gave particular attention to the rectification of undesirable tendencies in the cultural sphere. In this speech made to a forum on literature and art in Yenan, May, 1942, Mao reasserts the orthodox Communist view that art and literature must subserve the political ends of the revolution, but insists that art cannot be mere propaganda. He acknowledges that aesthetic criteria are distinct from political ones, that political correctness is not enough in works of art, and that they fail if lacking in "artistic quality." He does not, however, pursue the question of how such quality is to be achieved in the aesthetic form if the ideological content is so rigidly controlled, and therefore suggests no remedy for the sterilizing effect which such control has usually had on artistic creativity.

Note the attention given to the special need of cadres, as an elite group, for works of art representing cultural "elevation" rather than mere popularization.

[From *Selected Works*, IV, 69–86]

Comrades! We have met three times during this month. In the pursuit of truth, heated debates have taken place and scores of Party and non-Party comrades have spoken, laying bare the issues and making them concrete. I think this is very profitable to the whole artistic and literary movement.

In discussing any problem we should start from actual facts and not from definitions. We shall be following the wrong method if we first look up definitions of art and literature in the textbooks and then use them as criteria in determining the direction of the present artistic and literary movement or in judging the views and controversies that arise today. We are Marxists and Marxism teaches that in our approach to a problem we should start not from abstract definitions but from objective facts and, by analyzing these facts, determine the way we shall go, our policies and methods. We should do the same in our present discussion of art and literature. . . .

What then is the crux of our problems? I think our problems are basically those of working for the masses and of how to work for them. If these two problems are not solved, or [are] solved inadequately, our artists and writers will be ill-adapted to their circumstances and unfit for their tasks, and will come up against a series of problems from within and without. My conclusion will center round these two problems, while touching upon some other problems related to them.

I

The first problem is: For whom are our art and literature intended?

This problem has, as a matter of fact, been solved long ago by Marxists, and especially by Lenin. As far back as 1905 Lenin emphatically pointed out that our art and literature should "serve the millions upon millions of working people." [25] [pp. 69–70]

II

The question of "whom to serve" having been solved, the question of "how to serve" comes up. To put it in the words of our comrades: Should we devote ourselves to elevation or to popularization? [p. 75]

Though man's social life constitutes the only source for art and literature, and is incomparably more vivid and richer than art and literature as such, the people are not satisfied with the former alone and demand the latter. Why? Because, although both are beautiful, life as reflected in artistic and literary works can and ought to be on a higher level and of a greater power and better focused, more typical, nearer the ideal, and therefore more universal than actual everyday life. Revolutionary art and literature should create all kinds of characters on the basis of actual life and help the masses to push history forward. For example, on the one hand there are people suffering from hunger, cold, and oppression, and on the other hand there are men exploiting and oppressing men—a contrast that exists everywhere and seems quite commonplace to people; artists and writers, however, can create art and literature out of such daily occurrences by organizing them, bringing them to a focal point, and making the contradictions and struggles in them typical—create art and literature that can awaken and arouse the masses and impel them to unite and struggle to change their environment. If there were no such art and literature, this task could not be fulfilled or at least not effectively and speedily fulfilled.

What are popularization and elevation in art and literature? What is the relation between the two? Works of popularization are simpler and plainer and therefore more readily accepted by the broad masses of the people of today. Works of a higher level are more polished and therefore more difficult to produce and less likely to win the ready acceptance of the broad masses of people of today. The problem facing the workers, peasants, and soldiers today is this: engaged in a ruthless and sanguinary struggle against the enemy, they remain illiterate and uncultured as a result of the prolonged rule of the feudal and bourgeois classes and consequently they badly need a widespread campaign of enlightenment, and

[25] See V. I. Lenin, *The Party's Organization and the Party's Literature.*

they eagerly wish to have culture, knowledge, art, and literature which meet their immediate need and are readily acceptable to them so as to heighten their passion for struggle and their confidence in victory, to strengthen their solidarity, and thus to enable them to fight the enemy with one heart and one mind. In meeting their primary need, we are not to "add flowers to a piece of brocade" but "offer fuel to a person in snowy weather." Under the present conditions, therefore, popularization is the more pressing task. It is wrong to despise and neglect this task.

But popularization and elevation cannot be sharply separated. . . . The people need popularization, but along with it they need elevation too, elevation month by month and year by year. Popularization is popularization for the people, and elevation is elevation of the people. Such elevation does not take place in mid-air, nor behind closed doors, but on the basis of popularization. It is at once determined by popularization and gives direction to it. . . . This being the case, the work of popularization in our sense not only constitutes no obstacle to elevation but affords a basis for our work of elevation on a limited scale at present, as well as preparing the necessary conditions for our far more extensive work of elevation in the future.

Besides the elevation that directly meets the need of the masses, there is the elevation that meets their need indirectly, namely, the elevation needed by the cadres. Being advanced members of the masses, the cadres are generally better educated than the masses, and art and literature of a higher level are entirely necessary to them; and it would be a mistake to ignore this. Anything done for the cadres is also entirely done for the masses, because it is only through the cadres that we can give education and guidance to the masses. If we depart from this objective, if what we give to the cadres cannot help them to educate and guide the masses, then our work of elevation will be like aimless shooting, i.e., deviating from our fundamental principle of serving the broad masses of the people. [pp. 77–79]

. . . .

IV

One of the principal methods of struggle in the artistic and literary sphere is art and literary criticism. It should be developed and, as many comrades have rightly pointed out, our work in this respect was quite inadequate in the past. Art and literary criticism presents a complex problem which requires much study of a special kind. Here I shall stress only the basic problem of criteria in criticism. I shall also comment briefly on certain other problems and incorrect views brought up by some comrades.

There are two criteria in art and literary criticism: political and artistic. According to the political criterion, all works are good that facilitate unity and resistance to Japan, that encourage the masses to be of one heart and one mind, and that oppose retrogression and promote progress; on the other hand, all works are bad that undermine unity and resistance to Japan, that sow dissension and discord among the masses, and that oppose progress and drag the people back. And how can we tell the good from the bad here—by the motive (subjective intention) or by the effect (social practice)? Idealists stress motive and ignore effect, while mechanical materialists stress effect and ignore motive; in contradistinction from either, we dialectical materialists insist on the unity of motive and effect. The motive of serving the masses is inseparable from the effect of winning their approval, and we must unite the two. . . . In examining the subjective intention of an artist, i.e., whether his motive is correct and good, we do not look at his declaration but at the effect his activities (mainly his works) produce on society and the masses. Social practice and its effect are the criteria for examining the subjective intention or the motive. . . . According to the artistic criterion, all works are good or comparatively good that are relatively high in artistic quality; and bad or comparatively bad that are relatively low in artistic quality. Of course, this distinction also depends on social effect. As there is hardly an artist who does not consider his own work excellent, our criticism ought to permit the free competition of all varieties of artistic works; but it is entirely necessary for us to pass correct judgments on them according to the criteria of the science of art, so that we can gradually raise the art of a lower level to a higher level, and to change the art which does not meet the requirements of the struggle of the broad masses into art that does meet them.

There is thus the political criterion as well as the artistic criterion. How are the two related? Politics is not the equivalent of art, nor is a general world outlook equivalent to the method of artistic creation and criticism. We believe there is neither an abstract and absolutely unchangeable political criterion, nor an abstract and absolutely unchangeable artistic criterion, for every class in a class society has its own political and artistic criteria. But all classes in all class societies place the political criterion first and the artistic criterion second. The bourgeoisie always rejects proletarian artistic and literary works, no matter how great their artistic achievement. As for the proletariat, they must treat the art and literature of the past according to their attitude towards the people and whether they are progressive in the light of history. Some things which are basically reactionary from the political point of view may yet be artistically good. But the more artistic such a work may be, the greater harm will it do to the people, and the more reason for us to reject it. The contradiction between reactionary political content and artistic form is a common characteristic of the art and literature of all exploiting classes in their decline. What we demand is unity of politics and art, of content and form, and of the revolutionary political content and the highest possible degree of perfection in artistic form. Works of art, however politically progressive, are powerless if they lack artistic quality. Therefore we are equally opposed to works with wrong political approaches and to the tendency towards so-called "poster and slogan style" which is correct only in political approach but lacks artistic power. We must carry on a two-front struggle in art and literature. [pp. 84–86]

On the Correct Handling of Contradictions Among the People

This speech, popularly known by the catch-phrase "Let A Hundred Flowers Bloom," is one of Mao Tse-tung's most important theoretical statements since the consolidation of Communist power on the mainland of China and since the death of Stalin left Mao as perhaps the dean of Communist theoreticians. It was clearly occasioned in part by the shock of the uprising in Hungary late in 1956, which showed the degree of pent-up dissatisfaction possible under even a seemingly well-established Communist regime. If Mao's gesture was meant to encourage the "letting off of steam," those who took advantage of the offer found, after a brief period of forbearance by the Party, that they would be subjected to severe attack and penalized for their outspokenness.

We are not concerned here with the immediate political or tactical implications of this episode for the period in question or for the Communist world as a whole. In long-range terms its significance would seem to lie, not in any liberalization or loosening of Communist ideological control, but precisely in its reaffirmation of the importance Mao attaches to unity in matters of theory and doctrine. As we have already seen, for Mao and for Liu Shao-ch'i, the principal means of preserving that unity as a dynamic force has been ideological struggle. Yet under conditions of Party dominance the threat of stagnation is always present. Consequently for Mao, always concerned to keep his cohorts in battle-readiness, the question is how to stimulate the airing of contradictions without allowing them to become antagonistic, how to obtain the benefits of struggle without running the risks.

Subsequent reports from Peking have indicated that Mao is still wrestling with this problem and might still find a use for "nonantagonistic" criticism as an outlet for discontent. When, however, the Party stands as sole judge of what is antagonistic or not, and has made such an object lesson of those who unknowingly overstepped the invisible line earlier, it seems unlikely that this particular contradiction can be easily resolved.

This speech was originally delivered on February 27, 1957, before a large audience at a Supreme State Conference. When finally published at the end of June, it had been substantially revised and probably represented a much more guarded statement of policy than the original lecture. The purpose was now less to encourage "fragrant flowers" and more to identify "poisonous weeds."

[From Mao, *Let A Hundred Flowers Bloom,* ed. by G. F. Hudson, pp. 14–50]

TWO DIFFERENT TYPES OF CONTRADICTIONS

Never has our country been as united as it is today. The victories of the bourgeois-democratic revolution and the socialist revolution, coupled with our achievements in socialist construction, have rapidly changed the face of old China. Now we see before us an even brighter future. The days of national disunity and turmoil which the people detested have gone forever. Led by the working class and the Communist Party, and united as one, our 600 million people are engaged in the great work of building socialism. Unification of the country, unity of the people, and unity among our various nationalities—these are the basic guarantees for the sure triumph of our cause. However, this does not mean that there are no longer any contradictions in our society. It would be naive to imagine that there are no more contradictions. To do so would be to fly in the face of objective reality. We are confronted by two types of social contradictions—contradictions between ourselves and the enemy and contradictions among the people. These two types of contradictions are totally different in nature. [pp. 14–15]

The contradictions between ourselves and our enemies are antagonistic ones. Within the ranks of the people, contradictions among the working people are nonantagonistic, while those between the exploiters and the exploited classes have, apart from their antagonistic aspect, a nonantag-

[272]

onistic aspect. Contradictions among the people have always existed, but their content differs in each period of the revolution and during the building of socialism.

In the conditions existing in China today, what we call contradictions among the people include the following:

Contradictions within the working class, contradictions within the peasantry, contradictions within the intelligentsia, contradictions between the working class and the peasantry,. contradictions between the working class and peasantry on the one hand and the intelligentsia on the other, contradictions between the working class and other sections of the working people on the one hand and the national bourgeoisie on the other, contradictions within the national bourgeoisie, and so forth. Our People's Government is a government that truly represents the interests of the people and serves the people, yet certain contradictions do exist between the Government and the masses. These include contradictions between the interests of the state, collective interests, and individual interests; between democracy and centralism; between those in positions of leadership and the led, and contradictions arising from the bureaucratic practices of certain state functionaries in their relations with the masses. All these are contradictions among the people; generally speaking, underlying the contradictions among the people is the basic identity of the interests of the people.

In our country, the contradiction between the working class and the national bourgeoisie is a contradiction among the people. The class struggle waged between the two is, by and large, a class struggle within the ranks of the people; this is because of the dual character of the national bourgeoisie in our country. In the years of the bourgeois-democratic revolution, there was a revolutionary side to their character; there was also a tendency to compromise with the enemy—this was the other side. In the period of the socialist revolution, exploitation of the working class to make profits is one side, while support of the Constitution and willingness to accept socialist transformation is the other. The national bourgeoisie differs from the imperialists, the landlords, and the bureaucrat-capitalists. The contradiction between exploiter and exploited which exists between the national bourgeoisie and the working class is an antagonistic one. But, in the concrete conditions existing in China, such an antagonistic contradiction, if properly handled, can be transformed into

[273]

a nonantagonistic one and resolved in a peaceful way. But if it is not properly handled, if, say, we do not follow a policy of unity, criticizing and educating the national bourgeoisie, or if the national bourgeoisie does not accept this policy, then the contradictions between the working class and the national bourgeoisie can turn into an antagonistic contradiction as between ourselves and the enemy. [pp. 16–18]

There were other people in our country who took a wavering attitude toward the Hungarian events because they were ignorant about the actual world situation. They felt that there was too little freedom under our people's democracy and that there was more freedom under Western parliamentary democracy. They ask for the adoption of the two-party system of the West, where one party is in office and the other out of office. But this so-called two-party system is nothing but a means of maintaining the dictatorship of the bourgeoisie; under no circumstances can it safeguard the freedom of the working people. As a matter of fact, freedom and democracy cannot exist in the abstract; they only exist in the concrete. . . .

Those who demand freedom and democracy in the abstract regard democracy as an end and not a means. Democracy sometimes seems to be an end, but it is in fact only a means. Marxism teaches us that democracy is part of the superstructure and belongs to the category of politics. That is to say, in the last analysis it serves the economic base. The same is true of freedom. Both democracy and freedom are relative, not absolute, and they come into being and develop under specific historical circumstances.

Within the ranks of the people, democracy stands in relation to centralism, and freedom to discipline. They are two conflicting aspects of a single entity, contradictory as well as united, and we should not one-sidedly emphasize one to the denial of the other. Within the ranks of the people, we cannot do without democracy, nor can we do without centralism. Our democratic centralism means the unity of democracy and centralism and the unity of freedom and discipline. Under this system, the people enjoy a wide measure of democracy and freedom, but at the same time they have to keep themselves within the bounds of socialist discipline. All this is well understood by the people. [pp. 21–22]

Marxist philosophy holds that the law of the unity of opposites is a fundamental law of the universe. This law operates everywhere, in the natural world, in human society, and in man's thinking. Opposites in contradiction unite as well as struggle with each other, and thus impel all things to move and change. Contradictions exist everywhere, but as things differ in nature so do contradictions in any given phenomenon or thing; the unity of opposites is conditional, temporary and transitory, and hence relative, whereas struggle between opposites is absolute. Lenin gave a very clear exposition of this law. In our country, a growing number of people have come to understand it. For many people, however, acceptance of this law is one thing and its application, examining and dealing with problems, is quite another. Many dare not acknowledge openly that there still exist contradictions among the people, which are the very forces that move our society forward. Many people refuse to admit that contradictions still exist in a socialist society, with the result that when confronted with social contradictions they become timid and helpless. They do not understand that socialist society grows more united and consolidated precisely through the ceaseless process of correctly dealing with and resolving contradictions. For this reason, we need to explain things to our people, our cadres in the first place, to help them understand contradictions in a socialist society and learn how to deal with such contradictions in a correct way. [p. 26]

ON 'LETTING A HUNDRED FLOWERS BLOSSOM' AND 'LETTING A HUNDRED SCHOOLS OF THOUGHT CONTEND' AND 'LONG-TERM COEXISTENCE AND MUTUAL SUPERVISION'

"Let a hundred flowers blossom" and "let a hundred schools of thought contend," "long-term coexistence and mutual supervision"—how did these slogans come to be put forward?

They were put forward in the light of the specific conditions existing in China, on the basis of the recognition that various kinds of contradictions still exist in a socialist society, and in response to the country's urgent need to speed up its economic and cultural development.

The policy of letting a hundred flowers blossom and a hundred schools of thought contend is designed to promote the flourishing of the arts and the progress of science; it is designed to enable a socialist culture to thrive in our land. Different forms and styles in art can develop freely, and different schools in science can contend freely. We think that it is harmful to the growth of art and science if administrative measures are used

[275]

to impose one particular style of art or school of thought and to ban another. Questions of right and wrong in the arts and sciences should be settled through free discussions in artistic and scientific circles and in the course of practical work in the arts and sciences. They should not be settled in summary fashion. A period of trial is often needed to determine whether something is right or wrong. In the past, new and correct things often failed at the outset to win recognition from the majority of people and had to develop by twists and turns in struggle. Correct and good things have often at first been looked upon not as fragrant flowers but as poisonous weeds; Copernicus's theory of the solar system and Darwin's theory of evolution were once dismissed as erroneous and had to win through over bitter opposition. Chinese history offers many similar examples. In socialist society, conditions for the growth of new things are radically different from and far superior to those in the old society. Nevertheless, it still often happens that new, rising forces are held back and reasonable suggestions smothered.

The growth of new things can also be hindered, not because of deliberate suppressions but because of lack of discernment. That is why we should take a cautious attitude in regard to questions of right and wrong in the arts and sciences, encourage free discussion, and avoid hasty conclusions. We believe that this attitude will facilitate the growth of the arts and sciences.

Marxism has also developed through struggle. At the beginning, Marxism was subjected to all kinds of attack and regarded as a poisonous weed. It is still being attacked and regarded as a poisonous weed in many parts of the world. However, it enjoys a different position in the socialist countries. But, even in these countries, there are non-Marxist as well as anti-Marxist ideologies. It is true that in China socialist transformation, in so far as a change in the system of ownership is concerned, has in the main been completed, and the turbulent, large-scale, mass class struggles characteristic of the revolutionary periods have in the main concluded. But remnants of the overthrown landlord and comprador classes still exist, the bourgeoisie still exists, and the petty bourgeoisie has only just begun to remold itself. Class struggle is not yet over. . . . In this respect, the question of whether socialism or capitalism will win is still not really settled. Marxists are still a minority of the entire population as well as of the intellectuals. Marxism therefore must still develop through struggle. Marxism can only develop through struggle—this is true not only in the past and present, it is necessarily true in the future also. What is correct always develops in the course of struggle with what is wrong. The true, the good and the beautiful always exist in comparison with the false, the evil and the ugly, and grow in struggle with the latter. As mankind in general rejects an untruth and accepts a truth, a new truth will begin struggling with new erroneous ideas. Such struggles will never end. This is the law of development of truth, and it is certainly also the law of development of Marxism. [pp. 44–46]

People may ask: Since Marxism is accepted by the majority of the people in our country as the guiding ideology, can it be criticized? Certainly it can. As a scientific truth, Marxism fears no criticism. If it did and could be defeated in argument, it would be worthless. In fact, are not the idealists criticizing Marxism every day and in all sorts of ways? As for those who harbor bourgeois and petty-bourgeois ideas and do not wish to change, are not they also criticizing Marxism in all sorts of ways? Marxists should not be afraid of criticism from any quarter. Quite the contrary, they need to steel and improve themselves and win new positions in the teeth of criticism and the storm and stress of struggle. Fighting against wrong ideas is like being vaccinated—a man develops greater immunity from disease after the vaccine takes effect. Plants raised in hothouses are not likely to be robust. Carrying out the policy of letting a hundred flowers blossom and a hundred schools of thought contend will not weaken but strengthen the leading position of Marxism in the ideological field.

What should our policy be toward non-Marxist ideas? As far as unmistakable counter-revolutionaries and wreckers of the socialist cause are concerned, the matter is easy; we simply deprive them of their freedom of speech. But it is quite a different matter when we are faced with incorrect ideas among the people. Will it do to ban such ideas and give them no opportunity to express themselves? Certainly not. It is not only futile but very harmful to use crude and summary methods to deal with ideological questions among the people, with questions relating to the spiritual life of man. You may ban the expression of wrong ideas, but the ideas will still be there. On the other hand, correct ideas, if pampered in hot-houses without being exposed to the elements or immunized against disease, will not win out against wrong ones. That is why it is only by employing methods of discussion, criticism, and reasoning that we can really foster correct ideas, overcome wrong ideas, and really settle issues. [pp. 47–48]

On the surface, these two slogans—let a hundred flowers blossom and a hundred schools of thought contend—have no class character; the proletariat can turn them to account, and so can the bourgeoisie and other people. But different classes, strata, and social groups each have their own views on what are fragrant flowers and what are poisonous weeds. So what, from the point of view of the broad masses of the people, should be a criterion today for distinguishing between fragrant flowers and poisonous weeds?

In the political life of our country, how are our people to determine what is right and what is wrong in our words and actions? Basing ourselves on the principles of our constitution, the will of the overwhelming majority of our people and the political programs jointly proclaimed on various occasions by our political parties and groups, we believe that, broadly speaking, words and actions can be judged right if they:

1. Help to unite the people of our various nationalities, and do not divide them.

2. Are beneficial, not harmful, to socialist transformation and socialist construction.

3. Help to consolidate, not undermine or weaken, the people's democratic dictatorship.

4. Help to consolidate, not undermine or weaken, democratic centralism.

5. Tend to strengthen, not to cast off or weaken, the leadership of the Communist Party.

6. Are beneficial, not harmful, to international socialist solidarity and the solidarity of the peace-loving peoples of the world.

Of these six criteria, the most important are the socialist path and the leadership of the Party. These criteria are put forward in order to foster, and not hinder, the free discussion of various questions among the people. Those who do not approve of these criteria can still put forward their own views and argue their cases. When the majority of the people have clear-cut criteria to go by, criticism and self-criticism can be conducted along proper lines, and these criteria can be applied to people's words and actions to determine whether they are fragrant flowers or poisonous weeds. These are political criteria. Naturally, in judging the truthfulness of scientific theories or assessing the esthetic value of works of art, other pertinent criteria are needed, but these six political criteria are also applicable to all activities in the arts or sciences. In a socialist country like ours, can there possibly be any useful scientific or artistic activity which runs counter to these political criteria? [pp. 49–50]

CONCLUSION

Having concluded our survey of the Chinese tradition with an. examination of Chinese Communism, we return to our initial question: What has the one to do with the other? Does Chinese Communism represent a complete departure from tradition? Is it not, after all, far more Communist than Chinese?

The record to date—certainly as revealed in the writings above—indicates clearly enough the anti-traditionalist character of Chinese Communism. It is not just that revolutionary changes have been effected in Chinese society, and especially in institutions closely bound up with traditional ideologies (the family with Confucianism, for instance), but more directly that a deliberate attempt has been made to efface from Chinese minds whatever influence traditional religious and philosophical systems might still exert upon them.

Then too, above and beyond this overt hostility—Mao's scorn for Confucius and his contempt for religious "superstition"—there is also his positive commitment to a new orthodoxy which must be considered, for it is an orthodoxy which not only dispenses with the sanction of Chinese tradition, but feels little need even to reckon with it. Thus, with minor concessions to popular attitudes and modes of expression, the textbooks of Chinese Communism betray little self-consciousness over their break with the past. Mao's style of writing, his political vocabulary, his sources of authority, and his whole frame of reference are in most respects so foreign to Chinese tradition as to suggest an altogether different orientation of mind. More significant, therefore, than the explicit rejection of the past is the very small place it has occupied in Communist thinking. As Mao himself puts it, the past is of little concern; the important thing for Chinese Communists is to look to the future.

Nevertheless, it would be wrong to imply that Mao's rejection of the past is total. Certain aspects of traditional Chinese culture he does find worthy of admiration, and the new culture fostered by Communism must, he insists, preserve what is valuable in the old at the same time that it discards what is debased. Chinese Communists should therefore "throw away the feudal dross and absorb the democratic essence" of the earlier culture. Without doubt, this concession to history, which Mao says must be "respected" and from which the Chinese "cannot cut themselves adrift," does indeed leave room for future adaptation. In the definition of what is "feudal" and what "democratic," for example, there is a loophole through which much of Chinese tradition could be drawn, if that proved desirable. Indeed the very application of such terms as "feudal" and "democratic" to Chinese history suggests a flexibility of interpretation great enough to permit further adjustments if the need arises.

Allowing this much, the question still remains—and it is a large one—whether at present the Chinese Communists show any inclination toward making such adjustments, and if so, on what basis. Would gestures made toward Chinese tradition reflect a genuine respect for it? Would future adaptations represent the actual influence of traditional values, or rather mere accommodations to national feelings? That the whole process of adaptation or synthesis in regard to Chinese culture might be guided by aims quite foreign to Chinese tradition is a possibility which Mao's own remarks on the subject make very real. There can be no doubt that, in his mind at least, the process of sifting and selecting from Chinese culture should be governed, and most stringently so, by the criteria of Marxism-Leninism. Under such circumstances much that had been honored by tradition would have difficulty gaining recognition, while much else would probably be transformed or contorted beyond recognition.

Examples of the kind of approach which Chinese Communists might take to this problem are not lacking to us. In regard to the classical schools of Chinese philosophy, for instance, there has been a noticeable sympathy among Communist writers for the Taoists, and particularly for "Lao Tzu," as representing an opposition to Confucius and a radical critique of the established order. In such an appreciation, however, the underlying mysticism and quietism of "Lao Tzu" quickly becomes obscured as his new admirers hasten to claim him for the "democratic" tradition.

How much, indeed, of "Lao Tzu" survives when he must serve as spokesman for the oppressed masses, as the voice of social revolution?

Liu Shao-ch'i, on the other hand, offers an example somewhat in contrast in his *How To Be a Good Communist*. Here Confucian sources are drawn upon in explaining the nature and significance of Communist self-cultivation. While obviously Liu adapts traditional concepts to a most untraditional purpose (there is nothing in his sources which would allow for such complete subordination of the individual conscience to political authority, rather than to a presumed set of moral constants), the concepts are still half-recognizable. Confucian cultivation had attempted a delicate adjustment between the claims of the individual and those of his society. With Liu the adjustment is subtle and it involves the individual, but the balance is totally destroyed. The individual life has value now only in social terms (its value to the Party and state), not in human terms (its intrinsic personal worth or "humanity").

Whatever the incidental uses to which tradition has thus been put by Chinese Communists, and whatever allowances must be made for misappropriation (perhaps no more than for previous dynasties, since tradition has been less valued), still even this minimal recognition of the past helps to keep tradition alive. "Lao Tzu" may not be truly appreciated today, but he has survived his misinterpreters before. Liu Shao-ch'i may not quite rank Confucius and Mencius with Lenin and Stalin, and may decide all points of difference in favor of his latter-day sages, but he cannot speak of the two together without doing some honor (among Communists) to the earlier sages. The question is whether tradition kept alive on such a precarious basis will be sufficient for survival in a modern totalitarian society. Minor concessions of this sort could easily be lost in the general destruction of everything that has served to perpetuate tradition in the past.

Apart from such open expressions of the Communist outlook on tradition, there is at least one further approach which might be made to our problem. The evidence may be overwhelming that Chinese Communist thinking has been formed within the tradition of Marxism-Leninism, but is that tradition wholly at variance with the Chinese? In the institutional sphere the character of Communist rule bears strong resemblance to bureaucratic despotisms in the past. May not certain features of Communist thought also have an appeal for the Chinese precisely because they conform to traditional habits of mind or approximate traditional ideals? Here we are on much more speculative ground, but some points of correspondence can at least be suggested:

1. The possibility of achieving the ideal society—perfect peace and order, and eventually a minimum of government—has been a central theme of Chinese political thought for centuries. Where other traditions have placed their final hope in Heaven or Nirvana, the kingdom in which the Confucianists hoped was very much of this world. Again and again Confucian idealism has expressed its belief that such an ideal was attainable, and has inspired numerous (and usually naive) plans for the perfectly ordered and controlled society. The Communists, though condemning Confucian "idealism," have undoubtedly appealed to much the same idealistic hope, as indeed did the similarly anti-Confucian Taipings.

2. In addition to this political idealism, the Communists have probably appealed in their own way to the kind of moral idealism which Confucianism always fostered. The dedication of the Confucian *chün-tzu* to the service of state and society is matched by that demanded of the Communist cadre to the Party and state. Ethically these two forms of idealism rest on very different bases, but Liu Shao-ch'i had good reason to invoke for his cadres Fan Chung-yen's definition of the *chün-tzu* as one who is "first in worrying about the world's troubles and last in enjoying its pleasures." Such a lofty conception corresponded closely to Liu's idea of the good Communist, who accepts rigorous self-discipline and self-denial in the service of the revolution.

3. One aspect of this traditional moral idealism had been its emphasis on the pursuit of what is right rather than of what is profitable. In the past this principle had often been applied to the detriment of commercial activity and to the enhancement of state power in the economic sphere, presumably on the theory that the ruling elite acted in the interests of all but the merchant only in his own. In more recent times, owing to the prevalence of this idea, socialism has enjoyed a discernible advantage over "laissez-faire" liberalism and free enterprise in gaining general acceptance, and the acquisition by the state of great economic powers has conformed to, not violated, the traditional pattern.

4. Closely related to the moral idealism referred to above is the tradi-

tional Confucian ideal of the ruling elite. Despite important ideological differences, the new Communist elite resembles the old one in its combination of ideological and political authority, in its identification with a specific intellectual orthodoxy, and in its claim to qualify for leadership by conforming to a rigorous code of conduct.

It would be possible to list more such correspondences between Communist and Chinese traditions—similarities which can hardly be interpreted as traditional influences on the new ideology, but do suggest the perpetuation of certain general attitudes from the past into the immediate present. Since the list of dissimilarities is even longer and more obvious, we shall not attempt to prepare an inventory here. What is important to recognize ultimately is the superficial character of such resemblances as do exist, in so far as they might seem to bear upon the continuity of Chinese tradition or to endow Communist rule with a traditional character. Chinese Communism may have been the beneficiary of certain deep-rooted attitudes among the people, but it enjoyed this advantage without incurring a corresponding obligation, without binding itself to any of the traditional restraints upon the exercise of great power. As a consequence it has felt free to remake China as it pleased, without reference to traditional values or standards. It has known a degree of authority which yielded nothing to the admonitions of past sages, and it has possessed a degree of control over the lives of men which recognized none of the privileged sanctuaries of private and family life, wherein much that was most noble and gracious and humane in Chinese life had been preserved, even under earlier despotisms.

In the final analysis it must be admitted that the Chinese tradition, if it exists at all today in recognizable form, is in a stage of such rapid and violent flux that predictions have little value. As our introduction and the preceding chapters seek to make clear, this revolutionary process has been in motion since long before the rise of Chinese Communism, and its unsettling effects on tradition have been so severe that any assumption of a continuity in thought or of intellectual influence is extremely dubious. Whether the future belongs to Communism, some modification of it, or something wholly unforeseen, there is no sign yet that the forces of change are spent.

Perhaps this alone may be confidently believed: that a tradition so rich and diverse, and in many ways profound, cannot for long remain submerged. And if the condition of its re-emergence is that it join hands with other traditions, East and West, which share its basic humanistic values, this the Chinese tradition has already shown a capacity to do, for the benefit not of the Chinese alone but of all the world.

APPENDIX:

POPULAR RELIGION AND SECRET SOCIETIES

For the most part this book has been concerned with the great movements of thought among the educated elite of China. In such movements, however, the great masses of common people were rarely caught up. What filtered through to them was a much simplified and sometimes distorted view of the teachings which had found favor among those with some education and prestige. Such notions were quickly adapted to the needs of those indigenous, and somewhat heterogeneous, religious cults which have subsisted among the people for centuries.

POPULAR RELIGION

From the earliest times in China we hear of shamans, magicians, interpreters of dreams, and diviners who presided over a variety of religious cults and commanded the respect and awe not only of the common people but even at times of members of the aristocracy. Though Chinese historians, themselves mostly followers of Confucianism, have seldom deigned to notice these popular cults and superstitions, popular literature reveals a widespread belief among the common people of China in a host of benevolent and baleful gods and spirits, and the prevalence of numerous practices such as the making of offerings to win their aid or the observance of taboos to escape their wrath. Government officials have occasionally moved to curb the grosser forms of superstition or have taken active steps toward suppression when some popular cult assumed a dangerously political tone. But generally the ruling class has been content to leave the common people to their own beliefs.

While educated Chinese have paid homage only to Heaven and their ancestors, and sometimes to Confucius, Buddha, Lao Tzu, and a few other historical personages, the common people have believed in the existence of thirty-three Buddhist Heavens, eighty-one Taoist Heavens, and eighteen Buddhist hells, and put faith in astrology, almanacs, dream interpretation, geomancy, witchcraft, phrenology, palmistry, the recalling of the soul, fortune telling in all forms, charms, magic, and many other varieties of superstition. They have regularly visited temples and shrines of all descriptions which the educated generally avoided. Often fatalistically, they have believed that spiritual beings controlled their fortunes and must therefore be continually consulted, coddled, and appeased. While the literati have regarded Confucianism, Buddhism, and Taoism essentially as systems of philosophy, the common people have embraced them as religions and regarded their founders as supernatural beings.

Thus there has been a strong tendency in China for the educated and uneducated to go their separate ways in matters of religion. Unquestionably this has deeply affected the character of popular religion in China, which has been deprived of intellectual guidance and been forced to subsist on a low cultural level. By the same token, scholar-officials have had less influence in religion than they might otherwise have exerted, for the state cult of Confucius, to which they adhered, had little to offer the people at large.

It is clear that neither the intelligentsia nor the common people could be called Confucianists, Buddhists, or Taoists exclusively, for they have accepted all three systems as "different roads to the same destination." Aside from 600,000-odd Buddhist monks and nuns, 3 or 4 million Buddhist lay devotees or "disciples at home," several hundred thousand Taoist priests and "vegetarian women," 20 million or so Muslims, about 3½ million Roman Catholics, and close to 600,000 Protestants, all of whom were identified with a single religion in 1949, the majority of China's millions have "worn a Confucian crown, a Taoist robe, and a pair of Buddhist sandals," as the saying goes.

The pattern of folk beliefs reflects this facile syncretism. Generally their ethical notions have had a Confucian tone, while their views of the supernatural have been derived mostly from religious Taoism, itself more closely related to the complex of primitive Chinese religion than to philosophical Taoism. In spite, however, of these common elements in popular religion, individual cults have varied greatly among themselves, emphasizing this or that aspect of a rather shapeless tradition according to the needs of the particular group or locality concerned.

Perhaps the clearest expression of these beliefs is to be found in two tracts that have for centuries been influential among the Chinese population as a whole, the *Treatise of the Most Exalted One on Moral Retribution,* which is part of the Taoist canon, and *The Silent Way of Recompense,* which, though largely Taoistic, reflects the teachings of all three religions. In these two short treatises, Confucian social and moral ideals, the Buddhist teaching of noninjury to any form of life, the Taoist worship of stars and various gods as well as its merit system, the doctrine of recompense, the worship of Heaven, the belief in Heaven and hell, and the hope for everlasting life are all expressed in short, epigrammatical sentences that for centuries have been familiar to the common people whether literate or illiterate.

The Treatise of the Most Exalted One on Moral Retribution

This popular treatise has sometimes been considered the work of Lao Tzu, though its actual date and authorship are unknown. Since it is listed in the bibliographical section of the *History of the Sung Dynasty,* it dates at least from the thirteenth century and is probably much earlier. Millions of copies of this work, and of *The Silent Way of Recompense* which follows here, have been distributed over the years by men and organizations of good-will. They are standard texts in most popular cults, and would probably be found in any rural village which possessed even a few books.

[From *T'ai-shang kan-ying p'ien, Tao-tsang,* pp. 834–39]

The Most Exalted One said: "Calamities and blessings do not come through any [fixed] gate; it is man himself that invites them." [1] The reward of good and evil is like the shadow accompanying the body. Accordingly there are in Heaven and earth spiritual beings who record a man's evil deeds and, depending upon the lightness or gravity of his transgressions, reduce his term of life by units of three days. [2] As units are taken away, his health becomes poor, and his spirit becomes wasted. He will often meet with sorrow and misery, and all other men will hate

[1] *Tso chuan,* Duke Hsiang 23.
[2] There are differing theories concerning the length of the units of time used here and in the following.

him. Punishments and calamities will pursue him; good luck and joy will shun him; evil stars will harm him. When the allotted units are exhausted, he will die.

Furthermore, there are the Three Ministers of the Northern Constellation residing above man's head. They register his crimes and sins and take away from his term of life periods of three hundred or three days. There are also the Three Worm-Spirits residing inside man's body. Whenever the fifty-seventh day [of the sixty-day cycle, the day characterized by severity and change] comes around, they ascend to the court of Heaven and report man's sins and transgressions. On the last day of the month, the Kitchen God does the same. When a man's transgressions are great, three hundred days are taken away from his term of life. When they are small, three days are taken away. Great and small transgressions number in the hundreds. Those who seek everlasting life on earth must first of all avoid them.

Go forward if your deed follows the Way (Tao) but withdraw if it violates it. Do not tread evil paths. Do nothing shameful even in the recesses of your own house. Accumulate virtue and amass merits. Have a compassionate heart toward all creatures. Be loyal to your sovereign, filial to your parents, friendly to your younger brothers, and brotherly to your older brothers. Rectify yourself and so transform others. Be compassionate to orphans and sympathetic to widows. Respect the old and cherish the young. Even insects, grass, and trees you must not hurt. You should grieve at the misfortune of others and rejoice in their good fortune. Assist those in need and save those in danger. Regard others' gain as your own gain and their loss as your own loss. Do not publicize their shortcomings nor boast of your own superiorities. Stop evil and promote good. Yield much but take little. Accept humiliation without complaint and favor with a sense of apprehension. Bestow kindness and seek no recompense. Give without regret.

He who is good is respected by all men. The way of Heaven helps him, happiness and wealth follow him, all evil things shun him, and spiritual beings protect him. Whatever he does will succeed. He may even hope to become a god or an immortal.

He who seeks to become an immortal of Heaven should perform 1,200 good deeds. He who seeks to become an immortal of earth should perform 300.

But if he acts contrary to righteousness or behaves improperly. . . . [Here follows a long list of sins and crimes to be avoided, similar to that given in Pao-p'u Tzu [3] concluding with:] if he is insatiably covetous and greedy or takes oaths and swears to seek vindication; if he loves liquor and becomes rude and disorderly or is angry and quarrelsome with his relatives; if as a husband he is not faithful and good, or as a wife she is not gentle and obedient; if the husband is not in harmony with his wife; if the wife is not respectful to her husband; if he is always fond of boasting and bragging; if she constantly acts out her jealousy and envy; if he behaves immorally toward his wife and children; if she behaves improperly toward her parents-in-law; if he treats with slight and disrespect the spirits of his ancestors or disobeys the commands of his superiors; if he occupies himself with what is not beneficial to others or cherishes a disloyal heart; if he curses himself and others or is partial in his love and hatred; if he steps over the well or hearth [which should be taken seriously because water and fire are indispensable to life] or leaps over food [served on the floor] or a person [lying on a floor mat]; if he kills babies or brings about abortion or does many actions of secret depravity; if he sings or dances on the last day of the month or year [when the end should be sent off with sorrow] or bawls out or gets angry on the first day of the year or the month [when the beginning should be welcomed with joy]; if he weeps, spits, or urinates when facing north [the direction of the emperor] or chants and laughs facing the hearth [which should be treated solemnly because the family depends on it for food]; and, moreover, if he lights incense with hearth fire [a sign of disrespect] or uses dirty fuel to cook food; if he shows his naked body when rising at night or executes punishment on the eight festivals of the year; if he spits at a shooting star or points at a rainbow; if he suddenly points to the three luminaries or gazes long at the sun and the moon; if in the spring months [when things are growing] he burns the thickets in hunting or angrily reviles others when he faces north; if without reason he kills tortoises or snakes [which are honored along with the Northern Constellation], if he commits these or similar crimes, the Arbiter of Human Destiny will, according to their lightness or gravity, take away from the culprit's term of life periods of three hundred or three days. When these units are exhausted, he will die. If at death there

[3] See Vol. I, pp. 262–63.

remains guilt unpunished, the evil luck will be transferred to his posterity.

Moreover, if one wrongly seizes another's property, his wife, children, and other members of his family are to be held responsible, the expiation to be proportionate up to punishment by death. If they do not die, there will be disasters from water, fire, thieves, loss of property, illness, quarrels, and the like to compensate for the wrong seizure.

Further, he who kills men unjustly puts a weapon into the hands of others who will turn on him and kill him. He who seizes property unrighteously is like one who relieves hunger with spoiled food or quenches thirst with poisoned wine. He will be full for the time being, but death will inevitably follow. . . .

If one has already done an evil deed but later repents of his own accord and corrects his way, refrains from doing any evil and earnestly practices many good deeds, in time he will surely obtain good fortune. This is what is called changing calamities into blessings.

Therefore the man of good fortune speaks good, sees good, and does good. Every day he has three kinds of goodness. At the end of three years Heaven will send down blessings on him. The man of evil fortune speaks evil, sees evil, and does evil. Every day he has three kinds of evil. At the end of three years Heaven will send down calamity on him. Why not make an effort to do good?

The Silent Way of Recompense (Yin-chih wen)
(popularly attributed to the Taoist deity, Wen ch'ang)
[From Chou Meng-yen (ed.), Yin-chih wen kuang-i]

The Lord says: For seventeen generations I have been incarnated as a high official, and I have never oppressed the people or my subordinates. I have saved people from misfortune, helped people in need, shown pity to orphans, and forgiven people's mistakes. I have extensively practiced the Silent Way of Recompense and have penetrated Heaven above. If you can set your minds on things as I have set mine, Heaven will surely bestow blessings upon you. Therefore, I pronounce these instructions to mankind, saying. . . .

Whoever wants to expand his field of happiness, let him rely on his moral nature.

Do good work at all times, and practice in secret meritorious deeds of all kinds.

Benefit living creatures and human beings. Cultivate goodness and happiness.

Be honest and straight, and, on behalf of Heaven, promote moral reform. Be compassionate and merciful and, for the sake of the country, save the people.

Be loyal to your ruler and filial to your parents.

Be respectful toward elders and truthful to friends.

Obey the purity [of Taoism] and worship the Northern Constellation; or revere the scriptures and recite the holy name of the Buddha.

Repay the four kindnesses [done to us by Heaven, earth, the sovereign, and parents]. Extensively practice the three religions.

Help people in distress as you would help a fish in a dried-up rut. Free people from danger as you would free a sparrow from a fine net.

Be compassionate to orphans and kind to widows. Respect the aged and have pity on the poor.

Collect food and clothing and relieve those who are hungry and cold along the road. Give away coffins lest the dead of the poor be exposed.

If your own family is well provided for, extend a helping hand to your relatives. If the harvest fails, relieve and help your neighbors and friends.

Let measures and scales be accurate, and do not give less in selling or take more in buying. Treat your servants with generosity and consideration; why should you be severe in condemnation and harsh in your demands?

Write and publish holy scriptures and tracts. Build and repair temples and shrines.

Distribute medicine to alleviate the suffering of the sick. Offer tea and water to relieve the distress of the thirsty.

Buy captive creatures and set them free, or hold fast to vegetarianism and abstain from taking life.

Whenever taking a step, always watch for ants and insects. Prohibit the building of fires outside [lest insects be killed] and do not set mountain woods or forests ablaze.

Light lanterns at night to illuminate where people walk. Build river boats to ferry people across.

Do not go into the mountain to catch birds in nets, nor to the water to poison fish and shrimps.

Do not butcher the ox that plows the field. Do not throw away paper with writing on it.

Do not scheme for others' property. Do not envy others' skill or ability.

Do not violate people's wives or daughters. Do not stir up litigation among others.

Do not injure others' reputation or interest. Do not destroy people's marriages.

Do not, on account of personal enmity, create disharmony between brothers. Do not, because of a small profit, cause father and son to quarrel.

Do not misuse your power to disgrace the good and the law-abiding. Do not presume upon your wealth to oppress the poor and needy.

Be close to and friendly with the good; this will improve your moral character in body and mind. Keep at a distance from the wicked; this will prevent imminent danger.

Always conceal people's vices but proclaim their virtue. Do not say "yes" with your mouth and "no" in your heart.

Cut brambles and thorns that obstruct the road. Remove bricks and stones that lie in the path.

Put in good condition roads that have been rough for several hundred years. Build bridges over which thousands and tens of thousands of people may travel.

Leave behind you moral instructions to correct people's faults. Donate money to bring to completion the good deeds of others.

Follow the principle of Heaven in your work. Obey the dictates of the human heart in your words.

[Admire the ancient sages so much that you] see them while eating soup or looking at the wall. [Be so clear in conscience that] when you sleep alone, you are not ashamed before your bedding, and when you walk alone, you are not ashamed before your own shadow.

Refrain from doing any evil, but earnestly do all good deeds.

Then there will never be any influence or evil stars upon you, but you will always be protected by good and auspicious spirits.

Immediate rewards will come to your own person, and later rewards will reach your posterity.

A hundred blessings will come as if drawn by horses, and a thousand fortunes will gather about you like clouds.

Do not all these things come through the Silent Way of Recompense?

RELIGIOUS SECTS

For centuries there has been a multitude of religious sects in China. Some are specifically affiliated with the great religions of the past, such as the Ten Schools of Buddhism (now virtually reduced to four) and the Northern and Southern Schools of Taoism. Others are syncretic in character, drawing upon different religious traditions, ancient and modern. In them the drive toward fusion and reconciliation is often far stronger than the desire for clarity or purity of doctrine. This is partly because such sects or societies have drawn most of their support from the uneducated, who have been generally uninterested in or incapable of articulating a systematic body of belief, and who have had difficulty preserving definite traditions. For the same reason, and because they were wholly or in part secret cults, these sects have remained shrouded in mystery, ignored by scholars and historians. A recent study of one area revealed fourteen religious societies previously unknown to the outside world. It is evident that, in recent times at least, such movements have risen to popularity and then disappeared again with astonishing swiftness.

As an example of the newer societies there is the Society of the Way (*Tao yüan*), or Society of the Way and Its Virtue (*Tao-te she*), which originated in Tsinan, North China, about 1921. Its buildings consist of five halls, one each for worship, scripture reading, meditation, preaching, and charity. On its altar are the names of Confucius, Lao Tzu, and the Buddha, and symbols representing Christianity and Islam. Its teachings emphasize the community of Heaven and man in matters of the spirit, and the spirit of world brotherhood. For its members, it urges meditation, cultivation of the inner life, the belief in planchettes,[4] and the use of spirit photography. For others, it practices charity and other forms of social service, operates hospitals, and establishes banks with small deposits for poor people. Its Decalogue reads: 1) Do not dishonor par-

[4] Boards used to obtain mediumistic messages like the Ouija boards of the West.

ents; 2) Do not lack virtue; 3) Do not lack goodness; 4) Do not lack righteousness; 5) Do not lack mercy; 6) Do not conceal the goodness of others; 7) Do not be cruel; 8) Do not have secrets; 9) Do not have envy or spite; and 10) Do not blaspheme.

The Fellowship of Good (*T'ung-shan She* or Society for Common Good) was started around 1918 in Peking. It advocates the "internal meritorious deeds" of worship, meditation, and vegetarianism, and the "external meritorious deeds" of charity and maintaining schools. It follows all three religions but strongly opposes monasticism and the renunciation of the family. Its Ten Ideals are: a straight heart, a high type of service, unrestricted virtue, clear instruction, observance of law, diligence in moral culture, desire for progress, harmony, maintenance of high ideals, and the unification of the soul. It believes that illness can be cured by quiet sitting. Until very recently it had branches in all parts of China, including Manchuria, but now it hardly exists.

Of the old societies, the most important is the White Lotus, chiefly because of its many branches both past and present. According to one account, it was founded in 1133 as a Buddhist sect emphasizing repentance, suppression of desires, vegetarianism, and abstinence from alcohol and the taking of life. It attracted many people, especially peasants, and soon spread from North to East and Central China. In addition to the use of prayers, incense, charms, and incantations, members also practiced boxing and fighting with spears, for the avowed purpose of resisting the invading Jurchen barbarians and supporting the Sung dynasty. In the last seven hundred years the society has rebelled against the Mongols and Manchus a number of times, especially in 1794, 1801, and 1813. In the early decades of this century, the society was strong in North China but rather weak in the lower Yangtze area. It was strongly organized on a local basis, with a leader who exercised absolute power. It is difficult to tell whether any of this has survived vigorous attempts at suppression by the Communists.

The White Lotus has branched into many sects such as the Red Scarf Society, the Eight Trigram Society, the Yellow Society, the notorious Boxers who rose to expel foreigners in 1900, and the Society of the White Robe. One of the more prominent ones in the last several decades has been the Tsai-li (Principle Abiding) Society. It obeyed the Law of Buddhism, observed the practice of Taoism, and followed the social rites of Confucianism. Its members abstained from smoking and drinking, did not burn incense or worship idols, but used many incantations and charms. The sect encouraged its members to be diligent and thrifty, and many poor and lazy people became hard-working and well-to-do under its influence. For this reason it had a strong appeal in rural areas, especially in North and West China. Members were mostly from the artisan and laboring classes, followed by farmers and merchants, and a few intellectuals.

Another important branch of the White Lotus in recent times has been the Way of Pervading Unity (*I-kuan Tao*). While other societies were declining, the Way gained strength and extended its activities during the Second World War. Like the Tsai-li, its origin is traced to the White Lotus but it is more likely that it evolved from secret activities started by some elements of the Boxers after the Revolution of 1911. The sect believes that the One is the root of all things and as a principle penetrates and pervades all existence. The universe evolves from the realm of *li* (principle or law), which is infinite and prior to the realm of *ch'i* (material-force), through its active and passive principles (yin-yang), and then to the phenomenal world. We are now in the midst of the third catastrophe in the history of human existence, and it is through the mercy of the Mother of No-birth, the Creator of all, and our own moral and spiritual efforts that the world will be saved. All systems— Confucianism, Taoism, Buddhism, Christianity, and Islam—with all their sages, gods, and Buddhas, are vehicles for this salvation. In the end all people will be saved.

Followers of the sect have emphasized internal and external meritorious deeds equally. The former includes self-cultivation, purification of the heart, reduction of desires, and control of the mind. The latter includes the use of charms and planchettes, the practice of the "three secrets" of finger signs and magic phrases, abstinence from meat, tobacco, and alcohol, incantation, worship of all religions, offering and sacrifice, study and recitation of Buddhist and Taoist canons, preaching and charity. Like most secret religious societies, it has attracted chiefly the ignorant and illiterate. There is no way of reckoning the number of its followers or its temples. During the Second World War it was very active in almost the entire territory occupied by Japan, especially in North China. Since the war, however, it has been suppressed and its activities have died down. How it has fared under the Communist regime is hard to ascertain.

The Way of Pervading Unity is specially significant for us because it is both old and new, old because of its origin in the White Lotus and new because of its recent appearance. While the literature of other societies either is so cryptic as to be untranslatable or is unavailable to us, that of the Way is accessible and is clearly expressive of the major beliefs and practices of these various religious societies. For these reasons we have translated below excerpts from several of its tracts. Note the various interpretations of Tao, the doctrine of three stages in each historical cycle, the Neo-Confucian philosophy of human nature and natural principle, the Buddhist gospel of universal salvation and its injunction against taking life, the Taoist technique of inner and outer meritorious deeds including alchemy and quiet sitting, the theory of retribution, and the harmony of the three religions.

Questions and Answers on the Way of Pervading Unity
[From *I-kuan tao-li wen-ta*, pp. 1–20]

Friend asked: It has not been very long since I joined the Way. I am ignorant about everything. Please enlighten me as to what the Way (Tao) really is.

I answered: Our Way is called the Way of Pervading Unity. If you ask about its whats and whys, their answers are many. Let me select and comment on the most essential as an introduction for you.

The Way is the general name for all goodness; all charitable work may be called the Way. It is also the ultimate principle; whatever conforms to the principle conforms to the Way. It is also the correct principle, such as parental love for the father, filial piety for the son, righteousness for the husband, obedience for the wife; loyalty, obedience, love, and virtue are all the Way. It is also the natural principle. There is the principle of Heaven in Heaven, the principle of earth in earth, the principle of human nature in human beings. We also say that the nature is the embodiment of the Way. What is inborn in us is born of heavenly nature. The nature of man is originally derived from the principle of Heaven. If we cultivate our nature with the principle of Heaven as our guide, we will fulfill the Way. . . .

I have heard my teacher say that Yao and Shun were born at high noon. Our epoch is at the transition from the high noon [of history] to the next period [1:00 to 3:00 P.M. of history]. When noon reaches its height, sunshine is full and complete. Hence the possibility of universal salvation in three stages and the reclarification of the Way of Pervading Unity. By the three stages is meant that Fu Hsi drew the eight trigrams and inaugurated culture and civilization, thus constituting the first stage. Confucius edited the Classics, formulated rites, developed moral principles, and established social standards, thus constituting the second stage. At present there are many religious societies both at home and abroad, each rectifying man's nature and destiny and probing into the nature and the principle, thus constituting the third stage. Since you, Sir, live in this generation, it means that circumstance brings you and the Buddha together. You should cultivate the Way with special effort, for happy circumstances should not be passed over. The nature is derived from the principle of Heaven; it is shared by all men. Who is he who cannot achieve a good and virtuous life? When one practices the Way, even if he cannot become an Immortal or a sage, he still can avoid bringing shame to his ancestors or causing trouble to his descendants, and become a perfect man. There are now many religious tracts available. If you want the best, search extensively.

Friend said: I have heard you say that Confucianism is a religion. How about Buddhism and Taoism? Are they orthodox or heterodox systems? Kindly tell me.

I said: The Way is in essence the nonultimate and the one principle. The one is divided into three, as a man's person is divided into essence, vital force, and spirit. At first the one is divided into three, and now the three are united as one, which is the sign of perfect culmination.

However, among the three religions, the Law of the Buddha is the highest. For this reason, at all times past and present, the great leaders of religion have been Buddhists. The *Hsien-chieh Scripture* says: "When the universe was formed out of chaos, it was decided that there would be ten Buddhas ruling the universe and there have already been seven." This can be proved by the fact that there are seven Buddhas in the Ta-hsiang Temple in the Fen-yang district of Shansi and also the Temple of Seven Buddhas in Ying Village of Ma-chuang in the Hsiao-i district of Shansi. In early times there was no written language and therefore their names are difficult to find out. The remaining three Buddhas are the Dīpankara Buddha, Tathāgata Buddha and Maitreya Buddha. Dīpankara ruled for 1,500 years and Tathāgata Buddha ruled for 3,000 years. The accounts of Maitreya need not be told here. He has already assumed the rule in his hands.

The Tathāgata Buddha was born on the eighth day, the fourth month, in the year 1027 B.C. His father's name was Ch'a-li [Shuddhodana], meaning pure rice, and his mother's name was Lady Maya. He left home at the age of nineteen. Having received instructions from Dīpankara, he preached for forty-nine years and wrote scriptures and left them for the salvation of the world throughout 10,000 years. His way is to point directly to one's nature and to become a Buddha, to explore directly to the source, to wipe out [the phenomenal characteristics of] sound and color, and to remove the distinction of the self and the other. Later generations call him the Founder of Buddhism. The *Record of the School Sayings of Confucius*[5] says: "There is a sage in the west whose name is Buddha. Without uttering a word, he speaks the truth. He transcends both chaos and order, for his is the way of nonaction (*wu-wei*)." He also left these words: "My way runs in cycles of 3,000 years—1,000 years of Correct Law, 1,000 years of Semblance of Law, and 1,000 years of Decay of Law. After the period of Decay of Law, the period of Correct Law will begin again." This is the same as the principle of jointly observing the three religions today.

Lao Tzu's surname was Li, his name was Erh, his style-name was Po-yang, and his posthumous name Tan. He was born in the Ch'en district in the state of Ch'u in 604 B.C. He was once King Yu's custodian of documents. His father's surname was Han, private name K'un, and style-name Yüan-pi. His mother's name was Ching-fu. She was pregnant for eighty years before he was born under a plum (*li*) tree. For this reason he changed his surname from Han to Li. After Confucius interviewed him about rites, because of the stupidity of King Yu, he mounted a buffalo and rode through Han-ku Pass to the west where he converted the barbarian King Yin-hsi. His way is to nourish the mind through simplicity. Its method is to draw water to supplement fire [to balance the passive and active forces of yin-yang]. When fire and water are harmonized, then one proceeds to refine gold fluid and reconvert cinnabar [after it has been turned into mercury which, in Taoist alchemy, represents the acme of the way to immortality]. He left the *Tao-te ching*, the *Classic of Purity*, the *Treatise of the Most Exalted One on Moral Retribution*,

---

[5] The *K'ung Tz'u chia-yü*, a spurious work from the Han dynasty.

and the *Silent Way of Recompense,* which now circulate throughout the world. As to Confucius, his work covers both government and religion and need not be recounted here.

The fundamental ways of the three religions are all directed at the nature and the principle. Their ethical standards and moral principles all flow out of the heavenly nature. When the substance of the nature is understood, moral principles will be correctly comprehended even without study. As is often said, when the substance is understood, the function is comprehended, and when the root is firm, the branches flourish. This is only natural.

Unfortunately, Buddhism has lost its wonderful truth and Taoism has lost its practice of alchemy and magic formulas. Their followers merely recite scriptures and chant vows and beg food from people. Confucianism has lost its central principles of the nature and the principle. Even world-renowned writers do nothing more than search for paragraphs and pick up sentences. If you ask them about the practice of "knowing where to rest," "unperturbedness," "tranquillity," and self-introspection, or the method for the investigation of things, or complete development and nourishment and fulfillment of human nature, few can answer. The result is that the three religions have almost completely disappeared.

In our Way all three religions are observed. We practice the social rites and moral principles of Confucianism, utilize the methods of the Founder of Taoism, and follow the rules of Grand Old Buddha. When these are applied on a small scale, one's years will be increased and life prolonged. When applied on a large scale, one will be enlightened in the Way and become a pure being [a saint]. This is the work of re-clarifying the principles of Pervading Unity.

Friend said: Since there is Pervading Unity in the three religions, do all of them require vegetarianism?

I said: Abstinence. There are the Five Precepts in Buddhism, and not to kill is the first. Man exists for only a few scores of years and should not become an enemy of animals. The main thing is of course universal salvation. There are, I am afraid, cases where a person is not free [to abstain] and because of his vegetarianism his cultivation of the Way is sometimes hampered. Therefore while the discipline is there, its application must be flexible. Nevertheless, people who are cultivating the Way must hold compassion as fundamental. An insect or a bird shares

[299]

with us the same heavenly nature. It is only because they differed in merits and demerits in their previous lives that they have changed in this life. If we kill and eat them, we are obstructing the principle of Heaven. [The Immortal] Lü Tsu wrote a poem which says:

> My flesh is the same as the flesh of all creatures;
> Its shape is different but its principle is not.
> Do not let Yama [Ruler of Hell] judge you.
> Ask yourself what you should do.

If you, Sir, are willing to give up some enjoyment of the mouth, please burn incense in front of the altar and take vows [not to eat meat]. I shall report to the Hall of Lao Tzu where your meritorious deed will be recorded. . . .

Friend said: If one wants to go ahead, what should be the first step?

I said: Build up a firm faith. Faith is the mother of the Way and the source of meritorious deeds. If a man has no faith, even divination will not be effective for him. It must be realized that all people are sufficiently endowed with the nature of Heaven, and Taoist immortals and Buddhas are identical in reality. It is due to various degrees of ignorance or enlightenment that we have become different. The round head and square feet of man resemble Heaven and earth. His inhaling and exhaling are symbolic of yin and yang. His two eyes are comparable to the sun and the moon, and his five internal organs correspond to the five elements. His pleasure, anger, sorrow, and joy are no different from wind, clouds, thunder, and rain, and his [four moral virtues of] humanity, righteousness, decorum, and wisdom are basically the [four aspects of] origination, development, adaptation, and correctness [of the universe]. Babies at birth are of the same reality as Heaven and earth, and the sages Yao, Shun, Confucius, and Mencius are no different from the common man. Those who understand the principle will become immortals and Buddhas, while those who violate it will become earthly spirits and wandering souls. Follow it and cultivate it—this is the Way. It is the unalterable principle. Do you believe in it?

Friend said: According to your theory, all scriptures are useless.

I said: Scriptures are a means. The great Way must be cultivated and intuited by oneself. A Buddha can show us the direction but cannot do the cultivation for us. The recitation of scriptures is merely a means whereby we may intuit the Law, that is all. If reciting the scriptures can always lead to an understanding of the Way, then what scriptures did the Buddhas of old have to recite? We should not avoid reading, but should not rely on it. Therefore it is said that reading scriptures is not so good as preaching them, and preaching them is not so good as acting according to them.

Friend said: The Deity we worship is called on the one hand the Twice Shining Lord on High, and, on the other, the Infinite Mother. Please tell me whether the Deity is male or female.

I said: By Twice Shining is meant that the Deity has shone and yet shines again. By being infinite is meant having no limit. It is called Mother because it is its nature to create. Heaven, earth, and man above and below, immortals and Buddhas, heavenly and earthly spiritual beings, and all things with intelligence are creatures of the one Mother. Hence modern scholars speak of the 400,000,000 people as uterine brothers, and in Kuan-ti's altar instructions there is the saying: "Your nature is originally my nature; you and I are essentially no different."

. . . .

Friend said: In past years when there was no kerosene in this country, our sesame oil and hemp-seed oil were very cheap. When opium poppy was grown everywhere, the price of rice was very low. At that time the cash was the unit and there was much money in circulation. Now that we light our lamps with kerosene, the opium poppy has disappeared, and a copper is worth ten cash, things should be much cheaper. How is it that money is scarce and droughts and floods are unduly severe?

I said: Gold and silver are the spirit of the universe. A person's spirit declines when he gets old. It is the same with the universe, and for the same reason the times are bad. Droughts and floods are determined by the state of the people's mind. Among the five elements, water is produced by Heaven. When rain fails to fall or when it falls at the wrong time, it is all because the people's minds are perverted and no longer in harmony with the mind of Heaven. There is only one way to restore normal conditions: it is goodness or moral character. Heaven can send down calamity, but can also bestow blessings. Just as water can overcome fire, so goodness can deliver us from suffering. Goodness in the person can protect the person. Goodness in the family can protect the family. If everyone is good, the world will be peaceful before sundown.

[301]

Chu Hsi said: "Our mind is one with the mind of the universe." If man's mind is good, the mind of the universe is also good. The universe and all things form one body with me. As to things being expensive when they should be cheap—well, it does not matter. People who cultivate the Way only think of good and evil, and therefore what they enjoy is quite free from the price of things. All of us must be good in order to restore normal conditions.

Methods of Religious Cultivation
[From Kuo Ting-tung et al., *I-kuan tao i-wen chieh-ta*, pp. 8a–9b]

How should male and female friends of the Way practice meritorious deeds?

In practicing such deeds, male and female friends should divide the burden but work together, the total membership being mobilized. Some may take up the responsibility of Heaven, earth, and man and write letters to propagate the principles of moral reform. Others may lecture on the teachings of the scriptures and propagate the gospel. Those with money may contribute according to their capacity to print holy scriptures and books of instruction. Those with energy may go in all directions to persuade and lead their good relatives and friends to join the Way as soon as possible. Some may donate money to build Buddha Halls to help a great number of people to practice meritorious deeds. Others may uphold with all their heart the Law of the Buddha so that the work of the Way will expand and grow daily. Some may be determined to practice earnestly and to abide reverently by the orders of the teacher. Some may cultivate the Way all their lives, thus setting an example for others. All these methods should be followed by male and female friends of the Way in their own ways to attain the fruits of goodness. . . .

What are internal meritorious deeds?

Cultivating the person, perfecting the self, seeing to it that all one's conduct conforms to the principle, making one's mind pure and desires few, and "seeking the lost mind"—all these are internal meritorious deeds.

What is the way to seek the lost mind? Can you tell me the method?

The method of seeking the lost mind is simply the way of controlling the mind. Of course, the most important way to control the mind is quiet sitting. For wisdom is born of the spirit, and the spirit is born of peace and quiet. To refine one's essence in order to transform it into energy, to refine energy in order to transform it into spirit, and to refine spirit so that it may return to vacuity, there is no other way than quiet sitting.

To practice quiet sitting, sit cross-legged and erect, both in the morning and in the evening, with eyes closed in order to nourish the spirit, and with the tongue touching the roof of the mouth. Let the mind be calm and breathing be quiet. Get rid of all impure thoughts and erroneous ideas. Think neither of good nor of evil. Neither move nor shake, breathe neither in nor out. When sitting reaches the point that not a single thought arises and all anxieties have ceased, then there will be profound peace and purity and nothing inside or outside [the mind]. . . .

What are external meritorious deeds?

Exhort others to do good and bring them to perfection. Enable all living creatures to be saved and everyone to turn toward the good. Do the work of assisting people and benefiting living beings. Harbor the thought of helping others in misfortune and saving the world. First rectify oneself and then rectify others. Deeds like these are external meritorious deeds.

What is the proper way of practicing an external meritorious deed?

In practicing an external meritorious deed, one must not have any intention of seeking for fame, and, what is more, one must not say any unkind word or show any angry expression. If one does a deed for the sake of fame, there is no merit in it to speak of. If one tries to exhort others with a bad temper or an angry expression, one is no longer a practitioner of the Way. In short, doing a meritorious deed, one must obey the holy teachings of the three religions and make the best real effort. Copying religious tracts, building Buddha Halls, propagating the doctrines of the Way so as to enlighten people—all these are meritorious deeds of the first order. We must realize that to transform a person so that he achieves the Way [and becomes a saint] is to make it possible for his ancestors of nine generations to ascend to Heaven, and to copy a sentence from a religious tract is better than to utter 10,000 words. Even the sages of the three religions did not go beyond this. As to the worldly work of rendering assistance in emergencies, helping people in their misfortunes, relieving others and removing danger, donate money to do it yourself if the need is small, and raise money and work with others if the need is great. Other meritorious deeds that require no money should be practiced whenever and wherever the occasion arises.

SECRET SOCIETIES

Secret societies have existed in China since ancient times but their activity and numbers increased markedly from the time when the Sung dynasty was invaded by barbarians from the North. Because of the secrecy which has surrounded them and because scholars have regarded them as unworthy of attention, little reliable information about these societies has come down to us. However, generally speaking, they are represented by two broad movements, the White Lotus and the Hung Society. The White Lotus Society has predominated in the North. It has been chiefly religious (though it has started and participated in many revolutions) and has a great number of branches loosely organized and related to one another. The Hung Society, on the other hand, has predominated in South, West, and Central China. It has been primarily political, though with a religious coloring, and has branched into several well-organized groups. The White Lotus and some of its offshoots have already been mentioned. In this section, we shall confine ourselves to the Hung Society.

The Hung Society (*Hung men*) may possibly have its origin in the White Lotus, though more probably it was organized in the middle of the seventeenth century by supporters of the Ming dynasty with the avowed purpose of overthrowing the Manchus and restoring Chinese rule. According to the society's own account, it was founded by a scholar named Yin Hung-sheng in 1631, whom its members consider to be their First Founding Father. In the declining years of the Ming, Yin rallied a number of prominent scholars about him in an effort to save the dynasty. His efforts were unsuccessful, however, and he died in 1645. A decade or so later, a group of monks in the Shao-lin Temple in Fukien secretly organized for revolution. In 1672 when the Manchu emperor called for volunteers to fight an invasion by a western tribe, they answered the call and expelled the invaders. But when it was finally discovered that they were actually rebels in search of an opportunity for an uprising, their temple was surrounded and burned. Five monks (later honored as the

"Five Early Founding Fathers") escaped, hid under a bridge, and were saved by five brave men (the "Five Middle Founding Fathers"). These were later joined by five other monks (the "Five Later Founding Fathers"). After much fighting against the Manchus, they met Abbot Ten-thousand-Cloud Dragon (Wan Yün-lung) and Ch'en Chin-nan (the "Great Ancestor"), who started an independent uprising. Ch'en and the Five Early Founding Fathers plotted their revolution in the Red Flower Pavilion in present Hupei province. In the second period (1:00–3:00 A.M.) of the twelve-period day cycle on the twenty-fifth day of the seventh month in 1674 they and their followers formally took a vow to be fraternal brothers, overthrow the Manchus, and restore the Ming. The conspiracy spread to South China. By 1698 Ch'en had died but his successors continued the fight. Members of the society worshiped Heaven as father and earth as mother and for this reason the society is also called the Heaven and Earth Society (*T'ien-ti hui*).

It is doubtful if any of this account is reliable. Even the origin and meaning of the name Hung is in dispute, but the majority opinion holds that it refers to the reign Hung-wu of the founder of the Ming dynasty. At any rate the story of the burning of the Shao-lin Temple has become a colorful and exciting part of Chinese folklore dramatized in endless variations on the popular stage and in story telling, and the Bridge and the Pavilion have been adopted as sacred symbols in the society's ceremonies. The movement, starting in Fukien, spread later to Formosa, to East, South, and West China, and finally to the far Southwest and Northwest. The society participated in many revolts, notably those of 1774 and the Taiping Rebellion.

Like most secret societies, the *Hung men* has developed into many branches, such as the Double Sword Society, Dagger Society, and the Clear Water Society. Their history is vague and their relationships are uncertain. Two branches of the society, however, stand out prominently and are known at least in broad outline. One of these is the Triple Harmony Society (*San-ho hui,* referring perhaps to the harmony of Heaven, earth, and man; or to the three "rivers," also pronounced *ho,* where the rebels met). It is also called the Triad Society (*San-tien hui,* referring perhaps to the three dots on the left side of the Chinese character *hung*). The other branch is the Elders Society (*Ko-lao hui*). The Triad Society was strong in South China, especially among farmers and working people, as well as among the overseas Chinese. In the United States it has branched into or affiliated with the Chih Kung Tong ("Society to Bring About Justice"), which is now no longer secret but a purely charitable organization. In recent years the Triad Society took an active part in the Revolution of 1911 led by Sun Yat-sen, in the revolution against Yuan Shih-k'ai's attempt to become emperor in 1915, and in resisting the Japanese invasion in the Second World War.

The Elders Society, variously named in different parts of China, originated in Fukien somewhat later than the Triad Society. One theory is that in 1853 when the Triad Society was resisting the Manchus in South China, the Elders Society arose in Central and North China in sympathetic response. In any case it spread over most of the country but became particularly strong in Central, North, and West China. It is said to have been so powerful in the nineteenth century that even leading government generals such as Tseng Kuo-fan (1811–1872) and Tso Tsung-t'ang (1812–1885) were obliged to join it. In recent times it was the most extensive, well organized, and influential of China's secret societies.

The ideals of the Hung Society may be summed up as patriotism, chivalry, fraternity, and traditional morality. The spirit of patriotism of the society needs no comment, except to add that the society worships Emperor T'ai Tsung (r. 627–644), founder of the T'ang dynasty. Like other secret societies, it employs pass words, hand signs, signs by arrangement of tea cups, and so on, about which members are pledged to keep absolute secrecy or suffer death. Unlike other secret societies, however, the combined spirit of chivalry, fraternity, and patriotism makes the Hung Society unique. It regards as its model the famous fraternity of the Peach Garden, where Kuan Kung (d. 219, erroneously called in the West the God of War) and two other heroes vowed to be brothers and to defend the Han dynasty, and also the well-known 108 rebels vividly described in the novel *Shui-hu chuan* (*The Water Margin* or *All Men Are Brothers*).

Certain numbers are regarded by the society as sacred. One of these is 108, which may refer to the rebels just mentioned or may be the sum of 36 and 72, which in their turn probably refer to the 36 gods in Heaven and the 72 gods on earth. Hence these numbers are used for the punishments specified below. The documents that have been selected for translation represent those most expressive of the ideals and attitudes of the society.

They are oaths taken by candidates and "commands" given by the Worshipful Master at various stages in the initiation ceremony. Besides oaths and commands, there are many poems, questions and answers, and other sayings used in meetings, most of them so cryptic as to be unintelligible to an outsider. The documents selected below are those common to the Hung Society as a whole.

The Thirty-Six Oaths of the Hung Society
[From Chu Lin, *Hung men chih*, pp. 26–30]

We, sharing fortune and misfortune, are dedicated to the restoration of the Ming dynasty which belonged to Heaven and earth and all existence, to the destruction of the barbarian bandits [the Manchus], and to waiting for the true mandate of Heaven. We reverently worship the Lord of Heaven and the Sovereign of Earth, the spirits of mountains and rivers and grain, the spirits of the Six Powers, the spirits of the Five Dragons in the five directions, and the infinite number of spiritual beings. Since the establishment [of our Society] hundreds of activities have been promoted. What the ancients knew to be worthy of teaching to later generations, we pass on.

Brethren! I shall now lead you again into the midst of loyalty to country and devotion to friends. We swear before Heaven on High in the spirit of sharing life and death. Tonight each of us recommends several new followers to the Heaven and Earth Society, follows the example of the fraternal pledge in the Peach Garden, and vows to be a Brother to the others, takes Hung as his family name, Gold-and-Orchid as his private name,[6] and forms one family. After entering the Hung Society, you must be of one body and one mind, each helping the other, and never allowing any distinction between one another to be made.

Tonight we worship Heaven as our father, earth as our mother, the sun as our brother, and the moon as our sister. We also worship before our First Founding Father, the Five Founding Fathers, Ten-thousand-Cloud Dragon, and others, and all spiritual beings of the Hung family. As we kneel in worship before the altar tonight, our minds and spirits are suddenly pure and clear. Each shall cut his finger, suck his blood, and take the oath of living and dying together.

[6] Gold standing for the solidity of friendship and orchid for its fragrance.

We consider the second period [1:00–3.00 A.M.] of the twenty-fifth day of the seventh month, 1674, as the time of our birth. Spread over the two capitals [Nanking and Peking] and the thirteenth provinces [in South, East, West, and Central China], we form one body and one mind, all seeking happiness for one another and each assuming his burden without any carelessness or failure. As soon as the kings and dukes of the present regime are no longer truly kings and dukes, and generals and prime ministers no longer truly generals and prime ministers, and the people begin to show unrest, that is the sign given us by Heaven that the Ming dynasty is to be restored and the barbarian bandits destroyed. We should be determined to carry out the command of Ch'en Chin-nan, which he gave many years ago, construct pavilions and build bridges [as stations in this lodge], establish the City of Universal Peace, re-enact the drama, travel over the five lakes and the four seas to search for the heroic and the brave, hold firmly in hand the authority of the City of Willows, burn incense and take the oath that will last as long as our land. Let each new member attend to his task in his respective sphere, and carry out the principle [of revolution] according to the will of Heaven. "Those who obey Heaven shall live and those who disobey shall perish."[7] All those who can restore the Ming dynasty, avenge our grievance, wipe out our disgrace, and establish the order of Universal Peace will themselves receive the titles of king and duke and their posterity will be prosperous throughout all generations. Whoever violates this principle shall be destroyed beneath swords and halberds and have his heirs cut off. Only people with a heart of loyalty and spirit of devotion may receive eternal blessing. We receive our lives from Heaven and earth and exist under the light of the sun and the moon. After we join in fraternity, we now suck our blood, make our pledges, and take our vows. We look upward and invite the spiritual beings to descend and bear witness. Each shall show his sincerity and take the Thirty-six Oaths:

1. From the time I enter the Hung Society, your parents are my parents, your brothers and sisters are my brothers and sisters, your wife is my sister-in-law, and your sons and nephews are my sons and nephews. If I violate this oath, may I be destroyed by the five thunders.

2. Whenever [a fellow Brother's] parents or brother pass away and there is no fund for burial, every Brother must immediately make known

[7] *Mencius*, IV A, 7.

the fact as soon as the white silk flies [an emergency call for help arrives] so that those with money may contribute money and those without money may contribute their energy. If a Brother [conceals the fact] and pretends ignorance, may he be destroyed by the five thunders.

3. Whenever any of the Hung family Brothers in the provinces or abroad arrives, whether he be a scholar, farmer, artisan, merchant, or tramp, he must be received, accommodated for the night, and given meals. If a Brother pretends ignorance and treats a fellow Brother as an outsider, may he perish beneath 10,000 swords.

4. Even though a Brother may not be acquainted with a fellow Brother of the Hung family, if the fellow Brother hangs up his signboard or utters a password and he still does not recognize the fellow Brother, may he perish under 10,000 swords.

5. Affairs of the Hung family may not be divulged or confided to one's father, son, brother, or relative. If a Brother privately passes on or tutors others in the Society's underwear [secret documents] or waist-bands [membership certificates], or uses them for the purpose of making money, may he perish beneath 10,000 swords.

6. Brothers of the Hung family may not secretly act as leads for the arrest of a fellow Brother. Even if there is accumulated enmity, the matter should be presented to the Brethren for a just settlement, and by no means should hatred be retained in one's heart. If by chance an arrest is made by mistake, the fellow Brother must be set free at once. If a Brother violates this oath, may he be destroyed by the five thunders.

7. Whenever a fellow Brother is in financial difficulty, a Brother must come to his assistance. He must do his best to provide the fellow Brother with money for his expenses or fare, whether the amount is large or small. If he shows no consideration in this, may he be destroyed by the five thunders.

8. If a Brother fabricates stories about a fellow Brother violating his human obligations, plotting to assassinate the Incense Master [Worshipful Master], or committing a murder, may he perish beneath 10,000 swords.

9. If a Brother violates a fellow Brother's wife, daughter, or sister, may he be destroyed by the five thunders.

10. If a Brother appropriates a fellow Brother's money or property [entrusted to him for safe keeping], or deliberately fails to deliver the same as requested, may he perish under 10,000 swords.

11. If a Brother does not devote all his mind and energy when a fellow

Brother entrusts his wife or children to his care, or important matters to his handling, may he be destroyed by the five thunders.

12. If anyone joining the Hung Society this evening lies about the date and hour of his birth, may he be destroyed by the five thunders.

13. Having joined the Hung Society this evening, one must have no regret or sigh. If a Brother entertains such a state of mind, may he perish beneath 10,000 swords.

14. If a Brother secretly assists an outsider [against a fellow Brother] or robs him of money or possessions, may he be destroyed by the five thunders.

15. A Brother must not force a fellow Brother to sell him goods or force him out in order to make a sale. If he relies on his strength and oppresses a weak Brother, may he perish beneath 10,000 swords.

16. A Brother must return the money or things borrowed from a fellow Brother. If he goes contrary to his conscience and appropriates the money or things, may he be destroyed by the five thunders.

17. When in a robbery a Brother takes money or things from a fellow Brother by mistake, they must be returned at once. If he intends to appropriate them, may he perish under 10,000 swords.

18. If a Brother is captured by a government official, he must bear the consequences for what he has done himself and must not involve a fellow Brother because of any enmity. If a Brother violates this oath, may he be destroyed by the five thunders.

19. When a fellow Brother is murdered or arrested, or when he has gone away for a long time, and the family he has left behind becomes destitute, a Brother must take steps to render assistance. If he pretends ignorance, may he be destroyed by the five thunders.

20. When a fellow Brother is abused by others, a Brother must go forward to help him if he is in the right or arbitrate if he is in the wrong. If a fellow Brother is repeatedly abused by other people, the Brother must not pretend ignorance but must inform the Brethren so they may consult and decide on a course of action, with everyone contributing money and those without money contributing energy to strive for his glory. If a Brother violates this oath, may he be destroyed by the five thunders.

21. Whenever a Brother learns that a fellow Brother from the provinces or from abroad is to be arrested, he must lose no time in informing the fellow Brother so he may escape as soon as possible. If the Brother pretends ignorance, may he perish beneath 10,000 swords.

22. A Brother must not conspire with an outsider to cheat a fellow Brother of money in a place of gambling. If he commits this crime knowingly, may he perish beneath 10,000 swords.

23. A Brother must not fabricate stories or twist the words of fellow Brothers so as to set them apart. If he violates this oath, may he perish beneath 10,000 swords.

24. A Brother must not illegally proclaim himself a Worshipful Master. When the mourning period [period of training] of three years since initiation into the Hung Society is over, if he is truly loyal to the Society and devoted to the Brethren the Worshipful Master will tutor him in the literature of the Society, and eventually he may be promoted to be the Worshipful Master either through transmission or through the recommendation of the three Deacons. If he acts [as a Worshipful Master] without proper authority, may he be destroyed by the five thunders.

25. After joining the Hung Society, all enmity among Brothers must be wiped out. If a Brother violates this oath, may he be destroyed by the five thunders.

26. When a Brother's own brother is involved in a dispute or lawsuit with a fellow Brother of the Hung family, the Brother must try to reconcile them and must not render aid to either side. If he violates this oath, may he be destroyed by the five thunders.

27. A Brother must not, under any pretext, invade the territory held by a fellow Brother. If he pretends ignorance and places the fellow Brother in danger, may he be destroyed by the five thunders.

28. A Brother must not be jealous of the money or things acquired by a fellow Brother or plot to share his spoil. If he has such intentions, may he be destroyed by the five thunders.

29. A Brother must not betray the secret or harbor any bad intention when a fellow Brother makes some fast money. If he violates this oath, may he perish beneath 10,000 swords.

30. A Brother must not secretly help an outsider to oppress fellow Brothers of the Hung family. If he violates this oath, may he perish beneath 10,000 swords.

31. A Brother must not oppress people because of the power or the huge membership of the Hung family, and, what is more, he must not do violence and behave like a despot. Instead he must mind his own business. If he violates this oath, may he perish beneath 10,000 swords.

32. A Brother must not breed hatred of fellow Brothers because they do not lend him money. If he violates this oath, may he be destroyed by the five thunders.

33. If a Brother rapes a fellow Brother's young child, may he be destroyed by the five thunders.

34. A Brother must not accept or buy a fellow Brother's wife or concubine as his own spouse. Neither may he commit adultery with them. If he commits such a crime knowingly, may he perish beneath 10,000 swords.

35. A Brother must be very careful in his speech and may not carelessly use the words, phrases, and other secrets of the Hung family, so as to prevent outsiders from penetrating our mysteries and to avoid inviting trouble with them. If he violates this oath, may he perish beneath 10,000 swords.

36. Whether a Brother is a scholar, a farmer, an artisan, or a merchant, he should attend to his own occupation. Having joined the Hung Society, the first emphasis must be loyalty to the Society and devotion to the Brethren, and the cultivation of fellowship with all Brothers within the four seas. When the time of uprising comes, all Brothers must be of one mind and united effort to destroy the Manchu role, restore the Ming empire as soon as possible, and avenge the burning of the Five Early Founding Fathers. If in an emergency a Brother is hesitant or divided in his mind, escapes from his responsibility, and makes no effort, may he perish beneath 10,000 swords.

The Ten Prohibitions of the Hung Society
[From Chu Lin, *Hung men chih,* pp. 32–33]

1. Wives of Brothers must cultivate correct behavior and married Brothers must not be given to sexual promiscuity. If wives do not cultivate correctness, both of their ears will be cut off. If [married] Brothers are sexually promiscuous, they will be punished by death.

2. When a Brother's parent dies and he lacks money for the funeral and asks Brothers for financial help, all should do their best to help him. Those who refuse will have both ears cut off.

3. When a Brother makes a plea of poverty and appeals for a loan, he may not be refused. Those who hold him in contempt or sternly refuse him will have both ears cut off.

4. Brothers may not purposely cause a fellow Brother to lose money in a place of gambling or secretly cheat him. Those who commit this offense will be beaten with a bamboo 108 times.

5. After joining the Hung Society, no Brother may secretly divulge the Society's regulations to outsiders. Those who commit this offense will be punished by death.

6. When a Brother entrusts money or documents in the course of his business or dealings with people abroad, they may not be secretly used or appropriated. Those who commit this offense will have both ears cut off.

7. When a Brother engaged in a fight with outsiders comes for help, aid must be rendered. Those who pretend not to know him will be beaten with a bamboo 108 times.

8. Any Brother who, because of his superiority, oppresses his inferiors, or because of his strength maltreats the weak, will have both ears cut off. In addition he will be beaten with a bamboo 72 times.

9. When a Brother is in distress, aid should be given immediately. Those who violate this will be beaten with a bamboo 108 times.

10. When a Brother is in danger or has been arrested by a government official, all Brothers must take steps to save him. Those who shirk responsibility under any pretense will be beaten with a bamboo 108 times.

The Ten Disciplines of the Hung Society
[From Chu Lin, *Hung men chih*, pp. 35-36]

1. It is not permitted to injure or destroy a fellow Brother [that is, in the Society's secret language, be disrespectful to him].

2. It is not permitted to curse or scold parents.

3. It is not permitted to stir up a lamp or put out a light [stir up trouble].

4. It is not permitted to oppress others because of one's superiority.

5. It is not permitted to deceive Heaven and cross the river [cheat people].

6. It is not permitted to skim off the fat and leave the soup [take the best for oneself].

7. It is not permitted to be inhumane and unrighteous.

8. It is not permitted to pick the red and take what is submerged in water [take illegal fees or compensation].

9. It is not permitted to struggle to go ahead when walking with others [push ahead for personal glory].

10. It is not permitted to usurp any position in the Society.

The Eight Virtues of the Hung Society
[From Chu Lin, *Hung men chih*, p. 141]

1. Be absolutely loyal and dedicated to the country.
2. Be filial and obedient to parents.
3. Instruct and teach your wife and children.
4. Be harmonious with your brothers.
5. Be harmonious with your neighbors.
6. Help people in distress and save people in danger.
7. Sincerely advise your friends.
8. Protect the rich and help the poor.

INDEX

[315]

Chu Yüan-chang, 133
Ch'u Ch'eng-po, 74-76
Ch'ü Yüan, 159
Chuang Tzu (or Chuang Chou), 168
Chuang Tzu, study of, in third and fourth centuries, 158
Ch'üan-hsüeh p'ien: Exhortation to Learn (Chang Chih-tung), 81-87
Ch'un-ch'iu: Spring and Autumn Annals, commentary on, 69-70
Chung-kuo che-hsüeh shih ta-kang: Outline of the History of Chinese Philosophy (Hu Shih), 182
Civil service examination system, abolition of, xi, 197; *see also* Education
Clan, *see* Family or clan system
Class society, Communist ideas on, 204, 230, 231, 236, 241, 243; *see also* Social order
Colonialism, 197, 223; *see also* Imperialism —Western
Commerce, state control of, 1
Communism, Chinese, 196-284; establishment of headquarters at Yenan, xii; compared with Taiping movement, 31; Sun Yat-sen and, 105-6; Chiang Kai-shek and, 138, 144-45; nature of revolution, 200-32; new-democratic revolution, 221-28; dictatorship of the people, 229-32; theory and practice of, 232-79; and Chinese tradition, 279-84; *see also* Chinese Communist Party; Kuomintang-Communist collaboration
Communist Party, Chinese, *see* Chinese Communist Party
Communist Party of the U.S.S.R., inter-Party struggle in, 260
Confucianism: influence in Taiping ideology, 28-30; K'ang Yu-wei's resolution of problem of change and, 65-69; superiority of, 79-81; attitudes of Sun Yat-sen and Chiang Kai-shek toward, 135-36, 138; attack on, 151-56; Liang shu-ming's conversion to, 187; Communism and, 279-84 *passim;* literati and, 286; interpretation of, in cults and secret societies, 296-304 *passim*
Confucius, teachings of, 151, 174, 175, 186, 189-91
Confucius As a Reformer: K'ung Tzu kai-chih k'ao (K'ang Yu-wei), xi, 63, 65, 68-69
Constitution, Five-Power, 112-13
Cults and secret societies, 285-314
Cultural Construction (magazine), 192
Cultural Construction on a Chinese Basis

(1935), Declaration for, 192-94; Hu Shih's criticism of, 194-95
Culture: Chinese and Western, debated, 152, 184-95; Mao on peasants' cultural movement, 214-15; in New Democracy, 226-28; *Cheng-feng* movement and, 266

Darwin, Charles R., 170, 173
Decorum, *see Li* (rites)
Democracy: Sun Yat-sen's principle of, 109-13; guided, 117; or absolutism, 124-36
Democratic centralism, 222, 224-25
Democratic League, 125
Democratic revolution, 228-32
Demon worship, Hung Hsiu-Ch'üan's mission to destroy, 19-20
Dewey, John, 152, 157, 167, 171-72
Dictatorship, 127-34 *passim,* 224-25, 229-32
"Doubting of antiquity" movement, 152, 182-84
Dreams, 286
Duty, 139*n*

Economic planning, 136
Economics: the Taiping program, 30-33; K'ang Yu-wei's plans for reform of, 64, 71-73; in Sun Yat-sen's program, 113-17; in New Democracy, 225
Education: need for reform in, 64, 71-73; expansion of, in republican era, 157; Mao on, 214-15; *see also* Civil service examination system
Eight Characters, 213
Eight Trigram Society, 294
Elders Society (*Ko-lao hui*), 305, 306
Elite, the, 282-83; *see also* Class society
Emperor, *see* Ruler
Empress dowagers, 64
Engels, F., 237-42, 244
Essentials of the New Life Movement (Chiang Kai-shek), 137, 138-44
Eucken, Rudolf, 186
Europe, Liang Ch'i-ch'ao's travel impressions of, 185-87; *see also* West, the
Evolutionism, 186
Examination system, *see* Civil service examination system
Exhortation to Learn: Ch'üan-hsüeh p'ien (Chang Chih-tung), xi, 81-87

Family or clan system, 67; overthrow of authority of, 210-14; *see also* Filial piety
Fan Chung-yen, 282

Industry, nationalization of in Communist plan, 222
Institute of Marxism-Leninism in Yenan, 249
Institute of Rural Reconstruction, 188
Institutional reform, 55-73
Intuition, 174, 179
Irrigation, encouragement of, under Manchus, 44
Islam, rise of, compared with Taiping movement, 24; see also Muslims

James, William, 167, 171
Japan: occupation of coastal China and Yangtze valley, xii; comparison of reforms in late Manchu China and Meiji, 59-60, 63-64; as example of successful modernization, 121-23; Nationalists in, 137
Jen: as humanity, T'an Ssu-t'ung's study of, 88-91; Liang Shu-ming on, 190
Jen-hsüeh: The Study of Humanity (T'an Ssu-t'ung), 88-91
Jesus, teaching of universal love, 174, 175
Juan Yüan, 54n
Jung Lu, 73, 74

K'ang Nan-hai tzu-pien nien-p'u: Autobiographical Chronology (K'ang Yu-wei), 62
K'ang Yu-wei, xi, 60-73, 74, 87, 91; Chu I-hsin's letter to, 76-79
Kant, Immanuel, 167
Kiangsi Soviet, xi
Knowledge, action and, 121-24
Kokutai (national polity), 59
Kokutai no hongi: Fundamentals of Japan's National Polity, 137
Ko-lao hui (Elders Society), 305, 306
Kropotkin, Peter, 173
Ku Chieh-kang, 182-84
Kuan Kung, 306
Kuan Tzu, 140
Kuang-hsü, emperor, 64, 71, 87
K'ung Fu-tzu, see Confucius
K'ung Tzu Kai-chih k'ao: Confucius As a Reformer (K'ang Yu-wei), xi, 63, 65, 68-69
Kuomintang: Sun Yat-sen and, 98-99; becomes National People's Party, 105; political tutelage a key doctrine of, 124-29; Lo Lung-chi on, 125-29; and absolutism, 129-34; Chiang and, 138, 148-50; revolutionary aims of, 198; Manifesto of the First National Congress of, 225

Kuomintang-Communist collaboration, xi, 106, 204, 221, 243

Lambert, Johann H., 174
Land: reclamation and development under Manchus, 44; taxation of, 114; reform, 114-16, 222; nationalization of, 100, 104-5; tenure system, 225
Land System of the Heavenly Kingdom, The: T'ien-ch'ao t'ien-mu chih-tu, 30-33
Landlordism, 103, 104-5
Languages, 157, 163-67; study of Western, 44, 45, 48-51
Lao Tan, see Lao Tzu
Lao Tzu (Lao Tan): Communist writers on, 280; treatise attributed to, 287
Laski, Harold, 125
League of Common Alliance, see T'ung-meng hui
Legge, James, 55
Lenin, V. I., 232-42 passim, 267-68; see also Marxism-Leninism
Let a Hundred Flowers Bloom (Mao Tse-tung), 271-79
Levenson, Joseph, 92n
Li (rites; decorum), Chiang Kai-shek on, 136, 139-44
Li chi: Book of Rites, Li yün section of, 69
Li Hung-chang, xi, 22, 43, 49-51
Li Meng-yang, 161
Li Po, 158
Li Ta-chao, 200-3
Li-yün ("Evolution of Rites"), section in Book of Rites, 69
Liang Ch'i-ch'ao, xi, 87, 91-97, 172, 180, 184-87
Liang Shu-ming, 185, 187-91
Liberalism, Mao Tse-tung on, 263-66
Lien, meaning of, 139-44
Lin Tse-hsü, xi, 4-10
Literary revolution, xi, 151, 156-67
Literature: aristocratic, 162; "forest," 162-63; Mao Tse-tung on, 266-71; popular, 285; of cults and secret societies, 296-314
Liu Shao-ch'i, 248-63, 281, 282
Liu Tsung-yüan, 62, 159
Liu Yü, 133
Lo Lung-chi, 125-29
Love, Confucian idea of, 174, 175

Magic, belief in, 286
Manchu dynasty: reform and reaction under, 43-97; overthrow of, 98, 101-2

Phrenology, 286
Planchettes, belief in, 293, 295
Political parties, 154
Political tutelage, 119-36
Polygamy, condemnation of, 24
Positivism, 198
Pragmatism, 167, 169-72, 173, 186, 198
Press, public, 55, 64; see also specific periodicals, e.g., *New People*
Primer in Verse: Yu-hsüeh shih, 28-30
Principle (Tao), *see* Tao
Principles of the Heavenly Nature: T'ien-ch'ing tao-li shu, 33-42
Program of National Reconstruction, A (Sun Yat-sen), 117
Protestants, number of, in China, 286
Protests from the Study of Chiao-pin: Chiao-pin lu k'ang-i (Feng Kuie-fen), 45-49

Rationalism, 245
Red Army, 204
Red Scarf Society, 294
Reform: movements under Manchus, 43-97; Hsüeh Fu-ch'eng on, 51-55; Wang T'ao on, 55-59; institutional, 59-73; Kang Yu-wei's, 60-73; conservative reactions to, 73-87; of men's minds, 74-76; extremist position on, 87-97
Religion: influence in Taiping Rebellion, 18-42 *passim;* Communist attitude toward, 210-14 *passim,* 228, 279; attitudes of literati and common people toward, 285-87; popular, 285-314; *see also specific religions,* e.g., Buddhism
Religious cultivation, methods of, 302-4
Religious societies, number of, 293
Republican era, 151-95, 197
Republicanism: T'an Ssu-t'ung's advocacy of, 87-88; one of Sun Yat-sen's Three Principles, 98, 100, 102-3
Revolution: Sun Yat-sen's three stages of, 117-21; and absolutism, 129-32; Mao Tse-tung on nature and aims of, 208-9, 215-21
——— *Chinese:* Nationalist, 64, 98-150 *passim;* Communist, 196-97, 222-24, 228-29
Righteousness, see *I*
Rites, see *Li* (rites); *Li chi* (*Book of Rites*)
Rites of Chou, 67
Roberts, Issachar J., 19
Roman Catholics, number of, in China, 286
Ruler(s), T'an Ssu-t'ung on, 89-90; *see also* Government

Russell, Bertrand, 152, 167
Russia, Tsarist, 238
Russian Revolution, 105, 130-31, 132
Russo-Japanese War, as impetus to revolutionary nationalism, 99

Sa Meng-wu, 192-94
Sabbath, observance of, 24
Sakuma Shōzan, 12
Salvation, in Buddhist sects, 295
San-ho hui (Triple Harmony Society), 305-6
San min chu-i: Three People's Principles (Sun Yat-sen), 105-6; *see also* Three People's Principles
San Min Chu I Youth Corps, *see* Youth Corps
San-tien hui (Triad Society), 305
Schiffrin, Harold, 103n
Schopenhauer, Arthur, 174
Science(s): study of Western, 44, 45-48, 49-51; and philosophy of life, 151, 152, 172-81; Ch'en Tu-hsiu's attitude toward, 167; Hu Shih on, 169-71; metaphysics and, 172-81
Secret societies, 285-314 *passim*
Self-cultivation, 248-56 *passim*
"Self-strengthening" movement, 45-73 *passim*
Shao-lin Temple, burning of, 304-5
Sheng-wu chi: Military History of the Ch'ing Dynasty (Wei Yüan), 11
Shih ching: Book of Odes or Book of Poetry, 250
Shih Nai-an, 159, 161
Shui-hu chuan (*The Water Margin* or *All Men Are Brothers*), 306
Sian incident, xii
Silent Way of Recompense, The, 287, 290-93
Sino-Japanese War, xi, 60, 73
Slave ownership, bans on, 24
Smuggling, 2, 4
Social Interpretation of History, The (William), 114
Social order, Sun Yat-sen's program for reform of, 117-18; *see also* Class society
Socialism: in Sun Yat-sen's program, 113-14, 136, 197; Liang Ch'i-ch'ao on, 186; Communism and, 231, 240 (*see also* Communism)
Society of the Way (*Tao yüan*), 293
Society of the Way and Its Virtue (*Tao-te she*), 293
Society of the White Robe, 294

Victoria, Queen, Lin Tse-hsü's letter to, 5-9

Wan Yün-lung, 305
Wang Chung-hui, 145
Wang Fu-chih (Wang Ch'uan-shan), 88
Wang Hsien-ch'ien, 73
Wang T'ao, xi, 55-59, 61, 65, 66
Wang Ts'an, 159
Wang Yang-ming (Wang Shou-jen), philosophy of, 121-24
War, Lin Tse-hsü's recognition of necessity for adoption of western methods of, 9-10
Warlordism, 197
Waseda University, 173
Way, the, see Tao, the
Way of Pervading Unity, The (I-kuan Tao), 295-302
Wei Yüan, xi, 4, 10-17
Well-field system: Mencius on, 67; K'ang Yu-wei on, 67; Hu Han-min on, 104; Hu Shih's study of, 182-83
Wen ch'ang, 290
West, the: opening of China to, 1-17; comparison of civilizations of China and, 12-17, 187-92; Taipings and, 22; increased contact with, 43-97 passim; influence on students sent to, 50-51; Sun Yat-sen and, 99-100, 106, 107-8, 197; Chiang Kai-shek and, 134-50 passim; influence in republican era, 151-95 passim; Communist attitude toward, 227 (see also Imperialism—Western)

White Lotus Society, 294-304
Will of Sun Yat-sen, 252
William, Maurice, 114
Williams, Harold, 203
Wine, bans on, 24
Witchcraft, 286
Women: greater equality for, under Taipings, 24; liberal attitude toward, 154-56; Mao Tse-tung on position of, 210-12
World War, First, aftermath in China, 151-52
Wu Chien-jen, 161
Wu Chih-hui, 173, 178-79, 180
Wu P'ei-fu, 130

Yang Hsiu-ch'ing, 21, 23, 34
Yeh Te-hui, 73, 79-81
Yellow Society, 294
Yen Fu, 61
Yin Hung-sheng, 304
Yokohama, 100
Youth Corps, San Min Chu I, 148-49
Yu-hsüeh shih: Primer in Verse, 28-30
Yüan (Mongol) dynasty, 164
Yuan Shih-k'ai, xi, 130, 151, 152, 306